International Relations in Southeast Asia

ASIA IN WORLD POLITICS
Series Editor: Samuel S. Kim

International Relations in Southeast Asia

The Struggle for Autonomy

Third Edition

Donald E. Weatherbee

ROWMAN & LITTLEFIELD
Lanham • Boulder • New York • London

Published by Rowman & Littlefield
A wholly owned subsidiary of The Rowman & Littlefield Publishing Group, Inc.
4501 Forbes Boulevard, Suite 200, Lanham, Maryland 20706
www.rowman.com

Unit A, Whitacre Mews, 26-34 Stannary Street, London SE11 4AB, United Kingdom

Copyright © 2015 by Rowman & Littlefield
First edition 2005. Second edition 2009.

British Library Cataloguing in Publication Information Available

Library of Congress Cataloging-in-Publication Data
Weatherbee, Donald E., author.
 International relations in Southeast Asia : the struggle for autonomy / Donald E. Weatherbee. — Third edition.
 pages   cm. — (Asia in world politics)
 Includes bibliographical references and index.
 ISBN 978-1-4422-2299-1 (cloth : alk. paper) — ISBN 978-1-4422-2300-4 (pbk. : alk. paper) — ISBN 978-1-4422-2301-1 (electronic)
 1. Southeast Asia—Foreign relations. 2. Southeast Asia—Politics and government—1945- 3. ASEAN. I. Title.
 DS526.7.W44 2015
 327.59—dc23

2014034407

Printed in the United States of America

Contents

Tables and Boxes

TABLES

BOXES

Preface to the Third Edition

Although the thematic framework and intellectual argument of this revised third edition of *International Relations in Southeast Asia: The Struggle for Autonomy* is the same, in many respects it is a new book in its comprehension of regional developments over the past half decade. The step-by-step building of the ASEAN Community, with its December 2015 target date, is taking place in a dynamically evolving regional security environment. The "peaceful rise" of China is showing a darker side with its aggressive pursuit of territorial and jurisdictional claims to 80 to 90 percent of the South China Sea. The American Obama administration, freed from the wars of its predecessor, is resisting China's effort to exclude the United States from Southeast Asia. The regional "pivot" or "rebalancing" of American power is designed as a demonstration of the intention to defend US great-power stakes in the region's future. At a time when ASEAN solidarity and coherence is required in its great-power dealings, divergent national interests among the member states threaten to undermine the ASEAN Community and the regional struggle for autonomy—or in ASEAN parlance, its claim to centrality in regional international relations—in ways not manifest in the earlier editions.

In addition to my scholarly debts acknowledged in the previous editions, in preparing the third edition, I would like to add my thanks to Ambassador Tan Chin Tiong, director of Singapore's Institute of Southeast Asian Studies (ISEAS), for the invitation to join ISEAS as a visiting professorial fellow for three months in 2013. The resources and support provided by Director Tan and his staff during my tenure at ISEAS are deeply appreciated. Special thanks go to Mr. Daljit Singh, coordinator of ISEAS's Regional Strategic and Political Studies Program, for his interest and assistance in my work and links to Singapore policy officials. In Jakarta, I am indebted to Ms. Hazel Margaretha and her staff at the Jakarta office of the United States–Indonesia

Society (USINDO) for the logistical support that allowed me to maximize my schedule there in April 2013. I also appreciate the invitation from Dr. Vikram Nehru of the Carnegie Endowment for International Peace to participate in two sessions in February 2014, where a number of the book's issues and arguments were presented for discussion and critical commentary.

Every step of the way, from the proposal to the completed manuscript, I have again had critical input and feedback, both in substance and style, from Professor Epsey Cooke Farrell. I have also been fortunate to have enjoyed both the encouragement and patience of Susan McEachern at Rowman & Littlefield.

Donald E. Weatherbee
Morristown, NJ, and Jamestown, RI

Preface to the Second Edition

In preparing this revised second edition of *International Relations in Southeast Asia: The Struggle for Autonomy*, I have had the benefit of critical commentary on the first edition as well as feedback from instructors who have used it as a text. Those familiar with the first edition will find a number of changes, and in many respects it is a new book. This edition is single authored. I would again thank Ralf Emmers, Mari Pangestu, and Leonard Sebastian for their contribution to the first edition. Chapters 6 and 7 contain entirely new material. In this edition, there is less emphasis on the war on terror. There is a more structured discussion of human security as an issue area in international relations in Southeast Asia. The new ASEAN Charter and the ASEAN community-building process are highlighted. There is a more extended consideration over the course of the text of the China–ASEAN–United States triangle. And, of course, all of the topics and issues have been updated. On the basis of suggestions from users, I have added more footnotes to primary sources and secondary sources available on the Internet.

To my scholarly debts acknowledged in the preface to the first edition, I would add my thanks to Dr. Thitinan Pongsudhirak, director of ISIS Thailand, and Dr. Susuma Snitwongse, chairperson of the Advisory Board, ISIS Thailand, for inviting me to participate in the ISIS October 2006 conference on Democracy and Human Security in Southeast Asia. I would also like to acknowledge the stimulation provided by the Columbia University Southeast Asia Seminar.

The stylistic skills of Dr. Epsey Cooke Farrell of Seton Hall University's Whitehead School of Diplomacy again improved the text chapter by chapter. I also appreciate the encouragement and patience of Susan McEachern and the assistance of Alden Perkins at Rowman & Littlefield.

Donald E. Weatherbee
Morristown, NJ, and Jamestown, RI

Preface to the First Edition

This book is designed as an introduction to the issues and dynamics of international relations in contemporary Southeast Asia. Its goal is modest. Planned as a textbook, it does not pretend to present new research findings or theoretical insights. Footnotes have been held to a minimum with an emphasis on directing the reader to documentary sources available on the Internet. The hope is to stimulate deeper investigation by interested students into the topics covered, perhaps recruiting members of a younger academic generation to consider further study of Southeast Asian politics and international relations.

When initially approached to do the book, I hesitated, uncertain as to whether I wanted to devote the time and discipline required for a textbook. What convinced me to do it were the expressions of interest from faculty currently involved in basic Southeast Asia–related courses who felt that it would fill a gap in available text resources. Rather than country-by-country case study chapters, the book is thematically organized around some of the central policy questions facing Southeast Asia's decision makers. The scope extends beyond the problem of security that has historically dominated the academic study of international relations in Southeast Asia to include nontraditional issue areas in international relations. I have also tried to bring the state as the primary actor in international relations in Southeast Asia back into focus to balance the great academic attention that has been given to ASEAN—the Association of Southeast Asian Nations—the collective framework for intraregional and international interaction.

The intellectual genesis of the work is four decades of teaching courses on Southeast Asian international relations to upper-division undergraduate and graduate students with an interest in Southeast Asia. The scholarly debts I have accumulated in a career devoted to studying, teaching, and writing about politics and international relations in Southeast Asia are profound and many. I acknowledge my gratitude to the late Richard Louis Walker who created at the University of South Carolina's Institute of International Studies, now bearing his name, a collegial and supportive base for many years. I also give due to generations of my students whose own interests and enthusiasms helped keep mine alive. Over the years, I have enjoyed the company, wisdom, and expertise of hosts of academic counterparts and government officials in the United States, Europe, and Southeast Asia. They are too numerous to even begin to think of singling out. I am particularly grateful for my long-standing associations with the Institute of Southeast Asian Studies in Singapore, the Center for Strategic and International Studies in Jakarta, and the Institute of Strategic and International Studies in Bangkok.

In preparing the manuscript for the book, I am indebted to Dr. Ralf Emmers and Dr. Leonard Sebastian in Singapore and Dr. Mari Pangestu in Jakarta for their generous willingness to provide what are chapters 6 and 7. In addition to the helpful comments and criticisms of the anonymous reviewers of the draft manuscript, I would also mention Dr. Epsey Cooke Farrell, who teaches the kind of course at which this book is aimed. Both her classroom feedback and stylistic skills improved the text chapter by chapter. I also appreciate the encouragement and patience of Susan McEachern and Jessica Gribble at Rowman & Littlefield.

> Donald E. Weatherbee
> Columbia, S.C.
> Jamestown, R.I.

Selected Abbreviations

AADMER	ASEAN Agreement on Disaster Management and Emergency Response
AC	ASEAN Community
ACCORD	ASEAN and China Cooperative Operations in Response to Dangerous Drugs
ACD	Asian Cooperation Dialogue
ACMECS	Ayeyawady–Chao Phraya–Mekong Economic Cooperation Strategy
ADB	Asian Development Bank
ADIZ	air defense identification zone
ADMM	ASEAN Defense Ministers' Meeting
AEC	ASEAN Economic Community
AEM	ASEAN Economic Ministers' Meeting
AEMM	ASEAN – EU Ministerial Meeting
AFAS	ASEAN Framework Agreement on Services
AFP	Armed Forces of the Philippines
AFTA	ASEAN Free Trade Area
AHRD	ASEAN Human Rights Declaration
AIA	ASEAN Investment Area
AICHR	ASEAN Intergovernmental Commission on Human Rights
AMBDC	ASEAN Mekong Basin Development Cooperation
AMF	ASEAN Maritime Forum
AMM	ASEAN Ministerial Meeting
AMMDM	ASEAN Ministerial Meeting on Disaster Management
AMME	ASEAN Ministerial Meeting on the Environment

AMMTC	ASEAN Ministerial Meeting on Transnational Crime
AMRO	ASEAN+3 Macroeconomic Research Office
APEC	Asia-Pacific Economic Cooperation
APSC	ASEAN Political-Security Community
APT	ASEAN + 3
ARF	ASEAN Regional Forum
ARMM	Autonomous Region in Muslim Mindanao (Philippines)
ASA	Association of Southeast Asia
ASCC	ASEAN Socio-Cultural Community
ASEAN	Association of Southeast Asian Nations
ASEM	Asia–Europe Meeting
ASG	Abu Sayyaf Group (Philippines)
ASOD	ASEAN Senior Officials on Drug Matters
ASOEN	ASEAN Senior Officials on the Environment
AWG	ASEAN working group
BIFF	Bangsamoro Islamic Freedom Fighters
BIMP-EAGA	Brunei–Indonesia–Malaysia–Philippines East ASEAN Growth Area
BIMSTEC	Bay of Bengal Initiative for Multi-Sectoral Technical and Economic Cooperation
CAB	Comprehensive Agreement on the Bangsamoro
CBM	confidence-building measures
CEPEA	Comprehensive Economic Partnership in East Asia
CEPT	common effective preferential tariff
CGDK	Coalition Government of Democratic Kampuchea
CLMV	Cambodia, Laos, Myanmar, Vietnam
CLV-DT	Cambodia–Laos–Vietnam Development Triangle
CMI	Chiang Mai Initiative
CMIM	Chiang Mai Initiative Multilateral
CNRP	Cambodia National Rescue Party
COBSEA	Coordinating Body on the Seas of East Asia
COC	Code of Conduct (in the South China Sea)
COMMIT	Coordinated Mekong Ministerial Initiative against Trafficking
CPP	Cambodia People's Party
CPP-NPA	Communist Party of the Philippines/ New People's Army
CSCAP	Council for Security Cooperation in the Asia-Pacific
CTF	Commission on Truth and Friendship (Indonesia–Timor-Leste)
CTI	Coral Triangle Initiative
DOC	Declaration on Conduct (in the South China Sea)

EAEG	East Asia Economic Group
EAFTA	East Asia Free Trade Area
EAMF	Expanded ASEAN Maritime Forum
EAS	East Asia Summit
EASG	East Asia Study Group
EAVG	East Asian Vision Group
ECCC	Extraordinary Chambers in the Courts of Cambodia
ECOSOC	[United Nations] Economic and Social Council
EEZ	exclusive economic zone
EPA	economic partnership agreement
EPG	Eminent Persons Group
ESCAP	[United Nations] Economic and Social Commission for Asia and the Pacific
EU	European Union
FDI	foreign direct investment
FLEG	Forest Law Enforcement and Governance
FPDA	Five Power Defence Arrangement (Australia, Great Britain, Malaysia, New Zealand, and Singapore)
FRETILIN	Frente Revolutionária do Timor Leste Independente (Revolutionary Front for an Independent East Timor)
FTA	free trade agreement
FTAAP	Free Trade Area of the Asia Pacific (proposed)
FTO	foreign terrorist organization
FUNCINPEC	Front Uni National pour un Cambodge Indépendent, Neutre, Pacifique, et Coopératif (United National Front for an Independent, Neutral, Pacific, and Cooperative Cambodia)
GAM	Free Aceh Movement (Indonesia)
GCTF	Global Counterterrorism Forum
GDP	gross domestic product
GMS	Greater Mekong Subregion
HDI	Human Development Index
IAI	Initiative for ASEAN Integration
IBRD	International Bank for Reconstruction and Development
ICC	International Criminal Court
ICJ	International Court of Justice
IDP	internally displaced persons
IMB	International Maritime Board
IMF	International Monetary Fund
IMS-GT	Indonesia–Malaysia–Singapore Growth Triangle (= SIJORI)
IMT-GT	Indonesia–Malaysia–Thailand Growth Triangle

INGO	international nongovernmental organization
INTERFET	International Force for East Timor
IOM	International Organization for Migration
IOR-ARC	Indian Ocean Rim Association for Regional Cooperation
ISF	International Stabilization Force
ISG	Inter-Sessional Support Group (ARF)
ISM	Inter-Sessional Meeting (ARF)
ITLOS	International Tribunal for the Law of the Sea
ITTA	International Tropical Timber Agreement
ITTO	International Tropical Timber Organization
JCLEC	Jakarta Center for Law Enforcement Cooperation
JDA	joint development area
JI	Jema'ah Islamiyah
JIM	Jakarta Informal Meeting
JSOTF-P	Joint Special Operations Task Force–Philippines
JWG	joint working group
KR	Khmer Rouge
LMI	Lower Mekong Initiative
LPDR	Lao People's Democratic Republic
MALSINDO	Malaysia, Singapore, Indonesia (patrols)
MAPHILINDO	Malaysia, Philippines, Indonesia (nonpolitical confederation)
MDG	Millennium Development Goals
MDT	mutual defense treaty
MGC	Mekong–Ganga Cooperation grouping
MILF	Moro Islamic Liberation Front (Philippines)
MNLF	Moro National Liberation Front (Philippines)
MOU	memorandum of understanding
MRC	Mekong River Commission
MSG	Melanesian Spearhead Group
MSP	Malacca Strait Patrols
NAM	Nonaligned Movement
NGO	nongovernmental organization
NLD	National League for Democracy (Myanmar)
ODA	official development assistance
OIC	Organization of Islamic Cooperation
OIC-PCSP	OIC Peace Committee for the Southern Philippines
OPM	Organisasi Papua Merdeka (Free Papua Organization)
PCA	Permanent Court of Arbitration
PICC	Paris International Conference on Cambodia
PIF	Pacific Islands Forum

PKI	Indonesian Communist Party (Partai Kommunis Indonesia)
PMC	Post-Ministerial Conference (ASEAN)
PNG	Papua New Guinea
PNTR	permanent normal trade relations
PPP	purchasing power parity
PRC	People's Republic of China
PTA	Preferential Trade Arrangement (ASEAN)
PULO	Patani United Liberation Organization (Thailand)
RCEP	Regional Comprehensive Economic Partnership
ReCAAP	Regional Cooperation Agreement on Combating Piracy and Armed Robbery against Ships in Asia
REDD	Reducing Emissions from Deforestation and Degradation
ROK	Republic of Korea
RTA	regional trade agreement
SARS	severe acute respiratory syndrome
SCS	South China Sea
SEAC	South-East Asia Command
SEANWFZ	Southeast Asian Nuclear Weapons Free Zone
SEARCCT	Southeast Asia Regional Center for Counter-Terrorism
SEATO	Southeast Asia Treaty Organization
SIJORI	Singapore–Johor Baru–Indonesia growth triangle (= IMS-GT)
SLORC	State Law and Order Restoration Council (Myanmar)
SOM	Senior Officials' Meeting
SPDC	State Peace and Development Council (Myanmar)
SRV	Socialist Republic of Vietnam
TAC	Treaty of Amity and Cooperation in Southeast Asia
Tcf	trillion cubic feet (natural gas)
TIFA	trade and investment framework agreement
TIP	trafficking in persons
TOC	transnational organized crime
TPA	Trade Promotion Authority
TPP	Trans-Pacific Partnership
TP-SEP	Trans-Pacific Strategic Economic Partnership
TPS-OIC	Tariff Preference System–Organization of Islamic Cooperation
TRIPS	trade-related intellectual property rights
UNAIDS	United Nations Joint Program on HIV/AIDS
UNAMET	United Nations Assistance Mission in East Timor
UNCHR	United Nations Commission on Human Rights

UNCLOS	United Nations Convention on the Law of the Sea
UNDP	United Nations Development Program
UNEP	United Nations Environment Program
UNFCCC	United Nations Framework Convention on Climate Change
UNGA	United Nations General Assembly
UNHCHR	United Nations High Commissioner for Human Rights
UNHCR	United Nations High Commissioner for Refugees
UNHRC	United Nations Human Rights Council
UNIAP	United Nations Inter-Agency Project on Human Trafficking in the Greater Mekong Subregion
UNMISET	United Nations Mission in Support of East Timor
UNMIT	United Nations Integrated Mission in Timor-Leste
UNODC	United Nations Office on Drugs and Crime
UNOTIL	United Nations Office in Timor-Leste
UNSC	United Nations Security Council
UNTAC	United Nations Transitional Authority for Cambodia
UNTAET	United Nations Transitional Administration in East Timor
UPR	Universal Periodic Review (UNHCR)
VAP	Vientiane Action Programme
VFA	Visiting Forces Agreement (US–Philippines)
WCD	World Commission on Dams
WHO	World Health Organization
WPNCL	West Papuan National Coalition for Liberation
WTO	World Trade Organization
ZOPFAN	Zone of Peace, Freedom, and Neutrality
ZoPFFC	Zone of Peace, Freedom, Friendship and Cooperation

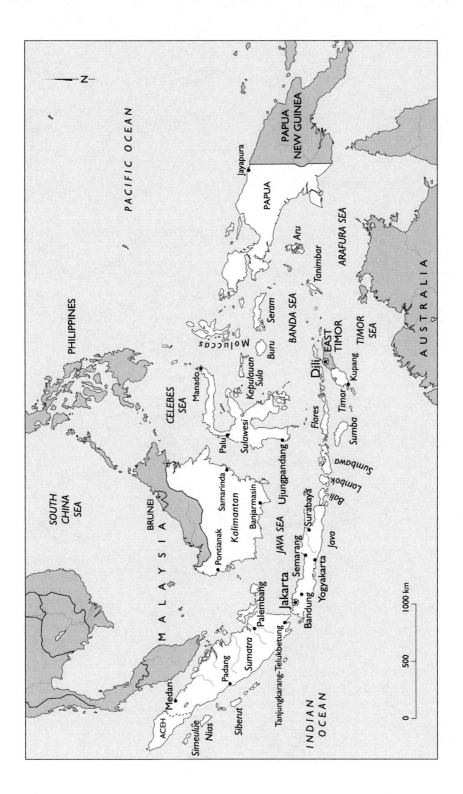

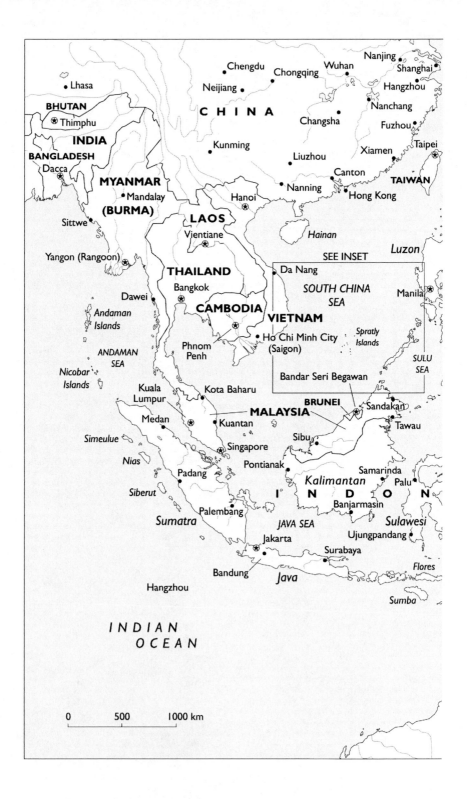

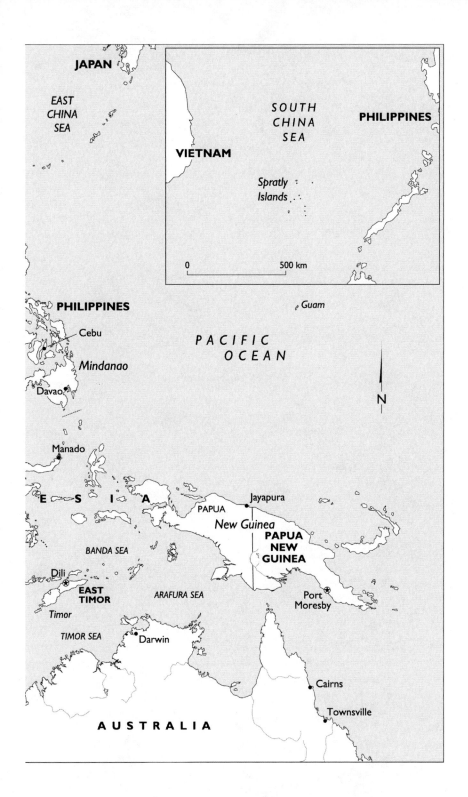

Chapter One

Introduction: The What and Why of Southeast Asia

On 31 December 2015, the Association of Southeast Asian Nations (ASEAN) will celebrate the establishment of the ASEAN Community (AC), designed to be a dynamic, cohesive, resilient, and integrated institutional expression of soft regionalism. It is "soft" in the sense that the members do not give up any of their independent sovereign rights through multilateral cooperation. The AC itself is a tripartite entity composed of an ASEAN Political-Security Community (APSC), an ASEAN Economic Community (AEC), and an ASEAN Socio-Cultural Community (ASCC) (chapter 4).

The emergence of the AC comes eight years after the ten Southeast Asian states belonging to ASEAN adopted the ASEAN Charter in 2007. This gave ASEAN an international personality as a treaty-based regional organization.[1] The reinvention of ASEAN in the 2007 charter came forty years after the foreign ministers of Indonesia, the Philippines, Singapore, and Thailand, and the deputy prime minister of Malaysia issued the Bangkok Declaration on 8 August 1967 establishing ASEAN.[2] The core five ASEAN states were joined by Brunei (1984), Vietnam (1995), Myanmar and Laos (1997), and Cambodia (1999). Waiting in the wings are Timor-Leste and, less probable, Papua New Guinea.

Although the ASEAN Charter proudly proclaims that it is a product of "We the peoples" of ASEAN—or more accurately the separate ASEAN states—the peoples have had little input in shaping its form or functions. ASEAN is the creature of the elite leaderships of its member states acting together on issues in functional areas where national interests converge and cooperation can further the pursuit of national interest under a veil of regional interest. The evolution of ASEAN, from its 1967 foundation to an ASEAN Community nearly a half century later, does not reflect an internalized ASEAN regionalist dynamic. It is a result of the foreign policy outputs of the individual

1

member states as they each adjust to and accommodate the changes and challenges to national interests in the Southeast Asian regional international environment. In the interval between 1967 and the present, the political and economic context of regional international relations has been dramatically altered, although the tools of national policies, even as they might be deployed through ASEAN, are largely the same.

It was at the height of the Cold War in Southeast Asia in 1967 when the United States, the predominant regional political and strategic presence, looked across the battlefield divide of Vietnam to its Cold War antagonists, the USSR and the People's Republic of China. The dominant economic presence was Japan, which through trade, investment, and official development assistance (ODA) was seemingly turning Southeast Asia into an economic dependency. Today, the great-power equation has fundamentally changed. The USSR has been replaced by a Russian Federation which has yet to reemerge as a great-power actor in Southeast Asia. Just as dramatic has been the rise of China as a regional great-power economic and political actor, eclipsing Japan and challenging the relative power position of the United States. Not to be overlooked as a possible future regional great-power actor, India too is rising. What has not changed historically for the states of Southeast Asia is the policy problem of how to pursue their national interests within the constraints of the dynamics of the great powers' presence in the region.

Table 1.1.   The Southeast Asian States

Country	Capital City	Area (sq mi/sq km)	Population (millions)*
Brunei	Bandar Seri Begawan	2,227/5,765	0.4
Cambodia	Phnom Penh	69,900/181,040	15.5
Indonesia	Jakarta	735,358/1,904,569	253.7
Lao PDR	Vientiane	91,430/236,800	6.8
Malaysia	Kuala Lumpur	127,316/329,749	30.1
Myanmar (Burma)	Nay Pyi Taw†	261,969/678,500	55.7
Philippines	Manila	198,117/513,120	107.7
Singapore	Singapore	271/704	5.6
Thailand	Bangkok	98,270/514,000	67.4
Timor-Leste	Dili	5,794/15,007	1.2
Vietnam	Hanoi	127,243/331,114	93.4
Total Population Southeast Asia			637.5

Source: US Central Intelligence Agency, World Factbook 2013.

*Est. July 2014.

†Official spelling (often Nay Pyi Daw).

The original invention of ASEAN was in large measure a response to the regional uncertainties of the Cold War. The contemporary reinvention of ASEAN in the AC is a response to the political and strategic uncertainties of the rise of China and the reactive American and Japanese postures. For the Southeast Asian states the goal has been to create in ASEAN a regional framework for greater maneuverability among the great powers: to augment—but certainly not replace—traditional bilateral diplomacy. This is now explicit in the ASEAN Charter, which states as one of its purposes: "To maintain the *centrality* and *proactive* role of ASEAN as the *primary driving force* in its relations and cooperation with its external partners in a regional architecture that is open, transparent and inclusive" (emphasis added). At the same time, however, tensions created by great-power policies have thrown into relief divergent interests among the ASEAN states that threaten the comity of the ASEAN Community.

Since ASEAN's creation, international relations in Southeast Asia have played out at two levels: the state-to-state bilateral level and the ASEAN multilateral level. At each level there are two sets of relationships. At the bilateral level, there are the relationships among the Southeast Asian states themselves and the relationships of the Southeast Asian states to external actors, in particular the great powers. At the ASEAN level, there are the relationships of the member states to ASEAN and ASEAN's relationship to the external world, again particularly the great powers. An analysis of Southeast Asia's international relations has to address the question of how the two levels with the four categories of transactions mutually interact in terms of behavior at one level influencing behavior at a different level. As will be illustrated, the quality of Southeast Asian states' bilateral relationships with a great power can disrupt the coherence and proactivity of ASEAN.

If, as noted, ASEAN claims to be the central driving force of the region's relations with its external partners, what is the basis of its "centrality" given the real power asymmetries between ASEAN and the great powers? Two hypotheses can be advanced. First, ASEAN is emerging as a hub of its own global network with spokes of different sizes running to all of the great- and not-so-great-power actors and is becoming the fulcrum of a regional balance of power. A second hypothesis suggests that because of their own competitive rivalries, the great powers have implicitly granted to ASEAN by default the right to define the terms of an amorphous regionalism in which real commitment is limited and poses no threat to great-power interests.

Both hypotheses assume that the state actors are seeking to promote their national interests. At one level, there are interests originating in a dominant international system driven by the great powers and potent stateless transnational forces which are summed up in the term "globalization." Southeast

Asia, particularly with the evolution of ASEAN, might be considered a subordinate subsystem of the dominant system.[3] In the Southeast Asian subsystem, there are local national interests derived not just from the economic, social, and political requirements of a modern state, but also from each state's unique matrix of history, culture, and religion. One of the dynamics of international relations in Southeast Asia is how global and local interests complement or conflict with one another at both the bilateral and ASEAN regional levels.

SOUTHEAST ASIA AS AN INTEREST AREA

The Southeast Asian subsystem is becoming an increasingly important unit of the international system. This is the result of three interrelated developments. It is derived in part from key regional states' increasing capabilities and national ambitions. Indonesia and Vietnam are examples. It also reflects the interdependencies being established as the ASEAN region is integrated into the global economy. Finally, Southeast Asia has become a stage where great-power rivalries and competition for influence are being played out. The details of the script are constantly changing, and past interactions of the external actors with the countries of the region will be different in the future. The historical constant for both the regional and extraregional actors is national interest, which with respect to policy choices is defined by national decision makers.

Security Interests

In Southeast Asia, the traditional security concerns involving the threat and use of force by one state against another state have waned but not been eliminated. The regional perils presented by the Cold War conflicts that pitted the great powers and their local surrogates against one another are no longer present (chapter 3). A controlling interest that underpinned those conflicts was strategic access to Southeast Asia, and that is still a great-power interest. It is most obviously at work in shaping policies for maritime security in the South China Sea (chapter 6). Within ASEAN itself, it has been argued that a durable security community has been constructed on the basis of the collective acceptance of the norms of peaceful change and nonuse of force in international relations. This remains to be demonstrated, since the potential for intra-ASEAN armed clashes exists (chapter 5). From the ASEAN vantage, there is an assumption that all countries with interests in Southeast Asia have a common interest in a peaceful, politically stable, and open strategic regional environment. That assumption is being tested (chapter 6). The ASEAN states have also joined their security interests to the wider East Asia and Pacific security environment in the ASEAN Regional Forum (ARF) (chapter 5) and the East Asia Summit (EAS) (chapter 4).

Economic Interests

The rapidly growing economies of Southeast Asia have become an integral part of the East Asian regional and global markets (chapter 8). Even the states left behind, like Myanmar and Laos, have rich potential for resources exploitation to fuel the growth industries of their neighbors (chapter 10). By the end of the Cold War, the five newly industrializing economies of Southeast Asia—Indonesia, Malaysia, the Philippines, Singapore, and Thailand—had achieved sustained levels of relatively high economic performance based on strategies of export-led growth. The local economic "Crash of '97" followed by a wider global economic downturn gave them a reality check, but firm platforms for recovery for future growth were quickly put in place. The laggard socialist states have largely abandoned the command model of development, hoping to emulate the successes of their regional partners. Vietnam now outpaces Thailand and the Philippines in economic growth.

The ASEAN states have tried to expand intraregional trade through a variety of initiatives. The earlier, hesitant efforts at regional integration have evolved to the current goal of an ASEAN Economic Community by the year 2015. In theory, the AEC would create a single market and production base, strengthening the region's capabilities to deal with the international economy. The more economically advanced ASEAN countries have forged numerous bilateral free trade agreements (FTAs) with external trading partners and in their collective format have negotiated ASEAN + 1 regional trade agreements (RTAs). Two proposed comprehensive RTAs have brought great-power tensions into economic play: the China-backed Regional Comprehensive Economic Partnership (RCEP) and the US-proposed Trans-Pacific Partnership (TPP) (chapter 8).

Political Interests

As the new millennium began, it was thought that important Southeast Asian countries had been lapped by a "third wave" of democratization.[4] Only Indonesia stands out as a democratic model. With the exception of Myanmar, little if any democratizing change has taken place in Southeast Asia's undemocratic and authoritarian states. The formal elective representative democratic frameworks for the governments of Cambodia, Malaysia, Singapore, and Timor-Leste mask an undemocratic reality. The once-praised democracies of the Philippines and Thailand have been severely eroded by coups and leadership failings. Jakarta's efforts to translate its democratization process to its ASEAN neighbors and to ASEAN itself have had only mixed success. There has been no "Southeast Asia spring." Nevertheless, even though democratic change has been resisted by ruling elites, a democratic political culture is gradually spreading among the people in Southeast Asia. Civil societies are emerging in the most economically dynamic states from new modern social classes and networks facilitated by the phenomenal spread of social media. The frequent use of harsh repressive measures by ASEAN governments defending against democracy activists clashes with Western liberal interests in promoting democracy and defending human rights.

Efforts to apply Western-defined standards of civil and political rights as a benchmark for the quality of bilateral political relations have become the most visibly contentious part of the political agenda (chapter 9). China, on the other hand, has no problem with democracy and human rights issues in its relations in Southeast Asia. It joins with ASEAN in asserting noninterference in the internal affairs of a sovereign country. China's unconditional approach stands in sharp contrast to Western governments' stances conditioned by nontraditional liberal international relations agendas.

Nontraditional Interests

Even as the states of the region grapple with the traditional transactions of international relations involving security, high politics, and economic advantage, they are confronted by a nontraditional contemporary agenda. International relations have been redefined in the context of globalism. The successes of their economic development strategies have enmeshed Southeast Asian governments in a transnational nexus of economic, social, and cultural interests and norms articulated by the liberal democratic West. Issues having to do with narcotics trafficking, gender discrimination, environment, minority rights, refugees, migrant labor, and child labor have become part of international relations in Southeast Asia (chapters 9 and 10). The concept of security has been broadened to include human security as a goal of the international community. The politics of this agenda challenges the adaptive capabilities of the regional states' policy makers. It also calls into question the immutability of sovereignty, the founding principle of the modern state, and the concomitant claim to noninterference in matters of domestic jurisdiction. In many policy conflicts arising out of the nontraditional agenda, Southeast Asia finds China, a strong advocate of sovereign boundary maintenance, an ally while the United States and the European Union (EU) can be adversaries.

Before examining in the succeeding chapters the working out in Southeast Asia of the traditional and nontraditional international relations agendas, it is first necessary to test two underlying assumptions informing both the preceding paragraphs and the book. The premise is that the eleven countries of Southeast Asia can be treated as part of a definable international political/economic region, and that the Southeast Asian region itself objectively exists for extraregional international actors.

DEFINING THE SOUTHEAST ASIAN "REGION"

The concept of Southeast Asia as a geopolitical region is a product of World War II in the Pacific. In the Allies' war against Japan, a South-East Asia Command (SEAC) was created in 1943. Headquartered at Kandy in Ceylon (now Sri Lanka), SEAC did not fully geographically correspond to today's Southeast Asia. It did, however, give a political context to the notion of a region with political and strategic coherence that was barely hinted at in the travelogues and anthropological use of the term "Southeast Asia" before the war.[5]

At the outset of World War II, the Kingdom of Thailand was the only independent Southeast Asian state, and its independence was qualified by unequal treaties and imperialist pressures. There was no political or economic sense of a coherent Southeast Asian region. It was a geographic area where European states and America had carved out sovereign domains, connected not to each other but to faraway metropolitan capitals. Foreign empire did not disrupt any existing Southeast Asian regional political order. There was no overarching Southeast Asian unifying geopolitical structure. Before the Europeans there were indigenous claimants to empire whose historical memories are evoked in modern nationalisms: Cambodia's Angkor, Indonesia's Majapahit, Thailand's Ayudhya, and Myanmar's Bagan. To dynastic China, the precolonial kingdoms in Southeast Asia were considered to be vassal tributaries located in the "Southern Ocean" (*nanyang*).

After the 1945 defeat of Japan, the returning European colonial powers faced nationalist resistance to the reimposition of alien rule. The imperial responses to the local waves of nationalism differed. The United States had committed itself before the war to Philippine independence. This was accomplished in 1946. A war-weakened Great Britain, once shorn of India in 1947, did not resist independence for Burma in 1948. Malaya's independence from Britain was delayed until 1957, while Malay and British Commonwealth forces fought a communist insurgency, known as the "Emergency." The British decolonized Singapore, Sarawak, and British North Borneo (Sabah) in

1963 by incorporating them with Malaya into a new federal Malaysia. After only two years, Singapore and Malaysia parted ways, and Singapore became independent in 1965. Little oil-rich Brunei, a British protectorate sandwiched between Sabah and Sarawak, refused to join the new Malaysian Federation and reluctantly became independent in 1984. Fearful of designs on it by its Malaysian and Indonesian neighbors, it was reassured by a residual British defense commitment.

The road to independence was not that smooth for the Netherlands Indies and French Indochina, comprised of Vietnam, Cambodia, and Laos. In August 1945, Indonesia proclaimed its independence. The Dutch used military force to try to restore their authority. After two Dutch "police actions," stout Indonesian resistance, and strong international pressure, the Netherlands was forced to cede sovereignty in 1949, retaining, however, Dutch New Guinea until 1963 (chapter 3). Finally, in the wake of the overthrow of dictatorship in Portugal, after four centuries of Portuguese rule East Timor declared independence in November 1975. This was followed one month later by an Indonesian invasion and absorption into the Indonesian state. East Timor reemerged as independent Timor-Leste in 1992 under UN auspices after international intervention (chapters 2 and 9).

France fought a costly war in Vietnam for nearly a decade against a nationalist–communist coalition led by Ho Chi Minh. This was the First Indochina War. During the course of that war, Cambodia and Laos were able to throw off French rule. France gave up in Vietnam in 1954, and the United States picked up the struggle in a partitioned Vietnam, with extensions into Laos and Cambodia, until 1973. This was the Second Indochina War. After three decades of war and tens of thousands of casualties, it was only in 1975 that a unified independent Vietnamese state emerged (chapter 3).

At independence, the leaders of the new states of Southeast Asia faced similar tasks. First, authority had to be consolidated in states that were weak and vulnerable. Revolutionary violence and separatist urges threatened their territorial and political integrity. The old nationalism had been built on opposition to imperialism. A new nationalism had to be founded on real achievement in nation building. Second, working relationships had to be established with former colonial rulers on the basis of sovereign equality rather than colonial dependence. Third, they had to obtain access to international sources of capital and markets in order to deliver on the promise to their populations of economic development and social welfare. Trade, aid, and foreign direct investment were the mantras of the economic planners. Finally, having been long separated by history and imperialism, the new states of Southeast Asia had to establish relations with each other. This was no easy task given historical antagonisms and contested borders.

It was only with the post–World War II emergence of the newly independent nation-states of Southeast Asia that makers of foreign policy and students of international relations began to think of this group of countries as an international region. The external awareness of a Southeast Asian region at this early point was primarily a product of its geostrategic position in the Cold War (chapter 3). In today's very different global international political context, a first question to be asked in examining international relations in the Southeast Asian region is, what kind of region is it?

The Geographic Region

Geographic proximity is a basic criterion of a region. On a map, Southeast Asia lies within the space roughly bounded in the north by China, the east by the Pacific Ocean, the southeast by Australia, the south by the Indian Ocean, and the southwest by the Bay of Bengal and India. Southeast Asia is a physical region. Its climate is humid and tropical. It experiences the annual alternation of the wind patterns from continental Asia, the northeast or wet monsoon, and from the Australian continent and Indian Ocean, the southwest or dry monsoon. The monsoon pattern dominates Southeast Asia's agricultural calendar. Even though agriculture as a percentage of gross domestic product (GDP) is steadily diminishing, it is still the source of livelihood for tens of millions of Southeast Asians and irrigated rice the main staple food of the populations.

The geographic region is resource rich. Its rapidly depleting forests are the world's principal source of tropical hardwoods. Deforestation has become a major issue in the dialogues on climate change (chapter 10). Southeast Asia is an important producer of oil and natural gas. A factor in the competition for jurisdiction in the South China Sea is the prospect of oil and gas fields under the seabed (chapter 6). Mineral deposits include commercially valuable tin, nickel, copper, and gold. Southeast Asian fisheries, both natural and farmed, provide the major source of protein in the people's diet as well as export earnings. Aggressive exploitation of fisheries has become a source of political irritation as countries seek to defend their law of the sea–defined maritime exclusive economic zones (EEZs) (chapter 10).

Nesting inside the Southeast Asian geographic box are two smaller boxes: continental or mainland Southeast Asia and maritime or island Southeast Asia. This has led to competitive strategic perspectives within ASEAN.[6]

Continental Southeast Asia

Continental Southeast Asia has been the historical seat of civilizations, empires, and states centered on the valleys, plains, and deltas of north–south running great rivers: from west to east, the Irrawaddy and Salween in Myanmar, the Chao Phraya in Thailand, the Mekong, and Vietnam's Red River. The Mekong River is the central artery of mainland Southeast Asia, giving it whatever natural unity it might possess. Rising in Tibet, the mighty Mekong runs more than three thousand miles from China, touching Laos, Myanmar, Thailand, and Cambodia before emptying into the South China Sea at delta Vietnam. It is the twelfth longest river in the world, and in volume of flow it is the tenth greatest world river. The Mekong drainage basin is the focus of overlapping ambitious developmental planning frameworks that envision it as a liquid engine of economic activity (chapters 4 and 10). North of the Mekong Delta, Vietnam is cut off from its continental neighbors by a chain of hills and mountains. It shares, however, a key strategic feature with the others. Bordering and politically looming above continental Southeast Asia is the Chinese land and population mass. From a Beijing perspective, the Mekong region might be considered part of a greater Yunnan.

Maritime Southeast Asia

Maritime Southeast Asia has margins on the South China Sea as a common natural feature. Depending on the controlling political perspective, the states of this subregion are joined or separated from each other by the two great archipelagoes of the Philippines and Indonesia; East and West Malaysia divided by the southern reach of the South China Sea; island Singapore off the tip of peninsular Malaysia; Brunei wedged between the East Malaysian Sabah and Sarawak states; and Timor-Leste, trapped in the Indonesian archipelago. Maritime Southeast Asia's political patterns historically evolved from networks of coastal trading points that from the end of the first millennium BCE were engaged in commercial exchange with India and China. These waters are the commercial and naval links between Northeast Asia and South Asia, the Middle East, and on to Europe. Maritime Southeast Asia's strategic outlook is fastened on the South China Sea, most of which is claimed by China (chapter 6).

The Human Geography of Southeast Asia

Bounded geography, climatic similarities, common ecological features, and other observable shared natural characteristics of the states of Southeast Asia are not enough to define a political region. The notion that a river of traditional cultural heritage and history runs beneath the modern politics in ASEAN and gives Southeast Asia a unique international identity, while romantic, cannot be empirically supported.[7] There must be other commonalities that relate to how the states behave politically toward each other and the extraregional international environment. In fact, beyond the macrogeographic unity of the latitude-longitude box, there are few qualities that we associate with a world region to be found in Southeast Asia. There is no regionwide identity—race, ethnicity, language, religion, culture, and history—such as we find in the Arab world, Western Europe, or, with the exception of Brazil, Latin America.

Ethnic Diversity

Complementing and partially overlapping the fragmented geography of Southeast Asia are its ethnic and cultural maps. In continental Southeast Asia, there are three major ethnic-linguistic groups with many languages and dialects reflecting its prehistoric population. The Austro-Asiatic language family includes Mon, Khmer (Cambodian), and Vietnamese. The Tibeto-Burman group has Burmese as its major language. Tai-speaking tribal groups from Southwest China were the latecomers, beginning to move into Southeast Asia at the beginning of the last millennium in a migration that continued into the last century. The largest number of Tai speakers is in Thailand, followed by Laos, and the Shan who straddle the Thailand–Myanmar border. The ethnic-linguistic roots of maritime Southeast Asia are found in the Austronesian migrations southward from a coastal China-Taiwan homeland that by 1500 BCE had spread its Malayo-Polynesian languages and culture through the archipelagoes to the South Pacific. The complexity of the ethnic-linguistic map is demonstrated by the fact that in Indonesia alone, up to three hundred distinct ethnic-linguistic groups have been identified.

We must add to the indigenous ethnic mix the generations of Chinese immigrants. They number about twenty-five million, or less than 5 percent of the total Southeast Asian population. Chinese trading settlements existed in precolonial Southeast Asia, but it was during the European imperialist period that the foundations for the contemporary Chinese communities in Southeast Asia were laid. The largest minority Chinese population by percentage of national population is the 24 percent in Malaysia. Singapore is a 77 percent majority Chinese state. Concentrated in urban areas and engaged in critical businesses and trade, the Chinese minority's economic influence is far out of proportion to its numbers. This has been a source of indigenous nationalist resentment since independence. There has also been a question of the loyalties of local Chinese. The issue was first raised in suspicions about a Chinese Trojan horse for communism. It has been reframed in terms of concerns about local Chinese links to the flow of Chinese trade and investment.

Religious Diversity

Differences in religious belief and practice in Southeast Asia roughly correspond to the continental–maritime geographic divide. On the mainland, Theravada Buddhism dominates in Myanmar, Thailand, Cambodia, and Laos. The Indic cultural background of most of continental Southeast Asia, excluding Vietnam, earned it the earlier soubriquet of "Farther India" or "India beyond the Ganges." It is a Western myth that Buddhists are inherently fatalistic, passive, and nonaggressive. As centuries of warfare have demonstrated, Buddhists can be just as savage as anyone else.

Islam is the predominant religion of maritime Southeast Asia. The aggregate Muslim population of Southeast Asia is 250 million, or 39 percent of ASEAN's total population.[8] Brunei, Malaysia, and Indonesia are Muslim-majority countries. Indonesia alone accounts for 88 percent of Southeast Asia's Muslim population. Arab and Indian traders brought Islam to the region as early as the thirteenth century. By the end of the sixteenth century, Islam had swept in a great arc from the Malay Peninsula through the archipelagoes. The vision of radical Islamist networks with links to terrorism is the unification of all Southeast Asian Muslims in a new caliphate transcending secular state boundaries. At both the western and eastern ends of the Islamic arc, the Muslim populations are restive national minorities in Myanmar, Thailand, and the Philippines (chapter 5). All Muslims in Southeast Asia have a transnational identity. They are part of the *ummat*, Islam's universal community of believers. They feel for, and support, the struggles of Muslims anywhere in the world. The perceived grievances of the *ummat* are a factor in shaping Islamic Southeast Asia's attitudes toward the United States' relations with the Muslim-majority Southeast Asian states. To many Muslims, American interventions in Muslim countries are viewed as war on Islam.

Vietnam and the Philippines are outliers from the Buddhist and Muslim cultural domains in the region. The traditional Vietnamese royal courts had been a southern extension of the Chinese cultural sphere. Among the population are Theravada Buddhists, Mahayana Buddhists, Christians, and Confucians. The different religions and sects in Vietnam have in common submission to the demands of a secular Leninist regime. The Philippines' population is more than 90 percent Christian with 80 percent Roman Catholic. Underneath the "great religions" of Southeast Asia there remain numbers of minority ethnic groups classified as animists, that is, propitiators of localized deities and spirits.

Historical Antagonisms

Even though the independent states of Southeast Asia are relatively new to the modern state system, they bring with them the baggage of a history of war. For centuries, Burmese and Thai armies laid waste to each other's territories. The Thais have not forgotten that Burma sacked their capital Ayudhya in 1767. Nor have the Laotians erased from their national memory the fact that an invading Thai army laid waste to Vientiane in 1827, carrying away the Jade Buddha, the national palladium. In the eighteenth and nineteenth centuries, Thai and Vietnamese dynasties wrestled for control of Cambodia. The blood-soaked traditional Cambodian–Vietnamese relationship, represented in the thirteenth-century sculpture at Angkor Wat, was continued in modern Cambodia by the wholesale murder of Vietnamese nationals in the aftermath of the 1970 military coup that installed a pro-American Cambodian government. At the primordial level of analysis, the Vietnamese invasion and occupation of Cambodia and ensuing Third Indochina War was a continuation of the conflict-filled traditional relationship. During World War II, Thailand, backed by Japan, grabbed back Cambodian, Laotian, Burmese, and Malayan territories wrested from it by French and British imperialism. They were returned as part of the postwar settlement. Thailand's irredentist past still fuels suspicions among its neighbors about its subregional ambitions.

In maritime Southeast Asia, the pan-Indonesia elements in the Sukarno era's radical nationalism raised fears among its neighbors that Indonesia sought to restore the supposed fourteenth-century "golden age" boundaries of Java's Majapahit Empire. These suspicions seemed confirmed when Indonesia used military force in the early 1960s to try to prevent the formation of Malaysia and were rekindled by Indonesia's invasion and occupation of the former Portuguese territory of East Timor in 1975 (chapter 3).

DIVERSITIES IN MODERN STATE DEVELOPMENT

The ethnic, cultural, and historical diversities in Southeast Asia are the background of relations among the contemporary states of the region. Since independence, the states have pursued different political and economic paths.

Political Diversity

There is no common Southeast Asian political culture. Until the 1990s, the internationally relevant macropolitical division of the region was between communist and noncommunist Southeast Asia. High politics was conducted along that divide with little reference to the internal political differences among the states on each side of the divide. The formal political institutions in Southeast Asia vary greatly: an absolute monarchy (Brunei), three constitutional monarchies (Malaysia, Thailand, and Cambodia), five republics (Indonesia, Myanmar, the Philippines, Singapore, and Timor-Leste), and two socialist states (Laos and Vietnam). In terms of governmental structure, Indonesia, Myanmar, and the Philippines are presidential. Cambodia, Malaysia, Singapore, Thailand, and Timor-Leste are parliamentary, headed by prime ministers. Laos and Vietnam are Leninist command states.

More important than the constitutional basis or institutional form given to authority in a state is the quality of the relationship of state authority to its population. The most significant distinguishing political factor for contemporary international relations is the degree to which governments are representative of and accountable to their citizens. Certainly for the liberal democratic countries of the West, attitudes about and policies toward the individual countries of Southeast Asia are influenced by the "democratic" content of their domestic politics. An important component of this is human rights (chapter 9). It also can impact the way Southeast Asian countries relate to one another.

Clark Neher and Ross Marley devised a scale for democracy in Southeast Asia which ranked the countries in four categories of democracy, semidemocracy, semiauthoritarian, and authoritarian based on citizen participation, electoral competition, and civil liberties.[9] Utilizing their methodology, in 2014 there was only one democracy in Southeast Asia—Indonesia. The semidemocracies are Malaysia, the Philippines, and Timor-Leste. The semiauthoritarian bracket contains Cambodia and Singapore. On the Neher-Marley spectrum, Brunei, Laos, Thailand, and Vietnam are authoritarian. Myanmar is in a democratizing transition from a military junta. It is too soon to tell whether its trajectory will be similar to Indonesia's post-Suharto or fall short of democracy. The scheduled 2015 elections will be an indicator.

Another measure of political diversity is Freedom House's annual report, *Freedom in the World*. The Freedom Index measures two dimensions, political rights (PR) and civil liberties (CL), and scores from 1 to 7, with 7 being the lowest score to determine whether a country is free (F), partly free (PF), or not free (NF). Table 1.2 shows the scores for Southeast Asia in the 2014 report. In 2013, Indonesia had been labeled free with an index rating of PR-2 and CL-3 but was downgraded in 2014 to partly free because of the passage of a restrictive civil society law in 2013. This raises the question of whether the Indonesian democratization process has stalled. The 2014 Thai coup will downgrade Thailand's standing on the index.

Economic Inequalities

At independence, the Southeast Asian states, with the exception of Brunei and Singapore, had similar economic problems, being classified as underdeveloped. This status was characterized by low per capita GDP, poor living standards, inadequate human resources, primary products exploita-

Table 1.2.   2014 Freedom Index for Southeast Asia

Country	PR Score	CL Score	Status
Indonesia	2	4	PF
Philippines	3	3	PF
Timor-Leste	3	4	PF
Malaysia	4	4	PF
Singapore	4	4	PF
Thailand	4	4	PF
Cambodia	6	5	NF
Brunei	6	5	NF
Myanmar	6	5	NF
Vietnam	7	5	NF
Laos	7	6	NF

Source: Freedom House, *Freedom in the World 2014.*

tion, few value-added industries, and other measures of low economic performance. A priority of the Southeast Asian states has been economic development.

Initially, divergent routes for development were chosen that can be roughly categorized as socialist/communist and mixed-capitalist. However, the Marxist programs failed and the mixed-capitalist model prevails. Four Southeast Asian nations—Cambodia, Laos, Myanmar, and Timor-Leste— are on the forty-nine-country United Nations list of Least Developed Countries (LDCs) where human security is most at risk (chapter 9). LDC status is based on the combination of extreme poverty, structural weakness of the economy, and lack of development capacity.[10] The World Bank's classification of country economies by income has four income categories: low, low-middle, upper-middle, and high.[11] In Southeast Asia the low-income countries are Cambodia, Timor-Leste, Laos, Myanmar, and Vietnam. Indonesia, the Philippines, and Thailand are in the low-middle-income bracket, and Malaysia is found in the upper-middle-income ranks. Brunei and Singapore are high-income countries. Table 1.3 illustrates some of the development differences in Southeast Asia. The Southeast Asian states' economic strengths and weaknesses contribute to their foreign policy capabilities and activities in the regional and international systems. The political adaptation to the discrepancies between the wealthier and poorer countries has been built into an economically tiered ASEAN system. The latecomers— Cambodia, Laos, Myanmar, and Vietnam, collectively called the CLMV countries—have been granted a longer period of time to meet the ASEAN regional integration targets.

Chapter One

Table 1.3.   Selected GDP Economic Indicators (2012 est.)

Countries	GDP (PPP)* $ Billion	World Rank (1–220)	Per Capita GDP (PPP) $ Thousands	World Rank (1–220)	GDP % Growth 2012 est.
Brunei	22.04	127	55,300	11	1.3
Cambodia	37.25	108	2,400	187	6.5
Indonesia	1,164.0	16	5,100	158	6.2
Lao PDR	19.52	137	3,100	176	8.3
Malaysia	506.7	38	17,200	78	5.6
Myanmar	90.93	77	1,400	209	6.3
Philippines	431.3	32	4,500	165	6.6
Singapore	331.9	41	61,000	7	1.3
Thailand	662.6	25	10,300	116	6.4
Timor-Leste	111.23	152	10,000	119	10.0
Vietnam	325.9	42	3,600	170	5.0

Source: CIA *World Factbook, July 2013.*

*GDP is given in purchasing power parity, a measure of relative purchasing power made by converting a currency's market exchange rate to a standardized weighted US dollar rate.

REGION AND REGIONALISM

It is clear from the above discussion that diversity rather than homogeneity is the compelling characteristic of Southeast Asia. In order to study Southeast Asia as a region, it will be necessary to identify unifying transactional or institutional patterns. One scholar paradoxically finds diversity itself as the unifying theme making Southeast Asia a region.[12] Another argues that "the notion of 'Southeast Asia' is more a result of American and European professors looking for a convenient way to study a geographic region than it is a meaningful term for an area that systematically shares commonalities."[13] A premise of this book is that the foundations of international relations in Southeast Asia rest on national diversities not regional unity. Southeast Asia can be conceived of as an aggregation of overlapping geographic, ethnic, cultural, political, and economic subregions. Potent divisive, not unifying, forces originate in these diversities. The idea of "unity out of diversity" is an elite conceit, not a natural political phenomenon.

Yet, despite the fact that Southeast Asia has few of the characteristics commonly utilized to define a political region, we continue to treat it as such. This is because of the existence of the Association of Southeast Asian Nations. ASEAN gives institutional expression to an essentially declaratory regionalism that originates not from natural circumstances, but in the political will of Southeast Asian policy elites. Very importantly, the Southeast Asian regional identity claimed by ASEAN has been nominally accepted by members of the global international system. Looking to the future, if one or more states reprioritizes its national interests in terms of its great-power relationships, its political commitment to ASEAN's expression of regionalism could waver. What we might call the Southeast Asian "virtual" or "imagined" region is a product of a process that is as much ideational as institutional. In fact, the term "ASEAN" itself is often used as a synonym for geographic Southeast Asia, even though Timor-Leste is excluded. Donald Emmerson described Timor-Leste as a "slippage between a spatial Southeast Asia and a political ASEAN."[14] ASEAN's insistence on defending the Myanmar junta's internationally embarrassing membership was in part an almost reflexive devotion to its founders' vision of a congruency of ASEAN with Southeast Asia.

In many respects, the idea of regionalism is more powerful than the loose, poorly articulated, voluntary institutions and multilateral structures that give it form. Nearly every Southeast Asian multilateral grouping, from chambers of commerce to educators, has been "ASEAN-ized," that is, notionally assimilated to a sense of regionalism that has its political expression in ASEAN. Annex 2 of the ASEAN Charter lists more than 70 "entities" officially associated with ASEAN. Since its creation in 1967, and particularly since the ending of the Third Indochina War followed by communist–noncommunist state reconciliation, ASEAN in its organizational framework embodies the analytical existence of a Southeast Asian region.

As already noted, ASEAN's regionalism is "soft" regionalism in that the member states have not delegated any of their authority to it. Because of the demonstrable relative lack of substantial regionalized real policy achievements, ASEAN's critics have trumpeted its failures. It has been called, for example, an "uncertain collocation of fragile states that connote the failed delusional entity of Southeast Asia."[15] Certainly, movement has been slow for regionalism as a process, in part because ASEAN is inner conflicted. Still, a Southeast Asian region exists because leaders have a minimum, lowest-common-denominator consensus on what regional interests are and some degree of collective expectations of how they should act in pursuit of those interests. Rather than considering ASEAN an example of failed regionalism, it is perhaps more accurate to view ASEAN in terms of aspirational regionalism, toward which progress is being made in achieving the diplomatic goals set forth by its founders, but not the integrative goals of theorists and bureaucratic proponents.[16]

THE STUDY OF INTERNATIONAL RELATIONS IN SOUTHEAST ASIA

International relations theories and analyses seek to explain how change occurs in relations among states to provide a basis for making probabilistic statements about state behavior.[17] A central concern is the mode of change in the quality of relations between national units, often reduced to a dichotomy of conflict or cooperation. The fact that the "virtual" region of ASEAN and the real geographic region of eleven very disparate sovereign states have policy coexistence complicates the study of international relations *in* Southeast Asia. Note the emphasis on the preposition "in" in the preceding sentence. This is because there is no international relations *of* Southeast Asia. ASEAN is the voluntary creation of its still fully sovereign state members and not an independent international actor. This presents a level-of-analysis question that influences the theoretical paradigm to be applied. Do we start with the states or the region?

The Realist Approach

The dominant paradigm for interpreting international relations in Southeast Asia has been realism. The pillars of realism are the sovereign state, national self-interest, and power. National elites acquire and mobilize national capabilities to pursue national interests in a competitive international environment in which there is no central governing order. For a state's relations with other states, national interest is defined by the elites who have authority in the state. National interests are not based simply on temporally situated pragmatic political or material goals. They are determined in a social and psychological context of history, culture, and religion that makes the definition of interest an exercise unique to each set of national policy makers.

At the heart of realist theory are security interests, usually narrowly defined as state independence, territorial integrity, and maintenance of the political system. The greatest part by far of the literature on Southeast Asian international relations is focused on security as traditionally defined. The most influential body of work on Southeast Asian international relations from a realist foundation is that of Michael Leifer.[18] He assigned great weight to the operation of the balance of power as the controlling political factor in Southeast Asian foreign policy decision making. As national interests clash and threats to security mount, nations resort to self-help, seek through alliances and alignment a balance of power, or shelter under hegemonic protection. There are more comprehensive definitions of security relating not just to the state but also to the political, economic, and social human conditions of the state's population. The "needs of the common man" as contained in the concept of human security is newly in vogue (chapter 9). Even if we adopt a people-centered approach as opposed to the traditional state-centric, it remains the fact that it is principally the state that negotiates the "people's interests" in the international system.

The unrelieved realist's Hobbesian view of international relations as an anarchic jungle is qualified by an approach that emphasizes cooperation among states as well as conflict as a way to pursue national interest. This involves a calculation of relative gains. International relations, rather than being a zero-sum game, can be win-win, although some win more than others. In this approach, ASEAN is a mode of international cooperation through which member states pursue national interests. With security still the realist heart of interest and the balance of power its mechanism, ASEAN as a regime for cooperative security can be placed in a realist balance-of-power perspective (chapter 5).[19] ASEAN's policy output cannot be explained without locating and understanding the different national interests being expressed through it. Whatever is understood as an ASEAN regional interest is based on the consensual harmonizing of national interests in order to present a formal united front.

Liberalism

With the advent of ASEAN, attention shifted from state actors to the assumed regional institutional actor. ASEAN was viewed through the lens of international integration studies, relying too much on analogy from the Western European experience. Functionalist theory was employed to suggest that through ASEAN specific transnational structures in the economic, technical, and social fields would evolve, to which ASEAN-wide decision-making authority would be transferred. This would build community from the bottom up. It was expected that institution building in the nonpolitical issue areas would spill over into more politically sensitive areas of states' interactions. However, after more than four decades, not one such structure can be located. For the liberal integrationists, for whom ASEAN has proved a theoretical disappointment, ASEAN's failure is the failure of the political will of leadership. For the realists, what integrationists call failure is in fact the political will of leaders at the state level who make conscious decisions based on national interest about which issues and at what level cooperation in ASEAN will be offered.

A different approach to ASEAN draws from regime theory, which looks at habit-forming experiences of cooperation over time. These create international regimes that are sets of implicit or explicit principles, norms, rules, and decision-making procedures around which participating actors' expectations converge in a given issue area.[20] Regime theory accepts the fact that states act on the basis of interest but are disciplined to the reciprocally understood obligations of the "regime." The sense of regime is unconsciously captured in the notion of an "ASEAN way" of addressing issue-specific problems through informal consultation and consensus. The most productive, but still unsatisfactory, effort to apply regime theory to Southeast Asia is in ASEAN as a security regime (chapter 5).

Constructivism

It is only a theoretical step from regime to community, but in practical policy terms a perhaps insurmountable gulf. A regime is founded on learned expectations about behavior in functionally specific state interactions. A community, on the other hand, is defined not so much by interests as by shared values and norms. An attempt to bridge that gulf intellectually is the separation of "interest" from "identity" found in constructivist theory.[21] Amitav Acharya's contributions laid the foundation for a constructivist view of ASEAN.[22] For constructivists, a community is socially constructed through knowledge, norms, culture, and other cooperative associations that over time cognitively promote a collective identity. For ASEAN, then, the lack of institutional progress is not important. What is important is mutual recognition of an ASEAN identity. It is this that leads to stability and consensus. The decoupling of identity from institutions, however, leaves open the question of what the link is from identity to state action. Outcome in terms of policy takes a backseat. For the constructivists, ASEAN "has had less to do with the coordination of cooperation for divvying up gains than it has with the facilitation of a dialogue on what region 'means' for them."[23] Critics also point out that any ASEAN "identity" is only one among the identities that leaders in Southeast Asia have—national, ethnic, religious, class—and that the ASEAN identity is not shared with their own populations, of which many have less than fully solidified national identities. A paradigm based on elites' hypothesized collective ASEAN identity is insufficient for understanding international relations in Southeast Asia. ASEAN identity is not superior to national interests when it comes to actual policy choices.

THE LINK BETWEEN STATE AND REGION

ASEAN is only one aspect of international relations in Southeast Asia. Academic concentration on ASEAN tends to obscure the fact that for Southeast Asian policy elites, critical areas of conflict and cooperation exist bilaterally and subregionally in both traditional interest areas and the new global agenda. ASEAN has proved itself singularly unsuccessful in dealing with political issues internal to the region since ASEAN's overriding organizational principle is the inviolability of member-state sovereignty. National leaders in Southeast

Asia rhetorically affirm the regional identity and cooperate where interests are served, but the state is still the primary actor. Former ASEAN secretary general Ong Keng Yong realistically recognized this fact in pointing out that membership in ASEAN was in addition to the national policies of each member government: "Each of the members has every right to formulate its own national position based on its circumstances *that will best serve its own national interests*" (emphasis added).[24]

Leaders in Southeast Asia consciously and rationally understand that there are national interests that can be promoted in concert with other Southeast Asian states having similar interests. The relationships in ASEAN are intergovernmental, which, as Leifer pointed out two decades ago, "means that while interests may be shared they are rarely held truly in common."[25] This is especially true with respect to bargaining with powers that have greater political, economic, and military capabilities. The member states can amplify their international voice through ASEAN as a kind of diplomatic caucus. Similar or complementary national interests can be translated to a regional interest even though the outcomes are received at the state level. The way that national interests are cooperatively associated through ASEAN represents the link between the levels of state–region analysis. The management of this depends on decision making at the state level.

THE ARGUMENT AND STRUCTURE OF THE BOOK

The chapters to follow will detail the major actors, interests, issues, key relationships, structures, and institutions involved in an understanding of international relations in Southeast Asia. The material is presented in the context of a thematic argument that gives a pattern to Southeast Asian international relations that includes "regionalism" as a variable but also accounts for the behavior of the state units as well as nonstate actors. The thematic proposition can be put simply. From independence, the states of Southeast Asia, individually and collectively, have struggled for policy autonomy in their international environments. By "autonomy" is meant the ability to pursue self-defined national interests within the limits of national capabilities, free from externally imposed political, economic, or military constraints. The initial external limits on autonomy were set in the context of the global Cold War and American security primacy in Southeast Asia. As US political hegemony has diminished in the post–Cold War era, Southeast Asia now sees on the policy horizon a prospective Chinese hegemony. The irony in the struggle for autonomy is that while Southeast Asian states enhance their capabilities through globalization, they meet new categories of nontraditional policy-limiting demands aggressively promoted not only by states, but also by international nongovernmental organizations that, unlike states, can penetrate sovereignty with direct links to domestic NGO counterparts.

It can also be asked whether and how a state's commitment to ASEAN itself might constrain the policy options of its member states. For example, Indonesia's foreign minister, Marty Natalegawa, asserted in 2013 that Indonesia "must become a country that shapes and moulds. We are not interested in responding in a passive way to developments."[26] Yet confined within ASEAN, Indonesia's pretension of active leadership faces the reality of consensus decision making and the ASEAN way.[27]

Chapter 2 introduces the state and nonstate actors whose actions shape foreign policy outcomes in Southeast Asia. Chapter 3 briefly reviews international relations in Southeast Asia during the Cold War. This background is necessary to comprehend the major discontinuities and reorientations in the post–Cold War era. Chapter 4 examines the structures of ASEAN-led regionalism in Southeast Asia. Chapter 5 addresses conflict and modes of conflict resolution in traditional areas of Southeast Asian security interests. The conflicts in the South China Sea with their implications for ASEAN solidarity and great-power competition are the subject of chapter 6. Nontraditional security issues such as terrorism and transboundary crime are treated in chapter 7. Southeast Asia's regional structures for international economic cooperation are the topic of chapter 8. Chapter 9 examines human security in Southeast Asia. Chapter 10 looks at environmental issues in Southeast Asian international relations as a nontraditional issue area. The concluding chapter 11 returns to issues raised in the introduction. It asks three questions, the answers to which will shape the future of international relations in Southeast Asia. Will national leaders succeed in reinventing ASEAN as a more effective collaborative mechanism? Can ASEAN maintain its claim to "centrality" in maneuvering between China and the United States? What are the possible outcomes as the struggle for autonomy continues?

NOTES

1. The text of the charter and its annexes can be accessed at http://www.asean.org/archive/publications/ASEAN-Charter.pdf.

2. "Bangkok Declaration," *Handbook on Selected ASEAN Political Documents*, I, accessed at http://www.asean.org/archive/pdf/HBPDR.pdf.

3. The concept of a subordinate Southeast Asian subsystem of the international system was introduced by Michael Brecher, *The New States of Asia: A Political Analysis* (Oxford: Oxford University Press, 1963).

4. Samuel P. Huntington, *The Third Wave: Democratization in the Late Twentieth Century* (Norman: University of Oklahoma Press, 1991).

5. Donald K. Emmerson, "'Southeast Asia': What's in a Name?" *Journal of Southeast Asian Studies* 15, no. 1 (March 1984): 1–21.

6. Geoffrey Wade, "ASEAN Divides," *East Asia Forum*, 15 January 2011, accessed at http://www.eastasiaforum.org/2011/01/15/asean-divides.

7. For a detailed discussion of this point, see Donald E. Weatherbee, "ASEAN's Identity Crisis," in *Legacy of Engagement in South East Asia*, ed. Ann Marie Murphy and Bridget Welsh (Singapore: Institute of Southeast Asian Studies [hereafter cited as ISEAS], 2008), 355–58.

8. Statistics on Southeast Asia's Muslim populations are based on the CIA's *World Factbook 2013*.

9. Clark D. Neher and Ross Marley, *Democracy and Development in Southeast Asia: The Winds of Change* (Boulder, CO: Westview Press, 1995), 193–95.

10. The full list and criteria for the LDC can be found at the website of the United Nations Office of the High Representative to the Least Developed Countries, Landlocked Developing Countries, and Small Island Developing Countries, accessed at http://www.unohrlls.org.

11. The World Bank's classifications can be accessed at http://www.worldbank.org using the data and research link.

12. Amitav Acharya, *The Quest for Identity: International Relations of Southeast Asia* (Singapore: Oxford University Press, 2000), 3.

13. Clark Neher, "Review of Acharya, *Quest for Identity*," *Journal of Asian Studies* 61, no. 3 (August 2002): 1101.

14. Donald K. Emmerson, "Challenging ASEAN: A Topological View," *Contemporary Southeast Asia* 29, no. 3 (December 2007): 427.

15. David Martin Jones and M. L. R. Smith, *ASEAN and East Asian International Relations: Regional Delusion* (Cheltenham, UK: Edward Elgar, 2006), 73.

16. Rodolfo C. Serverino, *Southeast Asia in Search of an ASEAN Community* (Singapore: ISEAS, 2006), 166, 372.

17. The pluralism that informs international relations theory in Southeast Asia is discussed by Alan Chong, "Southeast Asia: Theory between Modernization and Tradition," in *Non-Western International Relations Theory*, ed. Amitav Acharya and Barry Buzan (New York: Routledge, 2010), 117–47.

18. A major collection of Leifer's writings is in Chin Kin Wah and Leo Suryadinata, eds., *Michael Leifer: Selected Works on Southeast Asia* (Singapore: ISEAS, 2005). Leifer's influence is surveyed in Joseph Chinyong Liow and Ralf Emmers, eds., *Order and Security in Southeast Asia: Essays in Memory of Michael Leifer* (London: Routledge, 2005).

19. Ralf Emmers, *Cooperative Security and the Balance of Power in ASEAN and the ARF* (New York: RoutledgeCurzon, 2003).

20. Stephen Krasner, "Structural Causes and Regime Consequences: Regimes as Intervening Variables," *International Organization* 36, no. 2 (Spring 1982): 186.

21. Alexander Wendt, "Constructing International Politics," *International Security* 20, no. 1 (Summer 1995): 71–81; Jeffrey T. Checkel, "The Constructivist Turn in International Relations Theory," *World Politics* 50, no. 2 (January 1998): 324–48.

22. Acharya, *The Quest for Identity*; Amitav Acharya, *Constructing a Security Community in Southeast Asia: ASEAN and the Problem of Regional Order* (New York: Routledge, 2001).

23. Alice Ba, *[Re] Negotiating East and Southeast Asia: Region, Regionalism, and the Association of Southeast Asian Nations* (Stanford, CA: Stanford University Press, 2010): 41.

24. As quoted in the *Straits Times* (Singapore), 23 March 2003.

25. Michael Leifer, *ASEAN and the Security of South-East Asia* (London: Routledge, 1989), 148.

26. "Marty Urges Treaty to Ward Off Indo-Pacific Conflict," *Jakarta Globe*, 3 August 2013.

27. Donald E. Weatherbee, *Indonesia in ASEAN: Vision and Reality* (Singapore: ISEAS, 2013).

SUGGESTIONS FOR FURTHER READING

For Southeast Asian regional physical, economic, and human geography, see the relevant chapters in Barbara A. Weightman, *Dragons and Tigers: A Geography of South, East, and Southeast Asia*, 3rd ed. (Hoboken, NJ: Wiley, 2011). For a concise regional history, see Milton Osborne, *Southeast Asia: An Introductory History*, 11th ed. (Sydney, Australia: Allen & Unwin, 2013). D. R. SarDesai, *Southeast Asia Past and Present*, 7th ed. (Boulder, CO: Westview Press, 2012) examines the historical foundations of the modern states. Robert A. Daley and Clark Neher, *Southeast Asia in the New International Era*, 6th ed. (Boulder, CO: Westview Press, 2013) is organized on a country-by-country basis. N. Ganesan and Ramses Amer, eds., *International Relations in Southeast Asia: Between Bilateralism and Multilateralism* (Singapore: ISEAS, 2010) explores links between the theoretical literature and policy in the region. Amitav Acharya, *The Making of Southeast Asia: International Relations of a Region*, 2nd ed. (Singapore: ISEAS, 2012) explores the roots of a Southeast Asian regional identity.

There are a number of serial publications that contain current scholarship and opinion on problems and politics in Southeast Asian international relations. Singapore's Institute of Southeast Asian Studies publishes the quarterly journal *Contemporary Southeast Asia* which features analyses by foreign and Southeast Asian scholars. It also produces the annual volume *Southeast Asian Affairs* covering the important political, economic, and foreign policy events of the previous year on a country basis. Southeast Asia–related articles often appear in the University of California Press's bimonthly *Asian Survey* which also has an annual January/February number with a country-by-country retrospective. *Pacific Affairs*, published at the University of British Columbia, includes Southeast Asia in its scope. The *Pacific Review*, published in London, focuses on regional security and strategic issues.

The CSIS Pacific Forum publishes *Comparative Connections*, a triennial e-journal focused on key bilateral relationships, including the United States–Southeast Asia and China–Southeast Asia, accessed at http://www .csis.org/programs/comparative-connections. Other e-sources for commentary on contemporary affairs include the *New Mandala* (http://asiapacific .anu.edu.au/newmandala), *East Asia Forum* (http://www.eastasiaforum.org), *Asia Times* (http://atimes.com/atimes/Southeast_Asia.html), and *Asia Sentinel* (http://www.asiasentinel.com), to mention only a few. For daily regional news coverage, go to *Channel News Asia*, Asia-Pacific link (http://www .channelnewsasia.com) or *Asia News Network* (http://www.asianewsnet.net). There are English-language newspapers online from all of the Southeast Asian capitals. The better ones (fewer political constraints) are *Jakarta Post*, *Jakarta Globe*, *Bangkok Post*, *Nation* (Bangkok), *Daily Inquirer* (Manila), *Manila Times*, and *Straits Times* (Singapore).

Chapter Two

The International Actors in Southeast Asia

International actors in Southeast Asia, as elsewhere, can be grouped into two broad categories: state actors and nonstate actors. There are eleven state actors in Southeast Asia. Ten of them are joined in ASEAN. The eleventh, Timor-Leste, remains outside. The primary extraregional actors with significant national interests in Southeast Asia are Australia, China, Japan, India, and the United States. Their policies set the basic economic and political parameters for the autonomy of the Southeast Asian states. The Republic of Korea (South) has strong bilateral economic ties in the region as well as participating in various "plus 3" (China, Japan, ROK) ASEAN fora, but it is not directly engaged in the geopolitical/geostrategic tensions that define contemporary "high politics" in Southeast Asia. During the Cold War years, the old Soviet Union was an important actor, but its Russian successor state's political role is much more limited. Papua New Guinea's link to Southeast Asia is defined by its relationship to Indonesia. The EU, collectively acting for its member states, has important economic interests but, except for human rights and environmental issues, does not loom large politically. Finally, Taiwan has been effectively politically excluded from the region by the ASEAN states' acceptance of the one-China model.

Nonstate actors include international intergovernmental organizations, the majority of which operate under the umbrella of the United Nations system, and a wide variety of international nongovernmental organizations (INGOs) that are independent of government mandates. Multinational corporations (MNCs) are not included as a separate category in this international relations–focused book since, despite their local political, economic, and environmental impacts, their ultimate objectives are private economic interests, not public policy.

Finally, there is the question of what kind of international actor the regional organization ASEAN is. The ASEAN Community in 2015 will not change the regional organization's fundamental relationship to its member states. ASEAN will remain a "soft" multilateral structure through which the collective policy will of its member states is expressed in areas where there is multilateral consensus. While the ASEAN Charter confers an international personality on ASEAN, with ambassadors accredited to it, it has no legal or political capacity to act on behalf of its members in a binding fashion. The AC's operational code enshrines the principles of sovereignty, noninterference, and other prerogatives that guarantee the supremacy of the state in the conduct of international relations in Southeast Asia.

REGIONAL STATE ACTORS

Southeast Asia's states are incorporated in an international state system in which the basic principle governing state interaction is sovereign equality. Even though Southeast Asian states may challenge the Western bias in the workings of the international system, they fully embrace sovereign equality in their relations with each other and with extraregional state actors. It is obvious that despite the underpinning legal fiction of sovereign equality, all states in the Southeast Asian international subsystem are not equal in terms of capability to promote their national interests. This capability is usually termed "power." In discussions of state power, the elements making up power are often disaggregated into "soft" and "hard" power, with the former a measure of noncoercive influence and the latter military strength, with a different mix for each nation-state. Some states have more power than others, and power is relative in both bilateral and multilateral settings. For this chapter introducing the Southeast Asian state actors, it is necessary to choose an order of appearance. Adhering to the principle of sovereign equality, the states are ordered alphabetically, since to use power for ranking purposes would seem to ignore the fact of the relativity of power. The reality of power in international relations in Southeast Asia is demonstrated in the chapters that follow.

Brunei (Negara Brunei Darussalam [Abode of Peace])

Brunei is officially a Malay Islamic Monarchy (Melayu Islam Beraja). Its absolute ruler, Sultan Hassanal Bolkiah, came to the throne in 1967 as the twenty-ninth ruler in a dynasty that goes back to the fifteenth century. He is the longest-serving head of government in Southeast Asia. Brunei is a very rich microstate. Its small population sits atop large oil and natural gas

Table 2.1.   Southeast Asian Heads of Government and State (January 2014)

Country	Head of Government	Head of State
Cambodia	PM Hun Sen	King Norodom Sihamoni
Indonesia	Pres. Susilo Bambang Yudhoyono*	same
Lao PDR	PM Thongsin Thammavong	Pres. Choummaly Sayasone
Brunei	Sultan Hassanal Bolkiah	same
Malaysia	PM Najib Razak	King Abdul Halim Mu'adzam Shah
Myanmar	Pres. Thein Sein	same
Philippines	Pres. Benigno Aquino III	same
Singapore	PM Lee Hsien Loong	Pres. Tony Tan
Thailand	PM Yingluck Shinawatra†	King Bhumibol Adulyadej
Timor-Leste	PM Xanana Gusmão	Pres. Taur Matan Ruak
Vietnam	PM Nguyen Tan Dung	Pres. Truong Tan Sang

*Term in office expired October 2014 to be succeeded by Joko Widodo, elected in July 2014.

†Dismissed from office by the Constitutional Court, May 2014, followed by a military coup led by Gen. Prayuth Chan-ocha.

reserves. It is the fourth-largest producer of oil and natural gas in Southeast Asia, and, given low domestic consumption, it is the largest net exporter of oil in the Asia-Pacific region. Oil and gas account for 98 percent of Brunei's exports, 93 percent of revenue, and 60 percent of its GDP. The revenue earned gives the population one of the highest standards of living in the region. It is estimated that its hydrocarbon reserves will support current export levels until 2035. Brunei's political and economic foundations are more like the Middle East emirates than its Muslim-majority partners in ASEAN, Indonesia and Malaysia. Sharia (Islamic) law was imposed in Brunei on 1 May 2014.

Brunei was once a great maritime empire that reached to Manila. A history of political intrigue, succession struggles, and especially the depredations of colonialism left modern Brunei surrounded and partitioned by the East Malaysian Sarawak state. Brunei became independent from Great Britain on 1 January 1984, and a week later ASEAN's sixth member. In the years leading up to independence, Brunei as a self-governing British protectorate had contentious relations with Malaysia and Indonesia, the other occupants of the island of Borneo. ASEAN is important to Brunei in providing a multilateral framework within which it deals with its neighbors. Despite its limited human resource pool, Brunei participates fully in ASEAN. It chaired ASEAN in 2013 as the members worked toward the ASEAN Community and dealt with South China Sea issues (chapter 6). Brunei shares the strategic vulnerabilities of Singapore with which it has close political and defense ties. It also has a memorandum of understanding (MOU) with the United States on defense relations and regularly engages with US forces in exercises and training programs.

Cambodia (Kampuchea)

The contemporary Cambodian state was born in 1993, emerging from the political wreckage of the Indochina wars (chapter 3). Its midwife was the United Nations Transitional Authority for Cambodia (UNTAC). UNTAC was the international mechanism to reconcile the Vietnam-installed and former Khmer Rouge cadre Hun Sen–led government of the People's Republic of Kampuchea (PRK) and the ASEAN-sponsored—and American- and Chinese-supported—Coalition Government for Democratic Kampuchea (CGDK). UNTAC's effort to put in place a framework for democratic governance was unsuccessful. Although losing the 1993 UNTAC-organized elections, Hun Sen and his Cambodia People's Party (CPP) threatened to take up arms again, forcing UNTAC to impose a shared power arrangement with the winning FUNCINPEC (United National Front for an Independent, Neutral, Pacific, and Cooperative Cambodia) led by Norodom Ranariddh, a son of modern Cambodia's founding father Norodom Sihanouk.

In 1997, Hun Sen challenged the UN and ASEAN by a coup against Ranariddh. Threatened by international economic sanctions and denial of ASEAN membership, Hun Sen was forced to accept new elections in 1998. A new government was brokered with Hun Sen as sole prime minister, a position he has maintained to the present through a relentless and ruthless consolidation of power and rigged elections including the 2013 election. In protest, the opposition Cambodia National Rescue Party (CNRP) boycotted the parliament. With democratization now in progress in Myanmar, Hun Sen's Cambodia has replaced it as the primary example of the gulf between the ASEAN Charter's commitment to democracy and social justice and the reality of governance in Southeast Asia.

Cambodia is one of Southeast Asia's poorest states. Since regaining independence, the state has been dependent for more than 60 percent of its budget on international economic assistance. The discovery in 2005 of potentially large hydrocarbon deposits off Cambodia's southern coast prompted hopes for a new revenue flow. It was originally projected that production would start in 2010, but the lack of infrastructure has delayed production to 2016. Cambodia's continued dependency on external donors has not led to good governance. Reform is grudging. Transparency and accountability are lacking. Corruption is endemic as the country is plundered in a political culture of impunity. The economic links between the developed democracies and Cambodia have not been a lever for change as China has emerged as a giant economic partner to Cambodia. It is the largest investor in Cambodia with a total of $9.7 billion between 1994 and 2012, and it is second only to Japan in official development assistance (ODA) with an estimated $2.7 billion in the same period. Unlike the democracies, China's economic penetration of Cambodia comes with no contingent strings attached such as human rights, labor freedoms, or environmental concerns. China's economic standing in Cambodia has given it political influence in a possibly emerging patron–client relationship.[1] Through Cambodia, China has an invisible seat at the ASEAN foreign ministers' meetings (chapter 6).

Cambodia's relations with its eastern and western neighbors remain troubled (chapter 5). Historical ethnic animosity against the Vietnamese colors popular reactions to the government's conduct of bilateral relations. Long-standing grievances toward Thailand have inflamed a territorial dispute over the Preah Vihear temple, leading to a 2011 border war that undermined the credibility of ASEAN as a security community (chapter 5).

Indonesia

Indonesia's size, rich resource base, the world's fourth-largest population, burgeoning economy, and geostrategic location athwart the South China Sea and the Indian Ocean give it a natural claim to regional leadership. Added to these factors of power is the political quality of being a stable democracy—the world's third largest—and at the same time having the world's largest Muslim population. Indonesia prides itself as proving that democracy and Islam are not incompatible. Its asserted capability to be a bridge between the Western and Islamic worlds has yet to be validated. If ASEAN, as it claims, is central to the evolving international architecture of the Asia-Pacific, Indonesia is central to ASEAN. Two decades ago a prominent Indonesian foreign policy analyst wrote that ASEAN needs Indonesia more than Indonesia needs ASEAN.[2] This is even truer today. Both China and the United States see relations with Indonesia as a key element in the evolving great-power relationships in Southeast Asia.

Shortly before the toppling of the more-than-two-decades-old authoritarian government of General Suharto in May 1998, Indonesia had been characterized as a "pivotal state," one whose future was poised at a critical turning point and whose fate would strongly affect regional and even global international relations.[3] Indonesia had become the dominant regional power in Southeast Asia, a major player in the East Asian and Pacific region, and a leader among the nations of the South. All of this changed in the economic wreckage of the Crash of '97 (chapter 8), which laid waste to Indonesia's financial sectors, and the ensuing political turmoil of the end of Suharto's presidency.

Through 2004, there were three governments of post-Suharto presidents: respectively, B. J. Habibie, Abdurrahman Wahid, and Megawati Sukarnoputri. Caught up in the upheaval of the transition from Suharto to the volatile politics of democratization, their governments were characterized by leadership failure. Rather than a pivot of Southeast Asia, Indonesia became a problem—no longer a core for regional stability providing leadership in ASEAN. The importance of Indonesia was emphasized by the flow of ODA from donor nations and international financial institutions even in the absence of good governance and reform. Like Russia after the collapse of the communist regime, Indonesia post-Suharto was believed to be too big to fail.

Indonesia turned a page following its first direct presidential election in 2004. This brought to office President Susilo Bambang Yudhoyono, popularly known as SBY, who was reelected to a second and final term in 2009. The bleak picture of Indonesia's future at the beginning of the millennium has been relieved. In the Suharto years, Michael Leifer famously described Indonesian foreign policy as informed by a "sense of regional entitlement."[4] Rather than "entitlement," Indonesia's relative power provides a platform for Indonesia to reclaim its role as primus inter pares in ASEAN, thus regaining its "strategic centrality" in Southeast Asia.[5] The global recognition of the "rise" of Indonesia as an important middle power has not been matched by its ability to put its stamp on ASEAN. Self-constrained by the rules of consensus decision making in ASEAN, Indonesia's historical "free and active" foreign policy has been stressed by ASEAN inaction at critical junctures. The July 2014 presidential election was won by Joko Widodo, governor of Jakarta. Unlike Yudhoyono, Widodo brings no foreign policy experience to the presidency. The crucial question for future international relations in Southeast Asia is whether Indonesia's commitment to ASEAN, so much associated with SBY's government, will be as strong after 2014 in his successor's presidency.

Laos (Lao People's Democratic Republic [LPDR])

The LPDR is Southeast Asia's only landlocked country. On its borders, Thailand, Vietnam, and China compete for political and economic influence as the three strive for access to its markets and resources, particularly hydropower (chapter 10). At the cultural level, it is an unequal competition since the Thai and Lao share the same ethnic-linguistic and Buddhist background. Thailand is Laos's dominant trade partner. Laos has overcome its post–Vietnam War dependency on Vietnam as it has opened up to foreign investment. In the period 1989–2011, Vietnam's aggregate foreign direct investment (FDI) in Laos was $4.9 billion; Thailand's, $4 billion; and China's, $3.9 billion.[6] The United States' trade and investment relations with Laos are minimal.

Laos is the hub of Mekong Basin development schemes focused on building infrastructure linking southwestern China to mainland Southeast Asia as well as exploiting hydroelectric generating potential for export to Thailand and Vietnam (chapters 4 and 9). The risk in the competition for Laotian resources is that Laos will become simply a platform for projects benefiting its neighbors with little developmental payoff for Laos itself. A higher profile for China can be expected as it aggressively pursues its geostrategic interests in Laos. Construction of a high-speed rail link from Kunming to Vientiane began in 2014, with completion expected in 2019. Coming with the railroad will be up to twenty thousand Chinese workers to join the tens of thousands of Chinese who have already flooded into northern Laos and cities beyond, economically displacing native Lao.[7]

The LPDR is a diehard communist state. The Lao People's Revolutionary Party (LPRP) maintains an absolute monopoly of political power. Laos began experimenting with free market reforms in 1986, but the pace of change is slow and grudging. Laos was the last ASEAN state to join the World Trade Organization (WTO), becoming a member in February 2013. There is barely the beginning of a rudimentary civil society. The "enforced disappearance" in December 2012 of Magsaysay Award–winning Laotian civil rights activist Sombath Samphone became a cause célèbre for the worldwide rights community. It also demonstrated the inutility of the ASEAN Intergovernmental Commission on Human Rights (AICHR), which by its operating rules could not take up the issue (chapter 9).

Malaysia

Malaysia is a multiethnic state in which in 2010 indigenous Malays and other groups (Iban, Dayak, etc.)—the *bumiputra* (sons of the soil)—were 67.4 percent of the population, followed by Chinese (24 percent) and Indian (7.3 percent).[8] Among the *bumiputra*, Malay Muslims were a more than 90 percent majority. Islam is the state religion. Government and politics are organized in the framework of parliamentary democracy but function to assure Malay supremacy, even, if necessary, through the application of draconian internal security laws. As in Indonesia, Malaysia's leaders have to be attuned to the influence that international Islamic issues might have domestically. In domestic politics a conservative Islamic party, PAS, stands in opposition.

A watershed in Malaysia's foreign policy occurred on 31 October 2003, when Prime Minister Mahathir Mohamad handed over leadership to his deputy, Abdullah Badawi. For twenty-two years, Malaysia's international role had been defined by Mahathir, operating until 1998 in the international shadow of Indonesia's Suharto. Challenging Suharto's accommodation to the globalization agenda, Mahathir sought to elevate Malaysia's status in the so-called South and the Nonaligned Movement by rallying them in a tone and style that was outspokenly and deliberately confrontational with the West, particularly the United States.

Neither Abdullah nor since 2009 his successor, Najib Razak, vied for the international spotlight by using the United States as a whipping boy. A pragmatic bilateral relationship is now built on mutual recognition of convergent interests. The United States is the largest foreign investor in Malaysia both in current investment and total stock and is Malaysia's fourth-largest trading partner. Malaysia is negotiating membership in the US-sponsored Trans-Pacific Partnership (TPP) (chapter 8). The two countries cooperate and consult on security matters and programs of military-to-military bilateral and multilateral exchange and exercising. In August 2013, at a meeting of their defense ministers, it was agreed to bring the already strong bilateral military relationship to a higher level.[9] The new higher public visibility of a warmer and deeper US connection has been attributed to the concerns about regional stability raised by China's increasing assertiveness, forcing Malaysia "to refocus on enhancing its bilateral relationship with Washington."[10] This seems reflected in President Obama's state visit to Malaysia in April 2014, the first by an American president in half a century, and the elevation of the bilateral relationship to one of a "comprehensive partnership."

Malaysia has become a model of Southeast Asian hedging or balancing strategies as it calculates how its relations with one of the great powers impacts its relations with the other. There is a close economic relationship between China and Malaysia, with China being Malaysia's largest trading partner and Malaysia being China's largest economic partner among the ASEAN states. A goal has been set to expand two-way trade to $160 billion by 2017. During the October 2013 visit to Malaysia by China's President Xi Jinping, the two sides agreed to upgrade their relationship to a "Comprehensive Strategic Partnership" (CSP). Malaysians attached great significance to this as a sign of special ties. In fact, a CSP seems to be simply a label for an umbrella framework under which disparate existing and future programs can be clustered to give a sense of integrated planning and implementation as in the Indonesia–China CSP and the action plans for China CSPs with Vietnam, Laos, Cambodia, and Myanmar.

Greater political importance has been assigned to Malaysia's decision to enhance security cooperation with China, giving operational life to their 2005 MOU on defense cooperation. The first-ever Malaysia–China joint military exercise was scheduled for 2014. No specifics were given other than that it would include land, sea, and air forces. Defence Minister Hishammuddin invited his Chinese counterpart to visit the Malaysian naval base at Sepanggar Bay, Sabah, "to jointly launch the establishment of direct contact between

Malaysia's Naval Regional Command 2 (Mawilla 2) and China's Southern Sea Fleet Command."[11] The fact that Malaysia has a stake in South China Sea territorial and jurisdictional disputes has not been made an issue in Kuala Lumpur's relations with China—unlike Vietnam and the Philippines. Some immediate frissons of concern were stirred that this might signify a security reorientation on Kuala Lumpur's part. It is probably best explained, however, as an example of Malaysia's hedging and balancing policy that does not diminish the more robust American defense link.

In Malaysia's ASEAN regional environment, the residuum of past quarrels and clashes with Singapore, Indonesia, Thailand, and the Philippines is a background against which contemporary divergent interests are managed (chapter 5). Malaysia, with its Muslim credentials, has been called upon by non-Muslim Thailand and the Philippines to act as mediator and facilitator in peace processes to end Muslim separatist insurgencies in their countries (chapter 5).

Myanmar

Following elections in 2010, a newly elected civilian government led by President Thein Sein, a former general, took office in Myanmar in March 2011, ending twenty years of brutal rule by the military (Tatmadaw) that had led to the country's international ostracism. The resulting government won wide praise for its surprising opening of democratic space and political reform, including the release of thousands of political prisoners. By-elections in 2012 seemed to confirm the turn to democratization with the National League for Democracy (NLD), whose 1990 election victory had been crushed by the Tatmadaw, winning forty-three of the forty-four seats it contested. The NLD's democratic icon, Nobel Prize–winning Aung San Suu Kyi, emerged as a possible presidential candidate in 2015, but only if a constitutional amendment makes her eligible. This appeared more likely when, on New Year's Day 2014, Thein Sein said he would support amending the article barring from the presidency persons whose children were foreign citizens.[12]

Myanmar's contemporary international relations are inextricably intertwined with the struggle for democracy. The unrelenting reality of the junta's systematic human rights violations had made it a pariah state. It was economically sanctioned by the West and an embarrassment for ASEAN. Suu Kyi became the international symbol of democratic opposition to the junta. Only a lifeline from China and revenue from environmentally uncaring exploitation of natural resources kept the economy afloat. Even though Thein Sein and the junta leaders have not disclosed the motives for their political rethink, the factors of global economic and political isolation, an impoverished population, the impact of 2008 Cyclone Nargis (chapter 9), and growing popular resentment against Chinese economic penetration were probably at work.

The United States, the European Union, and other democracies cautiously welcomed the Myanmar about-face. As sanctions have been rolled back, Myanmar is being integrated into the global economy. Foreign investment has flowed into the country, almost overwhelming badly deteriorated economic infrastructure. Even with reopened economic links to the West, China's dominant role in the economy persists. A parade of foreign dignitaries, including President Barack Obama, has visited Nay Pyi Taw. In 2006, ASEAN had pressured Myanmar to forgo its scheduled chairmanship because of the expected negative international reaction. In 2014, confident that the democratization process is irreversible, ASEAN awarded its chairmanship to Myanmar.

China has adapted its bilateral relationship with Myanmar to a new normal after the shock of the suspension of the Myitsone mega-dam project (chapter 10). The reopening of Myanmar's windows to the West gives Nay Pyi Taw new economic opportunities and hedging capabilities. Myanmar's major foreign policy question is whether it can create a new political and strategic balance between the West and China while still remaining economically dependent on China.[13] A gradual political distancing from China would be welcomed by the United States, India, and ASEAN. They fear that a Chinese goal in its Myanmar policy is winning a strategic foothold on the Bay of Bengal. As Myanmar resets its relations with the West, it is not divorcing China. In a sense, Myanmar is reclaiming its historical nonaligned role of great-power equidistance.

Myanmar's democratization process has obstacles to overcome. There is still warfare on the margins of the state with stubborn ethnic insurgents (chapter 5). Thein Sein's government's ASEAN relations have been strained by the Buddhist violence against the Muslim Rohingya minority and other Myanmar Muslims (chapter 9). Despite the great strides that Myanmar has made, in May 2014 President Obama notified Congress that economic sanctions against Myanmar would be renewed because of "ongoing conflict and human rights abuses in ethnic minority areas, particularly in Rakhine State [the Rohingya]."[14] At some future point, it is likely that there will be calls in Myanmar for accountability for perpetrators of egregious human rights abuses. Any challenge to the entrenched interests of the Tatmadaw will be resisted. Speaking of the proud history of the military, Thein Sein said in 2013, "It will always have a special place in government."[15]

The Philippines

When President Benigno Aquino III took the oath of office in June 2010, he inherited two internal wars and an escalating contest with China in the

South China Sea (in Manila, the West Philippine Sea). Both of the internal wars, against the Communist Party's New People's Army (CPP-NPA) and the Muslim Moro insurgency in the South, are approaching the half-century mark. The situation in the South has been complicated by the presence of terrorist Islamic jihadists of the Abu Sayyaf Group (ASG), which is alleged to have Al-Qaeda links (chapter 7). The Moro insurgency is discussed at length in chapter 5, and the South China Sea conflicts are the subject of chapter 6. The Philippines is the only Southeast Asian country in which an armed communist insurgency persists. Since 1968, the CPP-NPA has waged a Maoist "people's war." Although their ranks have thinned to between four thousand and six thousand, NPA fighters still operate in more than two-thirds of the Philippines' eighty-one provinces, making random attacks on military, police, and government institutions. On-again, off-again peace talks between the government and the communists since 1986 have had little result. Talks in Oslo, Norway, that broke down in 2004 were restarted in February 2013 but collapsed within weeks. The Oslo process has been facilitated by a Norwegian special envoy. President Aquino still hopes to achieve some measure of peacemaking success by the end of his term in 2016.

Manila's principal foreign policy task has been to find a way to harmonize its relations with ASEAN, China, and the United States. In ASEAN, the Philippines has always been somewhat of an outlier, a follower of consensus, not a molder. Its international orientation was viewed from ASEAN as based on Manila's "special relationship" with the United States. Since 2011, the strategic gulf between the Philippines and ASEAN has widened as Philippines security dependence on the United States has increased. The Philippines has become a fulcrum of the American "pivot" to East Asia. China, trying to isolate Manila from ASEAN, has warned the other members that spillover into ASEAN of the China–Philippines South China Sea disputes would have a negative impact on regional relations.

Lying at the heart of the US–Philippines "special relationship" is the 1951 Mutual Defense Treaty (MDT), from which flows a variety of American security assistance to the Armed Forces of the Philippines (AFP). For the United States, what was special was extensive military basing rights that made the Philippines a key element in the American strategy of forward deployment in Asia during the Cold War. After the base rights were terminated in 1991, a 1999 Visiting Forces Agreement (VFA) restored American military training and joint exercising with the AFP. In 2002, the United States deployed Special Forces to support the AFP in its campaign against the ASG.

Manila's security concern about China's territorial and jurisdictional threats in the South China Sea has enhanced the value of the "special relationship" even if it complicates Manila's relations within ASEAN. Secretary of State Hillary Clinton, celebrating the sixtieth anniversary of the MDT, promised US support in the maritime domain.[16] Manila was heartened when President Obama said in 2011 to his Philippines counterpart that "we have a 60-year-old alliance that assures that we are looking out for each other when it comes to security."[17] President Obama's April 2014 visit to Manila coincided with the conclusion of an Enhanced Defense Cooperation Agreement that will allow an undisclosed, but large, number of rotations of US land, air, and sea forces through the Philippines' bases.

As the Philippines looks to the United States, and not to ASEAN, for support in defending its maritime territories and jurisdictions against Chinese encroachment, two questions about the MDT foundation of the security partnership stand out. Will the MDT deter Chinese use of force against the Philippines in the contested South China Sea zones? If the Philippines, confident of American support, takes what China has called "a fork in the road towards a military confrontation," will the United States confront China militarily to defend the Philippines in the South China Sea?[18] President Obama diplomatically evaded directly answering that question during his April 2014 Philippines joint press conference with President Aquino.[19] This did not stop Secretary of Foreign Affairs Rosario from issuing a terse statement that under the MDT, the United States will come to the assistance of the Philippines "if our metropolitan territory is attacked or if our armed forces are attacked in the Pacific area." Rosario added that in 1999, in a diplomatic letter, the United States affirmed that the South China Sea is considered a part of the Pacific area.[20]

Singapore

Security concerns animate Singapore's approach to international relations. It is, in the words of a Singapore analyst, "a very small island state perpetually haunted by its sense of vulnerability."[21] The ethnic dimension exaggerates its geostrategic vulnerability. It is a Chinese nut in the jaws of an Indonesian-Malaysian nutcracker. This was graphically illustrated by Indonesian president B. J. Habibie who in 1998, wanting Singapore to know its place, pointed to a map and said, "Look at that map. All the green [area] is Indonesia. And that red dot is Singapore."[22]

The independent state of Singapore was born in the political trauma of forced separation from Malaysia in 1965. Led at independence by Prime Minister Lee Kuan Yew, now minister-mentor to his son Prime Minister Lee Hsien Loong, Singapore has adhered to the principle that domestic political stability is the sine qua non of security and economic growth. To that end, the government has stifled political opposition through one-party electoral domination and application of its Internal Security Act (ISA). Its illiberalism makes it a target for rights NGOs. There is a determination to use its human, financial, and technical resources to build an economy that is a major regional, even global, player. Singapore strives to be the financial services, technology, and trading eye of Southeast Asia (chapter 8). In the metaphor of the "poison shrimp," Singapore has built credible armed forces with skills and weapons platforms second to none in ASEAN. Finally, as part of its strategy for survival, Singapore consciously practices balance-of-power politics with bigger and often unfriendly neighbors so that it is not isolated.

The many bilateral issues following the messy divorce from Malaysia impeded normal bilateral relations (chapter 5). Indonesia has been frustrated in its pursuit of "hot money" by Singapore's unwillingness to sign an extradition agreement. Its highly visible relations with China, the United States, and India are part of that balance. ASEAN gives it regional political equality. Even though there is no formal US–Singapore military alliance, Singapore has been named a Major Security Cooperation Partner and, with a 2005 Strategic Framework Agreement, is, excepting the Philippines, perhaps the closest US ally in Southeast Asia. By agreement in 2011, US Navy littoral combat ships (LCSs) have been deployed in Southeast Asia from Singapore's naval base. The first LCS arrived in April 2013.

Thailand

Historically, Thailand's foreign policy has been likened to the bending of bamboo in the wind, keeping its options open and siding with the stronger in its dealings with the great powers. During the Cold War, Thailand opted to ally with the United States, rather than balance through nonalignment. Communist victories in the Indochina wars made Thailand ASEAN's frontline state, with the American alliance for insurance. Thailand was designated a Major Non-NATO Ally of the United States in December 2003, and the alliance is still rhetorically, if not substantively, valued. The foundation of the alliance was the 1962 Rusk–Thanat communiqué (chapter 3), which was moved into the twenty-first century in a 2012 new "joint vision" for the alliance.[23]

The American–Thai connection was shaken in September 2006 when populist prime minister Thaksin Shinawatra's democratically elected government was toppled by a military coup. The immediate bilateral consequence was the invocation of US law prohibiting security assistance to a country whose elected government is deposed by a military coup. China quickly stepped in by offering a military assistance package to compensate for loss of US funding. Junta-appointed prime minister General Surayud

Chulanont traveled to China, where he signed a five-year joint strategic plan of action covering a variety of programs of functional cooperation. This began a reorientation of Thai great-power policy from the United States to China, a bending in the political breeze that persists. Thailand was the first ASEAN country to strike a free trade agreement (FTA) with China. The Thai business and political elite are heavily invested in China. Thailand has deeper military-to-military ties with China than any other ASEAN country. Chinese political influence can be discerned in Thailand's position on the South China Sea disputes (chapter 6).

From the end of the Third Indochina War in 1991 (chapter 3), Thailand had viewed itself as the leading center of a stable Southeast Asian continental bloc. However, the sustained political instability and weak governments resulting from the 2006 coup put an end to Thailand's pretensions as a contender for regional leadership. This was acknowledged in January 2008 by ASEAN secretary general Surin Pitsuwan, a former Thai foreign minister, who bemoaned the fact that because of its internal conflicts Thailand had lost its capability to contribute to regional development.[24]

After the return to civilian parliamentary government in 2007, deeply polarized pro- and anti-Thaksin factions mobilized their street fighters, the Red Shirts and Yellow Shirts. Since the 2006 coup, three pro-Thaksin prime ministers in popularly elected governments have been dismissed from office by the Constitutional Court whose allegiance has been to the established antidemocratic elite. Prime Minister Abhisit Vejjajiva's unelected Democrat Party government was met by Red Shirt opposition that marred Thailand's 2009 ASEAN chairmanship. The ASEAN Summit in Pattaya ended in shambles as the Red Shirts stormed the hotel venue, forcing the summit's cancellation and the evacuation of the leaders. Besieged domestically, Abhisit picked a territorial fight with Cambodia that led to a border war, and unconcernedly watched the military's approach to the Muslim insurgency in Thailand's southern provinces lead to the internal war's expansion and intensification (chapter 5).

In March 2010, the Red Shirts occupied Bangkok's central business district. The army was deployed, and in the ensuing violence 85 protesters were killed and over 1,300 injured. Elections in 2011 swept the latest version of the Thaksin party, the Phue Thai (For Thais) Party, into power. Thaksin's younger sister, Yingluck Shinawatra, was sworn in as prime minister. Proposed frameworks for reconciliation or amnesty were met with massive antigovernment demonstrations mobilized by the People's Democratic Reform Committee (PDRC) that morphed into nearly insurrectionary demands to abandon the democracy that had repeatedly returned Thaksin's surrogates to power. New elections in February 2014 were disrupted by PDRC violence and intimidation, and the outcome was annulled by the theoretically independent election commission. With no end to the political turmoil in sight, elements of both the Red Shirts and Yellow Shirts armed themselves, and the country verged on anarchy. In May, the crisis deepened when Prime Minister Yingluck was dismissed from office by the anti-Thaksin judiciary. On 22 May 2014, there was a military coup, leaving the political future of Thailand unclear, but given the probable US response to the death of democracy in Thailand, the country will probably move further into the Chinese orbit, leaving the ASEAN Community blemished.

Timor-Leste (East Timor)

Timor-Leste joined the Southeast Asian region as a fully independent actor on 20 May 2002 and shortly thereafter became the UN's 191st member. Its independence was, like Cambodia's, husbanded by a UN peacekeeping and political reconstruction mission. Ruled until 1974 by Portugal, it shares the island of Timor with Indonesia's West Timor. After Portuguese authority collapsed, an East Timor nationalist declaration of independence was nullified by an Indonesian invasion and absorption of the territory as Indonesia's twenty-seventh province (chapter 3). For a quarter century, Indonesia's rule was opposed by Timorese armed resistance and international condemnation. After the fall of Suharto, President B. J. Habibie, in desperate need of international assistance and political support, agreed to an internationally supervised referendum on the province's future.

On 30 August 1999, the East Timorese people overwhelmingly chose separation from Indonesia in a "popular consultation" supervised by the United Nations Assistance Mission in East Timor (UNAMET). A terrifying rampage by army-backed pro-Indonesian militias followed the referendum, killing thousands of East Timorese, destroying infrastructure, and uprooting a quarter of the population. A UN-sanctioned intervention by the Australian-led International Force for East Timor (INTERFET) restored order and prepared the way for UN peacekeepers and the United Nations Transitional Administration in East Timor (UNTAET). China's first international peacekeeping experience was a small detachment to UNTAET. UNTAET was succeeded by the United Nations Mission in Support of East Timor (UNMISET). That mandate ended in May 2005, to be succeeded by the United Nations Office in Timor-Leste (UNOTIL). Electoral political violence and civil strife in 2006 led to a second Australian-led peacekeeping intervention called the International Stabilization Force (ISF) and the UN Security Council's authorization of a fifth UN mission, the United Nations Integrated Mission in Timor-Leste (UNMIT), with an international police presence. After a decade of internationally assisted political development—and when necessary intervention—Timor-Leste's third national election in 2012 was an important, and successful, test for the fragile democracy. Both UNMIT and the ISF completed their missions in 2012.

Timor-Leste's first important foreign policy task was to regularize its relations with Indonesia. This was complicated by issues of reconciliation over the postreferendum Indonesian atrocities (chapter 9). A host of legal issues such as Indonesian assets, border demarcation, and maritime overlaps also needed to be addressed. Timor-Leste has sought membership in ASEAN since 2007 when it acceded to ASEAN's Treaty of Amity and Cooperation in Southeast Asia (TAC). Its candidacy has been strongly supported by Indonesia, but there was concern among other ASEAN members, especially Singapore, that it was not ready. At the April 2013 ASEAN Summit, with reference to the application, the leaders were encouraged by progress made and agreed to "explore" possible participation by Timor-Leste in ASEAN activities "within the context of its need for capacity building."[25]

Timor-Leste's long-term economic hopes are based on oil and gas revenues from the fields in the Timor Sea with its overlapping Timor-Leste–Australia maritime jurisdictions. Revenue sharing in the overlaps is governed by two treaties: the 2002 Timor Sea Treaty and the 2006 treaty of Certain Maritime Arrangements in the Timor Sea (CMATS). Production in the field covered by the CMATS has been delayed because Dili demands processing on Timor-Leste's south shore rather than the operator's floating platform. Dili has also threatened to tear up the CMATS because of alleged Australian espionage during its negotiation, and in April 2013 Dili applied to the Permanent Court of Arbitration (PCA) to have CMATS ruled invalid.[26]

Vietnam (Socialist Republic of Vietnam [SRV])

Vietnam's 1995 admission to ASEAN was the final act of regional political reconciliation following the Third Indochina War (chapter 3). Within ASEAN, Vietnam stands out from the other late-entry CLMV countries in its power and influence. In fact, it has been asserted that Vietnam has replaced the Philippines in the core group of consensus decision makers in ASEAN.[27] A special relationship between Vietnam and Indonesia has developed and in 2013 was institutionalized in the form of a "strategic partnership," Indonesia's only one with an ASEAN state.

The Communist Party of Vietnam still commands the undemocratic state. The economy has achieved rapid economic development. From 2000 to 2013 Vietnam's GDP growth rate averaged 6.2 percent. It is one of Southeast Asia's most attractive destinations for FDI. Vietnam's international credentials were validated by its election as a nonpermanent member of the UN Security Council for 2008–2009. Vietnam's economic takeoff first required normalization of relations with the United States, which did not happen until 1995. Vietnam is negotiating membership in the TPP (chapter 8).

China, Vietnam's giant neighbor to the north, looms largest in Vietnam's geostrategic perceptions. Vietnam forged its historical national identity in centuries of struggle to resist Chinese hegemony. Vietnam's consciousness of being Southeast Asian, according to one historian, is not for its own sake, "but rather for the refreshment and reinforcement it provides in the grim business of maintaining the northern border."[28] It was grim in February 1979, when China briefly pushed its military across Vietnam's northern border during the earliest stages of the Third Indochina War (chapter 3). Since normalization of China–Vietnam relations in 1991, Vietnam's stance toward China has been described as a mixture of deference and defiance.[29] Ideological affinity and growing economic interdependence in the bilateral relationship are matched by Vietnam's fierce defense of its sovereignty and territorial integrity in the contested South China Sea domain (chapter 6). Maritime clashes have led to occasional anti-Chinese protests by Vietnamese nationalists. Beijing has warned Hanoi that attempts to "internationalize" what China insists is a bilateral problem would have serious repercussions for the broader relationship. The relationship reached a nadir in May 2014 when a forceful Chinese breach of Vietnam's maritime waters provoked widespread Vietnamese anti-China demonstrations that threatened both regime stability and bilateral relations.

Until the collapse of the Soviet Union, communist-ruled Vietnam had relied on Moscow as its security patron. Russia still has a stake in Vietnam. President Vladimir Putin signed a "strategic partnership" pact with Vietnam during his 2001 state visit, which in 2012 was elevated to a "strategic comprehensive partnership." Putin's November 2013 visit to Vietnam reinforced the connection. Vietnam may view Russia as a hedge in its effort to balance the United States and PRC. A key item has been Russian promises to aid in the modernization of the Vietnamese armed forces. Vietnam is one of Russia's largest arms buyers, with 80 percent of its military purchases being Russian. Hanoi's $2 billion purchase of six Varshavyanka (Kilo) Class Project-636 submarines, to be delivered by 2016, is a reflection of its South China Sea concerns. The submarine has stealth quietness operating in relatively shallow water.

Washington sees Vietnam as important to its "pivot" to East Asia. Since 2004, there has been an annual bilateral defense policy dialogue. Defense cooperation was furthered by the 2006 authorization of defense sales to Vietnam. In 2012 both Secretary of State Hillary Clinton and Secretary of Defense Leon Panetta held talks in Hanoi with a China subtext. In Washington, in July 2013, President Obama and President Truong Tan Sang launched a US–Vietnam Comprehensive Partnership to deepen and expand the bilateral relationship. President Sang welcomed American support for Vietnam's stance on the peaceful resolution of East Sea [South China Sea] issues.[30] In December 2013, Secretary of State John Kerry traveled to Hanoi to underscore the "enduring US commitment to the Asia-Pacific rebalance."[31] Obstacles to the development of closer bilateral political relations are mistrust of the United States by communist hard-liners in Hanoi and persistent concerns in the US Congress about the human rights situation in Vietnam (chapter 9).

EXTRAREGIONAL STATE ACTORS

China (People's Republic of China [PRC])

Once viewed suspiciously by Southeast Asian leaders, China now is seen as a responsible major actor to which the future of Southeast Asia is crucially linked. Even so, there remains an undercurrent of concern about the PRC's ultimate political, military, and territorial ambitions that has been sharpened as China aggressively pursues its claim to sovereignty in the South China Sea (chapter 6). To allay these concerns, a steady stream of high-level official Chinese delegations has regularly traveled to ASEAN capitals with a focused message of common interest in regional peace and stability. In October 2013, the new leadership team in China, President Xi Jinping and Premier Li Keqiang, toured Southeast Asia reinforcing the Chinese message, along with promises of expanding trade and investment. For the past decade, under the umbrella of the 2003 ASEAN–China "Strategic Partnership for Peace and Prosperity," there has been a proliferation of bilateral and multilateral cooperative engagements over a wide range of functional activities. This has had the effect of creating a China-centric web of mutual interdependencies.[32] Ministry-to-ministry links are a regular feature of official intercourse. Although still wary of China in the long term, at both the bilateral and multilateral level of relations, the Southeast Asians are both accommodating and benefiting from a rising and proximate China.

The 1949 appearance of the PRC as a regional state actor led to fears that aggressive communist China might try to impose a Marxist-Leninist-Maoist version of the traditional Confucian regional order. Indigenous Maoist revolutionary warfare against Southeast Asian governments from the 1950s into the 1980s gave substance to these fears. Moreover, Chinese minorities with divided loyalties in host Southeast Asian countries were viewed as potential Trojan horses.

Contemporary China—although in politics still Leninist—has demonstrated to Southeast Asia that in most respects China is a "normal" country dealing with other countries on the basis of sovereign equality and behaving in accordance with accepted international norms. China's first official contact with ASEAN was at the July 1991 ASEAN [Foreign] Ministers' Meeting (AMM). This was after the 1990 establishment of diplomatic relations between the PRC and Singapore, the last of the ASEAN countries to do so. China attained full dialogue status in 1996. China joins the ASEAN chorus championing the principle of noninterference in issue areas on the West's interventionist social and political rights agenda. The ASEAN states unquestioningly accept that Taiwan is part of China, although still maintaining separate economic ties to Taiwan.

Among the ASEAN states, as has already been noted, China's tightest connections have been with Myanmar, Laos, Cambodia, and Thailand. The latter, as ASEAN's official coordinator of China relations, 2012–2015, has influenced the shaping of a rather uncritical ASEAN view of Chinese foreign policy. The friendly face that China projects to ASEAN is different from the uncompromising and threatening face seen by the ASEAN states with South China Sea claims. Both ASEAN and China have tried to keep the two policy areas separate. Wang Yi, China's foreign minister, made it clear to his ASEAN counterparts at the 2013 meeting celebrating the tenth anniversary of the strategic partnership that China opposed certain member nations [the Philippines and Vietnam] "trying to tout their own stand as that of the regional organization" on South China Sea issues since this will harm the common interests between China and ASEAN.[33] This is complicated by the interests of other powers, not just the United States, but Japan and India.

While it does not yet rival the United States in military power and political and economic reach, there is a sense in Southeast Asia that inevitably China— so large and so geographically close—will be the power to be reckoned with in the future. It is the need to adapt to that future that informs the present-day Southeast Asia–China relationship. This reflects, in part, Southeast Asian concerns that in its global preoccupations the United States had disengaged from the region. Kishore Mahbubani, a distinguished Singapore diplomat, wrote that "China's benign rise was the result of American neglect."[34]

From the Southeast Asian vantage, the central question of the future structure of great-power involvement in the region will be the evolution of the US–China relationship. It is understood in ASEAN capitals that as China's economic and military power grow, the United States cannot maintain the same level of preponderance it once enjoyed. However, American interests and capabilities will still make it a major actor. The issue for the ASEAN states is not the relativity of power, but whether the United States will accommodate to a real balance of power with China or seek to contain its rising power. The last thing that Southeast Asian leaders want is to be forced to choose between the two.

Japan

The election of Japanese prime minister Shinzo Abe in December 2012 turned a page in ASEAN–Japan relations. In the space of seventeen days in January 2013, Japan's deputy prime minister visited Myanmar; the foreign minister, the Philippines, Brunei, and Singapore; and Abe himself, Vietnam, Thailand, and Indonesia. In May, the prime minister was in Myanmar and in July, Malaysia, Singapore, and the Philippines. In October, he journeyed to Thailand, Cambodia, and Laos. The year was capped by a special Japan–ASEAN Summit in Tokyo commemorating forty years of Japan–ASEAN relations.

In what is being called the "Abe Doctrine," Japan's relations with Southeast Asia have been reset based on four principles: the promotion and protection of universal values, a maritime regime based on law and rules, promotion of economic integration through trade and investment, and strengthened cultural ties.[35] In policy, the doctrine is backed by a new security dialogue and flow of ODA. The mutual payoff can be seen in the outcome of the commemorative summit. Japan pledged $30 billion in ODA to Southeast Asian nations over five years as well as $100 billion to support the Japan–ASEAN integration fund. In turn, the Southeast Asian leaders promised to cooperate with Japan to ensure "freedom of overflight and aviation safety in accordance with universally recognized principles of international law."[36] Although China's imposition of its Air Defense Identification Zone (ADIZ) to include Japanese airspace was not directly mentioned, the statement represented cautious ASEAN support for Japan in its dispute with China.

The Abe Doctrine can be compared to the 1977 Fukuda Doctrine. Prime Minister Fukuda, still sensitive to emotions in Southeast Asia about Japan's role in World War II, was hesitant about asserting a regional political role. This was at a time when Japan was the economic engine for Southeast Asia, a relationship depicted in the "flying geese" metaphor: Japan at the head of the V and the rest of Asia following behind in the different echelons of the regional division of labor. In the post–Cold War world, however, Japan seemed more like a wounded goose than the leader of the flock. The relative lowering of Japan's profile in the region has been coincident with the rise of China's. Although linked with China in the regionalism of the ASEAN + 3 (China, Japan, South Korea) and the proposed Regional Comprehensive Economic Partnership (RCEP) (chapter 8), East Asian regional leadership has been transferred from Tokyo to Beijing.

The rise of China has altered Japan's strategic appreciation of Southeast Asia in its security policy. The international context of the Abe Doctrine is different than that of the Fukuda Doctrine. Abe, in an atmosphere of heightened nationalism, seeks to enhance Japan's self-defense capabilities and associates Japan's security interests with Southeast Asia. Japan is the region's second-largest trading partner, with nearly 15 percent of its total trade with ASEAN. Japanese investment in ASEAN is greater than in China. Japan has a vital interest in freedom of navigation through the South China Sea. In the Senkaku Islands, Japan is confronting China in the same kind of offshore territorial dispute as are the Philippines and Vietnam in the Spratly Islands (chapter 6). Japan has enhanced its dialogues with ASEAN with a new emphasis on maritime issues. While Tokyo would not agree with a Manila newspaper headline that claimed "Japan to defend PH from China,"[37] Japan is forcefully asserting that it is a security stakeholder as well as an economic partner in Southeast Asia.

The United States

Since 1945, the United States has been the dominant great power in Southeast Asia. The implementation of American Cold War global political/military containment strategy influenced the political and economic development of all of Southeast Asia (chapter 3). With the ending of the Cold War, the global threat posed by a bipolar confrontation with the Soviet Union was replaced by a vague, loosely articulated strategic concept initially articulated by President Bill Clinton in his 1993 vision of a Pacific Community. This rested on three pillars: economic growth, political democracy, and security.[38] The three pillars remain intact, but in contemporary Southeast Asia it is the firming up of the security pillar that drives American–Southeast Asian relations.

For the United States and the countries of Southeast Asia the central strategic issue is coping with the rise of China. The worst-case analysis is that China is rivaling the United States in a zero-sum game for influence and ultimately the exclusion of the United States from the regional economic and security architecture. Of particular concern has been the scope and pace of China's military buildup. In the first decade of the new millennium, policy elites in Southeast Asia viewed the rise of China as being paralleled by a waning of American interest and influence in the region. In the wake of 9/11, America focused on the war on terror, the Iraq war, and the war in Afghanistan, all consuming of attention and resources.

The George W. Bush administration did promote closer relations with ASEAN in a 2005 ASEAN–United States Enhanced Partnership, the first fruits of which were the 2006 ASEAN–US Trade and Investment Framework

Agreement (TIFA) and a 2008 US Comprehensive Development Assistance Program for ASEAN. While welcomed, these did not weigh in on the political side of the relationship which, from the Southeast Asian vantage, required maintaining, if not predominance, at least a balance of power with China. American political disengagement seemed underlined when American senior officials often missed important ASEAN gatherings.

In July 2009, Secretary of State Hillary Clinton arrived in Bangkok for her first dialogue with ASEAN counterparts. She declared, "We're back!" It was an announcement that the new Obama administration would give higher priority to Southeast Asia. The United States finally adhered to the TAC, which put it on the same ASEAN plane as China and opened the door to the East Asia Summit (EAS) (chapter 4). The decisive American decision that signaled the reorientation of US policy was the so-called "pivot" or "rebalance" by which American political and military resources would be shifted from concerns in the Middle East and South Asia to the Asia-Pacific. In a November 2011 speech to the Australian parliament, President Obama announced a "deliberate and strategic" decision for the United States to play a larger and long-term role in shaping the region's future. He asserted that the United States "has been, and always will be, a Pacific power," and that we are here to stay.[39] US defense and diplomatic officials in their many meetings with Southeast Asian counterparts have stayed on this message. One of the many tests of the US role in shaping the region's future is being played out in the South China Sea (chapter 6).

Real US security cooperation and engagement in Southeast Asia is on a bilateral basis. There is no collective ASEAN structure to incorporate an American security presence other than the rhetorical platforms in the various ASEAN-led "talk shops" and dialogue processes (chapters 4 and 5). The quality and intensity of each particular US bilateral relationship will depend on the domestic political conditions in the partner state measured by Congress and NGOs against the American political criteria of democracy and political and human rights. There also lingers in the region the question of the durability and sustainability of the American recommitment given the vagaries of the American domestic political process. China is quick to point out its proximity and political stability as opposed to the United States' distance and political unpredictability. The ASEAN leaders diplomatically understood why, but privately were disturbed, when President Obama, during the October 2013 government shutdown, abandoned his Southeast Asia state visits, the first US–ASEAN Summit, and the EAS. This left the field open to the Chinese leadership team to make their case for the unreliability of American promises to Southeast Asia.[40]

On the Margins

Australia

Australia's role in Southeast Asia is viewed ambivalently on both sides of the relationship. On the one hand, Australia has sought to define itself economically and quasi-politically as an Asian state. On the other hand, it has explicitly identified the United States as its vital security partner. This was reinforced in 2011 when President Obama launched his "pivot" from an Australian platform, which included rotating deployments of US Marines to Darwin. This seemed to some critics in Southeast Asia to echo a previous Australian government's pretension of being the American regional deputy sheriff.

The most important but problematic of Australia's relations in Southeast Asia is with Indonesia. Australian policy is founded on the premise that Indonesia is more important to Australia than Australia is to Indonesia. Although it is officially downplayed, there is a latent "northern threat" syndrome in Canberra inherent in the geostrategic setting of densely populated Indonesia sitting just above thinly populated northern Australia. The Indonesian connection was badly frayed by the 1999 East Timor crisis. Australians viewed their lead in INTERFET to be a UN-mandated humanitarian rescue of the East Timorese people. Indonesian nationalists portrayed it as a new colonialism. Denunciation of Australia became a staple of Indonesian political life.

A new chapter in the bilateral relationship was opened with the 2007 Lombok Pact which provided for bilateral cooperation in a wide range of security- and defense-related activities. The key for Indonesia was the mutual pledge not to support in any manner the activities of any person or entity that constitute a threat to the stability, sovereignty, or national integrity of the other party, including those who seek to use the territory of one party to encourage or commit separatism in the territory of the other party. The diplomatic target was Indonesian Papua. The 2013 Australian Defence White Paper states that "Australia's strong partnership with Indonesia remains our most important regional strategic relationship and the partnership continues to deepen and broaden in support of our significant shared interests."[41] However, interests are not always shared.

The most troubling contemporary issue has been the influx of asylum-seeking boat people through Indonesia to Australia. Successive Australian governments have sought bilateral mechanisms to stanch the flow (chapter 9). Both sides have given priority to managing the relationship in terms of stability. It was destabilized in November 2013 when Jakarta learned—courtesy of NSA leaker Edward Snowden—that President Yudhoyono had been a target of Australian electronic espionage. An angry Indonesia recalled its

ambassador and suspended all strategic cooperation with Australia including combating people smuggling, an Indonesian reaction that Australia's
prime minister Tony Abbott termed "singularly unhelpful." An Indonesian-
proposed six-point plan to normalize relations gained little traction when further material on Australian "spying on Indonesia" was revealed. Australia's
stonewalling Indonesian queries about its intelligence activities in Indonesia
did not help.

India

A founding member with Burma, Cambodia, and Indonesia of the Nonaligned
Movement, India later blotted its copybook in Southeast Asia by taking the
wrong side on two international issues important to ASEAN. India backed
the Soviet Union's invasion of Afghanistan and Vietnam's invasion and
occupation of Cambodia (chapter 3). In these cases, New Delhi's strategic
perceptions were fastened on China's ties to Pakistan and the Khmer Rouge.
As a result, until the end of the Cold War, ASEAN remained cool to Indian
overtures for closer association. With strong backing by Singapore, India's
reconciliation with ASEAN began as a sectoral dialogue partner in 1992, a
full dialogue partner in 1995, and annual ASEAN–India Summits beginning
in 2002. It acceded to the TAC in 2003. In 2003, a framework agreement for
a free trade agreement was signed, but it was only after years of tough negotiations that it went into effect in 2010. India is also linked to ASEAN states
in three overlapping trade- and investment-focused multilateral organizations: the Bay of Bengal Initiative for Multi-Sectoral Economic Cooperation
(BIMSTEC), the Mekong–Ganga Cooperation group (MGC), and the Indian
Ocean Rim Association for Regional Cooperation (IOR-ARC) (chapter 4).

In the background to expanding ASEAN–India ties have been both sides'
perceptions of Chinese political assertiveness. New Delhi watched warily
as China forged regional and bilateral partnerships with ASEAN. India was
in direct competition with China for influence in Myanmar. To safeguard
its economic and geostrategic interests in the region, India adopted a "Look
East" policy to enhance trade and strategic relations in Southeast Asia, to
expand markets, to compete with Chinese political influence, and to improve
India's standing as a regional power. ASEAN has encouraged a higher Indian
profile in the region as a "soft balance" to China. On an equal footing with
China in the multilateral security dialogues of the EAS and the ARF, India's
positions complement ASEAN's. Although India does not project its "Look
East" policy in terms of being a balancing mechanism, ASEAN strategic
thinkers view India as a future important strategic ally as they hedge against
a China-dominated East Asian region.

Papua New Guinea (PNG)

PNG's primary cultural identification is Melanesian, and its regional orientation is toward Australia, New Zealand, and the South Pacific. Its primary multilateral regional organization memberships are the sixteen-nation Pacific Islands Forum (PIF) and the five-member Melanesian Spearhead Group (MSG). It was given observer status in ASEAN in 1976 and special observer status in 1981. In 1987 it became the first non-ASEAN state to accede to the TAC. It is a member of the ARF and considers itself a candidate for membership in ASEAN. The PNG concept is of Port Moresby being the bridge between ASEAN and the South Pacific. Concerns about its poor governance and capacity to meet ASEAN obligations have kept ASEAN's doors closed to it. One analyst has likened the PNG's ASEAN membership aspiration to Turkey's "endless audition" for EU membership.[42]

PNG shares a 472-mile (760 km) border with Indonesia, dividing the island of New Guinea roughly in half. Relations with Indonesia have been dominated by Indonesia's diplomacy and intimidation to prevent the PNG side of the border from becoming a sanctuary for Free Papua Movement (OPM) separatist insurgents (chapter 5). Border sensitivity is heightened by the refugee camps strung out along the PNG side of the border housing thousands of West Papuan refugees. Successive governments in Port Moresby, while sympathetic to their Melanesian brothers' struggle, have realized that Indonesia would not hesitate to use self-help measures if PNG did not cooperate on border security. While the two countries are committed to "soft" border management to promote economic and social exchange, Indonesia's side of the border is militarized, and border harassment and cross-border incursions are not infrequent.

Russia

Although Russia is not the great-power actor in Southeast Asia that its predecessor the Soviet Union was, under President Vladimir Putin Russia still makes its presence known, not willing to simply leave great-power visibility to China, Japan, and the United States. Russia is a dialogue partner of ASEAN, has acceded to the TAC, and participates in the EAS, which President Putin has not attended. Moscow's determination to remain regionally relevant was demonstrated in the June 2003 signing of a joint declaration for an ASEAN–Russian Federation partnership to enhance Russia's cooperative engagements with ASEAN over the full spectrum of ASEAN's interests. Moscow has also broadened bilateral relations, particularly with Malaysia and Vietnam.

Russia's economic presence through trade and investment is modest when compared to ASEAN's major partners. Its greatest bilateral visibility in Southeast Asia has been in weapons sales. As Southeast Asian military expansion and modernization programs continue (chapter 5), Russia is an alternative, and cheaper, source for high-technology weapons platforms than the United States or Western Europe. For example, the Indonesian, Malaysian, and Vietnamese air forces fly Sukhoi Su 30 combat aircraft.

NONSTATE ACTORS

For purposes of this discussion, by "nonstate actor" we mean an intergovernmental or nongovernmental (NGO) agency or organization with a program of international activity in Southeast Asia defined independently of any state actor or subgroup of state actors.

The United Nations System

The United Nations and its specialized agencies have been active in Southeast Asia beginning with the decolonization process itself. Indonesian independence from the Netherlands was facilitated through the fifteen-member UN Security Council, as was the transfer of sovereignty of Dutch New Guinea to Indonesia. It was the Security Council that authorized the UNTAC in Cambodia and the UNTAET in East Timor. Southeast Asian states have been important contributors to United Nations peacekeeping operations (PKOs). In 2013, Southeast Asian contingents were part of the fifteen PKOs underway: Philippines (6), Indonesia (4), Cambodia (4), Malaysia (3), Thailand (1), and Timor-Leste (1).

Five of the ten nonpermanent members of the Security Council are elected each year to two-year terms on secret ballots by a two-thirds majority of the 193-member UN General Assembly (UNGA). The candidates for the nonpermanent seats are drawn from five regional groups, with each group allowed two nonpermanent members. Southeast Asian states are in the fifty-two-member Asia group. Table 2.2 shows the Security Council membership history of Southeast Asian states. In 2008, for the only time, both Asia group seats were held by Southeast Asian countries: Indonesia and Vietnam. Both Jakarta and Hanoi celebrated their elections as prestige-building proof of their rising global profile. The ASEAN states have agreed to support the following future Security Council nominations: Malaysia, 2015–2016; Thailand, 2017–2018; Indonesia, 2019–2020; Vietnam, 2020–2021; and the Philippines, 2027–2028.

Table 2.2.   Southeast Asian States' UN Security Council Membership

Country	Dates of Memberships
Indonesia	1973–1974, 1995–1996, 2007–2008
Malaysia	1965, 1989–1990, 1999–2000
Philippines	1957, 1963, 1980–1981, 2004–2006
Singapore	2001–2002
Thailand	1985–1986
Vietnam	2008–2009

In the UNGA, where sovereign equality is demonstrated by one country, one vote, the pattern of Southeast Asia's voting is similar to that of India, China, and other Asian and African members. In 2012, the coincidence of ASEAN's UNGA voting with the United States on eighty important roll calls was 15.3 percent, with a Thailand high of 33 percent and a Vietnam low of 0 percent.[43] The ASEAN members caucus and tend to vote as a bloc on issues affecting the region or a member, such as supporting Indonesia in its East Timor province and defending Myanmar against Western efforts to sanction the junta.

The fifty-four-member United Nations Economic and Social Council (ECOSOC) has oversight over the organization's specialized agencies, programs, and funds for development assistance and other social and economic issue areas. The members are elected for three-year overlapping terms, with the Asia grouping allocated eleven seats. Indonesia held a 2012–2014 seat. ECOSOC's Asia work is carried out by the United Nations Economic and Social Commission for Asia and the Pacific (ESCAP) headquartered in Bangkok. UN specialized agencies like the Food and Agriculture Organization (FAO) and the World Health Organization (WHO) have been deeply engaged in technical assistance and regional economic development. The former has worked for food self-sufficiency in Southeast Asia; the latter is most lately known for its work in the SARS, HIV/AIDS, and avian flu epidemics (chapter 9). The United Nations Development Program (UNDP), working with ESCAP and the Asian Development Bank (ADB), plays an important role in progress toward human security in Southeast Asia, particularly the achievement of the Millennium Development Goals (MDG) (chapter 9). Also under ECOSOC, the UN Environmental Program (UNEP) is the lead agency in supporting the members in adapting to climate change (chapter 10).

Two other UN agencies have been active in human security matters in Southeast Asia. The Office of the UN High Commissioner for Refugees (UNHCR) plays an important role in providing for refugee relief, resettlement, and repatriation. Despite its humanitarian mission, the UNHCR often finds itself colliding with agents of host governments (chapter 9). The Office of the United Nations High Commissioner for Human Rights (UNHCHR) has had a particularly testy relationship with Southeast Asian nations aggrieved by its activities and reporting. Finally, the secretaries general themselves have acted as agents for political change in Southeast Asia. They have used their post as a bully pulpit to urge recalcitrant Southeast Asian nations like Cambodia and Myanmar to abide by the commitments to the norms and goals they accepted as members of the United Nations.

Organization of Islamic Cooperation (OIC)

The Organization of Islamic Cooperation (formerly the Organization of the Islamic Conference) is a fifty-seven-state intergovernmental organization. Headquartered in Jeddah, Saudi Arabia, it is the collective voice of Muslim countries seeking to secure and protect the interests of the Muslim world. In Southeast Asia, Brunei, Indonesia, and Malaysia are members. The OIC has directly and indirectly intervened, often with the agency of its Southeast Asian members, in defense of Muslim minorities in the Philippines, Thailand, and Myanmar (chapters 5 and 9).

International Financial Institutions

As World War II ended, two important international financial institutions were founded: the International Bank for Reconstruction and Development (IBRD), now the core of the World Bank Group, and the International Monetary Fund (IMF). Their original purpose was to promote economic recovery from the war's destruction and rebuild the international economic system. Over time, their mandates expanded to include economic development and financial stability in the newly independent countries.

The World Bank Group

The World Bank Group consists of the IBRD, the International Development Association (IDA), the International Finance Corporation (IFC), the Multilateral International Guarantee Agency (MIGA), and the International Centre for the Settlement of Investment Disputes. The United States, the Bank's largest shareholder, has always provided the Bank's president. The IBRD and IDA are a major source for development assistance in Southeast Asia. Indonesia has been the largest single regional client. Table 2.3 shows the World Bank's lending commitments in Southeast Asia from 2009 to 2013. Historically the bank has concentrated on infrastructure development, which has made it a target for environmental activists. This is particularly

Table 2.3. World Bank Southeast Asia Fiscal Commitments, 2009–2013* (US$ Millions)

Country†	2009	2010	2011	2012	2013	Total
Cambodia	35	5	70	0		110
Indonesia	4,332	3,013	2,389	3,251	1,770	14,755
Lao PDR	29	126	82	11	79	327
Myanmar					520	520
Philippines	341	721	323	845	408	2,638
Thailand	2	79	1,000	1	3	1,085
Timor-Leste					54‡	54
Vietnam	1,170	2,132	2,389	1,153	2,011	8,855
Total	5,909	6,076	6,253	5,261	4,845	28,345

Source: World Bank Country Data.

*World Bank, IBRD, and IDA cumulative fiscal year.

†Malaysia has not had recent World Bank Group fiscal commitments.

‡Timor-Leste cumulative to April 2013.

the case in Southeast Asia where World Bank support for large-scale dam building has been vigorously protested (chapter 10). More recently the World Bank has invested in capacity building, including governance and human capital. The Bank works in close cooperation with individual donor nations and coordinates consultative donor groups, among others, the Consultative Group for Cambodia (CGC), which in 2007 became the Cambodia Development Cooperation Forum (CDCF); the Timor-Leste Development Partners' Meeting (TLDPM); and the Consultative Group for Vietnam (CGV). Until the Indonesian government decided in January 2007 that it was ready to "graduate" from World Bank and donor-monitored development consultation, the Consultative Group for Indonesia (CGI), the 1992 successor to the Inter-Governmental Group on Indonesia (IGGI), had been a model of World Bank–coordinated economic assistance harmonization.

The International Monetary Fund (IMF)

The original mission of the IMF was to promote foreign exchange stability and assist in balance-of-payments difficulties. It is now a critical player in managing financial rescues of failing economies. The Fund's support comes with conditions relating to structural reforms directed to underlying causes of poor economic performance. It closely monitors a client country's performance against its agreements with the Fund as set out in quarterly "letters of intent" to which both sides have to agree. Critics argue that the IMF's emphasis on fiscal discipline, free markets, and privatization ignores the social and human needs of impoverished populations to whom government austerity and laissez-faire economics mean greater pain. The IMF has been the target of antiglobalists who reject its explicit commitment to integrating Southeast Asian economies into the global market system. Southeast Asian reactions to the conditional strings attached to IMF intervention were an important element prompting creation of the Chiang Mai Initiative (CMI), an incipient regional alternative to the IMF (chapter 8).

Asian Development Bank (ADB)

The Manila-headquartered ADB was founded in 1966 as a regional multilateral development lending institution. It has sixty-seven country members—forty-eight regional states and nineteen outside the region. Japan and the United States are the largest financial backers of the ADB, and Japan always provides its president. As of 31 December 2012, Japan had contributed $25.6 billion in capital subscription and $18.75 billion to special funds resources. The equivalents for the United States were $25.45 billion and $27 billion. Table 2.4 shows the cumulative numbers and amounts of loans made to Southeast Asian states through 2012. The ADB has also promoted subregional economic groupings in Southeast Asia (chapter 8).

International Nongovernmental Organizations (INGOs)

INGOs can be roughly divided into three groups. First, there are the international philanthropic institutions and foundations devoted to broad programming for economic, social, and political development. Both the Ford Foundation and the Asia Foundation have operated from field offices in Southeast Asia for decades, as has the German Friedrich-Ebert-Stiftung. More recently,

Table 2.4. ADB Loans and Amounts to Southeast Asian States* (US$ Millions)

Country	No. Loans	Amount
Cambodia	68	1,510
Indonesia	317	28,305
Lao PDR	80	1,782
Malaysia	77	1,997
Myanmar	32	531
Philippines	216	13,541
Thailand	92	6,354
Timor-Leste	2	40
Vietnam	145	11,966
Total	1,029	66,027

Source: ADB Country Data.

*Cumulative from date of membership to 21 December 2012.

the Soros Foundation's Open Society Institute has been making grants targeting eight Southeast Asian states. Another set of INGOs is functionally specific and provides a particular service, often humanitarian, to a country or region. In many cases these kinds of INGOs become agencies for the delivery of services. Examples of this are the International Red Cross, International Catholic Charities, Doctors without Borders, Oxfam, World Vision, and others too numerous to name.

A third set of INGOs is thematic interest groups that seek to influence policy in their interest area. They are advocacy organizations that, while often in consultative status with governments and UN agencies, seek to influence the policy of extraregional states toward the regional states as well as the domestic policy of the regional states themselves. Their causes in Southeast Asia can be regionally oriented or country specific, often bringing them into conflict with national governments that have wider and competing ranges of interests. For example, it was the global networking of advocacy groups that kept the East Timor question alive for a quarter of a century even though governments wished it would go away. Two internationally significant issue areas in which advocacy INGOs have been intensely involved are human rights and the environment, both of which raise politically sensitive questions (chapters 9 and 10). INGOs do not necessarily respect the political boundaries set by state sovereignty and can penetrate functionally through links to domestic NGOs with like causes. Sometimes domestic NGOs have advisory or budgetary ties to foreign governments. This means their activities can be affected by the quality of the relationship between their own government and their foreign supporters.

NOTES

1. John D. Ciorciari, "China and Cambodia: Patron and Client?" (IPC Working Papers Series, no. 121, Gerald R. Ford School of Public Policy, University of Michigan, 14 June 2013), accessed at http://ipc.umich.edu/working-papers/pdfs/ipc -121-ciorciari-china-cambodia-patron-client.pdf.

2. Dewi Fortuna Anwar, *Indonesia in ASEAN: Foreign Policy and Regionalism* (New York: St. Martin's, 1995), 57.

3. John Bresnan, "Indonesia," in *The Pivotal States: A New Framework for US Policy in the Developing World*, ed. Robert Chase, Emily Hill, and Paul Kennedy (New York: Norton, 1999), 15–39.

4. Michael Leifer, *Indonesia's Foreign Policy* (London: Allen & Unwin, 1984), 173.

5. The concept of Indonesia's "strategic centrality" was developed by Anthony L. Smith, *Strategic Centrality: Indonesia's Changing Role in ASEAN* (Singapore: ISEAS, 2000).

6. The figures are from the LPDR Ministry of Planning and Investment as reported in "Vietnam, Thailand Top Laos FDI," *Bangkok Post*, 12 February 2013.

7. The depth of Chinese penetration of Laos is examined in a two-part article by David Eimer, "Crossing the Line: Laos Braces for the Mega Railroad Project," *South China Morning Post* (Hong Kong), 29 September 2013, and "Losing Ground," *South China Morning Post* (Hong Kong), 6 October 2013.

8. The population figures are from the 2010 decennial census as reported by the Malaysian Department of Statistics, accessed at http://www.statistics.gov.my.

9. "Transcript, Joint Press Conference, Secretary of Defense Hagel and Minister Hishammuddin," accessed at http://www.defense.gov/transcripts/transcript .apex?transcriptid=5293.

10. John Lee, "Malaysia 'Punching above Its Weight' . . . and Finally Hitting the Target," in *Southeast Asian Affairs 2011*, ed. Daljit Singh (Singapore: ISEAS, 2012), 159.

11. "Malaysia-China Ink Defence Pact," *New Straits Times* (Kuala Lumpur), 30 October 2013.

12. "Myanmar President Backs Constitutional Amendment," *Nation* (Bangkok), 2 January 2014.

13. John Lee, "Myanmar Pivots Awkwardly Away from China," *ISEAS Perspective* 24 (December 2014).

14. President Barack Obama, "Letter to the Congress—Continuation of the National Emergency with Respect to Burma," accessed at http://www.whitehouse .gov/the-press-office/2014/05/15/letter-congress-continuation-national-emergency -respect-burma.

15. "Burma's Thein Sein Says Military Will Always Have a Special Place in Government," *Washington Post*, 9 May 2013.

16. "Remarks Aboard USS *Fitzgerald* Commemorating the 60th Anniversary of the US–Philippines Mutual Defense Treaty," accessed at http://state.gov/ secretary/20092013clinton/rm/2011/11/177228.htm.

17. "Remarks by President Obama and President Aquino of the Philippines before Bilateral Meeting," 17 November 2011, accessed at http://www.whitehouse.gov/the -press-office/2011/11/17/remarks-president-obama-and-president-aquino-philippines -bilateral-meeti.

18. A 2012 article in the People's Liberation Army newspaper warned that the mentality of the Philippines–US military cooperation "will lead the South China Sea issue down a fork in the road towards military confrontation and a resolution by armed forces," as cited by Reuters, accessed at http://mobile.reuters.com/article/ idUSBRE83K08D20120421?irpc-932.

19. "Remarks by President Obama and President Benigno Aquino III of the Philippines in Joint Press Conference," 28 April 2014, accessed at http://www.whitehouse .gov/the-press-office/2014/04/28/remarks-president-obama-and-president-benigno -aquino-iii-philippines-joi.

20. "DFA Chief Clarifies US Support under Mutual Defense Treaty," *Philippine Star* (Manila), 20 May 2014.

21. Husain Mutalib, "The Socio-Economic Dimensions in Singapore's Quest for Security and Stability," *Pacific Affairs* 75, no. 1 (Fall 2002): 39.

22. Cited by Lee Kuan Yew, *From Third World to First: The Singapore Story, 1965–2000* (New York: HarperCollins, 2000), 283.

23. US Department of Defense, "U.S. Thai Leaders Move Defense Alliance into 21st Century," accessed at http://www.defense.gov/news/newsarticle .aspx?id=118550.

24. As quoted in "Surin: Thailand Lost Momentum," *Bangkok Post*, 7 January 2008.

25. Chairman's Statement, 22nd ASEAN Summit, accessed at http://www.asean .org/news/asean-statement-communiques/item/chairmans-statement-of-the-22nd -asean-summit-our-people-our-future-together.

26. Donald K. Anton, "The Timor Sea Treaty Arbitration: Timor-Leste Challenges Australian Espionage and Seizure of Documents," *ASIL Insights* 18, no. 6 (February 2014), accessed at http://www.asil.org/insights/volume/18/issue/6/timor-sea-treaty -arbitration-timor-leste-challenges-australian-espionage.

27. Ernest Z. Bower, "US-Philippine Alliance: A Statesman Is Born," accessed at http://www.eastasiaforum.org/2011/04/20/us-philippine-alliance-a-statesman-is -born.

28. Keith Weller Taylor, *The Birth of Vietnam* (Berkeley: University of California Press, 1983), xxi.

29. Le Hong Hiep, "Vietnam's Hedging Strategy against China since Normalization," *Contemporary Southeast Asia* 35, no. 3 (December 2013): 334.

30. "Remarks by President Obama and President Truong Tan Sang of Vietnam after Bilateral Meeting," 24 July 2013, accessed at http://www.whitehouse.gov/the -press-office/2013/07/25/remarks-president-obama-and-president-truong-tan-sang -vietnam-after-bila.

31. Department of State Fact Sheet, "US–Vietnam Comprehensive Partnership," accessed at http://www.state.gov/r/pa/prs/ps/2013/218734.htm.

32. David Shambaugh, ed., *Power Shift: China and Asia's New Dynamic* (Berkeley: University of California Press, 2006), 23.

33. "Don't Flaunt the ASEAN Banner on the South China Sea Issue," *China Daily News*, 30 August 2013, accessed at http://usa.chinadaily.com.cn/world/2013-08/30/ content_16930770.htm.

34. "While America Slept," *Foreign Policy*, 27 February 2013, accessed at http:// www.foreignpolicy.com.

35. Narushige Michishita, "Abe Doctrine to Remake Japan–Asean Relations," *Straits Times* (Singapore), 6 March 2013.

36. The commemorative summit's joint statement can be accessed at http://www .asean.org/news/asean-statement-communiques/item/hand-in-hand-facing-regional -and-global-challenges.

37. "Japan to Defend PH from China," *Manila Times*, 28 June 2013.

38. Clinton made his call for a new Pacific Community before the National Assembly of the Republic of Korea, Seoul, South Korea, 10 July 1993. The text can be accessed at http://1997-2001.state.gov/www/regions/eap/930710.html.

39. President Obama's speech can be accessed at http://www.whitehouse.gov/the -press-office/2011/11/17/remarks-president-obama-australian-parliament.

40. "Cancellation of Trip by Obama Plays to Doubts of Asia Allies," *New York Times*, 4 October 2013; "Cancellation of Obama's Southeast Asia Trip a Boost for Xi," *Los Angeles Times*, 4 October 2013.

41. Australian government, Department of Defence, *Defence White Paper 2013*, 11, accessed at http://www.defence.gov.au/whitepaper/2013/docs/WP_2013_web .pdf.

42. Sean Jacobs, "No Thanks, Not Yet: PNG's ASEAN Bid," *East Asia Forum*, 4 December 2012, accessed at http://www.eastasiaforum.org/2012/12/04/no-thanks -not-yet-pngs-asean-bid.

43. US Department of State, "2012 UN Voting Practices Report," accessed at http://www.state.gov/documents/organization/208072.pdf.

SUGGESTIONS FOR FURTHER READING

Basic background data and statistics on each of the Southeast Asian coun-tries can be found in the US State Department's "Background Notes" on the country link at http://www.state.gov/p/eap; in the CIA's *World Factbook*, ac-cessed at http://www.cia.gov/publications/factbook; and through the country links on the ASEAN home page: http://www.asean.org. Economic data can be found on the country pages of the World Bank (http://www.worldbank .org) and the Asian Development Bank (http://www.adb.org).

The contemporary domestic political settings for the countries are out-lined in Jacques Bertrand, *Political Change in Southeast Asia* (New York: Cambridge University Press, 2013) and William Case, ed., *Contemporary Authoritarianism in Southeast Asia* (New York: Routledge, 2010). For China and Japan in Southeast Asia, see Ian Storey, *Southeast Asia and the Rise of China* (New York: Routledge, 2010) and Peng Er Lam, *Japan's Relations with Southeast Asia* (New York: Routledge, 2013). Natasha Hamilton-Hart, *Hard Issues, Soft Illusions* (Ithaca, NY: Cornell University Press, 2012) is a critical political economy analysis of US–Southeast Asian relations.

Some specific country studies are Sophal Ear, *Aid Dependence in Cambo-dia: How Foreign Assistance Undermines Democracy* (New York: Columbia University Press, 2013); Donald E. Weatherbee, *Indonesia in ASEAN: Vision and Reality* (Singapore: ISEAS, 2013); Vatthana Pholsena, *Post-war Laos: The Politics of Culture, History, and Identity* (Ithaca, NY: Cornell University Press, 2006); Johan Saravanamuttu, *Malaysia's Foreign Policy: The First Fifty Years* (Singapore: ISEAS, 2010); Nick Cheesman, Monique Skidmore, and Trevor Wilson, eds., *Myanmar's Transition: Openings, Obstacles, and Opportunities* (Singapore: ISEAS, 2013); Rommel C. Banlaoi, *Philippines*

Security in the Age of Terror: National, Regional, and Global Challenges in the Post 9/11 World (Boca Raton, FL: Auerbach, 2009); N. Ganesan, *Realism and Interdependence in Singapore's Foreign Policy* (London: Routledge, 2005); Pavin Chachavalpongpun, *Reinventing Thailand: Thaksin and His Foreign Policy* (Singapore: ISEAS, 2012); Michael Leach and Damien Kingsbury, eds., *The Politics of Timor-Leste: Democratic Consolidation after Intervention* (Ithaca, NY: Cornell University Southeast Asia Program, 2012); and Bill Hayton, *Vietnam: Rising Dragon* (New Haven, CT: Yale University Press, 2010).

Chapter Three

The Cold War in Southeast Asia

The worldview shaping the first four and a half decades of post–World War II international relations in Southeast Asia was American. Its political and strategic underpinning was the "containment" of communism, a strategy most famously spelled out in George Kennan's 1947 "Mr. X" article in *Foreign Affairs*.[1] Containment's central proposition was that the Soviet Union's pressure against the West was something "that can be contained by the adroit and vigilant application of counter-force at a series of constantly shifting geographical and political points, corresponding to the shifts and maneuvers of Soviet policy." Kennan urged the United States to enter "with reasonable confidence upon a policy of firm containment, to confront the Russians with unalterable counter-force at every point where they show signs of encroaching upon the interests of the peaceful and stable world." After 1949, the People's Republic of China (PRC) was added to the communist threats that had to be contained.

The perceived threat of communism's advance in Southeast Asia was demonstrated early by attempted communist coups and insurgencies in Indonesia, Burma, Malaya, and the Philippines. In fashioning relations with the new states of Southeast Asia, the United States emphasized "mutual security" against the communist threat as the basis for a wide array of economic and political ties so important for national development. The American goal was to enlist the countries of Southeast Asia into the "free world." The pressure on Southeast Asian states to commit to that goal backfired in Indonesia and Burma.

In Indonesia, US insistence on tying economic aid to a mutual security framework created a leftist nationalist backlash that brought down a West-leaning government. The new government quickly balanced its relations by diplomatically recognizing the USSR and the PRC. Burma was the first noncommunist state to recognize the PRC. Retreating Chinese Nationalist forces carved out a sanctuary in Burma's northern Shan states from which they made cross-border incursions into China. The Nationalist forces had clandestine support from Taiwan, Thailand, and the United States. In 1953, an angry Burmese government terminated its American aid program and took the issue to the United Nations. Many of the Nationalist troops were eventually repatriated to Taiwan. Others were pushed by the Burmese army across the Thai border, where they settled down to opium production. The affair confirmed Burma in the correctness of its policy of strict neutralism and nonalignment. For nearly four decades Rangoon (now Yangon) isolated itself from the international politics of the region.

CONTAINMENT IN SOUTHEAST ASIA

From the outset of the Cold War, the focus of containment in Southeast Asia was on French colonial Vietnam. The French were fighting what became the First Indochina War against the Viet Minh nationalist/communist independence movement led by Ho Chi Minh.[2] An April 1952 US National Security Council memorandum outlined the American view of the strategic problem posed by communist expansion through Vietnam.[3] The document stated that "in the absence of effective and timely counteraction the loss of any single [Southeast Asian] country would probably lead to a relatively swift submission to or an alignment with communism by the remaining countries of this group." This was the core of the "domino theory" of the strategic interrelatedness of the Southeast Asian states. If the dominoes fell, then "communist domination, by whatever means, of all Southeast Asia would seriously endanger in the short term and critically endanger in the longer term United States security interests."[4]

The first domino was Vietnam. For Washington, all communist lines of command, including Ho Chi Minh's, ultimately ran back to Moscow. The establishment of the PRC provided the Vietnamese both material and technical assistance. China's 1950 intervention in the Korean War underlined for the United States the urgency of the task. Washington viewed the Korean War and the French struggle in Indochina through the same lens of communist threat. The United States did not recognize the new regime in China, blocked its entry into the United Nations, and diplomatically pressed the Southeast Asian states not to recognize the PRC government.

By 1954, the French were exhausted. The United States, unwilling to intervene directly in support of the French, had provided over a billion dollars of assistance. The United States participated in the 1954 Geneva Foreign Ministers' Conference which devised a compromise political settlement, the

Geneva Accords, to terminate the French military role in Indochina. The United States did not associate itself with the final document but in a separate statement declared that it would refrain from the threat or use of force to disturb the agreement. Washington warned that it would view "any renewal of the aggression" with grave concern and as threatening international peace and security.[5] Already in 1954, the United States was characterizing the Viet Minh's struggle for an independent unified Vietnam as "aggression."

For the purposes of an armistice and regrouping of military forces, the Geneva settlement partitioned Vietnam at the 17th parallel. From its Hanoi capital in the north, Ho Chi Minh's Democratic Republic of Vietnam (DRV), with its ties to China and the Soviet Union, faced the southern Government of Vietnam (GVN) ensconced in Saigon and backed by the United States. The Geneva Accords called for national elections in 1956, but they were never held, with both sides blaming the other. The former French Indochina protectorates Laos and Cambodia were theoretically neutralized.

The Southeast Asia Treaty Organization (SEATO)

In the wake of the French defeat, the United States mobilized allies to support containment to meet the threat that now seemed posed by the opening of a communist strategic window to Southeast Asia. In 1954, eight nations signed the Southeast Asia Collective Defense Treaty (the Manila Pact) and created the Southeast Asia Treaty Organization (SEATO).[6] Only two SEATO members, the Philippines and Thailand, were in fact Southeast Asian. The other signatories were the United States, Great Britain, Australia, New Zealand, France, and Pakistan (with an eye to India). The operative heart of the Manila Pact stated that the parties to the treaty recognized that aggression by armed attack in the treaty area on a party to the treaty or any state or territory unanimously designated by the parties would endanger the peace and safety of all. In that event, they would consult to meet the common danger. A separate protocol brought Laos, Cambodia, and the "free territory" of Vietnam under the SEATO cover. In an understanding to the agreement, the United States stated that the treaty obligations only applied to communist aggression.

SEATO was very different from NATO in Europe. No military units were assigned to SEATO, and there was no unified military command structure. The only obligation the allies had was to consult. SEATO's significance as an alliance was not really military; it was political. It provided a multilateral political framework for US containment strategy in Southeast Asia. American forward military deployment in Southeast Asia had been limited to the Philippines. American military base rights in the Philippines were provided for in the 1947 package of agreements linked to Philippine independence. A

1951 bilateral US–Philippines Mutual Defense Treaty, still in force, fixed US reciprocal obligations to the Philippines. The most important of the more than twenty American military facilities in the Philippines were the naval base on Subic Bay and the Air Force's Clark Field.

SEATO's first real test came in 1961–1962, when Thailand felt threatened by a communist Pathet Lao military offensive against the theoretically neutral Royal Lao government. Because SEATO action required a unanimity that was not forthcoming, the United States and Thailand undertook a bilateral commitment. In the March 1962 Rusk–Thanat communiqué, the United States declared that its obligation under the Manila Pact in the event of communist aggression "was individual as well as collective" and did not depend on prior agreement of the other SEATO members. In other words, the multilateral treaty would function as a bilateral security pact between the United States and Thailand. This was the foundation of a US–Thailand security relationship that endures to the present.[7]

Great Britain held the SEATO umbrella over Malaya and Singapore until their independence when they chose technical nonalignment. Both countries maintained a security relationship with British Commonwealth partners Australia and New Zealand in the 1957 Anglo-Malay Defence Agreement (AMDA). This provided the basis for Commonwealth military assistance to Malaysia during its 1963–1965 "confrontation" with Indonesia (discussed below). AMDA was succeeded by the 1971 Five Power Defence Arrangement (FPDA). The FPDA survived the end of the Cold War. It still provides a multilateral vehicle within which Malaysia and Singapore can militarily cooperate in the absence of bilateral military training links. By the middle of the 1950s the Cold War lines and structures were in place. The DRV and GVN faced each other across the 17th parallel. Through the DRV, the USSR and PRC faced the United States, bringing a strategic front line of the Cold War into Southeast Asia. In neutralized Laos, the revolutionary forces of the Pathet Lao menaced the status quo, and in neutral Cambodia, Prime Minister Prince Norodom Sihanouk diplomatically maneuvered to keep his country out of the fray.

The Bandung Conference

Beneath the great-power-inspired Southeast Asian Cold War security system, Southeast Asian states sought ways to relate to each other on an alternative basis rather than simply choosing Cold War sides. Gathering concerns over great-power conflict in Asia prompted consultations among India, Pakistan, Ceylon (now Sri Lanka), Burma, and Indonesia. In two meetings in 1954 their prime ministers declared opposition to interference in domestic affairs by external communist or anticommunist agencies. Looking to amplify their regional voice, in April 1955 they convened a meeting of twenty-nine African and Asian heads of government and foreign ministers in Bandung, Indonesia. Southeast Asia was represented by communist DRV; neutralist Burma, Cambodia, Indonesia, and Laos; and American allies, the Philippines, Thailand, and South Vietnam. The Asian-African Bandung Conference marked Indonesia's emergence as an important actor on the international scene. It was also the debut of communist China as a regional political actor. The conference was driven by the twin themes of anti-imperialism and peaceful coexistence. The final communiqué set forth ten principles—the Bandung Principles—by observance of which nations could live in peace with one another and develop friendly cooperation (box 3.1).[8] The Bandung Principles incorporated the Five Principles of Peaceful Coexistence set forth in the preamble to the 1954 India–China agreement regulating their relations in the Tibet region. A compromise was reached with the neutralists on the question of security agreements. The conference recognized the right of individual and collective self-defense but with "abstention from the use of arrangements of collective

---

Box 3.1.   The Bandung Principles

The normative basis for Southeast Asian international relations is set out in the Bandung Principles adopted 24 April 1955 at the Bandung, Indonesia, Asian–African Conference. The principles are

- respect for fundamental human rights;
- respect for sovereignty and territorial integrity of all countries;
- recognition of the equality of all races and nations;
- abstention from intervention or interference in the internal affairs of another country;
- respect for the right of each nation to defend itself singly or collectively;
- abstention from use of arrangements of collective defense to serve the interests of any of the big powers;
- refraining from acts or threats of aggression or the use of force against the territorial integrity or political independence of any country;
- settlement of all international disputes by peaceful means;
- promotion of mutual interests and cooperation; and
- respect for justice and international obligations.

defense to serve the particular interests of any of the big powers." Although the historical record shows that the Bandung Principles have been routinely violated in Southeast Asia, they nevertheless provided the ideal foundation for structuring international relations in the region and still remain a normative reference point for Southeast Asian bilateral and multilateral relations.

The Nonaligned Movement (NAM)

The Bandung Conference was the precursor to the 1961 Belgrade Conference that founded the Nonaligned Movement (NAM). The only Southeast Asian states represented in Belgrade were Burma, Indonesia, and Cambodia. Building on the Bandung foundation, the NAM adopted a theoretical position of security equidistance between the Cold War great powers with a platform of anti-imperialism and adherence to the Five Principles of Peaceful Coexistence. The United States viewed nonalignment with hostility, identifying it as a communist Trojan horse, since leading roles were played by states like Cuba and Vietnam. Over time, the NAM's agenda became increasingly more radical and anti-West. Burma, a founding member, withdrew from the NAM following the 1979 Havana Summit because it viewed the NAM as not truly neutral. With the ending of the Cold War the NAM sought to transform itself by shifting attention to social and economic problems in the developing world. All the ASEAN states are now among the 120 members.

The Second Indochina War: 1961–1975

After the 1954 Geneva Conference, the United States became the principal supporter of the anticommunist Government of Vietnam. American advisors and material assistance worked to build South Vietnamese political and military capabilities able to withstand an emerging internal war led by Viet Minh cadres left behind at partition. The revolutionary political structure was the National Front for the Liberation of South Vietnam (NFLSV). The armed insurgents were called the Viet Cong (Vietnamese communists). Both the NFLSV and the Viet Cong were directed by the DRV. When it became obvious that promised national elections were not going to be held, the communist strategists began a classic "people's war." By 1961, it seemed clear that the GVN would not be able to defeat the insurgency with its own resources. President John F. Kennedy decided to introduce fifteen thousand US military advisors. The US justified its position by reference to its SEATO obligations. Hanoi denounced the American role as imperialism.

The United States assumed major responsibility for the conduct of the war after Congress gave President Lyndon Johnson a blank check in the 1965

"Tonkin Gulf" resolution to use whatever force necessary to defeat communism in Indochina.[9] By 1967, nearly three-quarters of a million American forces were at war in South Vietnam, along with forces from Thailand, the Philippines, Australia, New Zealand, and South Korea. Regular North Vietnamese People's Army of Vietnam (PAVN) troops were operating in the South. The United States carried the war north in massive bombing campaigns. The conflict spilled over into Laos and Cambodia as the United States tried to interdict North Vietnamese supply lines to the South along the so-called Ho Chi Minh trail and to strike enemy cross-border sanctuaries.

In technically neutral Laos, the United States and Thailand joined forces in a "secret war" against the North Vietnam–allied Pathet Lao. Cambodia's Sihanouk desperately tried to maintain neutrality that was routinely violated by both warring sides. He was ousted in a 1970 coup led by General Lon Nol, who quickly aligned with the United States. In addition to PAVN operating from bases in eastern Cambodia, indigenous Cambodian communists called the Khmer Rouge waged their own military campaign to seize power in Cambodia.

As the American war in Vietnam escalated in cost and casualties, realist critics viewed it as a strategic mistake as it degraded US military capabilities to the advantage of the USSR and PRC. For the growing ranks of antiwar protesters, the war had become a moral monstrosity. American public support collapsed. The antiwar mood helped elect President Richard Nixon in 1968. Nixon had promised to end the war, but it took four years. President Nixon and Secretary of State Henry Kissinger tried to force the DRV to negotiate on terms that would still preserve American credibility. Pressure was kept on the North by heavy bombing, and the Sino-Soviet split was diplomatically exploited by beginning a process of normalizing US–PRC relations. The 1973 Paris Agreement gave the United States what it described as "peace with honor."[10] The termination of American support left the GVN to face its enemy alone. Within two years, southern resistance crumbled. Saigon fell on 29 April 1975. Nine months later, Vietnam was unified. Saigon was renamed Ho Chi Minh City. As the end game played out in South Vietnam, so did the sideshows in Laos and Cambodia, with the victories of the Pathet Lao and the brutal Khmer Rouge regime of Pol Pot.

The American war in Vietnam was the most controversial period in modern American political and military history. It impacted the formulation and conduct of American foreign policy for a generation. The battle cry "No more Vietnams" represented a new, limitationist view of an American interventionist role in the world that persisted to 9/11. The peculiarly American introspective and retrospective concerns that prompted the drawing of so many "lessons of Vietnam" were not shared by Southeast Asian elites. They drew different lessons. One was about the constancy of the American security presence. This was signaled in 1969 by the enunciation of the Nixon Doctrine which stated that in cases of aggression other than nuclear, the United States would provide military and economic assistance in accord with treaty commitments, but that the threatened nation had the primary responsibility for its defense.[11] This prompted a Southeast Asian reassessment of the integrity of the passive American security umbrella. The perceived abandonment of South Vietnam reinforced the insecurities. Secondly, the domestic American political dialogue raised fears in Southeast Asia that the United States was entering a period of neoisolationism.

SOUTHEAST ASIA AND
THE SECOND INDOCHINA WAR

The Philippines and Thailand were the only Southeast Asian countries allied with the United States in the Second Indochina War. The calculations of the leaderships in Bangkok and Manila—the former a military dictatorship, the latter, after 1972, Ferdinand Marcos's presidential dictatorship—had less to do with SEATO obligations than with obtaining a higher level of American political, military, and economic support. Malaysia's and Singapore's Commonwealth allies in the FPDA were also American allies. Burma had become a hermit nation. Indonesia, under President Sukarno until deposed in 1966, actively opposed the US role in Vietnam.

Indonesia under Sukarno

Between 1957 and 1965, Indonesia challenged the American-dominated status quo in Southeast Asia. Its nonaligned position had been translated by President Sukarno into the championing of a "Jakarta–Phnom Penh–Hanoi–Beijing–Pyongyang axis" to fight Western imperialism and neocolonialism. Sukarno declared martial law in 1957, terminating parliamentary government, and by decree began to build a left-trending "guided democracy" that gave a role to the Indonesian Communist Party (PKI). When regional revolts broke out in 1958, the United States provided clandestine support to the rebel forces. The regional uprisings were forcefully suppressed, but the grievance against American subversion lingered. Sukarno also threatened the use of force to wrest Dutch New Guinea from the Netherlands. The United States offered to mediate the conflict, hoping to head off a war in the rear of its war in Vietnam. An American-sponsored face-saving political solution transferred authority in the territory to the United Nations in 1962, which in turn transferred it to an Indonesian interim administration in 1963. Nascent Papuan nationalism was suppressed. In 1969, the territory was incorporated into Indonesia as a province, planting the seeds of separatism (chapter 5).

"Confrontation" with Malaysia

Sukarno's strident distancing from the noncommunist world reached its zenith in the crisis over the British plan to decolonize Singapore and its Borneo territories in a federal union with already independent Malaya. The new state was established in September 1963. Declaring Malaysia a "puppet" of British imperialism, Sukarno announced a campaign to "crush" Malaysia. In an undeclared war, called by the Indonesians *konfrontasi* (confrontation), Indonesian marines were infiltrated into peninsular Malaysia, and terrorist bombs were set off in Singapore.[12] By virtue of the AMDA, British Commonwealth forces fought Indonesian incursions along the Sarawak–Indonesian border. The PKI strongly supported confrontation, hoping to become a volunteer fifth armed force with weapons from China. When Malaysia was elected a nonpermanent member of the UN Security Council in December 1964, a defiant Indonesia quit the UN, the only nation ever to do so.

Although Sukarno framed the justification for confrontation in terms of anti-imperialism, other sources of Indonesian conduct can be identified as well. A pan-Indonesia was part of an ultranationalist vision that included the territories now incorporated in Malaysia. Indonesian leaders, aware of Malaya's anticommunism and its sympathies toward Sumatran regionalists, also feared that an economically successful greater Malaysia could become a magnet for future Indonesian separatists. In terms of Jakarta's own possible regional hegemonic ambitions, a fragmented Malaya, Singapore, Sarawak, Brunei, and Sabah, even if independent, would be satellites of Indonesia. Finally, the conflict over Malaysia shifted public attention from Indonesia's failing economy and diverted anger to a foreign target.

The Fall of Sukarno

By 1964, political competition in Indonesia had been reduced to the anticommunist army and the PKI, with Sukarno balancing in between. The PKI maintained close ties to its Chinese counterpart and had penetrated the military, particularly the air force and marines. For the United States, the specter of being outflanked in Southeast Asia was real. Against a tension-filled backdrop of undeclared war against Malaysia, economic failure, local PKI challenges to Muslim interests, and uncertainties about Sukarno's health, the army–PKI conflict bubbling below the surface erupted on 30 September 1965 when PKI-backed leftist military elements attempted a coup. The army's strategic reserve (KOSTRAD) under General Suharto quickly regained control of the situation. Although the full details of the coup and countercoup are still a matter of controversy, there is no doubt about the outcome. A nationwide bloody anticommunist campaign was sponsored by the army. The PKI and its associated fronts were wiped out. The thousands of deaths have only been surpassed in Southeast Asia by the Khmer Rouge's "killing fields." Sukarno, who many thought was complicit in the coup, was politically isolated. Step by step, the new anticommunist rulers stripped Sukarno's authority and transferred it to Suharto, first as acting president in 1967 and then president in 1968.

The discontinuity in Indonesian political life had a dramatic international impact as well as domestic. One of the first results was the ending of *konfrontasi*. The West, rather than being excoriated, was now tapped as a critical source of economic assistance. Diplomatic relations with the PRC were "frozen" because of the alleged PKI–Communist Party of China (CPC) links. Cold War nonalignment remained a pillar of foreign policy, but the United States replaced the USSR as Indonesia's major defense supplier. Finally, it was the toppling of Sukarno that made ASEAN possible.

The Creation of ASEAN

Two important policy concerns impelled the noncommunist Southeast Asian states in 1967 to intensify and regularize their political contacts in a structured multilateral setting. The first was the escalation of the US war in Vietnam with its uncertain regional consequences. The second was the need to integrate post-Sukarno Indonesia into a regional order in which it could collaborate but not dominate. Of the two, the Indonesian problem was the most exigent. In addition to the shared interests derived from generalized perceptions of the regional international environment, each country had particular interests in establishing ASEAN. For the Philippines, ASEAN was a vehicle for the assertion of a regional identity rather than just being seen as a trans-Pacific appendage of the United States. Thailand's membership in ASEAN gave a Southeast Asian balance to its SEATO alliance with the United States. ASEAN gave Singapore's new sovereignty regional recognition. Malaysia hoped to find in ASEAN a political alternative to its Commonwealth ties that had been weakened by the British retreat east of Suez. Indonesia's aspirations for regional leadership could play out through ASEAN in a nonthreatening political format that did not limit its options.

ASEAN's Antecedents

There were two earlier projects in regionalism from which the founders of ASEAN could draw. Between 1961 and 1963, Thailand, the Philippines, and Malaya joined in the Association of Southeast Asia (ASA). In the planning stage from 1959, the original anticommunist inspiration was diluted in an organizationally loose grouping in which the political agenda was hidden in its public goal of the promotion of economic, social, scientific, and cultural cooperation in Southeast Asia. This did not relieve it of the Indonesian charge that the ASA was a SEATO plot. Cooperation within ASA foundered on the Philippines' break with Malaysia when the disputed Sabah (North Borneo) territory was incorporated into Malaysia in September 1963 (chapter 5).

A second organization, MAPHILINDO, was stillborn at a Malaya–Philippines–Indonesia summit meeting in Manila, 31 July–5 August 1963. Theoretically, it provided a loosely articulated quasi-confederal framework for relations among the three nations. Actually, MAPHILINDO was a diplomatic device through which the Philippines and Indonesia sought to frustrate or delay the creation of the Malaysian Federation. The proclamation of Malaysia one month later extinguished MAPHILINDO. The language of the Manila Accords establishing MAPHILINDO had Sukarno's fingerprints all over it. With regard to the respective American and British security ties of the Philippines and Malaya, it was agreed that the bases were temporary and should not be used to subvert directly or indirectly the independence of any of the three countries. Invoking the language of the Bandung Principles, it was stated that the three countries would not use collective defense arrangements to serve the interests of any of the big powers.[13]

ASEAN's Purpose

The outlines of a regional diplomatic grouping within which post-Sukarno Indonesia could play an active role in regional affairs emerged in the diplomatic negotiations to end *konfrontasi*. The planning crystallized in a 1966 Thai draft proposal for a Southeast Asian Association for Regional Cooperation which outlined what became ASEAN. On 8 August 1967, the foreign ministers of Indonesia, the Philippines, Singapore, and Thailand, and the deputy prime minister of Malaysia issued the Bangkok Declaration establishing the Association of Southeast Asian Nations.[14] The goal was to promote regional cooperation contributing toward peace, progress, and prosperity while being determined to ensure the members' stability free from external interference. The problem was to find an organizational framework in which the differing patterns of nonalignment and alignment could be accommodated. The solution was to borrow the MAPHILINDO formula and affirm that "foreign bases are temporary" (with no time frame fixed) and not intended to be used to subvert the independence of other states in the region.

ASEAN's stated purposes were to promote active collaboration and regional cooperation on matters of common interest in the economic, social, cultural, technical, scientific, and administrative spheres in order to strengthen the foundation for a prosperous and peaceful community of Southeast Asian nations. The organization was left open to any Southeast Asian state that accepted ASEAN's aims and purposes. No mention was made of political cooperation, let alone security. ASEAN elites expressly and repeatedly denied that ASEAN was a security organization or alliance. In cases of defense cooperation between ASEAN members, great pains were taken to point out that these were not part of ASEAN. Yet, from its outset ASEAN functioned in terms of collective political security. A Malaysian foreign minister retrospectively underlined the fact that the creation of ASEAN was the political reaction of the noncommunist states of Southeast Asia to the perceived common threat of communism posed by the Sino-Soviet struggle, expansive Vietnam, and domestic communist insurgencies.[15] From its inception, ASEAN had two tracks. One was the program of functional cooperation stated in the Bangkok Declaration. The other was its implicit political function as a loose anticommunist regional diplomatic caucus. ASEAN was a creature of its members' foreign ministers, and politics was in control.

Zone of Peace, Freedom, and Neutrality (ZOPFAN)

Looking to a post–Indochina War international environment, the five ASEAN states tried to fashion a proactive regional strategy independent of the United States' security policy, one that would not be threatening to the Indochinese states and would insulate the ASEAN region from great-power intrusion. In the 1971 Kuala Lumpur Declaration, the ASEAN governments agreed to exert the necessary efforts "to secure recognition of, and respect for, Southeast Asia as a Zone of Peace, Freedom and Neutrality free from any form or manner of interference by outside powers."[16] The ZOPFAN proposal was ASEAN's first avowedly regional political initiative.

As a declaratory statement of a goal of neutralization, the ZOPFAN was not self-enforcing in the sense that the ASEAN states had the capabilities to force other nations to respect the zone. Vietnam attacked the ZOPFAN as support for American imperialism that would obstruct the legitimate struggles of the peoples of Southeast Asia. The ZOPFAN was essentially a rhetorical device requiring no real policy commitment by the signatories or change in their existing security arrangements including their military alliances. Each ASEAN state was free to construct its own meaning of the concept. Any attempt to be specific would have shattered the fragile consensus on ZOPFAN as an abstraction.

THE INTERWAR INTERVAL: 1975–1978

After the April 1975 communist victories in Vietnam, Laos, and Cambodia, the central problem of international politics in Southeast Asia was to devise structures to accommodate and mediate relations between the regional non-communist states and the Indochinese states, principally Vietnam. The revolutionary triumphalism of the new rulers in Indochina intensified ASEAN Southeast Asia's concerns about Vietnam's ambitions and intentions. Vietnamese and Chinese support for domestic communist insurgents elsewhere in Southeast Asia seemed even more threatening now that a strong communist subregion had been established in continental Southeast Asia. Hope in some ASEAN quarters that victories would moderate revolutionary ardor in Indochina was dispelled by the Khmer Rouge's attack on its own Cambodian population, the Vietnamese gulags, and the flow of refugees into ASEAN Southeast Asia (chapter 9).

The ASEAN states' adjustment to the new situation was immensely complicated by the great-power linkages in the region. Both Laos and Vietnam were in the Soviet camp. China was the patron of the Khmer Rouge regime in Cambodia and an obstacle to Vietnamese hegemony in Indochina. Despite perceptions of American strategic distancing, ASEAN leaders privately insisted that a continued US political role was an essential counterweight to the operation of the Sino–Soviet competition for influence in Southeast Asia. This highlighted Manila's real contribution to ASEAN. The US–Philippines bilateral alliance was the umbilical cord of the American security commitment to the region. The code words for ASEAN support for the Philippines bases were "an active US presence."

The normalization of US–China relations, signaled by the 1972 Nixon–Chou En-lai (Zhou Enlai) "Shanghai Communiqué," gave political space for three ASEAN states to reevaluate their lack of relations with the PRC. China and some ASEAN states looked to each other through new balance-of-power lenses. For China, improved relations in ASEAN Southeast Asia would outflank the USSR and Vietnam. Malaysia led the ASEAN recognition parade on 31 May 1974. The Philippines followed suit on 9 June 1975. President Marcos saw normalization of relations with China as giving Manila some diplomatic leverage with the United States. Finally, on 1 July 1975, Thailand established diplomatic relations with China. All three bilateral joint communiqués announcing the establishment of diplomatic relations contained the "antihegemony" clause that was part of the China–US Shanghai Communiqué, stating that the governments are "opposed to any attempt by any country or group of countries to establish hegemony or create spheres of influence in any part of the world."[17] This was correctly viewed by the USSR as a Chinese effort to limit Soviet influence in Southeast Asia. One of the important security consequences for Southeast Asia of normalization of relations with the PRC was cessation of Chinese support to Maoist communist insurgencies in the region.

Indonesia and Singapore did not follow suit in the sudden rush to normalization. In Indonesia, Beijing was unable to overcome the taint of its alleged complicity with the PKI. Indonesia's military leadership viewed the PRC as a politically and territorially unsatisfied revisionist power with expansionist designs. Singapore, in the shadow of its Indonesian neighbor and with its Chinese majority population, was not going to recognize China until Indonesia did. It would be another fifteen years before Jakarta defrosted its "frozen" relations with Beijing in 1999, with Singapore following suit. Only then could the PRC become organizationally associated with ASEAN.

The 1976 Bali Summit

The communist victories in Indochina in 1975 catalyzed the ASEAN states into urgent efforts for greater security cooperation. In February 1976, the ASEAN heads of government met in Bali, Indonesia, for the first ASEAN Summit. There they laid the foundations for stronger political and economic collaboration within ASEAN without closing the door to reconciliation with the Indochinese states. Two important political documents were endorsed in the pursuit of collective political security. The first was the Declaration of ASEAN Concord (Bali Concord I) which in its political program called for "strengthening of political solidarity by promoting the harmonization of views, coordinating positions and, where possible and desirable, taking common action."[18] Actually, that process was well underway. Beginning with an "informal" meeting of the ASEAN foreign ministers in April 1972, the ministers agreed to meet at least once a year to discuss international developments affecting the region. This became an annual ASEAN Foreign Ministers' Retreat.

The second Bali agreement was the Treaty of Amity and Cooperation in Southeast Asia (TAC).[19] The TAC, more fully discussed in chapter 5, promised noninterference in the internal affairs of one another, settlement of differences or disputes by peaceful means, and the renunciation of the threat or use of force. The TAC was left open for accession by other states in Southeast Asia. In the later expansion of ASEAN, accession to the TAC was a requirement of membership but not a guarantee of admittance. What was important in 1976 is that the TAC was an explicit gesture indicating willingness for peaceful coexistence between ASEAN Southeast Asia and communist Southeast Asia.

Indonesia and East Timor

Coincident with emerging Communist-ruled Indochina, the four-century Portuguese colonial rule in the eastern half of the island of Timor collapsed.

The change in the political status quo deep in the archipelago raised red flags in Jakarta. Rival indigenous political groups, pro- and anti-Indonesian, competed for power. The Revolutionary Front for an Independent East Timor (FRETILIN) won the struggle and proclaimed the Democratic Republic of East Timor (DRET). Indonesia recoiled at the possibility of a communist foothold in the heart of the archipelago. This perception was reinforced by the championing of the DRET by Beijing and Hanoi. Indonesia's policy moved from clandestine support for Timorese opponents of FRETILIN to military invasion in December 1975.

As documents declassified only in 2001 show, President Gerald Ford, accompanied by Secretary of State Henry Kissinger, met President Suharto in Jakarta on 6 December 1975 and promised not to interfere; this despite the fact that Kissinger had been alerted that such an invasion using American weapons would violate US law.[20] Even though friendly governments acquiesced in Indonesia's de facto new sovereignty in what became its twenty-seventh province, for liberal democrats around the world the invasion was blatant aggression. From a realist perspective, one of Australia's most senior diplomats argued that it was understandable that Indonesia's leaders considered that in the national interest "they were obliged to prevent by any means the establishment within their boundaries of the small, powerless, non-viable, hence unstable, but independent country that East Timor could become."[21] The annexation of Portuguese Timor also raised again within ASEAN the question of what Indonesia's ultimate territorial ambitions might be. Indonesia's rule in East Timor was contested in the UN, and its human rights record in the province remained an irritant in Jakarta's bilateral relations with Western democracies.

The "Peace Offensive"

The first official ASEAN pronouncement on the new international order in Southeast Asia after the fall of Saigon came at the May 1976 ASEAN foreign ministers' meeting. It called for a "friendly and harmonious" relationship with the Indochinese states on the basis of the Bandung Principles. Vietnam initially rebuffed ASEAN overtures, considering its leaders Washington's puppets. At the 1976 NAM Summit, Hanoi denounced ASEAN's Bali Summit and opposed ASEAN's ZOPFAN. On a state-by-state basis, Vietnam normalized relations with all of the ASEAN states during 1976. Vietnam began to ease its hostility toward ASEAN in 1977. This change had a number of causes: deterioration of Vietnam's relations with China, deterioration of Vietnam's relations with Khmer Rouge–ruled Cambodia, the Lao PDR's need for normal economic relations with Thailand, Vietnam's desire for technical and economic links to the developing economies of ASEAN, and a possible desire to offset Vietnam's deepening dependence on the Soviet Union. Whatever the mix of motives might have been, the ASEAN response was positive. The negotiating climate had improved with the termination of American bases in Thailand and the dismantling of the SEATO organization in 1976, although the Manila Pact remained in force as did American bilateral commitments to Thailand and the Philippines.

In a peace offensive, Vietnamese officials toured the ASEAN region in 1977 and 1978. The Vietnamese and their ASEAN counterparts entertained in their public rhetoric a vision of a future stable, peaceful, and secure Southeast Asia. There was a clear difference, however, in the proposed structures and instrumentalities to resolve the differences of interest between communist and noncommunist Southeast Asia. The ASEAN nations continued to advance their ZOPFAN concept. Vietnam surprised them by unveiling at the June 1978 UN Special Session on Disarmament its own proposal for a Zone of Peace, Genuine Independence, and Neutrality (ZOPGIN). The notion of "genuine independence" meant eliminating American forward basing in Southeast Asia and severing security ties with the United States. In his travels in the region, the Vietnamese prime minister indicated a willingness to begin a dialogue with ASEAN without preconditions. With respect to the competitive peace zones, he assured his suspicious counterparts that it was the intent that was important, not the wording, which could be mutually worked out through consultation.

THE THIRD INDOCHINA WAR

In December 1978, buttressed by a new military alliance with the USSR, Vietnam invaded Cambodia, expelling Pol Pot's Khmer Rouge regime and adding to Thailand's growing Cambodian refugee burden. Pro-Vietnamese ex-KR members—including Hun Sen—accompanied the 180,000-man occupying army. With Vietnamese "advisors" they established the People's Republic of Kampuchea (PRK). Because of the "peace offensive" and the existence of a climate of hope for normal relations with Indochina, Vietnam's invasion and occupation of Cambodia came as a disillusioning shock to ASEAN.

The Vietnamese decision to invade Pol Pot's Cambodia culminated a bitter and complex relationship between the two erstwhile comrades-in-arms. At the primordial level of relations, there were competitive nationalisms reinforced by centuries of ethnic antagonism. There was ideological rivalry. The KR refused to accept the political inequality inherent in its perception of Vietnamese hegemonic pretension through Vietnam's promotion of a Hanoi-

Box 3.2.   The Indochina Wars

The First Indochina War, 1945–1954

The anticolonial war for independence waged by Vietnamese nationalist/communist forces against the French. It ended with the 1954 Geneva Accords that led to the partition of Vietnam between North and South Vietnam.

The Second Indochina War, 1961–1975

The ground war in South Vietnam and air war in North Vietnam waged by the United States with extensions to Laos and Cambodia. The United States sought to prevent the unification of Vietnam by the communist Democratic Republic of Vietnam (North Vietnam) as part of the American strategy of containment. The American war ended with the 1973 US–DRV Paris Peace Accords. The Second Indochina War ended with communist victories in South Vietnam, Laos, and Cambodia in April 1975.

The Third Indochina War, 1978–1991

The Khmer nationalist resistance backed by ASEAN, China, and the United States, to Vietnam's December 1978 invasion and occupation of Cambodia. It ended with the 1991 comprehensive peace agreement that created the United Nations Transitional Authority in Cambodia (UNTAC) and a restored Kingdom of Cambodia.

centered "special relationship" among the three Indochinese states. There were territorial issues along a bleeding border inflamed by KR cross-border raids and Vietnamese hot pursuit. In December 1977, Phnom Penh put an end to any "special relationship" by breaking relations with Vietnam. Finally, there was Vietnam's analysis of the strategic threat posed by China's ties to Cambodia. Vietnam, an ally of the USSR, feared Chinese encirclement. This brought the Sino–Soviet conflict to Southeast Asia. The Vietnamese invasion launched the Third Indochina War. What Vietnam thought would be a swift and irreversible fait accompli provoked a military and political contest that dominated international relations in Southeast Asia for more than a decade.

The ASEAN Response

No matter Vietnam's motivation, for a worried ASEAN this was the worst-case scenario. In ASEAN eyes, the first Southeast Asian domino had fallen to aggressive Vietnamese expansionism spearheaded by Southeast Asia's largest army. The Thai–Cambodian border had become ASEAN's strategic frontier. ASEAN's response was swift. On 9 January 1979, Indonesian foreign minister Mochtar Kusumaatmadja, as chair of the ASEAN Standing Committee, issued a statement on behalf of ASEAN deploring the armed conflict between the two Indochinese states and calling upon the UN Security Council to take immediate steps to end the conflict. This was followed three days later by an emergency ASEAN foreign ministers' meeting that confirmed the right of the Cambodian people to self-determination and demanded the immediate withdrawal of Vietnamese forces. For ASEAN, Vietnam's fait accompli was the illegal consequence of Vietnamese military aggression. In June 1979, ASEAN foreign ministers promised firm support and solidarity in the preservation of Thailand's independence, sovereignty, and territorial integrity in the face of Vietnamese hot-pursuit cross-border incursions. This position hardened in a June 1980 ASEAN joint statement that declared that incursions of Vietnamese forces into Thailand "directly affect the security of the ASEAN member states."[22] At the 1980 meeting, American secretary of state Edmund Muskie made an unquali-fied pledge of American support if Vietnam should invade Thailand.

ASEAN decision making in the early phase of the Cambodian crisis marked a major turning point for the grouping. Setting ASEAN on a course of resistance to Vietnam's act in Cambodia made operationally explicit the basic political nature of ASEAN cooperation. Secondly, it gave policy substance to the political program of the Declaration of ASEAN Concord. Thirdly, in its stance vis-à-vis the threatening Vietnamese presence at ASEAN's front line on the Thai–Cambodian border, ASEAN, by its collective common political action, explicitly linked Thailand's security and territorial integrity to that of its fellow ASEAN members. This verged on collective defense. The external threat seemingly posed by Vietnam and its USSR ally had become internal political cement transforming ASEAN as a grouping into an international diplomatic/political caucus whose terms of reference were those of the high politics of traditional security interests, not the functional areas of coopera-tion stated in ASEAN's founding declaration.

ASEAN brought the Cambodia issue to the UN Security Council in spring 1979, where a resolution based on the ASEAN position was vetoed by the

USSR. In November 1979, the UN General Assembly adopted an ASEAN draft resolution by an overwhelming vote of ninety-one to twenty-one. The Vietnam-sponsored PRK government was denied Cambodia's UN seat still held by Democratic Kampuchea. In 1980, by a vote of ninety-seven to twenty-three, the UNGA called for a special conference on Cambodia. Over the ferocious objections and boycott by the communist bloc, the United Nations International Conference on Kampuchea (ICK) was held in July 1981. The ICK's final declaration internationally legitimized the ASEAN formula for settlement of the Cambodian crisis.[23] It called for a cease-fire and withdrawal of foreign (i.e., Vietnamese) forces under the supervision of a UN peacekeeping force. This would be followed by a UN-arranged and supervised free election allowing all Cambodians to exercise their right to self-determination. UN peacekeepers would ensure the security of the election and the establishment of the new government resulting from it. The ICK declaration became the basis of later ASEAN and UN terms for a comprehensive political settlement.

On the ground, ASEAN-sponsored anti-Vietnamese Khmer resistance forces operated in western Cambodia from Thai sanctuaries. The largest and most combat effective of the three resistance factions was the Khmer Rouge, supplied and advised by China. The other two were the royalist forces of Sihanouk's FUNCINPEC and the Khmer People's National Liberation Front (KPNLF) led by longtime political foe of Sihanouk, Son Sann. The resistance factions uneasily coexisted under the umbrella of a Coalition Government for Democratic Kampuchea (CGDK) cobbled together in 1982 by ASEAN diplomats. By bringing Sihanouk and Son Sann under the CGDK tent with Pol Pot's Khmer Rouge, it was easier to defend diplomatically the DK's claim to Cambodia's UN seat. ASEAN was in a difficult position. It needed the KR to give combat capability to the resistance, but at the same time it did not want the KR to return to power. This dilemma complicated the question of Vietnamese withdrawal from Cambodia. ASEAN insisted that Vietnam withdraw, but Vietnam, in defense of the PRK regime, demanded that the KR first be disarmed.

ASEAN's efforts to undo Vietnam's actions had the full political and material support of the United States and China. The United States provided nonlethal material assistance to the CGDK. The PRC delivered lethal assistance through the Thai army. In February 1979, China punctuated its alliance with Thailand by launching a large-scale attack on Vietnam's northern frontier. This was designed to take the pressure off Thailand's border. Its deterrent value was lessened when the Chinese army did not fare well against Vietnamese defenders. It sent counterproductive political signals to some ASEAN members who were negatively impressed by China's willingness to use force in Southeast Asia. At a special meeting, the ASEAN foreign ministers, without naming China, called on "countries outside this region to exert utmost restraint and to refrain from any action which might lead to escalation of violence and the spreading of the conflict."[24] The danger was not just the Chinese but a possible escalation of Soviet support for Vietnam.

Early in President Jimmy Carter's administration, a tentative effort to begin a diplomatic normalization process with Vietnam had begun. When the American administration decided in 1978 that normalization of relations with Vietnam might jeopardize the establishment of diplomatic relations with China, it was abandoned. A key issue in the Vietnamese negotiations was gaining Hanoi's cooperation in the accounting for American servicemen missing in action (MIA). To this now was added the demand for Vietnamese withdrawal from Cambodia. For Vietnam, the American deference to China's hostility to Vietnam meant that the American economic embargo would remain in effect indefinitely.

Diverging ASEAN Perceptions

The face of ASEAN's external solidarity concealed different internal strategic perceptions. Malaysia and Indonesia, alarmed at the great-power implications of confrontation with Vietnam, advanced at a March 1980 bilateral summit in Kuantan, Malaysia, the Kuantan Principle. Conceptually rooted in the ZOPFAN, it called for an end to Soviet influence in Vietnam but at the same time recognized Vietnam's security concerns with respect to China. It assumed a Vietnamese political sphere of interest in Cambodia in return for a peaceful Thai–Cambodian border. The Kuantan Principle did not become an ASEAN position because of Thai, Singaporean, and Chinese objections. Thailand followed China's hard line, and Singapore, sensitive to its own geostrategic vulnerability, demanded the enforcement of the ICK declaration.

The growing rift in ASEAN over approaches to a political solution that could accommodate Vietnam's interests was fully demonstrated in 1983. The foreign ministers of Malaysia and Vietnam met at the New Delhi NAM Summit and came up with a proposal for informal "bloc-to-bloc" talks between ASEAN and Vietnam, Laos, and Cambodia outside of the ICK formula. The "5 + 3" (or with Cambodia excluded, "5 + 2") was endorsed by Indonesia and Singapore. Thailand, backed by China, objected, and ASEAN solidarity required conformity to the status quo in the absence of a new consensus.

It was the sense of missed opportunities and the implicit Chinese veto wielded through Thailand that in part inspired Indonesia to open its own bilateral channels to Vietnam in the search for a modus vivendi. From Jakarta's perspective, the only winners in bleeding Vietnam would be the Chinese, whose strategic window to Thailand was troubling, and the Russians, entrenching themselves in Vietnam. Jakarta also chafed under the perceived conditions of ASEAN solidarity in which it was a follower, not a leader. Indonesia's open disaffection with the Thai frontline-state strategy (backed by China) became public when Indonesia's military chief, who was also President Suharto's political troubleshooter, General Benny Moerdani, made an official visit to Hanoi in February 1984. There, he said that Indonesia did not view Vietnam as a threat to Southeast Asia. Indonesia opened a dialogue with Hanoi that supplemented the consensual ASEAN approach. In order to avoid an overt breach in ASEAN solidarity, Indonesia's ASEAN partners incorporated Indonesia's dual-track diplomacy into their political strategy by terming Indonesia ASEAN's "interlocutor" with Vietnam. Vietnam became increasingly anxious to extricate itself from Cambodia, as the economic costs were great in a failing economy cut off from normal economic relations with most of the world. In 1985, Vietnam announced it would withdraw its troops from Cambodia by 1990.

The End Game

The negotiating problem lay in disentangling the levels of political conflict. ASEAN's formal stance was that the PRK was a creature of Vietnam, and ASEAN would negotiate only with Vietnam, not the PRK. From Hanoi's vantage, the PRK was the government of Cambodia, and ASEAN would have to deal with Phnom Penh. The breakthrough came in a July 1987 joint statement by Indonesia's foreign minister Mochtar and his Vietnamese counterpart Nguyen Co Thach proposing separating the "international" from the "internal" levels of the conflict. In "informal" settings the Cambodian factions would negotiate the ending of what was now diplomatically transformed into a civil war, to be joined by the other parties who provided external support to the combatants. In this way ASEAN did not have to recognize the PRK or Vietnam the CGDK factions as legitimate representatives of Cambodia. Indonesia's ASEAN partners reluctantly acceded to this arrangement. ASEAN's new flexibility also stemmed from Sihanouk's own overtures to the PRK that threatened to leave ASEAN alone with the dreaded Khmer Rouge.

The informal negotiating process began with the first Jakarta Informal Meeting (JIM I) in July 1988. Before JIM II met in February 1989, ASEAN's bargaining position had been transformed. Shortly after JIM I, the new Thai prime minister, Chatichai Choonhaven, opened his own extra-ASEAN bilateral channels to Phnom Penh and Hanoi, proclaiming that he wanted to turn the battlefields of Indochina into a marketplace. He shocked his ASEAN counterparts by inviting PRK president Hun Sen to Bangkok the month before JIM II. Chatichai's ASEAN detractors charged that his de facto recognition of the Hun Sen regime unilaterally undermined a decade of ASEAN diplomacy. Solidarity, however, required that ASEAN accept in negotiations the administrative reality in Cambodia of the PRK. The JIM process, however, stalled on the issues of whether Hun Sen's government should be dismantled before elections were held in Cambodia and the functioning of any international oversight mechanism.

As the JIM process faltered, the negotiation framework was enlarged in the nineteen-nation Paris International Conference on Cambodia (PICC), cochaired by Indonesia and France with strong Australian input.[25] Between the first sessions of the PICC, 30 July–30 August 1989, which ended in deadlock, and its reconvening in September 1991, at which a peace accord was formalized, the agenda had been seized by the permanent members of the UN Security Council. The great-power dynamics in the regional conflict had undergone significant change in the decade of the struggle over Cambodia's future. This was largely due to Soviet premier Mikhail Gorbachev's emphasis on rebuilding the USSR's economy and restructuring the state. For this, détente and normalization of relations with the PRC were important. At a 15–18 May 1989 Sino-Soviet summit meeting, Gorbachev and his Chinese counterpart, Deng Xiaoping, agreed to a basis for national reconciliation in Cambodia, internationally supervised elections, and the convening of an international conference. It was the decoupling of the Sino-Soviet relationship from the Southeast Asian conflict that promoted great-power consensus on the terms of settlement.

Following the collapse of the first PICC, the UN Security Council's Permanent Five produced a framework agreement for a comprehensive settlement that would allow all of the external participants to step back from the Cambodian imbroglio to let the Khmer people settle their own future. The settlement proposals were approved on 18 August 1990 by the Security Council and endorsed by acclamation at the UNGA on 15 October.[26] The Cambodian factions, threatened by isolation from their external supporters, had little option but to accept, although grudgingly by the KR and Hun Sen and his renamed State of Kampuchea. The comprehensive political settlement was ratified at the October 1991 second session of the PICC.[27] The Third Indochina War was over. It remained for the United Nations to secure the peace in Cambodia.

After more than a decade, both ASEAN and Vietnam got largely what they wanted. ASEAN's goals as laid out in the 1981 ICK Declaration had essentially been achieved. Vietnam was out of Cambodia. The UN through UNTAC and its peacekeepers organized and implemented a generally fair and free election. Under UNTAC, the KR was marginalized, refusing to compete in the internationally dictated political framework. It eventually surrendered to the new Cambodian government. It left, however, the problem of accountability for the crimes of its ruling years, a problem that is still being wrestled with by the international community (chapter 9). For Vietnam, a hostile Cambodia with strategic links to China no longer was a threat, and the door to economic development opened. Hun Sen was a winner as well. Although UNTAC was technically in charge in Cambodia, Hun Sen's government remained in place as day-to-day administrator, boosting his political fortunes in post-UNTAC Cambodia. As Thai, Singaporean, and Malaysian businessmen and investors competed for advantage in a peaceful Indochina, formal ASEAN–Vietnam reconciliation began with Vietnam's accession to the Treaty of Amity and Cooperation in 1992 and the granting to it of official ASEAN "observer" status. Vietnam became ASEAN's seventh member in 1995.

For the United States, the USSR, and the PRC, the Cold War strategic triangle that had made ASEAN, Cambodia, and Vietnam surrogates in a Southeast Asian conflict zone was succeeded by détente and a replacement of American containment policy in Southeast Asia through growing economic interdependencies as China and Vietnam abandoned their failed command economies for market-oriented economies. With a diminished Soviet presence in Vietnam, China established full diplomatic relations with Vietnam in 1991. US–Vietnam diplomatic relations were established in 1995. The Cold War in Southeast Asia was over.

SOUTHEAST ASIA AT THE END OF THE COLD WAR

The political cohesiveness that allowed ASEAN to present a common front in the struggle to oust Vietnam from Cambodia originated in perceptions of a direct threat to the regional international order. It was politically defensive and did not derive from any inherent regional integrative process. Although ultimately diplomatically successful, the success was more a function of the real capabilities and interests of the external partners linked to the regional protagonists than to the capabilities of the ASEAN states. Second, the experience of the Third Indochina War revealed that there was no common ASEAN strategic perception. ASEAN states had disparate strategic orientations toward the United States and China. Third, it became clear that when an ASEAN state decided that its national interests were jeopardized by consensual ASEAN policy, national interests would take priority.

With the ending of the Cold War and the Third Indochina War—the sources of ASEAN's original political cement—the question was what new cement might bind the multiple diverse national interests in the ASEAN framework. ASEAN's first effort to grapple with new tasks of cooperation was in the ASEAN Summit's 1992 Singapore Declaration. In it, the leaders pledged "to move towards a higher plane of political and economic cooperation to secure regional peace and prosperity."[28] A new relevance for ASEAN was to be found in meeting the challenges of a transforming regional and global international economic order.

The search for a "higher plane" took place in a fundamentally altered great-power presence in the regional international environment. The crumbling and ultimate disappearance of the USSR divorced the political relations of the United States and PRC in the region from Cold War and Third Indochina War alliances and alignments. The time was ripe for ASEAN to bolster the ZOPFAN with the Southeast Asian Nuclear Weapons–Free Zone (SEANWFZ). The SEANWFZ had been mooted by Malaysia in the 1970s and promoted by Indonesia in the 1980s. The models were the 1963 Treaty of Tlatelolco declaring Latin America a nuclear free zone and the 1985 Treaty of Rarotonga establishing the South Pacific Nuclear Free Zone (SPNFZ). ASEAN's version had been stymied by US-allied Philippines and Thai objections. The SEANWFZ Treaty was signed in December 1995, entering into force in 1997.[29] Like the ZOPFAN, it was not self-enforcing, calling for the nuclear powers to accede through a separate protocol. This they have proved reluctant to do, including the United States.

The changed post–Cold War strategic environment was underlined by the 1991 termination of US basing rights in the Philippines, a key element in the Cold War US security posture in Southeast Asia. This followed replacement of Marcos's presidential dictatorship by a new democratic political order. The 1947 US–Philippines Military Bases Agreement (MBA) had been scheduled to expire in mid-September 1991. In May 1990, difficult renewal negotiations began that ended in a proposed new treaty. It was not ratified by a deeply split Philippine Senate. Opposition focused on issues of sovereignty, the nonnuclear provision of the 1987 Philippine constitution, and American support of the Marcos regime. The government presented the United States with a three-year phaseout plan. The United States shortened this to one year, the end of 1992. The ending of the Cold War gave less importance to Subic Bay's strategic value, particularly with the Russians out of Vietnam's Cam Ranh Bay. Many of the functions performed at Subic, other than major ship repair, were picked up elsewhere: Japan, Okinawa, Guam, Singapore, Thailand, and even Malaysia. What was lost was the high-profile visible symbol of American commitment to the region.

The disappearance of the USSR and the lower profile of the United States gave greater relative importance to the emergence of China as an important actor in Southeast Asia with a full range of national interests: economic, political, and security. China was at peace with all of the ASEAN states, had been their strategic ally in the Third Indochina War, and shares many of the social and cultural interests of the developing countries of Southeast Asia. For the first time since World War II, the US preponderance of power in Southeast Asia might be challenged by a power whose reach, while not yet global, is East and Southeast Asia regional. The USSR's regional capability had been one dimensional—military. Japan's role had been one dimensional—economic. The United States' capabilities are multidimensional—political, economic, and military—but China now also has the full measure of capabilities. This is the new dynamic in great-power relations in Southeast Asia. How it is being managed by the regional actors will be explored in the chapters to follow.

NOTES

1. George F. Kennan, "The Sources of Soviet Conduct," *Foreign Affairs* 25, no. 4 (July 1947): 566–82.
2. "Viet Minh" is an abbreviation of "Vietnam Doc Lap Dong Minh Hoi" (League for the Independence of Vietnam).
3. National Security Council, "United States Objectives and Course of Action with Respect to Southeast Asia [April 1952]," document 2 in *The Pentagon Papers as Published by the New York Times* (New York: Bantam, 1971), 27–31.
4. The domino theory postulated the geostrategic consequences for what then was designated the "free world" if Indochina should fall to communism. President Dwight D. Eisenhower stated it at a 7 April 1954 news conference in response to a question about the strategic importance of Indochina to the United States. He framed his answer in terms of what he called "the falling domino principle," in which the first falling domino in a row of dominoes will certainly and quickly lead to the fall of the last domino. He enumerated the order as first Indochina, then Burma, Thailand, the Peninsula (Malaya and Singapore), and Indonesia, with the consequent threat to the defensive island chain from Japan, Taiwan, and the Philippines, to Australia and New Zealand.
5. "Final Declaration at Geneva Conference and U.S. Statement Renouncing Use of Force," document 14, *The Pentagon Papers*, 49–53.
6. 6 UST 81, *Treaties and Other International Acts Series* 3170.
7. The agreement between American secretary of state Dean Rusk and Thai foreign minister Thanat Khoman was an executive branch interpretation of the Manila Treaty. This interpretation was restated by every American government through the end of the Third Indochina War.
8. The communiqué can be found as appendix C in Russell H. Fifield, *The Diplomacy of Southeast Asia: 1945–1958* (New York: Harper & Brothers, 1958), 512–19. For details of the conference, see George McTurnan Kahin, *The Asian-African Conference; Bandung, Indonesia, April 1955* (Ithaca, NY: Cornell University Southeast Asia Program, 1956).

9. "Southeast Asia Resolution," Public Law 88-408. It was called the "Tonkin Gulf" resolution because it followed an alleged attack by DRV torpedo boats on US destroyers off North Vietnam's Tonkin Gulf coast.

10. "Agreement on Ending the War and Restoring Peace in Vietnam," 27 January 1973, 24 UST 4–23, *Treaties and Other International Acts Series* 7542.

11. The Nixon Doctrine was enunciated at a 25 July 1969 press conference on Guam (hence Guam Doctrine) following a meeting with South Vietnam's President Nguyen Van Thieu. It was reiterated in Nixon's address to the nation on Vietnam on 3 November 1969. The texts can be found in Richard Nixon, *Public Papers of the Presidents of the United States: Richard Nixon*, vol. 1, 1969 (Washington, DC: U.S. Government Printing Office, 1971).

12. That the wounds of history still impact contemporary relations was shown again in February 2014, when Indonesia decided to name a new naval vessel after two national heroes. These were the marines who set off explosives in 1965 in a Singapore office building killing three persons and wounding many more. The perpetrators were executed. An angry Singapore government viewed the ship naming as a provocative endorsement of Sukarno's policies.

13. Bernard G. Gordon, *The Dimensions of Conflict in Southeast Asia* (Englewood Cliffs, NJ: Prentice-Hall, 1966), 102.

14. The "Bangkok Declaration," in *Handbook on Selected ASEAN Political Documents*, I:7, accessed at http://www.asean.org/archive/pdf/HBPDR.pdf.

15. Tan Sri Ghazali Shafie, "ASEAN Today and Tomorrow," *Foreign Affairs Malaysia* 14, no. 3 (December 1981): 335.

16. "Kuala Lumpur Declaration of a Zone of Peace, Freedom and Neutrality," 17 November 1971, in *Handbook on Selected ASEAN Political Documents*, II:7, accessed at http://www.asean.org/archive/pdf/HBPDR.pdf.

17. The full texts of the respective communiqués are collected in appendixes 8, 13, and 16 of Leo Suryadinata, *China and the ASEAN States: The Ethnic Chinese Dimension* (Singapore: Singapore University Press, 1985), 183–85, 198–200, 207–9.

18. "Declaration of ASEAN Concord" [Bali Concord I], in *Handbook on Selected ASEAN Political Documents*, III:7, accessed at http://www.asean.org/archive/pdf/HBPDR.pdf.

19. "Treaty of Amity and Cooperation in Southeast Asia," in *Handbook on Selected ASEAN Political Documents*, IV:7, accessed at http://www.asean.org/archive/pdf/HBPDR.pdf.

20. The declassified documents were released by the National Security Archive at George Washington University and can be accessed at http://www2.gwu.edu/~nsarchiv/NSAEBB/NSAEBB62.

21. Alan Renouf, *The Frightened Country* (Melbourne, Australia: Macmillan, 1979), 441–42.

22. "Joint Statement by the ASEAN Foreign Ministers on the Situation on the Thai-Kampuchean Border," Bangkok, 25 June 1980, *ASEAN Document Series 1967–1988* (Jakarta: ASEAN Secretariat, 1988), XII.A, Kampuchea.

23. "Declaration on Kampuchea," *UN Monthly Chronicle* 18, no. 9 (September–October 1981): 37–39.

24. "ASEAN Statement on the Vietnam-China Border War," Bangkok, 20 February 1979, as reported in Foreign Broadcast Information Service, *Daily Report: Asia and Pacific*, 23 February 1979, A-1.

25. In addition to the ASEAN 6, Laos, Vietnam, PRK, and CGDK, the PICC involved the five permanent members of the UN Security Council (Great Britain, China, France, the United States, and the USSR), Australia, Canada, India, and Japan.

26. The framework agreement for the Comprehensive Political Settlement in Cambodia is contained in the *Official Records of the Security Council Forty-Fifth Year, Supplement for August–September 1990*, document S/216879, annex.

27. "Final Act of the Paris Conference on Cambodia," 23 October 1991, accessed at http://www.usip.org/sites/default/files/file/resources/collections/peace_agreements/final_act_10231991.pdf.

28. "Singapore Declaration of 1992," accessed at http://www.asean.org/news/item/singapore-declaration-of-1992-singapore-28-january-1992.

29. "Treaty on the Southeast Asia Nuclear Weapons-Free Zone," *Handbook on Selected ASEAN Political Documents*, VII:29, accessed at http://www.asean.org.archive/pdf/HBPDR.pdf.

SUGGESTIONS FOR FURTHER READING

An overview of American Cold War policy in the Pacific region is Robert McMahon, *The Limits of Empire* (New York: Columbia University Press, 1999). There is a voluminous literature on the US war in Vietnam. A good place to start is David L. Anderson, *The Columbia Guide to the Vietnam War* (New York: Columbia University Press, 2002). A balanced short survey is Gary Hess, *Vietnam and the United States: Origins and Legacy* (Boston: Twayne, 1990). His bibliographic essay is a useful overview of the range of materials on the major topics. For the causes and diplomacy of the Third Indochinese War, see David W. P. Elliott, ed., *The Third Indochina Conflict* (Boulder, CO: Westview Press, 1981); Donald E. Weatherbee, ed., *Southeast Asia Divided: The ASEAN-Indochina Crisis* (Boulder, CO: Westview Press, 1985); Nayan Chanda, *Brother Enemy: The War after the War* (New York: Macmillan, 1986). For the negotiations to end the war, see A. Acharya, P. Lizée, and S. Peou, *Cambodia—The 1989 Paris Peace Conference: Background Analysis and Documents* (Millwood, NY: Kraus International, 1991). For the view of a senior American participant in the diplomacy ending the war, see Richard H. Solomon, *Exiting Indochina: U.S. Leadership of the Cambodian Settlement and Normalization with Vietnam* (Washington, DC: United States Institute of Peace Press, 2000). New access to Russian, Chinese, and Vietnamese sources is utilized in Odd Arne Westad and Sophie Quinn-Judge, eds., *The Third Indochina War: Conflict between China, Vietnam and Cambodia* (London: Routledge, 2006). American intervention in Indonesia's regional rebellion is the subject of George McT. Kahin and Audrey Kahin, *Subversion as Foreign Policy: The Secret Eisenhower and Dulles Debacle in Indonesia* (New York: New Press, 1995). For the West New Guinea dispute, see John Saltford, *The United Nations and the Indonesian Takeover of West Papua, 1962–1969: The Anatomy of a Betrayal* (London: RoutledgeCurzon, 2004). Indonesia's confrontation with Malaysia is dealt with in J. A. C. Mackie, *Konfrontasi: The Indonesia–Malaysia Dispute, 1963–1966* (Kuala Lumpur: Oxford University Press, 1974).

Chapter Four

ASEAN and Regionalism
in Southeast Asia

Regionalism in Southeast Asia is understood in this book as the association of state actors in formal or informal structures in areas of state activities in which complementary national interests can be harmonized by collective decision making seeking to maximize national interest through regional cooperation. It also enhances through a kind of pooling process the capabilities of the individual states in their relations with extraregional powers with greater capabilities. There can be no operational regional policy relevance unless and until collective decisions at the regional level are translated into the national policies of the member states.

We have already identified ASEAN as the most significant expression of the regionalist urge in Southeast Asia. ASEAN is often deemed to be the most successful regional grouping in the developing world. Unfortunately, however, the all-too-frequent comparison with the EU leads to disappointed expectations about ASEAN. The European experience has been one of supranational integration requiring derogations of national sovereignty and delegations of authority to a regional authority, neither of which the member states of ASEAN have yet been prepared to do. A question to be raised in this chapter, and to be examined more fully in the chapters to follow, is how ASEAN's successes and failures are to be measured and what kind of role it might have beyond the Southeast Asian region. ASEAN regionalism as an international process in Southeast Asia is taking place in the context of a wider East Asia and Pacific economic regionalism (chapter 8). ASEAN's future depends in part on what continuing value its member states will put on a Southeast Asia–centered organizational unit as they are incorporated into more inclusive, expansive, and sometimes competitive regionalist patterns of state interaction. As ASEAN states recognize that their national interests require institutional engagements transcending the geographic limits of ASEAN, what will this mean for the claim of ASEAN's centrality?

ASEAN: FROM DIPLOMATIC CONCERT TO COMMUNITY

One of the considerations that enter into any evaluation of ASEAN's success as a regionalist enterprise is its durability over time despite internal and external challenges. In the course of its nearly five-decade history, ASEAN has become a fixture in the international relations of the region. That it survived the conflicting interests and divergent strategic perceptions of its members is attributable to the conscious efforts of its political managers to focus on noncontentious interest areas so that no member would feel its national interests threatened by collective decisions. This is at the heart of the so-called ASEAN way: consensus decision making that does not diminish sovereignty or interfere in the domestic arrangements of the member states. ASEAN's regionalism is a soft regionalism in which there is no regional organizational authority over the member states' policies or behavior.

An important reason for ASEAN's persistence has been that once reconciliation with postconfrontation Indonesia was achieved in 1967, the regionalist stimulus did not originate internally. If ASEAN's lasting power had only depended on internal stimuli for political and economic cooperation, it probably would not have survived into the new millennium. To date, ASEAN's compelling raison d'être is in being a diplomatic concert of weaker powers in a regional international system dominated by stronger powers. ASEAN's political cement has not been a cooperative, let alone integrative, economic, social, or cultural process. Its cement has been political solidarity in facing external challenges, and as those challenges have changed, so too has ASEAN. Today's external strategic challenges involving competitive American and Chinese interests, rather than promoting ASEAN solidarity, are threatening ASEAN's institutional political coherence (chapters 5 and 6). The question can be raised as to whether the centripetal force of economic, social, and cultural cooperation in the ASEAN Community will offset the centrifugal political force of great-power interests.

For liberal integrationists, ASEAN still retains its unfulfilled promise. For realists, it has become part of the balance of power. For Southeast Asian leaderships, ASEAN is a diplomatic tool. ASEAN is one of the foreign and economic policy outputs of the policy systems of its member states. Policy makers and analysts, although differing in their approaches to ASEAN and evaluations of its achievements, would agree that after so long a period of time and with so much effort and prestige invested in it, an ASEAN political collapse would be regionally destabilizing. An imminent issue is ASEAN's continued international political relevance—its claim to "centrality"—in light of the new challenges. Can it adapt to new regional and international circumstances? Will the tools of the ASEAN way overcome the pull of great-power attraction?

ASEAN: FROM FIVE TO TEN

When looking for examples of ASEAN's achievements, some observers, particularly in the ASEAN states, point to its membership expansion to include (with the exception of newly independent Timor-Leste) all of the sovereign states of Southeast Asia. The 1967 Bangkok Declaration left ASEAN membership open to all states in Southeast Asia subscribing to its aims, principles, and purposes. Brunei joined at independence in 1984. Vietnam's admission in 1995 gave final closure to the political gulf between communist and noncommunist Southeast Asia. Membership had been offered as an incentive to Vietnam in the negotiations for terminating the Third Indochina War. The Lao People's Democratic Republic was granted observer status in 1992, Cambodia in 1994, and finally Myanmar in 1996. The 1995 ASEAN Summit decided to achieve an inclusive "one Southeast Asia" by the year 2000. The subsequent 1996 informal summit meeting advanced the date to admit the three candidate members simultaneously at the 1997 ASEAN Ministerial Meeting (AMM). Because Laos and Cambodia as observer states had a longer lead time for technical preparation for membership, the linking of Myanmar's admission to theirs was unexpected. It had to do with opposition to Myanmar's membership in democratic ASEAN circles as well as the West because of the military junta's atrocious human rights record. The packaging of Myanmar with Laos and Cambodia held the membership of the latter two hostage. ASEAN made it clear that Myanmar's internal politics were not relevant to the question of membership. As it turned out, it was Hun Sen's 1997 coup in Cambodia that presented a challenge to the ASEAN way.

Myanmar

ASEAN accepted Myanmar as a full member in 1997, fully recognizing that by giving the ASEAN seal of approval to the Myanmar junta, its international image would be tarnished. This was coincident with the building by the United States and EU of a sanctions regime against Myanmar. The strongest advocate for Myanmar's membership was Malaysia's prime minister, Mahathir Mohammad. In his welcoming keynote address to the 1997 Kuala

Lumpur thirtieth AMM that admitted Myanmar, Mahathir said of Western objections to Myanmar's membership that "ASEAN must resist and reject such attempts at coercion."[1]

ASEAN's two-pronged defense of Myanmar's admission was logically inconsistent. On the one hand, it was argued that ASEAN did not interfere in the domestic affairs of other nations and that Myanmar's internal politics were not relevant to the question of ASEAN membership. The second argument was that by a policy of "constructive engagement" along a broad range of interests in an ASEAN framework, the junta would be moved in the direction of political change and greater respect for human rights. The policy also kept the doors open for investment and economic exploitation of Myanmar's resources, particularly from Singapore, Malaysia, and Thailand. The leaders also feared that if they had admitted Vietnam, Laos, and Cambodia to ASEAN but isolated Myanmar, the junta would become a Chinese client. Finally, there was resentment, most vehemently expressed by Mahathir, of the American Clinton administration's insistent human rights campaign. ASEAN's refusal to cave in to the American pressure illustrated the diminished American political leverage resulting from the end of Cold War security concerns. From the Myanmar side, ASEAN membership gave the junta a modicum of international legitimacy, indirect access to Western markets, and a hedge against China.

Because of Myanmar, ASEAN's institutional relations with the West suffered until the beginnings of a democratic transition in 2011. In ASEAN-controlled settings and agendas, Western representatives had no choice but to sit with Myanmar as coequals or boycott ASEAN. They lost no opportunity, however, to openly chide the Myanmar regime on its rights record, to the discomfiture of the junta's ASEAN partners. The real prospect of a Western boycott if Myanmar had assumed the chair of ASEAN in 2006, as was its right by alphabetical rotation, led ASEAN to persuade Myanmar to step aside in favor of the Philippines. After the junta's September 2007 crackdown on prodemocracy protests, President George W. Bush canceled a proposed US–ASEAN Summit. Formal ASEAN–EU institutional engagements were paralyzed by issues of Myanmar's involvement. Myanmar's ASEAN membership, rather than an asset, became a cancer eating away at ASEAN's credibility in the community of democratic nations. ASEAN's commitments to democratic values and human rights in its new charter were treated as hypocritical rhetoric.

Bilateral overtures from ASEAN partners, particularly Indonesia and Malaysia, for dialogue with the junta on political change were coolly received and rebuffed. The junta remained intransigent in the face of concern of some ASEAN countries about the damage that was being done to ASEAN's global standing. Individual ASEAN states had no levers to force change other than to threaten Myanmar's stake in ASEAN itself. This would have required a consensus on suspension or expulsion which, given support to Myanmar from Laos, Cambodia, and Vietnam, was not going to happen.

The internal political changes since the installation of the Thein Sein government in 2011 have altered the international landscape for Myanmar. Sanctions have been lifted. As a reward for the democratization process, ASEAN changed its chair rotation to give Myanmar the 2014 chairmanship. This gave Nay Pyi Taw the opportunity to establish its credentials as a responsible steward of ASEAN affairs.[2] Its first official act as chair was to host the January 2014 informal ASEAN foreign ministers' meeting. The issue of internal violence against the Muslim minority Rohingya clouded its chairmanship (chapter 9). Myanmar made it clear that the Rohingya problem would not be raised in any ASEAN meeting during its chairmanship even though there is increasing dismay among ASEAN Muslim-majority states about the status of their coreligionists in Myanmar. In the rotation for coordinating ASEAN dialogues, Myanmar replaced the Philippines (2009–2012) as the 2012–2015 coordinator of the ASEAN–US dialogue, which would have been unthinkable prior to regime change.

Cambodia

Two weeks before Cambodia's scheduled induction into ASEAN in July 1997, Co–Prime Minister Hun Sen's security forces hunted down the FUNCINPEC supporters of Co-Prime Minister Prince Ranariddh, violently ending the UNTAC-sponsored power-sharing agreement that followed the 1993 elections (chapter 2). Beneath the facade of coalition, a struggle for power had the country teetering on the brink of a new civil war in anticipation of the scheduled 1998 elections. Hun Sen struck a preemptive blow. Ranariddh fled the country, and FUNCINPEC loyalist supporters took up arms in northern and northwestern Cambodia to resist Hun Sen's quasi–coup d'état. The ASEAN foreign ministers were shocked. At a hastily convened meeting they reaffirmed their commitment to noninterference in the internal affairs of other states but then interfered by deciding "that in light of the unfortunate circumstances which have resulted from the use of force the wisest course of action is to delay the admission of Cambodia into ASEAN until a later date."[3] ASEAN saw political stability in continental Southeast Asia at risk. The foreign ministers designated their colleagues from Indonesia, the Philippines, and Thailand to act on ASEAN's behalf as mediators. The ASEAN troika's goal was to guarantee that free and fair elections would be held in Cambodia with the participation of Ranariddh and his party. ASEAN's hand was strengthened by donor nations led by Japan, the largest donor, which suspended aid and withdrew its personnel. Cambodia's UN seat was vacant as the General Assembly's Credentials Committee would not decide between a Hun Sen– or Ranariddh-backed delegation.

Internationally isolated and with ASEAN membership at risk, Hun Sen was forced to accept ASEAN-monitored elections in 1998. They were narrowly won by the CPP amid turmoil, intimidation, and vote rigging. The ASEAN troika, apparently believing a little democracy was better than no democracy, hammered out a new coalition government in which Hun Sen became sole prime minister and Ranariddh the speaker of the National Assembly. With its requirements fulfilled, ASEAN admitted Cambodia to membership in 1999. Prime Minister Hun Sen's rehabilitation was made complete in 2002 when he chaired the ASEAN Summit. Hun Sen ultimately forced Ranariddh out of legal politics and into exile in 2006.

Why did ASEAN act differently in the Cambodian case—delaying membership and requiring a monitored election—than in the Myanmar case? The fact that, for ASEAN, internal politics were relevant to membership in Cambodia's case and not Myanmar's was based more on strategic realities than principle. A new civil war in Cambodia would have had political and strategic consequences for the three bordering ASEAN states, a threat Myanmar did not pose. Thailand certainly was not prepared to deal with another flood of Cambodian refugees. ASEAN and the international donor consortium did not want to see the efforts at reconstruction of the shattered society wasted. The ASEAN position on Cambodia was not based on democratic ideology. ASEAN wished to undo the act of force that had led to political instability in the continental heart of the region. Finally, after taking so much heat on Myanmar, ASEAN did not want its international image further sullied by ignoring the events in Cambodia.

A Tiered ASEAN

ASEAN's membership expansion came with costs for cooperation in terms of programmatic coherence and political community. In the expanded ASEAN, the continental states sharing the Mekong River focused on economic access to China. The original ASEAN members shared an anticommunist ideology, experiences with communist insurgency, and security bonds with the West. No such new integral ideological and strategic cement bound the disparate national units of the expanded ASEAN. The economic gap between the new members—collectively called the CLMV countries—led to intra-ASEAN issues testing the ideal of equality in economic decision making. One result was special dispensations for the economically second-tier members, including longer target dates to achieve ASEAN's collective economic goals. It was understood that a widening of the economic division between the two tiers as the "little tigers" outperformed the economic laggards could undermine ASEAN solidarity. ASEAN tried to address the problem by launching in 2002 an Initiative for ASEAN Integration (IAI).[4] A six-year IAI project-specific work plan was drawn up with four priority sectors: infrastructure, human resources development, information and communications technology, and regional economic integration. A second IAI work plan was launched for the 2009–2015 period. The goal was to increase the capabilities of the CLMV states to meet ASEAN-wide targets and commitments. The IAI did not address the structural differences between the political economies of the core group and the CLMV countries, nor did it provide for integrative institutional cooperation. The ASEAN 6 provided $33.4 million and dialogue partners $20.3 million to support the undertaking.

In addition to economic differences, political differences between the ASEAN 6 and the CLMV countries were deep. These included domestic political systems and strategic perceptions. The overarching similarities of political economies and security concerns of the core members are what made the original ASEAN possible. The question was whether the greater dissimilarities in the expanded ASEAN would lead to division rather than consensus and to even greater obstacles to cooperation than those that prevailed in the past. Although ASEAN can rightfully claim that all of Southeast Asia has been brought under ASEAN's regional normative tent, this is no predictor of the real policy choices to be made by the individual states in reaction to collective decisions. Furthermore, in an ASEAN 10, those collective decisions have lowered the common denominator threshold for policy action.

ASEAN historically has been a political grouping reacting to a threat environment dominated by state actors with greater capabilities than ASEAN can collectively deploy, let alone the member states individually. In a search for security defined traditionally, the core five original members maintained a high level of externally focused solidarity. The new threat environment is more complex and nontraditional, with a multidimensional array of political, economic, social, and cultural challenges. It remains to be seen whether an ASEAN 10 can maintain the kind of solidarity that will be necessary to transform ASEAN from a balance-of-power mechanism to a political/economic community as it embarked in 2007 on a reinvention of itself in the new ASEAN Charter. ASEAN's already diminished consensual solidarity might be further attenuated either through future expansion (Timor-Leste and PNG) or functional absorption into wider forms of regionalism.

ASEAN'S ORGANIZATIONAL EVOLUTION

How ASEAN's record as a manifestation of regionalism is to be judged depends on the critic's analytical vantage. There is no question but that it has shown remarkable political staying power and has contributed to regional stability. If, however, the measure is real achievements in areas of functional cooperation spelled out in the Bangkok Declaration, then for its first three decades ASEAN fell far short of its aspirations. Efforts to reconcile competitive claims of self-interest and regional cooperation were disappointing and concrete achievements elusive. ASEAN's real achievement was its contribution to a regional international political order that has promoted a climate for economic assistance, trade, and FDI supporting national development programs.

One explanation—or apologia—for the lack of functionally integrative economic and political progress is that the political demands of the regional security environment diverted political resources away from ASEAN's nonpolitical tasks. This argument assumes that if there had been no external security challenges, national elites would have pursued patterns of closer functional cooperation. This is not self-evident. It also ignores the fact that decision making about the forms and substance of regional functional cooperation is itself political, especially given linkages to domestic interests. The retort can be made that rather than inhibiting economic and political regionalism, the emphasis on political cooperation in facing external security challenges was a necessary prerequisite for cooperation in other policy areas.

The problem for ASEAN's regionalists was dual: connecting the international political processes to the regional cooperative process and connecting regional cooperation to national development strategies. It was not for want of study that integrative cooperation faltered. ASEAN's documentary history is rife with academic studies, policy papers, conference reports, and workshops seeking to give flesh to the bare bones of the Bangkok Declaration. This was particularly true of what emerged as the key substantive issue area: economic cooperation in a regional environment of economic competition. In the words of a former ASEAN secretary general, to make real progress would have required "almost a new vision and a new sense of dedication on the part of the ASEAN heads of government. Vision, dedication and above all, a fresh infusion of political will."[5]

Until the 1992 Singapore Summit, the machinery devised by ASEAN founders to carry out its mission was relatively simple, reflecting, perhaps, the low expectations of the foreign ministers for a decentralized consultative grouping. The foreign ministers' control was institutionalized in the AMM, ASEAN's collective executive. The chairmanship of the AMM annually rotates through ASEAN's capitals. Meetings of the ASEAN foreign ministers are not limited to the AMM. Special meetings can be held as occasion demands, for example, the January 1979 meeting to formulate the official ASEAN position on Vietnam's invasion of Cambodia and the ASEAN position on Hun Sen's 1997 Cambodian coup (above). The AMM chair is the official spokesperson. Before the 2007 ASEAN Charter, the AMM chair convened the ASEAN Standing Committee (ASC) composed of ASEAN ambassadors accredited to the host country. In fact, regular direct contact was maintained among the foreign ministers and their senior officials, and the role of the ASC was diminished.

In ASEAN's first decade, the functional tasks of devising cooperative activities below the political level of consultation fell to permanent and ad hoc committees of officials and experts. By 1969, eleven permanent committees dealing with economic, social, and cultural matters had been established. Based in different ASEAN countries, the committees worked in bureaucratic isolation, and despite manifest functional overlaps, there was no horizontal integrative mechanism. Although the committees generated numerous plans, projects, and cooperative schemes, there were few approvals and little project implementation. Notably missing from the regionalist orientations of the functional committees was any agency to connect ASEAN's economic development planning to the national development priorities and programs of its member states. This was a fatal defect for future ASEAN initiatives. ASEAN's bureaucratic backstopping was decentralized in national secretariats tasked with carrying out the work of the organization on behalf of their country as well as servicing the AMM and other committees. The national secretariats have no horizontal links with each other or to any centralizing coordinating body above them. Their focus is indicated by the fact that all of the national secretariats are housed in the member nations' foreign ministries.

The Bangkok Declaration was not an enforceable treaty. The structure of ASEAN was one of voluntary association with no binding obligations on the member states. There was no delegation of authority to ASEAN, and decision making was by consensual unanimity. ASEAN adopted Indonesian terminology to explain the process: *musyawarah-mufakat* (consultation and consensus). This meant that ASEAN moved at the pace of its slowest member. The objective was to avoid compromising fragile political cohesion by conflicts over concrete functional programs and projects where competitive national interests would come into play. Disappointed integrationists blamed the failure of progress in building regional cooperative programs and institutions on the leadership's lack of "political will." In fact, the absence of substantial steps toward functional regionalism was an expression of the AMM's political will.

The 1976 Bali Summit and Bali Concord I

The heads of government of the five ASEAN states met as ASEAN's leaders for their first summit in 1976. The call for the summit, initiated by Indonesia's president Suharto, was prompted, as noted in chapter 3, by the communist victories in Indochina. The political centerpiece of the summit was the Declaration of ASEAN Concord. Often termed Bali Concord I, it gave ASEAN an explicit political face.[6] It called for the strengthening of political solidarity through the harmonizing of views, coordinating of positions, and, where possible, taking common action. The heads of state also called for continuing security cooperation among the member states "*on a non-ASEAN basis*" (emphasis added). In its early decades, ASEAN had resisted external impulses to transform itself into a military alliance. However, given the new security environment, the strengthening of regional military capabilities was encouraged. With respect to regional security, the Bali Summit saw the signing of the Treaty of Amity and Cooperation in Southeast Asia (TAC) (chapter 5) and the leaders' endorsement of the Southeast Asian Zone of Peace, Freedom, and Neutrality (ZOPFAN).

The Bali Summit established an ASEAN Secretariat to remedy the lack of a coordinating administrative center. A secretary general of the secretariat—not of ASEAN—was appointed on a country-rotating basis for a two-year term (extended to three in 1985 and five in 1992). The post had no executive or policy role. Its charge was to keep the paperwork flowing. The secretariat is permanently headquartered in Jakarta. ASEAN's lack of institutional autonomy was embarrassingly displayed when Indonesia dismissed the first secretary general, an Indonesian national, for Indonesian domestic political reasons.[7]

Finally, at the Bali Summit, the heads of state for the first time gave leadership impetus to regional economic cooperation by adopting in principle a UN team's blueprint for industrialization through market sharing and resource pooling (chapter 8). The first fruit of the new emphasis was the ASEAN Preferential Trade Arrangement (PTA), the precursor to the 1992 ASEAN Free Trade Agreement (AFTA) (chapter 8). At the second, 1977, Kuala Lumpur ASEAN Summit, the economic ministers became the coequal of the foreign ministers with their reporting line directly to the leaders, not through the AMM.

The 1992 Singapore Summit

If the 1976 ASEAN Summit was a politically evolutionary watershed for ASEAN, the 1992 Fourth ASEAN Summit in Singapore was its economic equal. This was the first opportunity for the ASEAN member nations to respond collectively to the restructuring of the regional international environment. The Third Indochina War had ended, and Cold War imperatives no longer dominated ASEAN's policy plate. There was a sense of urgency in finding a new meaning for ASEAN. A summit without new initiatives would have been a failed summit. It was an opportunity for the economic regionalists to redirect the agenda. The Singapore Declaration promised to move ASEAN to a higher plane of cooperation.[8]

With politics no longer in command, the new engine for ASEAN regionalism would be economic integration as laid out in a Framework Agreement on Enhancing ASEAN Economic Cooperation, with AFTA at its center. To give direction to this, the bureaucratic structure for cooperation was rearranged. The existing ASEAN economic committees were dissolved, and the Senior Economic Officials' Meeting was tasked with handling all aspects of ASEAN economic cooperation. A ministerial-level council was established to oversee the implementation of the AFTA. The AMM, ASEAN Economic Ministers' Meeting (AEM), and ASEAN Finance Ministers' Meeting (AFM) became the leading organs of ASEAN. They were paralleled by a burgeoning number of other functional ministerial meetings and councils. At the consultative level, at least, ASEAN's work program comprehended nearly all aspects of a state's national policy concerns. Yet there was no structured direct ASEAN link to the national bureaucracies charged with those functions.

The leaders showed their determination to take nominal charge of the functionally expanding organization by institutionalizing the ASEAN summits. It was decided to have a formal summit every three years with an informal summit in the intervening years. The distinction between formal and informal ended with the fourth informal summit in Singapore in 2000.[9] The summit is held in that year's ASEAN chair's country. At the summits, the heads of government review ASEAN affairs, ratify and endorse the various proposals and initiatives that are to be undertaken in the name of ASEAN, and take note of regional and global events having bearing on ASEAN interests.

Finally, at Singapore the ASEAN leaders addressed the problem of continuity and direction within ASEAN itself. The secretary general of the ASEAN secretariat was upgraded to the secretary general of ASEAN and given ministerial status and a five-year term. The secretary general's mandate was expanded to initiate, advise, coordinate, and implement ASEAN activities. The secretary general does this with a relatively small staff. In 2012 the secretariat operated with a budget of $16 million and only seventy professionals among its three hundred employees.[10] Most of the bureaucratic burden of ASEAN still rests with the ten national secretariats and relevant national ministries. The task of staffing the literally hundreds of ASEAN intergovernmental sessions, committee meetings, workshops, seminars, training programs, and so on puts an enormous strain on the bureaucratic human resources pool of ASEAN's second-tier members.

The most ambitious effort to give effect to the new emphasis was the 1997 "ASEAN Vision 2020" set out by the heads of government in which they pledged to move toward close economic integration.[11] A year later, the leaders adopted a detailed plan of action designed to implement Vision 2020. The "Hanoi Plan of Action" was peppered with statements of intentions to "foster," "promote," "study," and "strengthen" what are essentially intergovernmental cooperative activities, not regional integrative structures.[12]

The financial crisis of 1997–1998 and the political turmoil that followed challenged the political leaders of Southeast Asia. They quickly learned that multilateral frameworks for regional economic collaboration provided no cushions for the shocks to their economies. It was every nation for itself in a series of ongoing bilateral negotiations among governments, international agencies, banks, and other creditors. At the same time that the political elite faced external pressures, they had to cope with the domestic dislocations occurring after the sudden reversal of years of rapid economic growth, rising living standards, and expectations of a better future. Political anger, generated throughout the region, focused on both the remote structures of global capitalism and more narrowly on domestic individuals, groups, and classes who had benefited the most from Southeast Asia's integration into the global economy, but who now appeared to be the authors of economic disaster.

ASEAN's failure to construct a regional response to the Crash of '97 shook the foundations of the grouping as each country groped for solutions, sometimes at the cost of neighbors. Unilateralism reigned supreme under the watchful eye of the IMF. Questions were raised about the relevance of ASEAN. There were hints that a two-tiered ASEAN might become a three-tiered ASEAN. In the first years of the new millennium, Singapore and Thailand, frustrated by the slow pace of ASEAN trade liberalization, stood apart as they looked to bilateral FTAs with their major extraregional partners for the stimulus to economic growth. This contributed to an unraveling of the ASEAN consensus on AFTA, even as a booming China drew FDI away from Southeast Asia and competed with Southeast Asia in the global marketplace.

ASEAN's sputtering economic cooperation coincided with the political tumult over Myanmar's repressive government. By embracing the Yangon regime, ASEAN distanced itself from its Western democratic dialogue partners. What little collective bargaining power ASEAN might have had in its dealings with Europe and North America was diminished by its growing organizational inability to deal with political issues of great concern to its major dialogue partners—with the exception of China. The war on terrorism and war in Iraq deepened existing differences in strategic perceptions between the supporters of the United States—the Philippines, Singapore, and Thailand—and the rest of ASEAN. What some observers perceived as an erosion of ASEAN's underpinnings and its political devaluation in Europe and North America occurred at a time of a leadership void in ASEAN. Indonesia's president Suharto was off the stage, and his successors were preoccupied with domestic stability. Prime Minister Mahathir in Malaysia was a polarizing figure and on his way out. Thailand's prime minister Thaksin Shinawatra was an unknown quantity who seemed to have his eye on a larger international stage. Philippine presidents fended off mob rule and coup attempts. Singapore's prime minister Goh Chok Tong had always functioned in the shadow of his predecessor, Senior Minister Lee Kuan Yew. The CLMV countries did not have leaders with international stature or respect. In these circumstances, ASEAN sought to reinvent itself a second time.

The 2003 Bali Summit and Bali Concord II

In 2003, ASEAN's chairmanship passed from Prime Minister Hun Sen's Cambodia to President Megawati Sukarnoputri's Indonesia. This was the first opportunity for a post-Suharto Indonesian leadership to play an important role in shaping the region's future. The 2003, Bali, ASEAN Summit was capped by the signing of the Bali Concord II, signifying a rededication to the political, economic, and social goals expressed more than a quarter of a century previously in the Bali Concord I, but in a more structured format. The goal was to create a dynamic, cohesive, resilient, and integrated ASEAN Community by the year 2020.[13] The ASEAN Community was to be supported by three "entwined and mutually supportive" pillars: an ASEAN Security Community (later renamed an ASEAN Political-Security Community [APSC]), an ASEAN Economic Community (AEC), and an ASEAN Socio-Cultural Community (ASCC). Four years later, at the 2007 summit in Cebu, the Philippines, the timetable was advanced half a decade to 2015.[14] This reflected more the changes in the international environment than any progress in community building. Historically, ASEAN has always seemed to be trying to catch up to the external events affecting it.

By pledging in the Bali Concord II affirmative steps to tighten their internal ties through the AEC, APSC, and ASCC, the ASEAN states hoped to regain collective leverage with their external partners. The Bali Concord II was described by its authors as a historic moment for ASEAN, but there have been many such moments in ASEAN's history, since forgotten. All of the ideas and proposals embraced in the new community frameworks already existed in one form or another. However, in the articulation of an AEC,

APSC, and ASCC, for the first time the leaders of ASEAN officially introduced the concept of an ASEAN Community as an integrative endpoint for
intensified intergovernmental cooperation in ASEAN. Yet, even though the
notion of "community" had become part of the ASEAN lexicon, the leaders
in the Bali Concord II continued to describe their relationship as a "concert"
of Southeast Asian nations. Goals and strategies for the building of the three
"pillar" communities were set in the 2004 Vientiane Summit's Vientiane
Action Programme (VAP).[15] The details were laid out in "blueprints" for the
AEC, ASCC, and APSC, which together with the IAI laid out the "road map"
to the AC.[16]

Of the three communities, the ASCC proposal is the most nebulous. It is
intended to foster cooperation in addressing a grab bag of social and cultural
problems associated with rural poverty, population growth, unemployment,
human resources development, education, environment, and health. The programs are broadly conceived as the human security element of comprehensive security. Rather than ASEAN regionalization in terms of planning and
allocation of resources, the ASCC depends on the intensification of existing
national and local programs. The kinds of problems to be dealt with in the
framework of the ASCC are commonly those of low politics, not involving
competing vital national interests. Furthermore, it is in these functional areas
that extraregional sources of ODA and expertise can partner.

The AEC will be the most advanced, if still incomplete, of the three pillars by the end of 2015. The goal is to establish ASEAN as a single market
and production base through the free flow of goods, services, investment,
and capital. The AEC will be achieved largely through carrying out the
implementation of existing agreements on AFTA, services, and investment.
It will require a level of cooperation and liberalization that has been absent in
ASEAN's past. Whether political leaderships in the ASEAN states will have
either the will or capability to overcome domestic protectionist interests is
problematic. Also, how the AEC can be articulated with other, broader, regional free trade areas than ASEAN embraces remains to be seen (chapter 8).

The APSC concept was most vigorously promoted by Indonesia. Jakarta
was responsible for the initial draft, allowing Indonesia to reclaim its position
as the strategic center for regional security. The goal is heightened political and security cooperation. The starting point was that ASEAN members
should accept that community interests should prevail over national interests,
particularly in cases where domestic conflict could spill over to affect other
members of the community. Indonesian foreign minister Hassan Wirajuda
called for openness and transparency in the community, in which ASEAN
would be "enabled to discuss with candor sensitive issues and to resolve them
amicably instead of relegating them to the back burner."[17] This position was

viewed as at odds with the fundamental ASEAN principles of sovereignty and noninterference. The Indonesian draftsmen also wanted strong protections for democracy and human rights built into the APSC. Specifically, they advocated an independent human rights commission (chapter 9). ASEAN's processing of a bureaucratic consensus through senior officials to the foreign ministers eliminated any effective innovation that would seriously alter the status quo. One commentator suggested that the rejection of Indonesia's bold and visionary concept for the APSC was because it was viewed by Jakarta's peers "as a blatant and unacceptable bid to reassert itself over the rest of the region."[18]

THE ASEAN CHARTER

From the outset it was acknowledged that the building of the ASEAN Community would require the mobilization of a degree of national political wills and capabilities that had heretofore been lacking. It was also recognized that the loose, almost ad hoc, and poorly institutionalized framework of ASEAN was not up to the task of community building. Accordingly, the foreign ministers at the 2004 AMM called for the creation of a new ASEAN Charter for the establishment of an effective and efficient institutional framework for ASEAN. The charter would also give a new face to the organization whose credibility and relevance had been seriously diminished in the eyes of the West. The goal was a more formal, structured, treaty-based organization, with an international legal personality. At their 2005 AMM, the foreign ministers agreed to a draft text of a Declaration on the Establishment of an ASEAN Charter. This was promulgated by the heads of government at their 2005 Kuala Lumpur Summit.[19] The declaration promised a forward-looking, rules-based organization in a normative framework of democracy, transparency, and good governance. At the same time, it enshrined the ASEAN way of consensus decision making, respect for sovereignty, and noninterference.

The task of reconciling the ideal basis of a new charter to the reality of the ASEAN way was given to an Eminent Persons Group (EPG) that was charged with providing recommendations for the key elements to be included in the charter. The EPG was made up of former high officials of ASEAN governments. As the EPG met, rumors and leaks swirled around possible innovations in the ASEAN way with respect to voting, accountability, a human rights mechanism, compliance, and even sanctions. The EPG's report was given to the heads of government at their January 2007 Cebu Summit (actually the postponed December 2006 summit). They in turn passed the report to a high-level senior officials' task force that actually fashioned the final draft of the charter. The charter was presented to the heads of government for approval at the 2007 Singapore Summit. Although the opening words of the charter invoked "we the peoples" of the member states of ASEAN, the peoples had little input. Civil society groups in all but Indonesia and the Philippines were shut out of the process. The final document was the work of the ASEAN apparatchiks of the official task force operating by consensus who cut out of the EPG proposals anything that was unacceptable to the least democratic members. The ASEAN Charter became ASEAN law in December 2008.[20] Indonesia was the last to ratify what is sometimes called ASEAN's constitution. The ratification process in Indonesia, like the Philippines, involved persuading parliament to approve despite deep misgivings about the watering down of any safeguards for democratic governance and human rights. The ASEAN claim to be "people oriented" is belied by the fact that there is no structured institutional access to its workings for civil society groups.

In the new ASEAN the supreme policy-making body is the ASEAN Summit that meets biannually and, if necessary, on an ad hoc basis. Below the summit, an ASEAN Coordinating Council (ACC) comprised of the ASEAN foreign ministers manages ASEAN affairs in general and coordinates the work of the three ASEAN Community Councils: an APSC Council, an AEC Council, and an ASCC Council. The dual role of the foreign ministers in the Coordinating Council and the AMM guarantees that politics will still have priority. The community councils are at the ministerial level and will meet biannually, chaired by an appropriate minister from the member state holding the ASEAN chairmanship. The community councils have under their purview the relevant ASEAN sectoral ministerial bodies. The ministerial meetings are preceded by their Senior Officials' Meeting (SOM) to iron out the ministers' agreements and undertakings. ASEAN national secretariats are the organizational links between ASEAN and the domestic bureaucracies. Table 4.1 gives an overview of ASEAN's structure.

The ASEAN secretary general is ASEAN's chief administrative officer whose five-year term of office rotates alphabetically by country and who is nominated by that government. There are four deputy secretaries general (DSGs) of four different nationalities than the secretary general. Two are state-nominated and two are recruited on the basis of professional merit. A Committee of Permanent Representatives with ambassadorial status has replaced the ASEAN Standing Committee as the quotidian link between the member states and the secretariat. The United States was the first to recognize the new international personality of ASEAN by naming a resident ambassador to ASEAN in April 2011. By the end of 2013, seventy-four ambassadors were accredited to ASEAN, most of them already accredited ambassadors to Indonesia.

Table 4.1. ASEAN Community Basic Structure

ASEAN Summit		
ASEAN Coordinating Council		
ASEAN Community Councils*		
Political-Security Council	*Economic Council*	*Socio-Cultural Council*
ASEAN Intergovernmental Commission on Human Rights (AICHR) ASEAN Ministerial Meeting (AMM) ASEAN Regional Forum (ARF) ASEAN Defense Ministers' Meeting (ADMM) ASEAN Law Ministers' Meeting (ALAWMM) ASEAN Ministerial Meeting on Transnational Crime (AMMTC)	ASEAN Economic Ministers (AEM) ASEAN Free Trade Area (AFTA Council) ASEAN Ministers of Energy Meeting (AMEM) ASEAN Ministerial Meeting on Agriculture and Forestry (AMMAF) ASEAN Finance Ministers' Meeting (AFM) ASEAN Investment Area (AIA) Council ASEAN Ministerial Meeting on Minerals (AMMM) ASEAN Ministerial Meeting on Science and Technology (AMMST) ASEAN Mekong Basin Development Cooperation (AMBDC) ASEAN Transport Ministers' Meeting (ATMM) ASEAN Telecommunication and IT Ministers' Meeting (TELMIN) ASEAN Tourism Ministers' Meeting (M-ATM) Initiative for ASEAN Integration (IAI) and Narrowing the Development Gap (NDG) Sectoral Bodies under the Purview of AEM	ASEAN Ministers Responsible for Culture and Art (AMCA) ASEAN Ministerial Meeting on Disaster Management (AMMDM) ASEAN Education Ministers' Meeting (ASED) ASEAN Ministers' Meeting on the Environment (AMME) Conference of the Parties to the ASEAN Agreement on Transboundary Haze Pollution (COP to AATHP) ASEAN Health Ministers' Meeting (AHMM) ASEAN Ministers Responsible for Information (AMRI) ASEAN Labor Ministers' Meeting (ALMM) ASEAN Ministers' Meeting on Rural Development and Poverty Eradication (AMRDPE) ASEAN Ministerial Meeting on Social Welfare and Development (AMMSWD) ASEAN Ministerial Meeting on Women (AMMW) ASEAN Ministerial Meeting on Youth (AMMY)

*The listing of the units is not hierarchical.

The ASEAN Charter, Article 11, enhanced the status of the secretary general with a place at all of the ministerial tables. In particular, it gave him the authority to present the views of ASEAN to external parties in accordance with approved policy guidelines. From 2007 to 2012, the ASEAN secretary general was former Thai foreign minister Surin Pitsuwan. Surin brought to the office a political skill set and capabilities not equaled by his predecessors. Surin made the best use of the political space that the charter and the annual turnover of ASEAN chairs gave him. He became ASEAN's most accomplished promoter and defender in international circles. The high profile of the secretary general was one of the few substantive underpinnings to the claim of ASEAN's centrality. Within ASEAN, Surin sought—with the discreet backing of Indonesia—to advance a progressive ASEAN agenda, not just minding the store, sometimes to the discomfiture of the more illiberal member states. Even so, he had no plenipotentiary powers, and his influence on decision making was only indirect. As he departed office, he challenged ASEAN to strengthen the secretariat and to give the secretary general a greater policy role.[21] It remains to be seen if his successor, Le Luong Minh, a Vietnamese sub-cabinet-level career diplomat, will follow up on Surin's parting challenge, let alone his style. Just as Surin's neutrality in the Thai–Cambodian border war (chapter 6) was suspect in Phnom Penh, Le's Vietnam Ministry of Foreign Affairs background is viewed suspiciously in Beijing (chapter 6).

On its face, the ASEAN Charter, in explicitly confirming all previous ASEAN decisions, declarations, and initiatives, has simply rearranged the boxes on a table of organization. What had been trumpeted as a landmark breakthrough has been dismissed by many critics as old wine in new bottles, and for some observers that wine has gone bad. The charter upholds the right of every member state to lead its national existence free from external interference or coercion. Decision making remains consensual. Regimes like those in Myanmar, Cambodia, and Laos could sign off on a document that touts democracy, the rule of law, and fundamental freedoms because there is no way to hold them accountable within the organization. Even as a sop to Indonesia, a toothless human rights mechanism was pushed off to a future date (chapter 9). In the absence of a compliance mechanism, any member can pick and choose from the ASEAN plate of norms and values those to which it will adhere. In a scathing commentary, a leading Thai political scientist wrote that the "scarcely relevant" charter laid bare ASEAN's limitations and that its runaway ambitions had turned into "folly."[22] The charter project, in hindsight, he continued, "was misguided and naively conceived, broached by misplaced overconfidence and manifested in utter disappointment." This may be too harsh a judgment, but it illustrates ASEAN's historical problem of creating expectations that are dashed by the reality of intra-ASEAN relations. At best, the goals of the charter are aspirational and not yet operational.

ASEAN'S EXTERNAL RELATIONS

The decision to raise and expand the member states' bilateral connections with important economic and strategic partners to the ASEAN collective level was made at the 1977, Kuala Lumpur, second ASEAN Summit. This associational relationship with important external partners was formalized as the ASEAN dialogue process.

The Dialogue Partners

At the 1977 summit, the ASEAN heads of government met with the prime ministers of Australia, Japan, and New Zealand. The following year, the ASEAN foreign ministers met in a Post-Ministerial Conference (PMC) with their counterparts from Australia, Canada, the EU, Japan, New Zealand, and the United States as official "dialogue partners." Since then four other dialogue partners have joined: the Republic of Korea in 1991 and in 1996, China, India, and Russia. The administrator of the UNDP was also invited to the PMC as a guest of the host chair. Pakistan has been a "sectoral" dialogue partner of ASEAN since 1993 and has unsuccessfully put itself forward as a potential official dialogue partner. It attributes its lack of promotion to Indian propaganda and diplomacy.[23] Although other countries have knocked on the dialogue door, ASEAN has maintained a moratorium on new dialogue partners since 1999. In the official dialogue process, one ASEAN country acts as the coordinator for a dialogue partner in a three-year rotation. Over the years, the dialogue partners and ASEAN have fashioned agreements on formal partnerships. Box 4.1 lists the dialogue partnerships with their dates of signing and in brackets the country coordinator in the 2012–2015 period.

Originally, the PMC dialogues took place in two phases. First, the ASEAN foreign ministers met with their dialogue partner counterparts as a group (ASEAN + 10) in a closed session of wide-ranging discussion of international economic, political, and security issues. This was followed by separate sessions between the ASEAN ministers and each dialogue partner (ASEAN + 1) to examine their bilateral relationship. It should be understood that these relatively brief and scripted engagements were the product of intensive planning and coordination at the senior official level. The original agenda of the dialogues was restricted to matters of functional cooperation. ASEAN resisted early efforts to broaden the PMC's scope to include political and security matters. However, because these kinds of regional issues were important for some of the external partners, to keep the dialogue relevant, ASEAN expanded the topics to include regional security. This was the genesis of the annual separate security dialogue of the ASEAN Regional Forum (chapter 5). The PMC ASEAN + 10 format has been allowed to lapse. Between the

Box 4.1.   ASEAN Dialogue Partnership Agreements

ASEAN–China Strategic Partnership for Peace and Prosperity (2003) [Thailand]

ASEAN–Japan Declaration for a Dynamic and Enduring ASEAN–Japan Partnership (2003) [Cambodia]

ASEAN–Russia Partnership for Peace and Security, and Prosperity and Development in the Asia-Pacific Region (2003) [Malaysia]

ASEAN–Republic of Korea Comprehensive Cooperation Partnership (2004) [Indonesia]

ASEAN–India Partnership for Peace, Progress and Shared Prosperity (2004) [Brunei]

ASEAN–United States Enhanced Partnership (2005) [Myanmar]

ASEAN–Australia Comprehensive Partnership (2007) [Philippines]

ASEAN–EU Enhanced Partnership (2007) [Vietnam]

ASEAN–Canada Enhanced Partnership (2010) [Singapore]

ASEAN–New Zealand Enhanced Partnership (2010) [LPDR]

PMCs, dialogues continue at different levels of official contact, including the partners' ambassadors to ASEAN and ASEAN ambassadorial committees in the dialogue partners' capitals. There are also ASEAN committees at the Brussels headquarters of the EU and the United Nations European headquarters in Geneva.

The dialogue process for China, Japan, India, and South Korea has been enhanced by including them at the annual ASEAN Summit in a series of ASEAN + 1 summits. New Zealand and Australia held a commemorative summit with ASEAN in 2004, and another one is scheduled. The EU and ASEAN held a commemorative summit in 2007. An ASEAN–Russia Summit was held in 2005. Between 2009 and 2012 there had been four ASEAN–US "leaders' meetings." As part of the US determination to raise its profile in the region, the leaders' meeting was elevated to a formal first ASEAN–US Summit in Brunei in October 2013. Unfortunately, because of domestic politics, President Obama did not attend, leaving Secretary of State John Kerry to stand in for him.

ASEAN's dialogue process complements the ASEAN member states' interests in their bilateral relations with the dialogue states, which in functional political and economic terms are more immediately important. The undertakings at the ASEAN level are translated into action at the bilateral level. In a number of cases, the dialogue partners have negotiated at the bilateral level programs of strategic cooperation that mirror broad statements of partnership with ASEAN at the regional level. The dialogue partners also have to take into account how problems at the bilateral level might influence the dialogue at the regional level where ASEAN solidarity rules.

ASEAN + 3 (APT)

Since 1997, China, the Republic of Korea, and Japan have developed a special relationship with ASEAN formalized as the ASEAN + 3 grouping, or APT. The external stimulus was the financial crisis of 1997 and the effort to find a regional mechanism to deal with it (chapter 8). Since then the pattern of collaboration and consultation has expanded to nearly every area of state interaction. In 1998, the APT heads of government commissioned an EPG East Asian Vision Group (EAVG) to report on measures to intensify intergovernmental cooperative links between Southeast Asia and Northeast Asia. Even before the EAVG had completed its study, the heads of government in a Joint Statement on East Asia Cooperation adopted at the 1999 ASEAN + 3 Summit agreed to institutionalize the APT.[24] At the time, the EAVG saw the APT as the first step toward an East Asia Community. The APT consultative structures have penetrated ASEAN's operations at most consultative levels. An APT Summit meeting in addition to the ASEAN + 1 individual summits with China, South Korea, and Japan has become part of the annual ASEAN summitry. Important ASEAN ministerial meetings now have parallel APT formats.

ASEAN's strategy in the APT is to enhance Southeast Asia's significance as a grouping to the Northeast Asian powers. Like its other external regional associations, ASEAN insists on its central agenda-setting role. In the APT framework, ASEAN also is balancing the growing influence of China in other bilateral and ASEAN relationships with the consensus mechanism that includes South Korea and Japan. Worries that the APT could evolve into an integrative regional exclusive trade and market grouping analogous to the East Asia Economic Group (EAEG) once promoted by Malaysia's Mahathir overlook the deep political divides between China and Japan (chapter 8).

The East Asia Summit (EAS)

A new adjunct to the growing complex of summitry around the ASEAN Summit was added in December 2005 when the first meeting of the East Asia Summit (EAS) was held. The idea for the EAS had been mooted by Malaysia's prime minister Abdullah Badawi as a first step toward the EAVG's goal of an East Asia Community. The proposed membership format was the

ASEAN nations with China, South Korea, and Japan. It would have differed from the ASEAN + 3 in that the ten ASEAN nations would be associated in the EAS as individual states, not as ASEAN. Both Japan and Indonesia offered resistance to this structure. Japan feared that China would drive it. Indonesia opposed the exclusivity of a new grouping that was essentially a deconstruction of the APT. Consensus demanded a broader invitation list so that at the inaugural EAS in Kuala Lumpur, in addition to the APT countries, Australia, India, and New Zealand were present along with Russian president Vladimir Putin as a guest of the EAS. The United States was excluded until it acceded to the TAC, a ticket of admission. The United States and Russia officially became part of the EAS in 2010.

The EAS is billed as the leading forum for Asia-Pacific leaders to dialogue among themselves about important security and economic issues in which they have shared interests. At its sixth meeting in 2011, the first with Russia and the United States at the table, the leaders adopted a Declaration of the East Asia Summit Principles of Mutually Beneficial Relations, adding to the normative rules of state conduct already in place in the region.[25] The topics addressed, mostly noncontroversial, cover major areas in which frameworks for possible cooperation can be identified: energy, environment, finance, education, pandemics, and natural disaster relief. The EAS Summit has spun off an annual EAS Foreign Ministers' Meeting.

With the addition of the United States, terrorism, piracy, and maritime security, as well as nonproliferation, have been added to the EAS agenda. Maritime security became a focus of the 2011 EAS at the Bali ASEAN Summit when, over China's vehement objections, the chair, President Yudhoyono, allowed the South China Sea problem to be discussed. American president Obama forcefully supported the positions of the Southeast Asian maritime states, while China's premier, Wen Jiabao, essentially said it was none of America's business.[26] President Obama's absence from the 2013 EAS seemed to embolden Premier Li Keqiang to press the Chinese point that the United States was an outsider.

As the EAS continues, the question can be raised as to its function in adding a new layer to the multilateral architecture in Southeast Asia. Once it became clear that the EAS was not to be a political twin of the economics-centered APT, China's interest seems to have waned. For the United States, it is evidence of American intention to demonstrate its commitment to maintain its role as a legitimate regional great power. The Russian case is puzzling. Moscow lobbied for EAS membership, but since becoming a member in 2010, the Russian presidents—first Medvedev and then Putin—have been no-shows. Two possible reasons for this may be a lower order of security interests in the region as compared to the PRC and the United States and a wish not to be caught between China and the United States in such a setting.[27]

For ASEAN, the EAS is self-assurance of its claimed centrality in the shaping of regional international relations. However, sitting across from the extraregional leaders, there is no one ASEAN leader who can speak authoritatively as the organization's single voice on real political and security issues. Realistically, the EAS is not a seven-actor summit, but a meeting of sixteen leaders in which the interaction of the great powers overshadows the ASEAN 10.

ASEAN and Europe

ASEAN has transformed its dialogue process with Europe into a formal organizational relationship, although not as penetrating or elaborate as the ASEAN + 3. The twenty-seven-nation EU is ASEAN's second-largest export market and its third-largest trading partner. Europe is also viewed by ASEAN as a participant, albeit somewhat politically remote, in the balance of power with China, the United States, and Japan. For years, however, ASEAN's institutional relations with Europe have been constricted by the EU's position on Myanmar. Until Myanmar's democratic breakthrough in 2011, the relationship was marked by "years of futile and tedious jousting over participation and mutual allegations of arrogance and indifference."[28]

ASEAN–EU Ministerial Meeting (AEMM)

The first AEMM took place in 1978 and was institutionalized in the 1980 EC–ASEAN Cooperation Agreement.[29] The AEMM meets every two years, alternating between Southeast Asia and Europe. A Joint Cooperation Committee monitors the progress of ASEAN–EU economic cooperation. Between these meetings, the ASEAN Brussels Committee represents ASEAN at EU headquarters. In addition to trade and market issues, there is a political exchange that since 1997 had been preoccupied by the Myanmar junta's assault on democracy. The EU's unwillingness to sit with ASEAN partner Myanmar has been a source of contention. The issue of Myanmar's place at the table was settled at the 2004 Asia–Europe Meeting (ASEM) discussed below. An important element in the early AEMM had been a proposed Europe–ASEAN FTA. This was a stuttering process finally broken off in 2009, largely over the EU's insistence on excluding Myanmar which was under sanctions. With the change in Myanmar, it is now hoped that negotiations can begin again after the 2015 official debut of the AEC.

Asia–Europe Meeting (ASEM)

A new Asia–Europe forum was launched in 1996 with the first ASEM Summit meeting.[30] The ASEM Summit meets every two years, alternating between Europe and Asia. In years between summits, the ASEM foreign ministers meet. As many as fifty ministerial and senior official meetings take place in the biennial cycle. With the addition of Croatia in 2014, the number of participants is fifty-two. An agreement on the admission of Laos, Cambodia, and Myanmar as a package was deadlocked in 2003, with ASEAN holding the admission of ten new EU states hostage for Myanmar. Recognizing that both the ASEM and AEMM processes were at stake, a diplomatic compromise was reached over Myanmar's participation. The 2004 ASEM Summit expanded the grouping by admitting the EU 10 and the ASEAN 3. Myanmar's membership was given a political asterisk, however, with the expectation that its participation in the ASEM Summit would be lower than head of government.

In a sense, the ASEM's genesis was a deployment to Europe of the ASEAN + 3. Europe's interests in Asia go well beyond ASEAN, but ASEAN did not want to see Europe engaged in a Northeast Asia dialogue that excluded ASEAN. For the Europeans, the ASEM was conceived as a balance to the Asia-Pacific Economic Cooperation forum (APEC) from which it is excluded. The EU accepts ASEAN's position that the AEMM is the cornerstone of the EU's regional cooperation and dialogue with the ASEAN states.

SUBREGIONAL MULTILATERAL
FRAMEWORKS: THE MINI-ASEANS

The recommendations of the 1972 UN developmental blueprint for ASEAN noted the advantages to be gained by the crossing of national frontiers in ASEAN to enhance the productive use of different and potentially complementary endowments of raw materials, skills, and other resources in different geographic areas. This concept was vigorously promoted by the ADB before the Crash of '97.[31] The term "growth zones" or geometric metaphors—triangles, quadrangles, and even hexagons—were applied to these areas. The key to the strategy is the mobilization of complementary-factor endowments in the contiguous national territories. The theory is that freed from the barriers of national sovereignty, market forces would lead to productive and efficient utilization of the disparate economic factors. The governments of the different national territories are expected to facilitate the transnational integration of economic factors by providing infrastructure development, legal frameworks, and incentives to encourage the flow of private and quasi-private investment for zonal development.

The ADB model and most of the literature supporting it has been of an "all things being equal" nature; that is, if unhampered by the intervention of noneconomic variables, where transnational economic complementarities exist, economic rationality would lead naturally to localized or subregional integration. In the ASEAN experience the process seems reversed. The growth zones exist by virtue of political proclamation, not market forces. In the 1990s, four such subregional growth zones had officially been blessed by the ADB: the Indonesia–Malaysia–Singapore Growth Triangle (IMS-GT, or alternatively SIJORI); the Indonesia–Malaysia–Thailand Growth Triangle (IMT-GT); the Brunei–Indonesia–Malaysia–Philippines East ASEAN Growth Area (BIMP-EAGA); and the Greater Mekong Subregion (GMS) Growth Zone or "Growth Hexagon." Although not part of ASEAN's structure, the subregional zones are viewed as enhancing and adding capabilities to the ASEAN Economic Community. However, as a September 2013 ADB report points out, there is inadequate linkage and coordination at the interface between ASEAN and the subregional groupings.[32]

The IMS-GT

The Indonesia–Malaysia–Singapore growth triangle is the only Southeast Asian subregional growth zone that begins to approximate the theoretical model. Actually, the leaders' political endorsement in 1990 simply formalized at a governmental level the existing pattern of economic relations. Singapore's economy had long been linked to the proximate geographic regions of Malaysia's Johor State and Indonesia's Riau Archipelago. Singapore had capital, technology, and entrepreneurial skills. Johor and the Riau Archipelago, especially the island of Batam, had land, labor, and water. Singapore was the hub of two spokes to economic hinterlands that themselves remained largely unconnected. The GT formula gave a political semidisguise to Singapore's economic dominance.

Although the economic raison d'être for the IMS-GT had limited geographic scope, domestic politics demanded its expansion. West Sumatra was included in 1994, and in 1996, Malaysia's Malacca, Negri Sembilan, and Pahang states were added. A year later five additional Indonesian provinces sought inclusion: Jambi, Bengkulu, South Sumatra, Lampung, and West Kalimantan. Economically, however, the IMS-GT despite its geopolitical scope was still the original triangle. Rather than accept a boundaryless transnational melding with Singapore as the centerpiece, both Indonesia and Malaysia embarked on efforts to compete with Singapore at their ends of the spokes, rather than complement. The political luster of the IMS-GT wore off as noneconomic irritants have intruded to cool bilateral relations between Malaysia and Singapore and Indonesia and Singapore (chapter 5). Symbiotic economic ties still link the three economies, but without governmental cheerleading.

IMT-GT

The Indonesia–Malaysia–Thailand GT was initiated in 1993 to spur economic growth in the three countries' less-developed provinces: fourteen southern Thai provinces, eight peninsular Malaysian states, and ten Sumatran provinces. Malaysia provided the impetus for this "northern triangle" in an effort to balance developmentally Singapore's dominance in the "southern triangle." Neither Indonesia nor Thailand invested much political capital, let alone public investment, into infrastructure that might help attract private capital. Although politically modeled on the IMS-GT, the IMT-GT had few complementarities and no Singapore-like financial and transportation hub. The ADB has been the development partner of the IMT-GT since 2007 and has seemed to show more enthusiasm for it than the national partners.[33] The IMT-GT quickly became moribund. It lacked an operating framework and coherent strategy. Part of the problem was competitive, as opposed to complementary, isthmian development programs of Thailand and Malaysia.

New life was breathed into the project in December 2005, when the first IMT-GT Summit—meeting on the margins of the ASEAN Summit—sought to reinvigorate it, calling for a blueprint for development. At a second summit in 2007, the IMT-GT heads of government launched an ADB-prepared "Roadmap for Development," 2007–2011. The Center for IMT-GT Subregional Cooperation (CIMT), hosted by Malaysia, is tasked with coordinating and monitoring the subregional grouping's activities. The CIMT is paralleled by a Joint Business Council. Beyond the bureaucratic links, it is difficult to identify any concrete integrative regionalist projects developed through the IMT-GT and private sector–funded development.

BIMP-EAGA

The Brunei–Indonesia–Malaysia–Philippines East ASEAN Growth Area was officially launched in March 1994 at a ministerial meeting in Davao City, the Philippines. Its geographical scope contains the Sultanate of Brunei; Indonesia's Kalimantan, Sulawesi, Maluku, and Papua provinces; East Malaysia's Sabah and Sarawak states and the Federal Territory of Labuan; and the Philippines' Mindanao and Palawan islands. Since 2001, the ADB has been the regional development advisor for BIMP-EAGA. Theoretically it is market driven and private sector led. The formal structure includes annual summit meetings and annual senior official/ministerial meetings. It has working groups in four areas: transport and infrastructure, natural resources, tourism, and small and medium business enterprise.

The BIMP-EAGA has been described as "an association of neglected regions."[34] With the exception of Brunei, the territories are at the margins of their countries, far from any energizing core hub. The Philippines' effort to make Davao on Mindanao a gateway to BIMP-EAGA has been frustrated by Muslim insurgency. Continued tension between the Philippines and Malaysia over Sabah's sovereignty is also an inhibiting factor. The Sulawesi–Sulu Sea maritime environment is rife with transnational criminal activity (chapter 6). Indonesian official support has been only pro forma. Even more so than the IMT-GT, the region has poor infrastructure. Local enthusiasm for the BIMP-EAGA's aspirations has not been matched in their national capitals. Governments have not made public investments that would attract private capital. Given the relative remoteness of the zone from market and transportation centers, major investments in infrastructure—with the exception of ecotourism—could prove to be financial white elephants.

The Mekong River Basin

The end of the Indochina wars ushered in a time of hope and aspiration for internationally cooperative development of Southeast Asia's greatest underutilized economic resource, the Mekong River. Its natural potentials have been limited by the economic, political, and strategic competitions of its six riparian states: Laos, Myanmar, Thailand, Cambodia, Vietnam, and China's Yunnan Province. With regional peace, new opportunities opened for economic development in a region with some of the lowest per capita GDPs in the world.

Greater Mekong Subregion (GMS)

In 1992, prodded by the ADB, Cambodia, China-Yunnan, Laos, Myanmar, Thailand, and Vietnam agreed to a program of subregional cooperation to enhance economic relations among them and to provide international recognition of a subregional growth zone. From the birth of the GMS, the ADB, functioning as the GMS secretariat, has been the lead agent for coordination, promoting cofinancing, obtaining ODA, strategic planning, and technical assistance.[35] A major development area has been the creation of hydropower dams in a strategic thrust that has put at risk the region's ecosystems. The Mekong River Commission (MRC), which has a regional international riverkeeping role, stands outside of the GMS (chapter 10).

Beginning in 2002, a triennial GMS Summit gives strategic direction to the relevant ministers and senior officials in the functional areas of cooperation embraced by the GMS. At the fourth summit in Nay Pyi Taw in December 2011, the leaders endorsed the new 2012–2022 GMS Strategic Framework. There is an annual ministerial meeting at which the nuts and bolts of cooperative programs are signed off on. At the nineteenth annual GMS Ministerial

Conference in 2013, a $50 billion Regional Investment Framework (RIF) was approved. A goal of the projects to be funded by the RIF is to complete road and rail transport corridors in the Mekong Basin and turn them into cross-border economic corridors. The political impacts of China's economic penetration of the Mekong Basin through the GMS and the bilateral ties facilitated under the GMS big tent are putting strains on ASEAN solidarity.

In an effort to link ASEAN—particularly Singapore and Malaysia—to the GMS, the 1995 ASEAN Summit created the ASEAN–Mekong Basin Development Cooperation (AMBDC). From the southern vantage, Thailand's status in the MRC and GMS gave it an advantaged gateway into the Mekong zone. The backbone for the AMBDC was a proposed railway corridor from Singapore to Kunming, Yunnan, through peninsular Malaysia, Thailand, and Laos, with branches connecting Cambodia and Myanmar. Oversight of the AMBDC is assigned to the ASEAN finance ministers, who meet annually.

CLMV Cooperation Framework

Within the GMS there are sub-subregional cooperation programs directed specifically toward the CLMV countries. A CLMV Summit in 2004 followed by an informal summit on the margin of the 2005 Kuala Lumpur ASEAN Summit produced an action plan for CLMV enhanced economic cooperation and integration. The explicit goal for closer CLMV cooperation was to help close the development gap between the CLMV countries and their more developed ASEAN partners. It also laid the basis for a new approach for ODA under the broader GMS umbrella. Japan is the primary donor with its Mekong–Japan Cooperation Fund. At the first Japan–Mekong Summit in 2009, the Japanese pledged $5 billion to support the Mekong–Japan Action Plan for 2010–2013. At the 2012 fourth Japan–Mekong Summit, the pledge for 2013–2016 was increased to $7.4 billion, a commitment Prime Minister Abe reinforced at the Japan–Mekong Summit in 2013. Japan's high ODA profile in the CLMV domain seeks to balance the more natural geoeconomic ties enjoyed by China.

Cambodia–Laos–Vietnam Development Triangle (CLV-DT)

A subset of the GMS is the CLV-DT. The heads of government of the CLV countries had prepared a Master Plan for the CLV Development Triangle to be presented at a CLV–Japan summit on the margin of the 2004 ASEAN Summit in Vientiane. The target areas were the border provinces of the three states. Japan is the most important strategic partner of the GMS, having pledged in 2004 $1.5 billion for Mekong development over three years. In January 2007, Japan announced a new Mekong–Japan Partnership Program under which $40 million in new ODA would go the CLMV countries and of which $20 million would go to the CLV-DT.[36]

Ayeyawady–Chao Phraya–Mekong Economic Cooperation Strategy (ACMECS)

Until the political collapse at its center, Mekong Basin development fit fully into Bangkok's "Thailand-plus" foreign economic strategy. Already in 1993, Thailand had initiated with China, the Lao PDR, and Myanmar the Quadripartite Economic Cooperation Plan, popularly called the "Golden Quadrangle," for the development of the upper reaches of the Mekong. In 2003, Thai prime minister Thaksin Shinawatra promoted a new development plan called the Ayeyawady–Chao Phraya–Mekong Economic Cooperation Strategy (ACMECS) linking Thailand, Myanmar, Cambodia, the LPDR, and Vietnam and named after the region's principal rivers. The ACMECS was formalized at a November 2003 summit meeting with the Bagan Declaration.[37] This Thai-centered, core–periphery geoeconomic structure ostensibly would promote mutual benefits through cross-border trade, transport, and finance cooperation and enterprise. A darker view was one of Thai exploitation of weaker partners. The ACMECS holds a triennial summit, the last in 2013. The cooperative goals of the multiple Mekong subregional development groupings overlap, as do the interests of the involved states, including the great powers. It is not coincidental that the leaders' summits and foreign ministers' meetings of the CLMV Cooperation Framework, the CLV Development Triangle, and the ACMECS coincide in place and date.

Lower Mekong Initiative (LMI)

In July 2009, American secretary of state Hillary Clinton and her counterparts from Cambodia, Laos, Thailand, and Vietnam held the first US–Lower Mekong Ministerial Meeting to discuss areas of cooperation in environment, health, education, and infrastructure development. Since regime change in Myanmar, it has been included in the LMI. Concept papers and plans of action have been prepared for capacity-building projects for which US Agency for International Development's (USAID) expertise and funds are made available. Secretary of State Kerry headed the American delegation to the sixth LMI Ministerial Meeting in July 2013. American involvement in Mekong development is seen as an opportunity to demonstrate US political commitment to the subregion.

TRANSREGIONAL COOPERATIVE FRAMEWORKS

ASEAN member states belong to a number of other regional groupings that are not institutionally linked to ASEAN in a dialogue format. An ASEAN state's membership reflects national interests that are not fully served through ASEAN membership.

The Asian Cooperation Dialogue (ACD)

In an express desire to bridge the missing links between Northeast Asia and South Asia and the Arab Gulf states, Thailand's prime minister Thaksin launched the Asian Cooperation Dialogue (ACD) in 2002. It reflected Thaksin's itch for a larger stage than ASEAN. As conceived, the ACD was meant to be an informal forum for Asian foreign ministers to exchange views and promote cooperation to strengthen the "voice of Asia."[38] Despite a lukewarm ASEAN reception, Bangkok pressed forward toward the inaugural ACD Foreign Ministers' Meeting with the ASEAN states, Bahrain, Bangladesh, China, India, Japan, Pakistan, Qatar, and South Korea. In 2003 Kazakhstan, Oman, and Sri Lanka were added; in 2004, Bhutan, Iran, Kuwait, Mongolia, and the UAE; in 2005, Russia and Saudi Arabia; in 2006, Tajikistan and Uzbekistan; in 2008, Kyrgyzstan; and in 2012, Afghanistan, for a total of thirty-two members. Notionally, the ACD encompasses the members of the ASEAN + 3 grouping, the Shanghai Cooperation Organization (SCO), the South Asia Association for Regional Cooperation (SAARC), and the Gulf Cooperation Council (GCC). The ACD is coordinated from the Thai foreign ministry. The first ACD Summit was held in Kuwait in 2012. Most of the non-Gulf states were represented at the vice or deputy foreign minister level. Thai prime minister Yingluck Shinawatra was the only Asian head of government to attend. A 2015 ACD Summit is planned for Thailand.

Bay of Bengal Initiative for Multi-Sectoral Technical and Economic Cooperation (BIMSTEC)

In 1997, Bangladesh, India, Myanmar, Sri Lanka, and Thailand joined in a cooperative format to promote trade, investment, and tourism.[39] Bhutan, the Maldives, Nepal, and Myanmar have since joined. There are annual foreign ministers' meetings, senior officials' meetings, and working and experts' groups in areas promoting functional cooperation. Thailand hosted the first BIMSTEC Summit in 2004 and India the second summit in 2008. The third summit took place in Myanmar in March 2014. One observer noted BIMSTEC's egregious failure to achieve anything of significance.[40] A framework agreement for a regional FTA was signed in 2004, but expected dates for completion have not been met. BIMSTEC's administrative center is a working group composed of the member states' ambassadors to Thailand, who are coordinated from the Thai foreign ministry. BIMSTEC can be viewed as the conjunction of New Delhi's "Look East" policy and Thaksin's "Look West." In BIMSTEC, India also has isolated Pakistan from the SAARC. It also provides Myanmar with a multilateral format not shared with China.

Mekong–Ganga Cooperation (MGC)

The Mekong–Ganga Cooperation grouping was founded in 2000 and links India to the five continental Southeast Asian states—Myanmar, Thailand, Laos, Cambodia, and Vietnam. It was the brainchild of then Thai foreign minister Surin Pitsuwan. The originally proposed name was the Mekong–Ganga Suvarnabhumi, but the notion of the "Golden Peninsula," redolent of Thai historical ambition, was rejected by Laos. India's multilateral linking to Laos, Cambodia, and Vietnam, which are not members of BIMSTEC, through the MGC gives it a political/economic presence in the entire Mekong Basin region where China has been an important strategic development partner. The MGC's policy organ is a foreign ministers' meeting that piggybacks on the annual ASEAN Ministerial Meeting (AMM) when the AMM host is an MGC member. Emphasis has been given to improving transportation links in an east–west highway corridor.

Indian Ocean Rim Association for Regional Cooperation (IOR-ARC)

Since March 1997, The Indian Ocean Rim Association for Regional Cooperation (IOR-ARC) links twenty Indian Ocean littoral states in Southeast Asia, South Asia, the Middle East, and Africa. In addition to ASEAN members Indonesia, Malaysia, Singapore, and Thailand, the IOR-ARC membership includes Australia, Bangladesh, Comoros, India, Iran, Kenya, Madagascar, Mauritius, Mozambique, Oman, the Seychelles, South Africa, Sri Lanka, Tanzania, the United Arab Emirates, and Yemen. The IOR-ARC dialogue partners are China, France, Egypt, Great Britain, Japan, and the United States. The secretariat is located in Mauritius.[41] The purpose of the IOR-ARC is to promote trade and investment among members. Policy guidance is given by the IOR Council [Foreign] Ministers who meet annually in an IOR country and on the margins of the UN General Assembly. It is an open forum which by charter avoids bilateral issues. Three working groups have been established: a working group on trade and investment, a business forum group, and an academic group.

Southwest Pacific Dialogue

At Indonesian initiative, a formal Southwest Pacific Dialogue was established in 2002 at the foreign minister level between Australia, Indonesia, New Zealand, Papua New Guinea, the Philippines, and Timor-Leste. It has been institutionalized on the margin of the annual ASEAN Ministerial Meeting. This allows PNG and Timor-Leste, which are not ASEAN dialogue partners, to have a structured format for exchange of views with ASEAN member countries that share common regional concerns with them.

Coral Triangle Initiative (CTI)

The CTI is a six-nation partnership, launched in 2007, between the governments of Indonesia, Malaysia, PNG, the Philippines, the Solomon Islands, and Timor-Leste. Its objective is the safeguarding of the region's marine environment and resources. Brunei became a CTI observer in 2014. Its regional secretariat is located in Manado, Indonesia.

Forum for East Asia and Latin America Cooperation (FEALAC)

Since1999, through FEALAC, sixteen Asian countries (the ASEAN + 3 and Australia, New Zealand, and Mongolia) have had a tenuous consultative link with twenty Latin American countries.[42] Because of distance and relative lack of interdependencies, little has been accomplished in practical terms through multilateral programs.[43] It has, however, facilitated bilateral ties for ASEAN countries to Mexico and Brazil, prospective dialogue partners once the dialogue moratorium is lifted. Also, as noted in chapter 8, Chile, Costa Rica, Mexico, and Peru have FTAs with ASEAN states. For China, FEALAC provides another opportunity to extend its influence.

NOTES

1. Accessed through the AMM link at http://www.asean.org.
2. Moe Thuzar, "Myanmar's 2014 ASEAN Chairmanship: A Litmus Test of Progress?" NBR Commentary, December 2013, accessed at http://www.nbr.org/research/activity.aspx?id=377.
3. ASEAN foreign ministers' press statement after specially convened Kuala Lumpur meeting, 10 July 1997, as reported in the *Straits Times* (Singapore), 11 July 1997.
4. For details of the IAI, see David Carpenter, Rokiah Alava, and Isyan Zulkifli, "Regional Development Cooperation and Narrowing the Development Gap," in *Narrowing the Development Gap in ASEAN: Drivers and Policy Options*, ed. Mark McGillivray and David Carpenter (New York: Routledge, 2013), 163–69.

5. Narcisco G. Reyes, "The ASEAN Summit Syndrome," *Foreign Relations Journal* (Manila) 1, no. 2 (June 1986): 73.

6. The Bali Concord I can be accessed at http://www.asean.org/news/items/declaration-of-asean-concord-indonesia-24-february-1976.

7. A retired army general, Hartono Dharsono was removed as secretary general of the ASEAN Secretariat for supporting Indonesian students who opposed a third term for President Suharto.

8. The Singapore Declaration can be accessed at http://www.asean.org/news/item/the-fourth-asean-summit.

9. In the official enumeration of ASEAN summits, the May 2014 summit in Nay Pyi Taw was the twenty-fourth, but this does not include the 1996, 1997, 1999, and 2000 informal summits, which would bring the total summitry to twenty-eight.

10. The figures are as cited by Giovanni Campannelli of the Asian Development Bank Institute in "ASEAN Principles Need Efficiency Updates," *East Asia Forum*, 5 November 2013, accessed at http://www.eastasiaforum.org/2013/11/05/asean -principles-need-efficiency-updates.

11. ASEAN Vision 2020 can be accessed at http://www.asean.org/news/item/asean-vision-2020.

12. Hanoi Plan of Action, accessed at http://www.asean.org/news/item/hanoi -plan-of-action.

13. Declaration of ASEAN Concord II (Bali Concord II), accessed at http://www .asean.org/news/item/declaration-of-asean-concord-ii-bali-concord-ii.

14. Cebu Declaration on the Acceleration of the Establishment of an ASEAN Community by 2015, accessed at http://www.asean.org/news/item/cebu-declaration-on-the-establishment-of-an-asean-community-by-2015.

15. The VAP can be accessed in the *ASEAN Document Series 2004*, item 9 under Summit at http://www.asean.org.archive/ADS-2004.pdf.

16. The AEC blueprint can be accessed at http://www.asean.org/archive/5187-10 .pdf; the ASCC at http://www.asean.org/archive/5187-19.pdf; and the APSC at http:// www.asean.org/archive/5187-18.pdf.

17. "Keynote Address" by H. E. Hassan Wirajuda, minister of foreign affairs, Republic of Indonesia at the Fourth ASEAN–UN Conference on Conflict Prevention, Conflict Resolution and Peace Building in Southeast Asia, 23–25 February 2004.

18. Barry Wain, "Jakarta Jilted," *Far Eastern Economic Review*, 10 June 2004, 20.

19. The text of the Declaration on the Establishment of an ASEAN Charter can be accessed at http://www.asean.org/news/item/kuala-lumpur-declaration-on-the -establishment-of-the-asean-charter-kuala-lumpur-12-december-2005.

20. The ASEAN Charter can be accessed at http://www.asean.org/archive/publica tions/ASEAN-Charter.pdf.

21. "Dr. Surin Sums Up ASEAN Challenge in His Valedictory Briefing," accessed at http://www.aseanec.blogspot/2012/11/dr-surin-sums-up-asean-challenge-in.html.

22. Thitinan Pongsudhirak, "ASEAN's Bang Ends in a Whimper," *Bangkok Post*, 28 November 2007.

23. Rummana Zaheer, "Why Pakistan Is Interested to Join Asean," *IOSR Journal of Humanities and Social Science* 10, no. 4 (May–June 2013): 7.

24. The Joint Statement on East Asia Cooperation, accessed at http://www.mofa.go.jp/region/asia-paci/asean/pmv9911/joint.html.

25. Accessed at http://www.asean.org/images/2013/external_relations/eas%20declaration%20of%20principles%2019%november%202020aa.pdf.

26. Donald E. Weatherbee, "Southeast Asia and ASEAN: Running in Place," in *Southeast Asian Affairs 2012*, ed. Daljit Singh and Pushpa Thambipillai (Singapore: Institute for Southeast Asian Studies, 2012), 9.

27. Artyom Lukin, "Putin Skips East Asia Summit (Again)," *East Asia Forum*, 22 October 2013, accessed at http://www.eastasiaforum.org/2013/10/22/putin-skips-the-east-asia-summit-again.

28. Shada Islam, "Not Yet a 'Pivot'—But EU–Asia Relations Get More Active and Intense," *Friends of Europe*, 30 October 2013, accessed at http://www.friendsofeurope.org/Contentnavigation/Publications/Libraryoverview/tabid/1186/articleType/ArticleView/articleId/3587/Not-yet-a-pivot-but-EUAsia-relations-get-more-active-and-intense.aspx.

29. The EU–ASEAN home page is http://eeas.europa.eu/asean/index/_en.htm.

30. The ASEM home page is http://www.eeas.europa.eu/asem/index_en.htm.

31. Myo Thant, Min Tang, and Hiroshi Kakazu, eds., *Growth Triangles in Asia: A New Approach to Regional Economic Cooperation* (Manila: ADB Publishing, 1994).

32. ADB, *Regional and Subregional Program Links* (Manila: ADB Publishing, 2013).

33. ADB, *Indonesia–Malaysia–Thailand Growth Triangle: Theory and Practice* (Manila: ADB Publishing, 1996).

34. C. P. F. Luhulima, "A Strategic Overview of BIMP-EAGA," *Indonesian Quarterly* 24, no. 1 (January–March 1996): 65.

35. ADB, *Cooperation in the Greater Mekong Subregion* (Manila: ADB Publishing, 1996).

36. The Mekong–Japan Partnership is outlined at http://www.mofa.go.jp/region/asia-paci/mekong/goal.pdf.

37. Bagan Declaration, 12 November 2003, accessed at http://www.mofa.gov.mm/declarations/bagan_press_statement.html.

38. The ACD home page is http://www.acddialogue.com/index.php.

39. The BIMSTEC home page is http://www.bimstec.org.

40. DNA Edit (India), "Failure to Launch," accessed at http://www.bilaterals.org?failure-to-launch.

41. The IOR-ARC home page is http://www.iorarc.org.

42. FEALAC's "cyber secretariat" can be accessed at http://www.fealac.org.

43. Kavi Chongkittavorn, "East Asia and Latin America—A Bridge Too Far and Too Few," *Nation* (Bangkok), 17 June 2013.

SUGGESTIONS FOR FURTHER READING

A historical overview of the Southeast Asian region is Nicholas Tarling, *Regionalism in Southeast Asia: To Foster the Political Will* (New York: Routledge, 2006). For the motivations and challenges that have shaped ASEAN regionalism, see Christopher B. Roberts, *ASEAN Regionalism, Cooperation, Values, and Institutionalization* (London: Routledge, 2012). A positive and comprehensive discussion of ASEAN is Rodolfo C. Severino, *Southeast Asia in Search of an ASEAN Community* (Singapore: Institute of Southeast Asia Studies, 2006). A critical look at the ASEAN way is David Martin Jones and M. L. R. Smith, *ASEAN and East Asian International Relations: Regional Delusion* (Cheltenham, UK: Edward Elgar, 2006). Shaun Narine, *Explaining ASEAN: Regionalism in Southeast Asia* (Boulder, CO: Lynne Rienner, 2002) is another good survey of ASEAN's development. Sharon Siddique and Sree Kumar, eds., *The 2nd ASEAN Reader* (Singapore: Institute of Southeast Asian Studies, 2003) is a major compendium of articles on all aspects of ASEAN's regionalism. *ASEAN at 40: Progress, Prospects and Challenges* is a special issue of *Contemporary Southeast Asia* 29, no. 3 (December 2007). For the background to the ASEAN Charter, see Tommy Koh, Rosario G. Manalo, and Walter Woon, eds., *The Making of the ASEAN Charter* (Singapore: World Scientific Publishing Company, 2009). For a constructivist view, see Alice Ba, *(Re)Negotiating East and Southeast Asia: Region, Regionalism, and the Association of Southeast Asia Nations* (Stanford, CA: Stanford University Press, 2009).

Chapter Five

Conflict and Conflict Resolution in Southeast Asia

The patterns of conflict in Southeast Asia that have threatened regional order and stability are complex and can be examined at three levels. The first level is one in which great-power interests play out in the regional conflict zone. This is the case in the South China Sea disputes where Chinese and American interests are linked to the regional states' overlapping claims to sovereignty and jurisdiction. The escalating South China Sea tensions testing ASEAN's coherence and solidarity will be treated separately in chapter 6. At the intra-ASEAN level, there are numerous territorial and maritime jurisdictional disputes at various stages of dormancy, settlement, or contention. In these cases historical cultural and ethnic antagonisms can leave their impress, particularly as they take on new meanings in contemporary nationalism. Although member states' interests in the integrity of ASEAN may buffer the intensity of national interest competition at the intra-ASEAN level of conflict, it has not eliminated it. At the state level, the struggle for self-determination or even independence by ethnic and religious minorities can spill over into the regional international relations arena.

In the international system, there are a variety of mechanisms for managing conflicting interests: diplomacy, mediation, arbitration, adjudication, and the coercive threat or use of force. Added to this, Southeast Asian states have developed in the "ASEAN way" what they view as a unique approach to conflict management which seeks to apply norms prescribing the nonuse of force through conflict-avoidance structures rather than conflict-resolution mechanisms.

THE ASEAN WAY OF CONFLICT AVOIDANCE

The application of the ASEAN way has two strategic goals. The first is to not allow bilateral disputes between ASEAN states to disrupt wider regional stability and the functioning of ASEAN itself. The second is to not let bilateral issues between ASEAN states and non-ASEAN states negatively affect intra-ASEAN relations. The basic assumption is that the ASEAN states share a common interest in a peaceful, harmonious, and stable regional international order in which they interact with each other from a platform of shared acceptance of common behavioral norms. It has been argued from regime theory that the pattern of conflict avoidance and management present in ASEAN are those of a "security community," that is, "a group of states that have developed a long-term habit of peaceful interaction and have ruled out the use of force in settling disputes among other members of the group."[1] A security community is a *condition* of predictable peaceful relations among a defined group of states in which there is no expectation of the threat or use of force. It is the absence of force in interstate relations that proves the condition exists, creating an international environment in which economic and social development can be promoted.

In a constructivist mode of analysis, the condition of an ASEAN security community is achieved through the socialization of its leaders to a norms-based regional collective identity that is socially constructed through the interactions of the ASEAN political elites. Peace and amity follow since everyone is on the same page of rules as set out by the ASEAN Charter and other normative statements. In this analytic setting, the ASEAN identity seems to be a kind of invisible hand, the policy reality of which cannot be verified. There is no question but that Southeast Asian states' interests in maintaining the cooperative framework of ASEAN have resulted in a regional security environment in which a pattern of broadly generalized and defined common national interests has converged to reduce substantially—but not eliminate—the possibility of armed conflict among them. This outcome, however, is perhaps better explained in an analysis that is centered on the workings of national interest in shaping policy choices rather than hypotheses about an ASEAN identity that seem divorced from national interests and the national institutions that project them as policy.[2]

An analytical framework that more realistically characterizes ASEAN's security aspects is that of "cooperative security," meaning an association for political and security cooperation that concentrates on conflict avoidance and management.[3] With a focus on shared security interests, regional peace and stability are promoted through a political process that emphasizes dialogue, consultation, flexibility, and trust in dealing with competitive interests, as opposed to a notional abstract identity and the valuation of norms. As a practical matter, it is difficult to distinguish the devices and mechanisms of the ASEAN way as manifested in cooperative security from the tools of traditional diplomacy.

It is clear that the ASEAN way does not provide a problem-solving framework. It is a conflict-avoidance mechanism through which each member state's presumed national interests in a stable regional security environment have priority in its national leader's ends-means, risks-rewards calculations governing policy choices. Such calculations have to be made at two political levels: the ASEAN regional and the domestic. The policy maker's problem is to gain rewards at one level and minimize risks at the other, or in a best case, to be rewarded at both levels.[4] The most difficult and politically sensitive of these kinds of calculations are in cases in which competing interests and the possibility of conflict are rooted in the traditional concerns of national security managers: defending against threats to sovereignty, territorial integrity, and the political system—often defined in terms of perpetuation of the ruling elites. The most direct threat is one that seeks to deny sovereignty, contest territory, or overturn authority. In decision making in these contexts, ethnonationalism at the domestic level is likely to be a more potent ideational force then any purported ASEAN identity.

ASEAN's security managers have not neglected acquisition of the traditional tools to defend national interests by force if necessary in cases where the ASEAN way breaks down. The rate of defense spending in ASEAN is one of the fastest growing in the world. By 2016, the defense spending is expected to be $40 billion.[5] Singapore leads the way with a 2013 defense budget of $12.3 billion, an 8 percent increase over the previous year. It has the largest defense budget in ASEAN with a per capita cost exceeding even Israel's. Indonesia is second only to Singapore in regional defense spending. The two account for more than half of ASEAN's total defense spending. In a building program to achieve what it calls a minimum essential force by 2024, Indonesia's 2013 defense budget was $8.1 billion, projected to rise to $12.3 billion in 2014. This is more than double what it was in 2011. The explicit Indonesian strategic goal is to become the strongest military force in Southeast Asia.[6] Malaysia, Thailand, the Philippines, and Vietnam have also ramped up defense spending. Even poor Cambodia, with its eye on Thailand, has given priority to acquiring tanks and armored vehicles from Europe and China.

The attention currently given to maritime defense system upgrades may be explained in terms of heightened tensions in the South China Sea. However, the ongoing upgrades of conventional land and air warfare capabilities reflect in part the stubborn persistence of regional bilateral security tensions.[7] There are also national felt needs to maintain relative parity with other ASEAN states. As the director general of the International Institute of Strategic Studies (IISS) once commented, "Southeast Asia's military establishments are evidently watching their neighbors' defense programs closely, and in some cases reacting to them."[8] While the national defense programs of ASEAN member states are independent of ASEAN and ASEAN consensual decision making, they do have regional political consequences. The respected Stockholm International Peace Research Institute (SIPRI) concluded that "the current wave of South East Asia [weapons] acquisitions could destabilize the region, jeopardizing decades of peace."[9] The prospect of future enhanced Indonesian military capabilities, especially if linked to stronger nationalist leaders, might give pause in cases where soft power is not thought to be enough to achieve Indonesia's foreign policy ends. This may have been in the mind of the Indonesian minister of defense in his remarks to the 2013 IISS Shangri-La–Asian security dialogue. "We should be mindful," he warned, "that there are inherent sensitivities in military build-ups that could create miscalculations, misperceptions, and misjudgments."[10] In order to avoid a destabilizing arms race, he called for "strategic transparency." Closer military-to-military ties among some of the ASEAN states to China and the United States have the potential to escalate existing sensitivities in the Southeast Asian security complex and present the risk of emergent security dilemmas for Southeast Asia.

The Norms and Modes of the ASEAN Way

The normative frameworks providing the referents for the ASEAN way are both universal and regional. ASEAN documents are replete with invocations of the Charter of the United Nations, international law, the Bandung Principles (box 3.1), and what was inherent in the original 1967 ASEAN Declaration.

Treaty of Amity and Cooperation in Southeast Asia (TAC)

The ASEAN way is often treated as a socialized informal process of consultation and consensus. The TAC provided in theory a more formal setting. It purports to regulate the behavior of signatory states in the peaceful settlement of disputes among them.[11] It was a product of ASEAN's first summit in 1976. The TAC is the regional international legal framework within which the normative rules expressed in the ASEAN way have been institutionalized in theoretically binding treaty obligations.

The political background was to encourage Vietnam to associate peacefully with the ASEAN states. When ASEAN membership expanded after the Third Indochina War, accession to the TAC became a requirement of mem-

Box 5.1.   Principles of the TAC (Article 2)

- Mutual respect for independence, sovereignty, equality, territorial integrity, and national identity.
- The right of every state to lead its national existence free from external interference, subversion, or coercion.
- Noninterference in the internal affairs of one another.
- Renunciation of the threat or use of force.
- Effective cooperation among themselves.

bership. A 1998 amending protocol opened the TAC to accession by states outside of Southeast Asia. Papua New Guinea—looking across its Indonesian border—was the first non–Southeast Asian state to accede. Since then all of ASEAN's dialogue partners as well as other countries with regional interests have signed on. In 2003, China became the first ASEAN dialogue partner to accede. With Norway's 2013 accession, the number of TAC signatories reached twenty-eight. This included the EU after another amending protocol to the TAC allowed state-based regional organizations to sign on. Despite

Table 5.1.   Signatories of the TAC as of 2013

The ASEAN 10
Australia
Bangladesh
Canada
China
EU
France
India
Japan
Mongolia
New Zealand
Norway
Pakistan
Papua New Guinea
Russia
Sri Lanka
Timor-Leste
United Kingdom
United States

ASEAN urging, the United States, although claiming to respect the TAC's spirit and principles, held back from signing, anxious to maintain a posture of strategic independence. The rising Chinese profile in ASEAN frameworks and ASEAN concerns about the credibility of America's political commitment to regional security gave greater urgency to the symbolic value of American accession, particularly since it was a necessary condition for participation in the East Asia Summit (EAS) (chapter 4). The United States finally acceded to the TAC in 2010.

The TAC broke new ground by providing an ASEAN mechanism for the pacific settlement of disputes. Articles 14 and 15 call for the establishment of a High Council consisting of ASEAN ministerial-level representatives. Its brief is to take cognizance of disputes or situations likely to disturb peace and regional harmony and to recommend appropriate means of settlement. It was not until 2001 that the foreign ministers laid out the rules of procedure for the High Council.[12] According to Article 18, the settlement provisions of the High Council would apply only if all parties to the dispute agree to their application. Moreover, the High Council's decision making is stipulated to be consensual. The relationship of the non-ASEAN states that have acceded to the TAC to the dispute-resolution mechanism of the High Council was addressed in the first amending protocol. TAC Article 14 was amended to apply to acceding non-ASEAN states "in cases where the State is directly involved in the dispute to be settled through the regional process."[13] Despite the many disputes and situations disturbing regional peace and harmony since then, there has been no cognizance taken of any ASEAN dispute.

The ASEAN Charter

Even though the High Council is by institutional design an ineffectual dispute-resolution mechanism, it continues to be valued as an important, if unused, element in ASEAN's conflict management system. The components of the APSC as announced in the 2003 Bali Concord II (chapter 4) stated that the High Council of the TAC shall be an important component in the APSC "since it reflects ASEAN's commitment to resolve all differences, disputes, and conflicts peacefully."[14] The ASEAN Charter, although not mentioning the High Council, states that disputes not concerning the interpretation or application of any ASEAN instruments shall be resolved in accordance with the TAC and its rules of procedure (Article 24:2). This would include the High Council. The "blueprint" for the APSC is deliberately ambiguous. It praises the TAC provisions for pacific settlement of disputes through friendly negotiations and refraining from the threat or use of force. It also calls for strengthening existing modes of pacific settlement as well as considering new mechanisms.[15]

It seems clear from the history of threats and use of force by Southeast Asian states that they have not abandoned force as an ultimate tool for pursuing national interests despite their claimed adherence to ASEAN's and the TAC's principles. From the outset, ASEAN's search for mechanisms such as the High Council to resolve intra-ASEAN disputes and conflict was doomed to failure. In 1999, Thailand's prime minister Chuan Leekpai, taking his cue from ASEAN's role in the 1997 Cambodian coup (chapter 4), persuaded his colleagues at the 1999 ASEAN Informal Summit he chaired to establish the ASEAN Troika as an ad hoc ministerial body. The troika scheme was fleshed out in a "concept paper" adopted by the foreign ministers at the July 2000 AMM, chaired by host Thai foreign minister Surin Pitsuwan.[16] It would consist of past, present, and incoming chairs of ASEAN. It could be called into existence by ministerial consensus in the event that a situation of common concern arose likely to disturb regional peace and harmony. It would be specifically barred from addressing issues that constituted the internal affairs of ASEAN member countries, and it would act in accordance with ASEAN core principles of consensus and noninterference. Concerned that ASEAN's external relations were being seriously damaged by the Myanmar junta, in September 2000 Surin sought to activate the troika to discuss the situation in Myanmar. Vietnam, chairing ASEAN, refused to act, calling the problem a Myanmar internal affair.

Like the High Council, the ASEAN Troika was stillborn. The barrier to collective dispute resolution in ASEAN is its core principles of sovereignty, noninterference, and consensus. Even if this could be overcome, there would remain the issue of a compliance mechanism. The ASEAN Charter does provide recourse to extra-ASEAN agencies for dispute resolution. Article 28 of the ASEAN Charter states that members have the right to bring their disputes to the United Nations or to any other international legal structure to which the disputing members are parties. Although, as will be pointed out, this has happened, recourse to an external agency is viewed as an admission of the failure of ASEAN and a diminishing of its autonomous international image.

ASEAN leaders realize that events in one ASEAN country or between ASEAN countries can have serious negative effects on other ASEAN countries or the viability of the association. The preferred approach of the ASEAN way in cases of serious dispute or state behavior violating ASEAN norms is quiet informal diplomacy through which no party wins or loses but accepts outcomes that will not rupture regional harmony and stability. This can take the form of informal bilateral summits to address issues that have not been compromised at lower bureaucratic working levels. This requires both mutual respect and trust, which are not always present. Indonesia's president Suharto had the political gravitas to intervene as a conciliating third party in the so-called *empat mata* ("four eyes") format. There is no ASEAN leader today who possesses this kind of intangible authority. In the ASEAN way, constructive engagement is encouraged, but the threat of sanctions, however, is not in the ASEAN diplomatic vocabulary.

MULTILATERALISM AND ASEAN SECURITY POLICY

Leaders in Southeast Asia are well aware of the fact that their local security interests cannot be isolated from the wider complex of security concerns and conflicts in the Asia-Pacific region. In that arena, ASEAN's principal dialogue partners interact outside of any ASEAN framework in competitive interests and potential conflict situations that might affect or even spill over to disturb Southeast Asia's peace and security. At the state-to-state bilateral diplomatic level, there are regular informal political exchanges about shared concerns with interested state parties. In addition, the ASEAN states have engaged their external partners in the ASEAN way of conflict avoidance, with its strengths—multilateral consultation and declaratory acceptance of norms of behavior—and limitations of consensus and noninterference. The principal institutional frameworks for this are the ASEAN Regional Forum and the ASEAN Defense Ministers' Meeting–Plus.

ASEAN Regional Forum (ARF)

From its initiation in 1994, the ARF meets once a year as an adjunct to the AMM. At the twentieth ARF in 2013 there were twenty-seven states and the EU. In addition to the ASEAN 10, the members are ASEAN's ten dialogue partners and Bangladesh, Papua New Guinea, Mongolia, North Korea, Pakistan, Sri Lanka, and Timor-Leste. The purpose of the ARF is to foster dialogue on issues of regional peace and security in order to promote confidence building and transparency. ARF claims the role of being the primary venue for dialogue and cooperation on security issues in the Asia-Pacific region. The ARF is chaired by the host foreign minister of the AMM. Its official record is the Chairman's Statement, a consensual document released at the conclusion of the meeting. It is bureaucratically supported by the ARF Unit in the ASEAN Secretariat.[17]

The ARF developed from the 1992 Singapore ASEAN Summit's call for an intensified PMC on political and security matters. The first enhanced PMC took place after the 1993 AMM. That meeting agreed to constitute the ARF as a separate consultative framework, but maintaining a contextual ASEAN identity. The 1994 "Concept Paper" for the ARF assigned a "pivotal role" to ASEAN, which had undertaken the "obligation to be the primary driving force of ARF."[18] The ARF "concept" envisioned that its cooperative activities would be built in a three-stage process: (1) the promotion of confidence building, (2) the development of preventive diplomacy, and (3) the elaboration of approaches to conflict. After two decades, the ARF has not moved beyond the first stage. With ASEAN in charge and the ASEAN way, it was assured that the ARF moves forward "at a pace comfortable to all," with decision making by consensus. ASEAN's control of the agenda and the Chairman's Statement has meant that in terms of addressing conflict and security issues, ARF has not moved beyond a "talk shop" from which no country goes away angry or embarrassed.

The ARF's institutional concentration has been on the first stage. It has meetings of an Inter-Sessional Support Group (ISG) on Confidence Building Measures and Preventive Diplomacy. Realistically, however, no progress toward preventive diplomacy can be achieved as long as the ASEAN way frames the rules. In an effort to give the ARF a more proactive role in preventive diplomacy, the 2007 ARF adopted terms of reference for an institution known as the ARF "Friends of the Chair" (FOC). The FOC was designed as a quick-reaction group to be activated on an ad hoc basis by the ARF chairman in times of emergency or threats to regional peace and security. The Friends of the Chair were the past chair, the current chair, the incoming chair, and a foreign minister of a non-ASEAN country. At China's insistence, the ARF chair had to inform the ARF member countries in advance of his convening of the FOC. Like its model, the ASEAN Troika, the FOC has not been utilized.

In addition to the ISG, there are four Inter-Sessional Meetings (ISMs): the ISM on Counter-Terrorism and Transnational Crime, the ISM on Disaster Relief, the ISM on Marine Security, and the ISM on Non-proliferation and Disarmament. The ISMs have programmatic emphases. The ISG and ISMs meet biannually, alternating between the ASEAN and non-ASEAN cochair countries. There are also numerous seminars and workshops throughout the intersessional year. An innovative aspect of the ARF is the organization of its Track II component. This consists of a network of national security–oriented institutions in the Asia-Pacific region linked together in the Council for Security Cooperation in the Asia-Pacific (CSCAP).[19] CSCAP, established in 1993, predating ARF itself, provides a platform for a continuing structured expert dialogue free from the official constraints of politics and diplomacy.

ASEAN Defense Ministers' Meeting–Plus (ADMM-Plus)

In 2010, a new multilateral ASEAN-centered forum was launched for regional security-related dialogue and confidence building as an adjunct to the annual ASEAN Defense Ministers' Meeting (ADMM) that debuted in 2006.[20] In the new ADMM-Plus, the ASEAN ministers now are joined by their counterparts from Australia, China, India, Japan, South Korea, New Zealand, Russia, and the United States, thus duplicating the membership of the East Asia Summit (chapter 4). The second ADMM-Plus was in 2013, at which time the decision was made to change from a triennial meeting to biennial, with the next ADMM-Plus scheduled for 2015. In addition to the ADMM-Plus, there have been less formal ADMM + 1 meetings with China and the United States. While showing ASEAN's evenhandedness in dealing with China and the United States, these "plus 1" formats have led to pressure on the ADMM to extend the same "plus" access to its other dialogue partners, particularly Japan.[21]

The ADMM-Plus framework extends ASEAN's multilateral security diplomacy of the foreign ministers' ARF to the defense diplomacy of its defense ministers. The goal is the same: building trust and confidence through the promotion of security dialogue and cooperation among the stakeholders in regional peace and stability. Like the ARF's ISMs, the ADMM-Plus process has six functional expert working groups (EWGs): humanitarian assistance and disaster relief, maritime security, military medicine, counterterrorism, peacekeeping, and humanitarian mine action. Again like the ISMs, the EWGs have cochairs from an ASEAN and a "plus" country. It is obvious that the program activities of the ARF and ADMM-Plus overlap. Even though both are lodged in the APSC community structure, there is no coordination between them. The ASEAN Charter assigns to the foreign ministers the task of recommending to the leaders the strategic directions of ASEAN's international relations as well as assuring consistency and coherence in the conduct of relations (Article 41:6–7). The emergence of the defense ministers' defense diplomacy suggests that as the defense ministers' "plus" activity is institutionalized, the prospect of bureaucratic rivalry cannot be ruled out, as the defense ministers have independent lines to national leaderships.

The ASEAN Maritime Forum (AMF)

The AMF was established in 2010 as part of the growing network of maritime security–related fora in the Asia-Pacific region. In 2012, the AMF met in Manila with an Expanded AMF (EAMF) that was EAS inclusive. This was a response to the November 2011 Bali EAS at which the leaders encouraged "a dialogue involving EAS participating countries to utilize opportunities to address common challenges on maritime issues building on the existing ASEAN Maritime Forum."[22] The AMF is described as a Track 1.5 forum of officials at the deputy minister and departmental director general level and nonofficial experts. The AMF and EAMF meet back to back. Although not part of the ARF, the AMF's agenda overlaps the ARF's ISM–Maritime Security. The United States strongly supported the AMF's expansion, giving it another opportunity to demonstrate that it is an important regional actor.

For ASEAN, the importance of the security dialogues is that it allows the member states to voice their security interests in the wider Asia-Pacific region, not just Southeast Asia. Furthermore, the platforms confirm for ASEAN its centrality in the regional political architecture. More narrowly, in these ASEAN-centered structures China is engaged in multilateral security dialogues over a wide range of topics, testing Beijing's commitment to a "peaceful rise." US participation guarantees continuity in American involvement in the regional security environment. ASEAN's "ownership" of the processes has meant that the ASEAN way has effectively limited agendas and activities to nonsensitive and nontraditional security issues rather than the real security flash points that threaten to disturb regional peace and stability.

ASEAN's unwillingness to move the agendas toward preventive diplomacy and approaches to conflict has been what some non-ASEAN proponents of greater proactivity see as deference to China's sensibilities. Even so, Indonesia's foreign minister Marty Natalegawa proposed in 2013 to take the ASEAN way to the Asia-Pacific level of international relations through an all-inclusive "Indo-Pacific" treaty modeled on the TAC.[23] He left unstated why such a treaty would be any more effective in curbing conflict than the TAC itself. Minister Marty may have been reflecting impatience with consensus when he suggested that Indonesia should offer a preemptive mechanism for conflict prevention and resolution, adding that "we must become a country that shapes and moulds."[24]

INTRA-ASEAN CONFLICT

ASEAN's incapacity to move to a politically integrative level above sovereignty and noninterference in domestic affairs suggests that notwithstanding claims of community, international relations in the ASEAN region are not really different from relations among states in any world region—governed by calculations of national interest and relative power, particularly when historical and ethnic passions collide with contemporary interests.

Sensitive Borders

The criteria of a modern state include legally bounded territory. Borders symbolize the essence of sovereignty and are zealously defended. Imperialist-imposed land borders were laid down for economic and political benefit of the rulers. Hundreds of miles of these borders were simply lines on a map, never having been physically demarcated and having little impact on the political allegiances and economic activities of local populations. The contemporary demarcation of the international frontiers of the successor states can have serious political consequences.[25]

One of the elements provoking Vietnam's 1978 invasion of Cambodia was the Khmer Rouge's armed clashes and incursions across their French-defined border. Uprooting French border markers, the KR sought to reclaim Cambodia's sovereignty over land occupied by ethnic Khmer (Khmer Krom) in Vietnam's Mekong Delta. In 2010, Sam Rainsey, the leader of Cambodia's opposition party, pulled up stakes marking the border fixed by a Vietnam–Cambodia joint boundary commission. Rainsey, tapping ethnic Cambodian anti-Vietnamese sentiments, claimed that they were hundreds of yards inside the Cambodian border, accusing Prime Minister Hun Sen of selling out to Vietnam. Vietnam's leadership found itself in a similar position when it accepted in 2009 its newly demarcated land border with China. The announcement sparked violent anti-China street protests in Vietnam that accused China of forcing concessions on Vietnam.

Thailand, at the center of continental Southeast Asia, has had to manage borders with four neighbors, all of whom have territory that once belonged to Thailand before being sliced off by France and Great Britain. The poorly marked Thailand–Myanmar border is populated by transborder ethnic groups often at war with Myanmar's central government. The border environment has been characterized by insurgency, refugee flows, and narcotics trafficking (chapter 7).[26] Border management on both sides has largely been left to military and paramilitary forces in a relationship marked by tensions and corruption.

Thailand and Laos have a 456-mile (735 km) land border and a 688-mile (1,108 km) Mekong and Hueang rivers border set in the 1907 Franco–Siamese Treaty. A joint border commission was established in 1997, which had eight meetings through 2007, when its work was suspended. Work resumed in 2013 with an expectation of finalizing the land border demarcation in 2015 and the river in 2017. It is the river boundaries that have stalled the process. A river's channel is subject to avulsion, with islands appearing and disappearing. Thailand and Laos fought a three-month border war, from December 1987 to February 1988, over the Mekong River village of Ban Rom Klao. There were more than a thousand casualties. Thailand's southern border with Malaysia crosses the Kra Isthmus. Walled, fenced, and marked with twelve thousand pillars, it has been called a "model border."[27] This cannot be said of Thailand's western border with Cambodia, discussed later in the chapter.

In addition to land borders, disputes over delimiting Southeast Asia's maritime zones and competitive claims to their marine resources are sources of dispute and conflict. All of the Southeast Asian states except Laos have maritime borders. Maritime states seek to draw the most extensive baselines seaward from their utmost extreme coastal points, or in the case of an archipelago, their furthest-lying islands. The marine extension of baselines sets the geographic parameters for a state's twelve-mile territorial sea, its two-hundred-mile EEZ, and finally its continental shelf. In the case of overlaps, the United Nations Convention on the Law of the Sea (UNCLOS) established the rules for delimitation and resolution of conflict. It also created the Hamburg, Germany-based International Tribunal for the Law of the Sea (ITLOS). All of the Southeast Asian states, with the exception of Cambodia, have ratified the UNCLOS.

Of the more than sixty maritime boundaries in Southeast Asia, only a few have been fully determined.[28] Indonesia alone has maritime boundaries with ten countries, with many gaps along the borders of its EEZ. There are two categories of maritime boundary arrangements. The first is delimitation agreements in which boundaries are agreed on. The other is provisional arrangements in which no boundary is settled, but the states have agreed to some form of joint exercise of jurisdiction and resource management, in particular over hydrocarbon deposits.[29] In 2012, twenty-nine Southeast Asian delimitation agreements and eight provisional arrangements had been reached.[30] To this, we can add the 2014 demarcation of EEZs in the waters between the Philippines' Mindanao and Indonesia's Sulawesi islands after twenty years of negotiation. The majority of the achieved delimitation agreements have been continental shelf boundaries. The South China Sea boundaries, with China's expansive sovereign claims, have become a potential flash point for regional security (chapter 6).

Provisional arrangements for sharing jurisdiction and management of resources allow countries with overlapping boundaries to shelve boundary delimitation problems in favor of joint development (JD). The Timor-Leste–Australia Joint Development Area was noted in chapter 2. A regional model for joint development is the Malaysia–Thailand Joint Authority (MTJA), created in 1991, exploiting natural gas deposits in the Gulf of Thailand (chapter 6). The MTJA was the model for a Thailand–Cambodia 2001 "Provisional Arrangement" in the Gulf of Thailand for exploiting potentially rich hydrocarbon reserves beneath their 10,400-square-mile (26,000 sq km) overlapping claims area (OCA) in which they had both awarded conflicting exploration blocks. The cooperative process came to a halt after the 2003 diplomatic crisis (discussed below). An effort to revive talks on the OCA in 2011 died on the border battlefield of the Preah Vihear dispute. Brunei and Malaysia have also used the JD approach in resolving maritime overlaps (chapter 6), and it has been mooted—so far without success—for the Indonesian–Malaysian dispute in the Sulawesi Sea.

Malaysia–Singapore

If Thailand and Cambodia have the most contentious bilateral relationship in ASEAN, that between Malaysia and Singapore is second. Although geographically linked by a causeway and bridge across the Johor Strait, the cultural and political gulf between the two is enormous. The ethnic factor is fully in play, with each unsure of the loyalties of their respective Chinese and Malay minorities. Ever since separation in 1965, the leaders have viewed each other with suspicion. The long list of disputes over material interests is set in an economic rivalry in which each country views the other's development policies as "beggar your neighbor." It took years of bitter negotiation to settle all of the issues left by separation. For example, it was not until 2011 that the 1990 "Points of Agreement" on the disposition of the Malaysian railway's land in Singapore was finalized.

Singapore's dependency on water from the peninsula was a vulnerability that Malaysia used as a diplomatic weapon for years. This was made explicit at separation by Malaysia's prime minister Tunku Abdul Rahman, who stated, "If Singapore's foreign policy is prejudicial to Malaysian interests, we could always bring pressure to bear on them by threatening to turn off the water."[31] The terms and pricing of the supply of untreated water to Singapore were fixed in 1961 and 1962 agreements which were to run to 2011 and 2061 respectively. In 2002, Malaysia pushed the water question to the top of its Singapore agenda, insisting on the right of review of the price as well as raising questions about the terms of any renewal of water agreements. For Singapore, Malaysia's alleged unilateralism, throwing into doubt an assured supply of water in the future, was a matter of state survival. Singapore's answer was financial and technical investment in a domestic water industry that leads the world. When the 1961 water agreement expired in 2011, Singapore did not negotiate for renewal, having achieved 60 percent water self-sufficiency. It expects full sufficiency by the 2061 expiration of the second water agreement. The water issue cropped up again in early 2014, when Malaysia floated a possible increase in the price of raw water to Singapore. Singapore asserts that under the terms of the 1962 agreement pricing could not be reviewed. "How good is it [the legal position]?" Singapore's foreign minister asked. "It is good as long as both countries observe international law."[32]

The Pedra Branca (Batu Putih) Island Crisis

During the years that Mahathir Mohammad was Malaysia's prime minister—1981–2003—relations with Singapore were tension filled. In addition to existing issues, a dispute over sovereign ownership of the islet of Pedra Branca led to the threat of use of force. Pedra Branca (White Rock) is located where the Singapore Strait meets the South China Sea. Horsburgh lighthouse has stood on it since 1851, administered first by the British Straits Settlement and now Singapore. In 1979, Malaysia, after years of silence, suddenly claimed what it called Pulau Batu Putih (White Rock Island) as part of Malaysia's Johor State. By 2002, Malaysia's aggressive pressing of its sovereignty claim over Pedra Branca had become a strident nationalist campaign for its surrender by Singapore. Singapore's insistence on maintaining the status quo was denounced by Malaysian defense minister Najib as a "belligerent betrayal of the ASEAN way."[33] This was ironic, since the threat of force was coming from Kuala Lumpur. Malaysian naval patrols faced off with the Singapore Maritime Police. There was real danger of an armed clash that could have disastrous political spillover. Responding to a remark by Malaysia's foreign minister that Singapore had two choices, compromise or go to war, Singapore's foreign minister responded, "Loose talk of war is irresponsible and dangerous. It whips up emotion that could become difficult to control."[34] The escalation of the crisis by Malaysia and its linkage to other issues like water added to Singapore's sense of crisis. The two nations seemed caught in a classic security dilemma, where war can occur between two parties when neither desires such an outcome. At its core is each actor's uncertainty about the intentions of the other. Even though the ASEAN way was at stake, ASEAN was silent.

Singapore urged that the issue of sovereignty be submitted to the International Court of Justice (ICJ). It was not until 2003, and the leadership transition from Mahathir to Abdullah Badawi, that an agreement was reached to refer the dispute to the ICJ. Why would Malaysia finally go to the ICJ? Coming off its ICJ victory in its sovereignty dispute with Indonesia over the islands of Ligitan and Sipidan, discussed below, Kuala Lumpur might have felt emboldened. Also, the government may have felt boxed in by the precedent it had set by accepting ICJ jurisdiction in that case. The ICJ judgment was handed down in 2008, awarding sovereignty to Singapore.[35]

Singapore's Land Reclamation

Even as the Pedra Branca case was being referred to the ICJ, Singapore and Malaysia were arguing another case in the ITLOS over Singapore's land reclamation project in the Johor Strait. Of Singapore's 276-square-mile (714 sq km) land area, 18 percent is reclaimed, with another 7 percent enlargement projected by 2030. The sand needed for land reclamation came first from dredging within its limited territorial waters, followed by imports. Singapore's need for sand made it the largest sand importer in the world, depleting beaches and coastal islands in Vietnam, Cambodia, Malaysia, and Indonesia. In response to nationalist and environmental concerns, exporting countries tightened supplies or even banned sand exports. This led to expanded illegal dredging, often abetted by corrupt local officials. The issue, known as the "Sand War," was added to the litany of complaints in the Malaysian and Indonesian diplomatic discourse with Singapore.

The most controversial reclamation project was in Singapore's territorial waters bordering Malaysia's Johor coast. Malaysia vigorously protested, claiming environmental damage and hazards to navigation. Singapore, on the other hand, viewed the issue as one more Malaysian effort to curtail Singapore's development. In September 2003, Malaysia submitted its case to ITLOS, requesting a provisional suspension of all Singapore land reclamation activities in the area. In October 2003, while not ordering Singapore to cease its work, ITLOS called for the two states to establish a group of independent experts to monitor the project and cautioned Singapore "not to conduct its land reclamation in ways that might cause irreparable prejudice to the rights of Malaysia."[36] The experts group reported in December 2004 in such a way that both sides could claim victory. On the basis of the report, Singapore and Malaysia reached a 2005 settlement allowing the reclamation projects to go forward with Singapore cooperating with Malaysia to limit any adverse impacts. Ambassador Tommy Koh, who was Singapore's agent in the ITLOS proceedings and had been president of the UN conference that produced the UNCLOS, reflecting on the outcome, wrote that "it is not certain that the land reclamation case would have been settled amicably if Dr. Mahathir were still prime minister."[37] This underscores the importance of the broader political relationship between disputants, as well as prevailing institutions and norms, for peaceful resolution. Singapore's president Tony Tan, visiting Malaysia in September 2013, cautioned that positive relations between Singapore and Malaysia could not be taken for granted.[38]

Malaysia–Indonesia

Although sharing ethnicity, culture, and religion, the contemporary relationship between Malaysia and Indonesia has been marked by suspicion and antagonisms rooted in Indonesia's 1960s undeclared war to "crush Malaysia" (chapter 3). The latent mistrust is quick to surface when perceived slights to sovereignty or nationalisms, no matter how minor, stir up patriotic emotions. For example, the use of an Indonesian folk song in a 2007 Malaysian tourism promotion was treated in Indonesia as major cultural theft. More serious has been Indonesian outrage at alleged systemic mistreatment of Indonesian domestic help by Malaysian (and Singaporean) employers (chapter 9). In the post-Mahathir years, a stronger and more cooperative working relationship has been built which has contained two major problems that in other circumstances might have led to breakdowns in the regional order.

Ligitan and Sipidan

Ligitan and Sipidan are two small islands on Borneo's northeast coast off the land border between East Malaysia's Sabah State and Indonesia's North Kalimantan Province. They came into dispute between the two nations in 1969 during continental shelf discussions. The islands' geopolitical significance is as points from which baselines can run in defining territorial waters and EEZs in the Sulawesi Sea with its oil and gas potential. The smoldering quarrel over the islands irritated Malaysian–Indonesian relations for more than three decades. Although no shots were fired, Indonesia's navy patrolled in the vicinity of the islands, and secret landings were made to demonstrate occupancy. Kuala Lumpur in turn beefed up its security forces in southeastern Sabah.

Prime Minister Mahathir and President Suharto, in an *empat mata* (four eyes) setting, agreed in 1996 to settle the dispute once and for all. It was decided to refer the matter to the International Court of Justice. The Ligitan and Sipidan dispute was the first time two ASEAN member nations had referred a bilateral dispute to an external agency for settlement. The TAC mechanism was explicitly rejected. The case went to the ICJ in November 1998, and the court handed down its decision in favor of Malaysia in December 2002.[39] The ICJ decision did not resolve the maritime boundary between Malaysia and Indonesia in the Sulawesi Sea, however. A necessary component for the successfully adjudicated outcome of the Ligitan and Sipadan dispute was strong leadership on both sides that was willing to settle the problem judicially and which had the domestic political capacity to abide by a possibly adverse decision. The ICJ's judgment was not well received by Indonesian politicians. Although the government of President Megawati had not initiated the ICJ case, it did suffer a nationalist backlash demanding that urgent steps be taken to ensure Indonesian sovereignty on the margins of its archipelago. The political lesson learned was not to seek external third-party intervention.

The Ambalat Block

Malaysia and Indonesia have been embroiled in an overlapping maritime zone dispute in the Ambalat block area of the Sulawesi Sea. It began in 2005 when Malaysia granted an exploration concession in what Indonesia claimed was its jurisdiction. Indonesia's protest to Malaysia was accompanied by a military buildup on both sides. Gunboat diplomacy became a game of naval chicken between Indonesian and Malaysian warships backed up by jet fighters. The dangers of a serious incident were illustrated by a collision between a Malaysian and an Indonesian naval vessel. With his predecessor President Megawati politically burned by the Sipidan–Ligitan ICJ decision, President Yudhoyono's political space on the issue was narrow, pressed as he was by nationalist politicians and a military that did not want to back down. In an escalation of the crisis, the Indonesian navy seized a Malaysian reef on which it built a structure it called a "lighthouse."

Rounds of talks since 2005 have ended inconclusively with neither side willing to compromise, even though both sides agree that UNCLOS should be the basis for settlement. Indonesia has ruled out international arbitration or adjudication. No attention at all has been paid to ASEAN's TAC mechanism. It took summit diplomacy between Yudhoyono and his Malaysian counterpart Prime Minister Abdullah Badawi to move the conflict away from sovereign claims to the block's economic potential. The Ambalat block is said to potentially have reserves of as much as 746 million barrels of oil and 130 billion cubic meters of natural gas.[40] In a January 2006 meeting, while admitting that there had been no breakthrough, the two heads of government for the first time publicly discussed the possibility of joint development in disputed maritime zones. Even as technical talks about a JDA go on, naval patrolling continues. The stalled talks have discouraged potential foreign concessionaires. The sticking point seems to be Indonesia's reluctance to engage in any arrangement that could be considered a diminution of sovereignty.

The Philippines' Sabah Claim

The issues over what was thought to be the dormant claim of Philippine sovereignty over Malaysia's North Borneo Sabah State burst into regional headlines again in spring 2013 when a band of heavily armed Sulu Filipinos landed in southeast Sabah to advance the traditional claims of the Sultan of Sulu. Coming shortly before Malaysian elections, Kuala Lumpur responded with an overwhelming ground and air attack against the invaders. Describing the situation as "sensitive," Indonesia's president Yudhoyono moved to reinforce Indonesia's newly created North Kalimantan Province (Kalimantan Utara), split off from East Kalimantan (Kalimantan Timur) in October 2012. Part of the rationale for the new province was to better secure Indonesia's border "to counter the threats against the nation's unity from neighboring countries."[41]

Malaysian sovereignty over Sabah has been disputed by the Philippines since the creation of the federation in 1963. The basis of the Philippine claim is an 1878 agreement between the Sultan of Sulu and the proprietors of the North Borneo Company that transferred the administration of the Sultan's North Borneo territory to the company. The Philippines insists that once the British decided to relinquish the rights originally held by the company, those rights reverted to the Philippines as sovereign successor of the Sultan of Sulu and could not be transferred to another state. By constitutional law and domestic legislation, the Philippines maintains that it had acquired "dominion and sovereignty" in North Borneo by historic right and legal title. In 1961 Philippine president Diosdado Macapagal filed the Philippines' claim but did not pursue it. President Marcos's government's scheme to insert insurgents into Sabah collapsed, and he verbally renounced the Sabah claim at the 1977 ASEAN Summit in Kuala Lumpur. However, the claim remained alive in the Philippines constitution and statutes and on maps. In 2001, the claim was again advanced in the ICJ as the basis for a Philippines attempt to intervene in the Malaysia–Indonesia dispute over Sipidan and Ligitan (discussed above). The court denied Manila's application, saying that the Philippines did not have a legal interest specific to the dispute. What is important is that the two countries did not let the issue develop into a major crisis. Although relations have been cool, both parties seem reasonably satisfied to let the issue remain in the background of their wider range of ASEAN engagements. One factor limiting Manila's options is the fact that the United States explicitly excluded Sabah from the workings of the US–Philippines defense alliance. The situation is complicated by the more than four hundred thousand Filipino Muslim immigrants in Sabah. Manila has been concerned both by the use of Sabah as a sanctuary and training ground for Muslim insurgents and by local mistreatment of Filipinos in Sabah.

The 2013 military episode put the issue on the Filipino nationalist agenda with a clamor for renewed efforts to pursue the claim. There were inflammatory reports of the brutalization of all Filipinos in Sabah by Malaysian forces lumping immigrants with the invaders. President Benigno Aquino III has sought to reassure Kuala Lumpur that his government had no part in the assault. He raised eyebrows by suggesting it was part of a conspiracy by his political archenemy, former president Gloria Macapagal-Arroyo, to wreck the Malaysian-brokered peace process in the southern Philippines (discussed below).[42] Aquino did not raise the issue at the April 2013 ASEAN Summit in Brunei. The Philippines preferred to view it as a bilateral problem even though it again raised serious questions about the foundations of the APSC.[43] Even as President Aquino was on a state visit to Malaysia in February 2014, a presidential spokesman found it necessary to reassure Filipino nationalists that the Sabah claim had not been abandoned. A 2008 presidential order that prohibited any government official from recognizing a "foreign state's sovereignty" over Sabah remains in force.

Thailand and Cambodia: The "Border War"

Thailand and Cambodia have a long history of animosity predating the modern states. Although both are committed to ASEAN's normative rules, they remain unreconciled to the ASEAN way. In 2003, an alleged comment by a Thai TV actress that Angkor Wat belonged to Thailand led to Cambodian mob attacks on the Thai embassy and Thai businesses. The border was sealed and diplomatic relations frozen until Cambodia apologized and made reparations. Significantly, China's vice minister for foreign affairs summoned the Thai and Cambodian ambassadors, telling them that China hoped that normal relations could be reestablished as soon as possible. China's unprecedented diplomatic intervention into a bilateral dispute within ASEAN signaled its growing political interests in mainland Southeast Asia. The unparalleled crisis contradicted ASEAN's raison d'être, raising serious—but unaddressed—questions about its underlying political and security assumptions and questioning its capability to act to meet an existential organizational challenge.

That the challenge was not met seemed proved when the long-simmering dispute over the ownership of the border area in which the ancient Khmer temple of Preah Vihear sits erupted in 2011 into a border war between Thailand and Cambodia. Cambodian prime minister Hun Sen informed UN secretary general Ban Ki-moon that "these are not armed clashes. This is war."[44] In 1962, the ICJ had awarded the temple to Cambodia, stating that "the temple of Preah Vihear is situated in territory under the sovereignty of Cambodia," and ordered the withdrawal of Thai authority from the vicinity of Cambodian territory.[45] Unsettled, however, was the extent of Cambodian territory in the temple's vicinity. Thailand claimed it meant only the ground physically under the temple. The quarrel remained dormant until 2008, when Cambodia applied to UNESCO to have Preah Vihear declared a World Heritage Site. The Thai opposition Democrat Party accused the incumbent pro-Thaksin People's Power Party (PPP) elected government of country selling by accepting the Cambodian proposal. The border problem became a major element in the domestic struggle between the parties until a constitutional coup dismissed the PPP government in December 2008 in favor of the Democrat Party led by Prime Minister Abhisit Vejjajiva. As the pro-Thaksin Red Shirts and anti-Thaksin Yellow Shirts fought in the streets, Abhisit fanned the flames of nationalism over the temple. Trapped in anti-Cambodian rhetoric, the Abhisit government militarized the area bordering Preah Vihear.

Armed clashes began in February 2011. Cambodia immediately appealed for ASEAN intervention, and the ASEAN chair, Indonesia's foreign minister Marty Natalegawa, called for a truce. An unbending Bangkok, however, insisted that the border problem was solely a bilateral question. Cambodia's prime minister Hun Sen, conscious that there would be no ASEAN consensus, appealed to the UN Security Council. Over strong Thai objections, the UNSC took up the issue. Voicing its "grave concern," the UNSC expressed support for ASEAN intervention and encouraged Thailand and Cambodia to cooperate.[46] Armed with a UN mandate, Marty called a special ASEAN foreign ministers' meeting at which Thailand and Cambodia agreed to avoid further violence and to begin bilateral negotiations. The Thai side grudgingly accepted a role for Indonesian observers—specifically not peacekeepers. A nationalist and military backlash with anti-Indonesian undertones prevented Abhisit's government from following through.

The frailty of the Indonesian-brokered truce was demonstrated when wider-scale fighting resumed in April 2008. Cambodia turned, again not to ASEAN, but to the ICJ for an interpretation of the meaning of the 1962 statement "territory under the sovereignty of Cambodia." In July 2011 the court issued an interim order establishing a "provisional demilitarized zone."[47] Unarmed Indonesian truce observers were to have access to the zone, but in the absence of Thai approval no Indonesian observers were deployed. De facto control of the border zone remained in the hands of the Thai military, who viewed the issue as a Thailand–Cambodia affair regardless of the ICJ, ASEAN, and especially Indonesia. Even so, a tenuous peace was maintained. On 11 November 2013, the ICJ issued its judgment, declaring that Cambodia "had sovereignty over the whole promontory of Preah Vihear" and requiring Thailand to withdraw all government personnel from the territory.[48] It has been left to a Thai–Cambodian Joint Border Committee to draw the new border lines, but it remains to be seen whether this can be implemented in a Thai political atmosphere of collapsing central authority followed by the 2014 military coup.

THE INTERNATIONAL DIMENSIONS OF ETHNIC CONFLICT

Chapter 1 noted the ethnic/religious map of Southeast Asia and its lack of conformity to the political map. This has led to conflict between the state and ethnic minorities caught in political frameworks that usually are controlled by the dominant ethnic group. There are also ethnic groups that have been cut off from their own people by the borders of the modern state, for example, the Khmer minority in delta Vietnam or the Malay Muslims in the southern provinces of Thailand. Conflict ensues when minorities, either encapsulated in the state or transborder, add a political sense of "nationalism" to their traditional identities and begin demanding self-determination.

Ethnic and religious conflict impacts international relations in Southeast Asia when it alters the patterns of relations between nations either bilaterally or in ASEAN's multilateral framework. Southeast Asian nations cannot ignore events that touch on their national identity, sovereignty, or territorial integrity. On the whole, Southeast Asian governments have managed ethnic conflicts well in the sense that they have not allowed them to disturb unduly the normal flow of regional relations.

Even in cases in which Muslim-majority Southeast Asian countries have concerns about the welfare of Muslim minorities elsewhere, this has not been allowed to threaten ASEAN solidarity. As a collective body, ASEAN cannot be indifferent to wider international concerns about the political and human rights issues raised in ethnic conflict, Myanmar having been the most notorious case (chapter 9). In addition to Myanmar, there are two areas of ethnic conflict that have had the potential to disrupt regional stability and the ASEAN way. These are separatist conflicts in Thailand and the Philippines. Indonesia was once on this list, but the Yudhoyono government and the Aceh separatists resolved their conflict. In the wake of that settlement the question raised is whether the Aceh conflict-resolution model can be applied to other conflicts in Southeast Asia.

Indonesia

Indonesia has confronted ethnic and religious insurgency since the foundation of the independent state. The Darul Islam revolt on Java and the Christian-based separatism of the Republic of the South Moluccas immediately challenged the republic's legitimacy and integrity. As noted in chapter 3, regionalist and ethnic rebellion in Sumatra and East Indonesia between 1957 and 1962 had clandestine support from the United States. The Suharto regime's repressive security state effectively, if ruthlessly, quenched dissidence. Its collapse saw a recrudescence of ethnic and sectarian violence. The most critical areas of Indonesia's internal security problems for the regional international order were at its provincial extremities in Aceh and Papua.[49] The goals of the Free Aceh Movement (GAM) and the Free Papua Movement (OPM) were independence from Indonesia. East Timor's independence revitalized the aspirations of these long-standing separatist movements. Jakarta had committed to use whatever force was necessary to ensure that there was not another East Timor, but intervening political forces including democratization and international attention worked to modify this policy.

Aceh

The war in Aceh that began in 1976 was only the last phase of the struggle of the Acehnese people to throw off "alien" rule, beginning with the Dutch and continuing into Indonesia's independence. The Acehnese are strongly Islamic, but religion was not the only item on the GAM (Gerakan Aceh Merdeka [Free Aceh Movement]) separatist agenda. The Acehnese resented the fact that Javanese and other migrant Indonesians enjoyed the greatest ben-

Box 5.2. Aceh's Struggle

Aceh historically was a fiercely independent sultanate situated at the northern end of the island of Sumatra. It was among the earliest territories in Southeast Asia to be Islamized and has been called the "front porch of Mecca." Acehnese ethnicity is closely bound up in its Islamic identity.

   In the Aceh wars between 1873 and 1903, the Dutch, at great human cost, forcefully extinguished Aceh's independence. After World War II, the Acehnese struggled for autonomy in the new secular Republic of Indonesia. They felt betrayed when Islamic law (Sharia) was not given constitutional legal standing. Acehnese dissidents supported the Darul Islam revolt in West Java and the later regionalist rebellions on Sumatra. In 1959, Aceh was given the status of a "special territory," but this did not quell resentment against the Javanese-dominated central government. In 1976, under the leadership of Tengku Hasan di Tiro, a claimed descendent of the last Sultan of Aceh, the Free Aceh Movement (GAM) took up arms against what it saw as a new colonialism.

efits from the exploitation of Aceh's oil reserves. In the course of the struggle between GAM's demands for self-determination and Indonesia's insistence on the integrity of the unitary republic, more than ten thousand lives were lost and the human rights of the population ignored by both sides.

   The transition to a democratic Indonesia after the collapse of the Suharto government provided the opening for moving away from a purely military strategy toward Aceh. During B. H. Habibie's presidency, laws on decentralization were passed giving Aceh and other provinces greater control over resources. The succeeding Wahid government began a peace negotiating process with GAM, facilitated by the Swiss Henri Dunant Center. In 2001, President Megawati Sukarnoputri's government granted a new "special autonomy" to Aceh that included the introduction of Sharia (Islamic) law. In December 2002, the government and GAM reached a mediated Framework Agreement for the cessation of hostilities. It was to be monitored by a Joint Security Commission that included a small group of foreign military monitors, primarily Thai and Filipino. A Japan–US–EU-led Tokyo Conference on Peace and Reconstruction in Aceh promised a special aid package for the beleaguered province. Not surprisingly, the settlement collapsed within four months. Jakarta flooded the province with thousands of troops, declared martial law, and in May 2003 began an all-out offensive to wipe out GAM once and for all.

Jakarta hoped to deflect foreign criticism by labeling GAM a terrorist organization. Indonesia worked diligently within ASEAN and with donor nations to obtain declarations of support for Indonesia's national unity. After the start of the 2003 military campaign, the ASEAN foreign ministers reaffirmed their support for Indonesia's sovereignty and territorial integrity, recognizing the Indonesian efforts—implicitly the military campaign—to restore peace and order in Aceh. International insistence on Indonesian territorial integrity recognized that the breakup of Indonesia would be regionally destabilizing. The vision of the possible international outcome was more of a Balkans case than a USSR, since in a failed Indonesia there would be no Russia-like center. A success for separatism in Indonesia would be a model for separatist movements elsewhere in the region. A weakened Indonesia would present even more fertile ground for Islamic radicalism and terrorism. Although Jakarta considered the war in Aceh to be an issue of sovereign concern, it was effectively internationalized because of Indonesia's importance to the future of the region's international order.

As the months wore on, the government's timetable for victory became longer and longer, with martial law extended into 2004. Malaysia braced for a cross-strait flow of refugees. Donor nations feared that an East Timor–like human disaster was in the offing. In November 2003, the conveners of the Tokyo conference on Aceh issued a Joint Statement on Aceh expressing concern about the extension of the military emergency in the province and its implications for the well-being of the people of Aceh.[50] Jakarta denounced what it called foreign "meddling," pointing out that the role of the Tokyo conference cochairs had ended with the breakdown of the peace talks.

At the end of 2004, GAM and the people of Aceh were faced with two human disasters. The first was the military campaign the Indonesian army was carrying out. The second was the devastation brought to Aceh by the December 2004 Indian Ocean tsunami. The only way the people and economy of Aceh were going to recover would be in a stable political environment in which economic resources could be mobilized for Aceh's recovery and rehabilitation. The newly elected Yudhoyono government began a round of negotiations with GAM, facilitated this time by the Finnish Crisis Management Initiative led by former Finnish president Martti Ahtisaari. On 15 August 2005, an MOU was signed ending the separatist war—not with independence but with self-government and greater autonomy for Aceh. The demilitarization measures of the MOU were overseen by the EU Aceh Monitoring Mission, with personnel contributions from Thailand, Malaysia, Singapore, the Philippines, and Brunei. Indonesia's parliament passed the necessary autonomy legislation in July 2006, and in December 2006 Aceh's first directly elected governor was picked—a former GAM military commander. The circumstances that led to the resolution of the Aceh conflict do not seem to fit other cases of ethnic conflict in Southeast Asia. The Indonesian government and GAM did not have a deep religious divide—unlike Thailand, the Philippines, and other Southeast Asian states with rebellious ethnic minorities. Nor is it likely that another intervening variable as dramatic as the 2004 tsunami can be expected. Another analyst has pointed to a kind of "double defeat" of the contending militaries, forcing strategies to change. From 2003, GAM was losing the armed struggle in the province, but the Indonesian military was under pressure to reduce its role in a democratic society.[51]

Papua

The former Netherlands' territory of West New Guinea became an Indonesian province in 1967 following the beginning of an Indonesian war against the Dutch. American and UN intervention led to a transfer of sovereignty to Indonesia (chapter 3). Since then, an episodic, low-intensity armed struggle has been waged by the OPM (Organisasi Papua Merdeka [Free Papua Movement]) against Indonesian rule. Although the armed strength of the OPM numbers only in the low hundreds, its existence provides a nationalist armed core for a widely shared aspiration for self-determination. An aggressive Indonesian transmigration policy has relegated the indigenous Melanesian peoples to the economic and social margins of the society. Papuan nationalists view the Indonesian and foreign exploitation of the province's resources as a pillaging of their national patrimony. Harsh and abusive civil–military relations have aggravated the tensions. For the OPM and its Papuan supporters, Indonesia has turned Papua into an internal colony.

Papuan nationalists took heart in the turmoil of the post-Suharto democratic transition. In November 1999, thousands of Papuans rallied for independence. Indonesian president Abdurrahman Wahid, while apologizing for past human rights violations, ruled out independence as an option, a position crystallized in the government of his successor, President Megawati. The 2002 special autonomy granted to Aceh also included Papua. In violation of the special autonomy, the province has been split into two provinces, Papua and West Papua. In 2013, the Indonesian parliament approved the carving out of three new provinces. The motive was to weaken Papuan nationalism and dilute the impact of greater local control over resources. The beneficiaries of autonomy are not the Papuans, but the Indonesian migrant population.

Despite the West's concerns about rights issues in Papua, Indonesia has garnered consistent support for its sovereignty and territorial integrity from the ASEAN states, ASEAN's dialogue partners, and the ARF. Indonesia has

Box 5.3.   Papua's Struggle

Dutch and German imperialists partitioned the island of New Guinea in the nineteenth century. Its population is Melanesian. After World War I, Germany's eastern half of New Guinea became a British League of Nations Mandate administered by Australia. After World War II, it was a UN Trust Territory administered by Australia until it became independent as Papua New Guinea (PNG) in 1974. Newly independent Indonesia claimed Dutch New Guinea, the western half of the island, as part of its colonial legacy. As the Dutch began a belated effort to prepare the Papuans for self-government, Indonesia, under President Sukarno, prepared to use military force to assert its sovereignty over what it called West Irian (Irian Barat). With no support from its NATO allies, the Netherlands was forced to accept an American-brokered compromise. In October 1962, the Netherlands transferred the territory to a UN administration. Eight months later, the UN transferred administrative control to Indonesia, which promised an act of self-determination for the inhabitants by 1969. In that year an undemocratic "act of free choice"—dubbed by critics as an "act of no choice," organized by the Indonesian military—took place. It was an indirect and coerced plebiscite whose participants were 1,025 selected men who opted for integration into Indonesia as a province. Melanesian activists took up armed resistance to what they consider to be exploitative Indonesian colonialism.

neutralized support for GAM from across PNG's border, and in the 2006 Lombok Pact, Australia promised not to allow Indonesian separatists to operate from Australia (chapter 2). With the exception of Vanuatu, Jakarta has been able to deny the OPM any international personality. In Vila, Vanuatu's capital, there is a West Papuan People's Representative Office which houses the secretariat of the West Papua National Coalition for Liberation (WPNCL) that was formed as the OPM's international face in 2008. Vanuatu has pressed the WPNCL's application for membership in the Melanesian Spearhead Group (Fiji, PNG, the Solomon Islands, Vanuatu, and FLNKS [Front de Libération Nationale Kanak et Socialiste]). FLNKS, the New Caledonia independence party, also supports the WPNCL's admission. In January 2014, a delegation of the MSG's foreign ministers—minus Vanuatu—visited Papua and Jakarta where they met with President Yudhoyono. In a joint statement, the MSG delegation stated its respect for Indonesian sovereignty, unity, and territorial integrity.[52] The probability that the cause of self-determination for the indigenous Papuans will be successful seems remote as the social and cultural Indonesianization through migration buttresses the state's military- and police-backed political hold.

Muslim Separatism in the Philippines

For more than four decades, the Philippines' government has faced an armed Islamic insurgency in its southern Mindanao and Sulu provinces during which more than 150,000 people have died. The Muslim cause has been the creation of an independent Moro nation (Bangsamoro). Two principal political/military organizations claim leadership of the Moros, the Moro National

---

Box 5.4. The Bangsamoro

The Muslim minority in the Philippines numbers 4.5 million, or about 5 percent of the total population. The Muslims are concentrated in the southern islands, being a majority in four provinces in southwestern Mindanao and the Sulu archipelago and a minority in western and southeastern Mindanao. The Muslim population is collectively called Moro, a Spanish label derived from "Moor." Once a term of opprobrium, today it is used proudly to distinguish not only a people but their sense of nationhood (*bangsa*). The Moros can be broadly thought of as the northern extension of the Malay Islamic culture, but this is not an ethnic definition of a community. The Bangsamoro consists of ten ethnic-linguistic groups. When pressed by external non-Muslim forces, the commonality of Islam prevails over ethnic distinctions. Historically, it was the Moro sultanates that gave a supravillage political structure to precolonial Philippines. The Spanish aggressively spread crusading Christianity southward from Luzon, not completing the pacification of Mindanao until shortly before the United States replaced Spain as sovereign. American authority was imposed in the course of a fierce struggle against the Moros, who resisted the displacement of customary law and traditional authority in a secular colonial state. After Philippines' independence, the Moros continued to resist efforts to assimilate the South to rule from Manila. Large-scale migrations of Christian Filipinos after 1950 added a religious overlay to the underlying political and economic tensions in a Manila-centric system that favored the newcomers. Marcos's martial-law regime was the last straw.

Liberation Front (MNLF) and the Moro Islamic Liberation Front (MILF). A splinter group, the Bangsamoro Islamic Freedom Fighters (BIFF), carved out of the MILF, has complicated the peace process. Although not a part of the organized Moro struggle, the radical Islamist Abu Sayyaf Group (ASG) has taken advantage of insecurity in the Philippines' South to pursue its own jihadist agenda. The ASG's links to international Islamic terrorism prompted the United States to deploy a six-hundred-man Joint Special Operations Task Force (JSOTF-P) to the Philippines in 2002 (chapter 7). The unit was deactivated in 2014.

In 1973, the MNLF, led by Nur Misuari, took up arms against the Marcos dictatorship's martial-law regime. This was just the latest episode in the centuries-long Philippine Muslims' resistance to Manila's authority. Since then, an intermittent peace process has been punctuated by renewed violence. The diplomacy of the peace process has engaged the Philippines' ASEAN partners Indonesia and Malaysia as well as Libya and the Organization of Islamic Cooperation (OIC). Within the OIC, Indonesia and Malaysia acted to ward off sanctions against the Philippines but at the same time pressed Manila for concessions to Muslim aspirations.

The baseline for peacemaking is the 1976 Tripoli Agreement that was facilitated by the OIC-blessed good offices of Libya. The agreement provided for Muslim autonomy in those provinces and cities where there was a Muslim majority.[53] Indonesia, in its role of chair of the OIC's Peace Committee for the Southern Philippines (OIC-PCSP), played an instrumental role in converting the general terms of the Tripoli agreement into a 1996 Final Peace Agreement (FPA). The Indonesia-brokered FPA, signed in Jakarta and witnessed by President Suharto, created an Autonomous Region in Muslim Mindanao (ARMM).[54] An elected ARMM government took office with MNLF leader Nur Misuari as its first governor. The MILF competitor for Moro political allegiance did not accept the ARMM's formula for autonomy and attracted many MNLF dissidents. Manila did not deliver promised generous economic and social development funds, Islamic law was not enforced, and the ARMM was not allowed its own security force. Misuari's MNLF went back into revolt in 2002. However, effective Moro leadership and military forces in the armed struggle had passed to the MILF.

A new round of peacemaking began in 2001 when Philippines president Gloria Macapagal-Arroyo enlisted Malaysia as mediator and Kuala Lumpur as a neutral venue. Filipino nationalists still question Malaysia's motives: to neutralize the Sabah claim and gain economic access to Mindanao.[55] The United States, Japan, and Australia promised diplomatic and financial support to the peace process. In August 2008, a Memorandum of Agreement on the Muslim Ancestral Domain (MOA-AD) was reached that would create a new autonomous region, the Bangsamoro Juridical Entity (BJE).[56] As the Malaysia-brokered talks with the MILF were going on, Manila kept its line to the MNLF and the Indonesia chair of the OIC-PCSP open, a tactic the MILF viewed as trying to play the Moro factions off against each other.

The hope for peace was once more shattered when the Philippines Supreme Court ruled in October 2008 that the MOA-AD was unconstitutional, spurring a new round of fighting. President Benigno Aquino III came to office in 2010 promising a just and comprehensive peace settlement. A series of exploratory talks began which, with Malaysian facilitation, became a full negotiation. In a bold move, President Aquino flew to Tokyo in August 2011 for a face-to-face meeting with the MILF chairman Al Haj Murad Ibrahim. The two leaders agreed to fast-track the negotiations, which climaxed on 15 October 2012 with the signing of the Framework Agreement on the Bangsamoro, which established the parameters for the creation of a new Bangsamoro Autonomous Political Entity.[57]

The Framework Agreement was only a first step. The hard part was negotiating the details of the political entity in four Annexes on the Transitional Arrangements and Modalities of the Framework Agreement on transitional arrangements, revenue sharing, power sharing, and normalization. The last was the most contentious since it dealt with disarming the MILF and the creation of a Bangsamoro security force. The final accord on normalization was approved in January 2014. The "Comprehensive Agreement on the Bangsamoro" (CAB) was signed in Manila's presidential palace on 26 March with Prime Minister Najib Razak of Malaysia looking on. After seventeen years of fitful negotiations, five Philippine presidents, and three Malaysian prime ministers, peace may have come. In his speech at the CAB signing, President Aquino sternly warned that he "would not let peace be snatched from my people again."[58] The CAB faces the political uncertainty of congressional and judicial scrutiny. It is hoped that it can be fully implemented by the end of Aquino's term in 2016.

Not all Moros are satisfied with an MILF-dominated political framework. Claiming that the MNLF is still the OIC-recognized representative of the Moros, Misuari and his followers insist that any peace must be negotiated on the basis of the Tripoli Agreement and the subsequent FPA. With no stake in the CAB, the MNLF will continue to be a destabilizing presence with the potential to be a spoiler. In August 2013, the MNLF's forces launched a two-front attack in Sulu and Basilan. In January 2014, a new wave of military clashes with BIFF forces began. For the diplomacy of the OIC and its Indonesian OIC-PCSP chair, the peace issue now is intra-Moro relations and how to reconcile the MILF and MNLF in a way that might link the 1996 FPA to the 2012 Framework Agreement.[59] In December 2013, the Philippines

Department of Foreign Affairs officially requested the OIC to converge the FPA with the Framework Agreement. The OIC declined an offer to witness the signing of the CAB, continuing to recognize the 1996 Tripoli FPA as legal and binding.[60]

Patani Muslim Separatism in South Thailand

In 2004, the long-simmering tinderbox of discontent of the Muslim population of South Thailand burst into flames after the killing of 117 Muslim insurgents and protesters in incidents in Narathiwat and Pattani provinces.[61] By the end of 2013, the number of violent incidents reached nearly 16,000, with 5,900 deaths and 10,593 injured.[62] The region's Buddhist minority has been terrorized as increasingly capable insurgent forces violently attack the political and social institutions implanted in the South by the Thai government. Despite the South being flooded by tens of thousands of Thai army personnel, paramilitary forces, and police as well as continuous draconian "state of emergency" decrees, the insurgents have gained the tactical initiative and a strategic advantage. The insurgents' basic goal is Thai Malay Muslim self-determination, although the framework—administrative autonomy or separatism—is at issue within the ranks of the insurgent factions.

Box 5.5. The Patani Muslims

Thailand's Muslim population is more than three million, the great majority of whom are ethnic Malays living in Thailand's Deep South. They are concentrated in the provinces of Satun, Yala, Pattani, and Narathiwat, which, with the northern peninsular states of modern Malaysia, were part of the old Patani sultanate. In the nineteenth century, the sultanate had been tributary to the king of Siam (Thailand) who, in 1902, annexed it. Advancing British imperialism in the Malay states led to a 1909 Anglo-Siamese treaty in which Siam relinquished sovereignty in what are now the northern Malaysian states but kept control of the population and territories north of the new British-drawn border. Thailand seized back its lost Malay territories during World War II but was forced to return to the 1909 border in 1945. The Thai Malay Muslims, occupied in traditional subsistence agriculture, plantation agriculture, and fisheries, have resisted assimilation in a culturally Buddhist Thai state that aggressively defines a Buddhist Thai national identity in its language, education, and administrative policies in the Malay Muslim areas.

Successive Thai governments had treated the war in the South as an internal matter. The tone was set by Prime Minister Thaksin Shinawatra in 2004 when he threatened to walk out of the 2004 Vientiane ASEAN Summit if Indonesian president Yudhoyono and Malaysian prime minister Badawi put the situation in South Thailand on the agenda as a possible regional security issue. Because of ASEAN's golden rule, ASEAN has not taken cognizance of the conflict in South Thailand despite the implications for the ASEAN Political and Security Community. The situation in the South is treated in bilateral political exchanges between Thailand and its Muslim ASEAN partners. The neighbor with the greatest interest is Malaysia. The Thai Islamic insurgent groups have had long cultural ties to Malaysia's Muslims, often with family ties. Thai officials have been quick to charge that the Thai Muslim insurgents were operating from safe havens in Malaysia. A high-level Thailand–Malaysia security dialogue has called for greater cooperation along the border. Malaysia's security concerns are not just that of spillover of the war on the border. Both Malaysia and Indonesia also have concerns about the political impact of the Thai Muslims' struggle for their own Muslim populations.

Malaysia and Indonesia have sought to buffer Thailand against hard-line Arab states in the OIC. In a 2007 meeting with the OIC's secretary general, Thai prime minister Surayud Chulanont committed Thailand to allow Thai Muslims "to assume responsibilities over their domestic affairs through a decentralization process that allows the people to practice their own cultural and linguistic tradition and manage their natural resources in full respect of the sovereignty and territorial integrity of Thailand."[63] Thailand's failure to follow through on the commitment led to a condemnatory OIC resolution in 2012. Thailand's response was to threaten not to cooperate with the OIC in the future.

Since 2006, Thailand's governments and politicians, paralyzed by polarizing domestic antagonisms, have been content to allow the military to control the southern agenda. For the military, the bloodshed and flight of Buddhists from the South have become the norm. There was no political payoff for the government to challenge the military's defense of territorial integrity, sovereignty, and the king. A widening of the war in the southern provinces would strain not only Thailand's political resources in ASEAN but ASEAN itself, as a Muslim–non-Muslim breach is opened. It is tacitly understood that only a political solution can end the insurgency. It is also understood—but denied by ardent nationalists—that such a solution would have to involve some form of autonomy. Since 2006, different Thai governments have had secret contacts testing the negotiating waters. These have been facilitated by Indonesian and Malaysian connections. Indonesia has offered its good offices and its experience in resolving the Aceh conflict. Bangkok has been publicly conscious of

Malaysia's role in the Philippines–MILF peace talks. The domestic political context of the Indonesian and Philippine cases was quite different, however. In February 2013, preliminary peace talks began in Kuala Lumpur between the government and the insurgents. These have been facilitated by Malaysia's prime minister Najib. For Bangkok, the Malaysian role is problematic, with Kuala Lumpur being viewed more as a stakeholder than a neutral partner. The insurgents were represented by the BRN (Barisan Revolusi Nasional [National Revolutionary Front]). The degree to which the BRN, the main insurgent force, is coordinating with the other armed groups and can speak authoritatively for them is not known. Within six months the negotiations stalled. In September 2013, the BRN presented a package of preconditions for continuation of the talks (box 5.6) that raises questions as to how serious it is in reaching a negotiated settlement. If the purpose of the initial talks was to build trust and confidence, it was unsuccessful. If anything, the pace of violence has increased in the meltdown of central authority in Bangkok.

The prospect of any near-term breakthrough has become unlikely. It would require a strong, stable Thai government that could weather criticism from political opposition. The violent dismantlement of democracy in Thailand does not auger well for the emergence of such a government. As Bangkok is convulsed by schismatic politics, space is opened for the insurgents to maximize their bargaining positions. In the wake of the military coup in 2014, there has been an increase in insurgent violence. Even if the government could in the end agree on terms of an autonomous Muslim administrative district in the South, it might not satisfy bitter-end Muslim separatists or Thailand's Constitutional Court. If, as the insurgents threaten, a failure to make peace leads to a wider war, it would deepen the gulf between Muslim ASEAN and Buddhist ASEAN, being demonstrated as well by the plight of the Rohingya in Myanmar (chapter 9).

Box 5.6.   BRN Preconditions for Peace Negotiations

- The BRN to be recognized as liberators, not separatists
- Malaysia's role to be upgraded to mediator, not just facilitator
- Observers from ASEAN, the OIC, and NGOS during the dialogue process
- A special administrative platform to be set up under the Thai constitution
- All detained suspects and imprisoned insurgents to be unconditionally released

NOTES

1. Amitav Acharya, *Constructing a Security Community in Southeast Asia: ASEAN and the Problem of Regional Order* (London: Routledge, 2001).

2. For a fuller explication of this point, see Donald E. Weatherbee, "ASEAN's Identity Crisis," in *Legacy of Engagement in Southeast Asia*, ed. Ann Marie Murphy and Bridget Welsh (Singapore: ISEAS, 2008), 250–72.

3. Ralf Emmers, *Cooperative Security and the Balance of Power in ASEAN and the ARF* (London and New York: RoutledgeCurzon, 2003), 10.

4. For a seminal discussion of two-level game theory, see Robert Putnam, "Diplomacy and Domestic Politics: The Logic of Two-Level Games," *International Organization* 42, no. 3 (1988): 427–60. For applications in Southeast Asia, see Jörn Dosch, "The Impact of Democratization on the Foreign Policy of Indonesia, Thailand, and the Philippines," *Südostasien aktuell* 5 (2006): 42–70.

5. "Military Spending in Southeast Asia: Shopping Spree," *Economist*, 24 March 2012, 100.

6. As stated by Defense Minister Purnomo Yusgiantoro, "Indonesia to Have Strongest Military in Southeast Asia," *Jakarta Post*, 9 June 2013.

7. Comprehensive country and region defense data can be found in the International Institute for Strategic Studies (IISS.org) annual *Military Balance* and the Stockholm International Peace Research Institute's (SIPRI.org) annual *SIPRI Yearbook*.

8. John Chipman, press statement on the launch of *Military Balance 2008*, accessed at http://www.iiss.org.

9. SIPRI press release, 14 March 2010, "New SIPRI Data on International Arms Transfers Reflect Arms Race Concerns," accessed at http://www.sipri.org/media/pressreleases/2010/100315armstransfers.

10. Purnomo Yusgiantoro, "Military Modernization and Strategic Transparency," Third Plenary Session, Shangri-la Dialogue 2013, accessed at http://www.iiss.org.

11. "Treaty of Amity and Cooperation in Southeast Asia," *Handbook on Selected ASEAN Political Documents*, IV:21, accessed at http://www.asean.org/archive/pdf/HBPDR.pdf.

12. "Rules of Procedure of the High Council of the TAC," *Handbook on Selected ASEAN Political Documents*, XIII:96, accessed at http://www.asean.org/archive/pdf/HBPDR.pdf.

13. "Protocol Amending the TAC," *Handbook on Selected ASEAN Political Documents*, V:31, accessed at http://www.asean.org/archive/pdf/HBPDR.pdf.

14. Bali Concord II, paragraph A, 7, accessed at http://www.asean.org/news/item/declaration-of-asean-concord-ii-bali-concord-ii.

15. ASEAN Political and Security Community Blueprint, B.2.21–22, accessed at http://www.asean.org/archive/5187-18.pdf.

16. "The ASEAN Troika," concept paper adopted at the thirty-third AMM, Bangkok, 24–25 July 2000, in *Handbook on Selected ASEAN Political Documents*, XII:39, accessed at http://www.asean.org/archive/pdf/HBPDR.pdf.

17. The ARF's website can be accessed at http://aseanregionalforum.asean.org.

18. The ARF concept paper can be accessed at http://aseanregionalforum.asean .org/files/library/Terms%20of%20References%20and%20Concept%20Papers/Con cept%20Paper%20of%20ARF.pdf.

19. The CSCAP web page can be accessed at http://www.cscap.org.

20. The ADMM's website is http://admm.asean.org.

21. Termasak Chalermpalanupap, "ASEAN Defence Diplomacy and the ADMM-Plus," [ISEAS] *Perspective* 49 (26 August 2013): 3.

22. Chairman's Statement, Sixth East Asia Summit, 19 November 2011, accessed at http://www.asean.org/asean/external-relations/east-asia-summit-eas.

23. Foreign Minister Marty Natalegawa, "An Indonesian Perspective on the Indo-Pacific," keynote address to CSIS Indonesia Conference, 16 May 2012, accessed at http://www.csis.org.

24. "Marty Urges Treaty to Ward off Indo-Pacific Conflict," *Jakarta Globe*, 2 August 2013.

25. Ramses Amer, "The Association of South-East Asian Nations and the Management of Territorial Disputes," *Boundary and Security Bulletin* 9, no. 4 (Winter 2001–2002): 81–96.

26. According to Barry Wain, 98 percent of the border remains undemarcated. The two countries do not agree on its length: Myanmar's 1,313 miles (2,114 km) and Thailand's 1,491 miles (2,401 km). Barry Wain, "Latent Danger: Boundary Disputes and Border Issues in Southeast Asia," in *Southeast Asian Affairs 2011*, ed. Daljit Singh and Pushpa Thambipillai (Singapore: ISEAS, 2012): 42–43.

27. Ibid., 46.

28. See table 1, p. 16, in Sam Bateman, Joshua Ho, and Jane Chan, "Good Order at Sea in Southeast Asia" (RSIS Policy Paper, April 2009).

29. Tara Davenport, "Southeast Asian Approaches to Maritime Delimitation" (Asian Society of International Law, ASIL Working Paper 2012/7), 11–13.

30. Ibid, table 1, pp. 48–50.

31. As quoted in Mevotex, "Thanks to Malaysia's Dr. M Our Water Industry is Worth 10 Billion," accessed at http://www.malaysiafinanceblogspot.com/2012/11/ singapore-water-industry-thanks-to-you.htm.

32. As cited in "ASEAN Haze Watch System 'Delayed by Others,'" *Straits Times*, 7 March 2014.

33. "We'll Defend 'Sovereignty' over Pedra Branca: Najib," *Straits Times*, 15 January 2003.

34. Prof. S. Jayakumar, parliamentary speech, 25 January 2003, Singapore Parliament Report, 25 January 2003, accessed at http://www.parliament.gov.sg.

35. The judgment can be accessed at http://www.icj-cij.org/docket/files/130/14492 .pdf.

36. The order can be accessed at http://www.itlos.org/fileadmin/itlos/documents/ cases/case_no_12/Order.08.10.03.E.pdf.

37. Tommy Koh and Jolene Lin, "The Reclamation Case: Thoughts and Reflections," *Singapore Year Book of International Law* 10 (2006): 7.

38. As cited in *Today* (Singapore), 21 September 2013, accessed at http://www. todayonline.com/singapore/positive-spore-malaysian-relations-cannot-be-taken-for -granted-tony-tan.

39. Links to the full documentation of the ICJ adjudication of *Sovereignty over Pulau Ligitan and Pulau Sipidan (Indonesia/Malaysia)* can be accessed at http://www.icj-cij.org/docket/files/102/7714.pdf.

40. "North Kalimantan Becomes 34th Province," *Jakarta Post*, 27 October 2012.

41. These figures were given in Tunggadewa Mattangkilan, "Ambalat Border Dispute Ignored for Joint Indonesia/Malaysia Exploration Efforts," *Jakarta Globe*, 17 June 2013.

42. "Arroyo Denies Role in Sabah Standoff," accessed at http://globalnation.in quirer.net/67391/arroyo-denies-role-in-sabah-standoff.

43. Simon Tay, "Does Sabah Merit ASEAN's Attention?" *Nation* (Bangkok), 13 March 2013.

44. As quoted in "Cambodia, Thailand to Face UN over Border Dispute," *Channel News Asia*, 9 February 2011.

45. The summary of the judgment can be accessed at http://www.icj-cij.org/docket/files/45/4873.pdf.

46. "Security Council Urges Permanent Ceasefire after Recent Thai–Cambodian Clashes," *UN News Service*, 14 February 2011.

47. The terms of the court's interim order can be accessed at http://www.icj-cij.org/docket/files/151/16582.pdf.

48. The full decision can be accessed at http://www.icj-cij.org/docket/files/151/17704.pdf.

49. For concise discussions of the general problems of separatism in Aceh and Papua, see Anthony L. Smith, "Conflict in Aceh: The Consequences of a Broken Social Contract," *Harvard Asia Quarterly* 6, no. 1 (Winter 2002): 47–55, and David Webster, "'Already Sovereign as a People,' a Foundational Movement in West Papuan Nationalism," *Pacific Affairs* 74, no. 4 (Winter 2001–2002): 507–28.

50. "Joint Statement on Aceh by the EU, Japan, and the US," accessed at http://unpo.org/article/755.

51. Kirsten E. Schulze, "From the Battlefield to the Negotiating Table: GAM and the Indonesian Government 1999–2000," *Asian Security* 3, no. 2 (May–August 2007): 80–98.

52. "Melanesians Respect RI's Sovereignty," *Jakarta Post*, 16 January 2014.

53. The Tripoli Agreement can be accessed at http://www.gov.ph/1976/12/23/the-tripoli-agreement-december-23-1976.

54. The FPA can be accessed at http://pcdspo.gov.ph/download/2012/10.Final-Peace-Agreement-MNLF-September-2-1996.pdf.

55. Malaysia's Motive as Peace Broker under Question," *Manila Times*, 1 March 2014.

56. The MOA-AD can be accessed at http://www.muslimmindanao.ph/ances tral_domain.htm.

57. "The Framework Agreement" can be accessed at http://www.scribd.com/doc/137673080/Framework-Agreement-on-the-Bangsamoro.

58. "Enemies of Peace Beware—Aquino," Inquirer.net, 27 March 214, accessed at http://www.newsinfo.inquirer.net/589610/aquino-to-use-force-against-enemies-of-peace.

59. OIC Council of Foreign Ministers Resolution No. 2/39 on Question of Muslims in Southern Philippines, 17 November 2012, accessed at http://www.oic-oci.org/english/conf/fm/39/MM-DR-39CFM%20-FINAL.pdf.

60. "Bangsa Moro Deal Illegal—OIC," *Manila Times*, 22 April 2014.

61. In literature and reporting, both "Patani" and "Pattani" are used to identify the embattled region in South Thailand. The author uses "Patani" (Malay) which underlines the ethnic identity of the Malay Muslims whose culture and traditions are rooted in the Patani Sultanate which stretched to both sides of the modern border. "Pattani" is a transliteration of the Thai spelling of the Malay.

62. These figures from the Thai Internal Security Operations Command (ISOC) were reported by *Nation* (Bangkok), 2 January 2014.

63. As cited in Res. No. 1/35-MM on "Safeguarding the Rights of Muslim Communities and Minorities in Non-OIC Member States," thirty-fifth session of the OIC Council of Ministers, 18–20 June 2008, accessed at http://www.oic-coi.org/34cfm/resolutions/35-CFM-2008=MM-SG.pdf.

SUGGESTIONS FOR FURTHER READING

For detailed analyses of the status of contemporary ethnic and bilateral conflicts in Southeast Asia, the reporting of the International Crisis Group (http://www.crisisgroup.org) can be browsed by country links or by its search engine, with, for example, "Papua" or "Aceh" for Indonesia. The Honolulu/Washington, D.C.-based East–West Center publication series of *Policy Studies* has a number of studies dating from 2004 with issues on Southeast Asian ethno-conflicts. These can be accessed at http://www.eastwestcenter.org/publications. The PDF for a particular *Policy Studies* number has a free download. Of particular interest are Myanmar, nos. 31, 36, 39, 45, and 63; Papua, nos. 4, 5, 13, and 25; Aceh, nos. 2, 3, 8, and 47; and Mindanao, nos. 17 and 25. Ralf Emmers, *Comparative Security and the Balance of Power in ASEAN and ARF* (New York: RoutledgeCurzon, 2003) examines many of the issues raised in this chapter. Amitav Acharya, *Constructing a Security Community in Southeast Asia*, 3rd ed. (New York: Routledge, 2014) is an influential analysis of ASEAN's approach to security issues. For an overview of the evolution of the ASEAN way of problem solving, see Jürgen Haacke, *ASEAN's Diplomatic and Security Culture: Origins, Development and Prospects* (New York: Routledge, 2005). For the ARF, see Hiro Katsumata, *ASEAN's Cooperative Security Enterprise: Norms and Interests in the ASEAN Regional Forum* (New York: Palgrave Macmillan, 2009). The difficult relationships of Malaysia, Indonesia, and Singapore are explored in Joseph Chi Liow, *The Politics of Indonesia–Malaysia Relations* (New York: Routledge, 2005) and Lilly Zubaidah Rahim, *Singapore in the Malay World: Building and Breaching Regional Bridges* (New York: Routledge, 2007). Islam and regional conflict are examined in Joseph Camelleri and Sven Schottmenn, eds., *Culture, Religion and Conflict in Muslim Southeast Asia: Negotiating Tense Pluralisms* (New York: Routledge, 2013). For ethnic conflict, see chapters on Aceh, Mindanao, and South Thailand in Rajat Ganguly, ed., *Autonomy and Ethnic Conflict in South and Southeast Asia* (New York: Routledge, 2012). Duncan McCargo, *Tearing up the Land: Islam and Legitimacy in Southern Thailand* (Ithaca, NY: Cornell University Press, 2008) shows that the structure of the conflict is more complex than just religion. Kasetsir Charvit, Pou Sothivak, and Pavin Chachavipongpun, *Preah Vihear: A Guide to the Thai–Cambodia Conflict and Its Solution* (Bangkok: White Lotus, 2013) identifies the national interests at play. The chapters in Michelle Ann Miller, *Autonomy and Armed Separatism in Southeast Asia* (Singapore: ISEAS, 2012) discuss frameworks for peaceful settlement.

Chapter Six

The South China Sea Conflict Zone

The South China Sea (SCS) lies at the heart of Southeast Asia. With the exception of landlocked Laos, Myanmar on the Andaman Sea, and Timor-Leste in the east of the Indonesian archipelago, the remaining Southeast Asian states have shores that are washed, if only in part, by the gulfs, straits, and expanse of the South China Sea. It is technically a "semi-enclosed sea" as defined by UNCLOS, Article 122, in which, Article 123 states, the littoral states are encouraged to "cooperate with each other in the exercise of their rights and the performances of their duties."[1] Competition, rather than cooperation, however, has been the prevailing characteristic of the relations among the littoral states, with each one seeking to give real effect to their overlapping sovereign and jurisdictional claims.

Five of the ASEAN states—Brunei, Indonesia, Malaysia, the Philippines, and Vietnam—have maritime zone jurisdictions in the SCS that include, from the coast, territorial seas extending twelve miles, a two-hundred-mile exclusive economic zone (EEZ), and a continental shelf, the outer limit of which generally cannot exceed 350 miles from the baselines from which the territorial sea is measured.[2] In the EEZ, including the waters, seabed, and subsoil, the state has sovereign rights to explore, exploit, conserve, and manage natural resources whether living or nonliving. On its continental shelf, the state has sovereign rights to explore and exploit its natural resources. Where states' EEZs and continental shelves overlap, bilateral negotiations, as discussed in chapter 5, have been pursued for division or joint development following UNCLOS guidelines.

Scattered in the SCS are islands and island groups with contested claims to sovereignty as well as to the territorial seas and EEZs that might extend from them. The ASEAN states' jurisdictional and sovereign rights to zones are under great political, economic, and military challenges from China. The Chinese maritime map lies like a palimpsest over Southeast Asian jurisdictional maps. It includes a sweeping nine-dash-line arc enclosing 80 to 90 percent of maritime and land features of the SCS. Unlike UNCLOS-prescribed baselines fixing the ASEAN states' maritime zones, the nine dashes in China's maritime map are unrelated to any UNCLOS principles of demarcation. They are a graphic representation of a Chinese claim to historical dominion. China's unequivocal official position is clearly set forth in a 2009 submission to the UN which states that China has "indisputable sovereignty over the islands in the South China Sea and their adjacent waters and enjoys sovereign rights and jurisdiction over the relevant waters as well as the sea bed and subsoil thereof (see attached map)."[3] The attached map is that which is presented here as map 6.1.

China has elevated the importance of its SCS claims to a "core" national interest and wrapped it in the flag of ultranationalism. In February 2013, three Chinese warships patrolled off James Shoal at the southernmost point of the nine-dash line, only forty-eight miles (80 km) from the Sarawak coast, deep inside Malaysia's EEZ. The Chinese call James Shoal Zengmu Reef and have put a steel marker on it to assert ownership.[4] A ceremony was held on board during which the sailors pledged to "defend the South China Sea, maintain sovereignty, and strive toward the dream of a strong China."[5] The incursion and ceremony were repeated in February 2014.

It has been China's aggressive efforts to enforce its claims in the South China Sea that have pushed the SCS to the top of the list of Southeast Asia's potential flash points. It had been hoped in ASEAN, although without foundation, that the 2013 change of leadership in China might lessen tensions in the South China Sea. As actions in 2014 in the South China Sea and the East China Sea show, China's policies may become more assertive as China defends its nonnegotiable claims of sovereignty and jurisdiction in the South China Sea. This has created an existential crisis for ASEAN as the group wrestles with reconciling its functional embrace of China in ASEAN + 1 and ASEAN + 3 settings and the threat to ASEAN solidarity posed by nonresponse to China's salami-slicing of member states' jurisdictions. It has also escalated regional tensions with China inherent in the American "pivot" and defense of the strategic status quo.

WHAT'S AT STAKE?

The stakes are high in what might be a zero-sum game for some of the competitors who would contest with China in determining the territorial, eco-

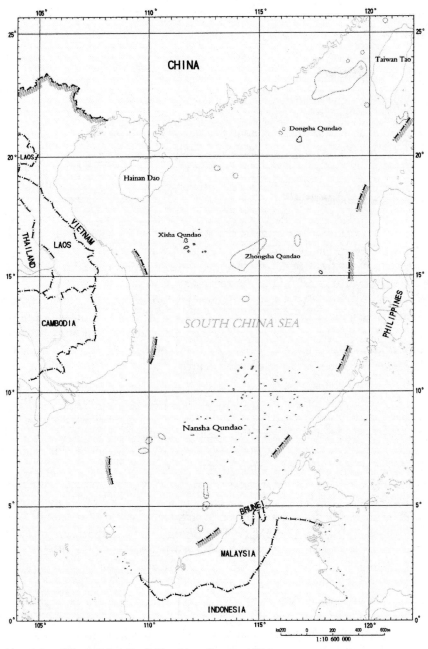

Map 6.1.   Chinese Nine-Dash-Line Map. *Source:* UN.

nomic, strategic, and political place of the South China Sea in international relations in Southeast Asia.

Territorial Stakes

Studded throughout the South China Sea are islands, islets, shoals, reefs, and rocks over which sovereignty is contested. There are four island groupings. The Pratas Islands, a choke point in the Taiwan Strait, are currently occupied by Taiwan but also claimed by China. The three other groups—the Paracels, Spratlys, and Macclesfield Bank/Scarborough Shoal—pit China's claims (mirrored in the background by Taiwan) against the claims of Vietnam, the Philippines, and Malaysia.

The Paracel Islands (China—Xisha, Vietnam—Hoang Sa), 130 coral islands and reefs in two clusters, the Amphitrite and Crescent, lie between Vietnam and Hainan Island. In January 1974, China wrested control of the Crescent group from South Vietnamese forces in what has been called the "Battle of the Paracels." Three Vietnamese ships were sunk and seventy-three Vietnamese killed. The post-1975 Vietnamese government had long ignored South Vietnam's defeat, but in the heat of its own SCS face-off with China, in January 2014 Hanoi allowed public commemoration of the fiftieth anniversary of the battle and the Vietnamese martyrs. Texts and exhibitions have reaffirmed Vietnam's sovereignty over Hoang Sa and the purported illegality of China's occupation.

Also in the north of the SCS, Macclesfield Bank (Zhongsha) and Scarborough Shoal (China—Huangyan, Philippines—Panatag) have been controlled by the Philippines but claimed by China. Uninhabited, their importance has been in fishery resources. Scarborough Shoal is well within the Philippines EEZ, 136 miles (220 km) west of Luzon. In April 2012, Philippines fishery officers tried to arrest Chinese vessels that were poaching protected species in the Scarborough Shoal atoll. Chinese maritime patrol vessels intervened to prevent the arrests. After a standoff, both sides agreed to withdraw. The Philippines did. The Chinese did not. Since then there has been a permanent Chinese armed maritime patrol presence that has prevented the Philippines from fishing in its own EEZ. China has de facto annexed the Scarborough Shoal to Zhongsha authority.

The Spratly Islands consist of 160 or so islands, islets, reefs, rocks, and sandbanks spread over 158,000 square miles (410,000 sq km) of the central South China Sea.[6] The Spratlys have become the major theater of a battle for sovereign rights and maritime jurisdictions. The islands are called Nansha by China, Truong Sa by Vietnam, and, in its claimed area, Kalayaan by the Philippines. Even the name of the sea in which the Spratlys are located has become part of the dispute. Hanoi's name for the South China Sea is Bien Dong (East Sea), while Manila now dubs it the West Philippine Sea. For the latter, the thought is that to accept the name South China Sea will somehow strengthen China's claims. Both China and Vietnam lay claim to the entire archipelago. Kalayaan overlays part of the Chinese and Vietnamese claims. The foundation for the claims of both China and Vietnam is historical presence, China's going back to the Han dynasty, twenty-three centuries ago. Vietnam's historical claim was bolstered by colonial inheritance from France. The Philippine claims reference discovery and proximity and date only from the 1950s. The Malaysia and Brunei claims are EEZ and continental shelf–extension based.

In terms of effective human occupation, as opposed to pillars, markers, and flagpoles, the Philippines has catalogued forty-three occupied sites.[7] Vietnam occupies twenty-one islands or reefs. They are administered as a district of mainland Khanh Hoa Province. Vietnam's June 2012 "Law of the Sea of Vietnam" restated in its first article that the Paracels and Spratly Islands were under the sovereignty and jurisdiction of Vietnam.[8] Predictably, this sparked an angry Chinese reaction. China's foreign ministry protested the "illegal and invalid" infringement on Chinese sovereignty, stating that China would resolutely safeguard its territorial sovereignty.[9] The Philippines has nine occupied sites that are grouped as the Kalayaan municipality, part of Palawan Province. Kalayaan became an integral part of the Philippines Republic by presidential decree in 1978, an act protested by both Beijing and Hanoi. Malaysia has five occupied sites in the southern Spratlys. Although Brunei's EEZ and continental shelf claims overlap Malaysia's, including the Spratlys' Louisa Reef and Rifleman Bank, neither of these has features to support a territorial claim. The largest and most heavily fortified island is Itu-Aba, occupied by Taiwan, at the north end of the Spratlys.

China occupies no true island but has constructed seven fortified facilities on reefs. The PRC's physical presence in the Spratlys began in 1988 when it ejected Vietnam from Johnson Reef and Fiery Cross Reef, sinking two Vietnamese ships at the cost of sixty-four Vietnamese lives. Some were shot while standing on Fiery Cross Reef defending the Vietnamese flag. In 1995, the Philippines' Mischief Reef, only 129 miles (239 km) from Palawan, was seized by China with only diplomatic resistance by Manila. China's escalation of its pressure on the Philippines, as was demonstrated at Scarborough Shoal, continues. In March 2014, the Philippines' occupation of Second Thomas Shoal, called Ayungin by Manila and Ren'ai Reef by China, came under Chinese siege. Philippine occupation is based on a rotating eight- to ten-man marine detachment on a rusting-out scuttled World War II LST. Chinese maritime forces tried to blockade efforts to resupply by the detachment.

The Chinese foreign ministry denounced the "illegal" Philippine presence and declaimed that "China will by no means allow the Philippines to seize the Ren'ai Reef in any form."[10]

The effort and cost of occupying such remote places has nothing to do with the value of the real estate. Its purpose is demonstrating effective occupation of sovereign territory from which baselines for EEZs and continental shelves might be drawn. This is limited by UNCLOS Article 121 (3) to land features that can "sustain human habitation or economic life of their own." This raises significant questions about the legal validity of some of the Spratly Islands' zonal claims.[11] However, Beijing has made it abundantly clear that the UNCLOS does not apply within the nine-dash line. Its 1996 ratification of UNCLOS declared that "the People's Republic of China reaffirms its sovereignty over all of the archipelagos and islands as listed in article 2 of the Law of the People's Republic of China on the territorial sea and contiguous zones."[12] The referenced Article 2 of China's law includes Xisha, Zhongsha, and Nansha.[13]

To give a legal administrative framework to its claims to sovereignty, in 2012 China established a civil government that placed Xisha, Nansha, and Zhongsha in a new Sansha Prefecture of Hainan Province. The garrisoned prefectural center is the upgraded Sansha City on Woody Island (Yongxing) in the Paracels. Beijing is making a major capital investment in Sansha City to make it the gateway to the South China Sea. With the creation of Sansha Prefecture, China upped the political ante to parallel the militarization of its South China Sea footprint. Given the tensions of cohabitation in the Spratlys, without dispute resolution acceptable to Beijing it seems only a matter of time before either Vietnam or the Philippines gives China a pretext to forcefully evict them or makes it too costly to hang on.

The Economic Stakes

The most important resources at stake in the competition for sovereignty are oil and natural gas reserves. Until there is a resolution of the sovereignty questions and resultant jurisdictional overlaps, large-scale exploration and exploitation of the sea's potential resources will be delayed. The presumption of vast energy resources in the contested South China Sea offshore basin is based largely on extrapolation from the existing proved reserves being worked in uncontested areas on the South China Sea littoral by Brunei, Malaysia, the Philippines, Vietnam, and Indonesia. The US Energy Information Administration estimated in 2013 that the SCS has proved and probable reserves of 11 billion barrels (bbl) of oil and 190 trillion cubic feet (Tcf) of natural gas.[14] Because there has been essentially no exploration in the central South China Sea, there are no reliable figures for undiscovered reserves. Speculative

Chinese National Offshore Oil Company estimates put undiscovered oil at 125 billion bbl and natural gas at 500 billion Tcf. The US Geological Survey has offered a much lower estimate for undiscovered reserves of between 5 and 22 billion bbl of oil and between 70 and 290 billion Tcf. Even though the Chinese estimates of oil and gas reserves are considered optimistic, the lure of tapping these potential reserves raises the stakes in the territorial and jurisdictional contest, particularly as energy demands and prices increase.

A significant part of the proved and probable oil and gas reserves are on the continental shelves beneath the EEZs of the ASEAN states. China's nine-dash line carves out large swaths of Indonesian, Malaysian, Bruneian, and Vietnamese hydrocarbon potential exploration and production blocks. At its southernmost extent, the line overlaps the blocks north of Indonesia's Natuna Islands. It was not until March 2014 that a senior military official publicly acknowledged a looming Chinese threat.[15] China has acted to impede oil and gas developmental activity in Vietnam's and the Philippines' EEZs by seeking to influence or ward off possible global partners and by harassment at sea, as well as offering Chinese oil blocks in the Vietnamese EEZ. Chinese aggressive behavior toward the Philippines seeks to deny the Philippines access to the potential hydrocarbons beneath the Reed Bank in the Philippines' EEZ. Major oil companies have not bid for Philippine blocks because of what Manila calls Chinese "intimidation." One oil energy research analyst explained that big oil companies "cannot afford to upset the Chinese and be marginalized in the Chinese market," adding that only businesses "with no chance in China" would bid.[16]

A second major economic resource at stake in the South China Sea competition is its fisheries, vital to Southeast Asian food security as well as an important export industry. With fish stocks threatened by overfishing and degraded environmental conditions (chapter 10), aggressive Chinese tactics for control of the fisheries within the nine-dash line in Southeast Asian EEZs puts at risk the littoral states' UNCLOS-guaranteed rights to exploit, conserve, and manage their EEZs' living resources. Vietnamese and Philippine fishing vessels have been coercively forced out of their traditional EEZ fishing grounds. China has arrested Vietnamese fishermen and in March 2013 fired flares and set a Vietnamese fishing boat ablaze. This led to anti-China protests in Vietnam. The Philippines' Scarborough Shoal has been mentioned above. Indonesia has been affected by China's claim to Indonesian EEZ fisheries. In 2010, with guns trained, a Chinese maritime enforcement cutter forced an Indonesian patrol vessel to release Chinese fishing boats apprehended in Indonesia's EEZ. Similarly, in March 2013, an Indonesian patrol vessel boarded a Chinese fishing boat in Indonesia's EEZ and arrested nine crewmen. An armed Chinese cutter arrived on scene and, weapons leveled, demanded the release of the prisoners. The Indonesian captain acquiesced in consideration of the safety of his crew.[17]

China has created a new legal framework to take upon itself the right to regulate fishing in the South China Sea. Beginning on 1 January 2014, all foreign fishing vessels within China's SCS waters—within the nine-dash line—would need to register and get approval from Chinese authorities of the Hainan provincial government.[18] It is too early to tell how vigorously or selectively China might try to enforce the fishery law—punish Manila but not push Jakarta. Enhanced Chinese capabilities may be reflected in the reorganization of its multiple maritime surveillance and enforcement agencies into a paramilitary Chinese Coast Guard under the Ministry of Public Security. The growing Chinese maritime presence in the SCS and its activities in enforcing its claims to sovereign rights and jurisdiction suggest that incidents at sea will increase. The Chinese stance has brought to the fore the strategic question of freedom of navigation.

The Strategic Stakes

China's assertion of its sovereignty and jurisdiction over the more than 1.4-million-square-mile (3.6 million sq km) South China Sea challenges not only ASEAN's maritime states but as well the members of the international community with important maritime commercial and military interests. The SCS is a vital waterway through which the sea routes from East Asia to the Middle East pass. For the United States, freedom of navigation in the SCS for American naval vessels is deemed a vital security interest. China's efforts to regulate the activities of foreign military operations in its claimed EEZs have already led to incidents between Chinese and US forces.[19] The UNCLOS provides for high seas navigational and other freedoms in the EEZ (Article 58, with reference to Article 87). If China's buildup of naval and air capabilities leads to even greater demands for regulatory control of the South China Sea's international waters, both China and the United States will face hard political and military choices. There was great concern in the region that Chinese unilateral imposition of an air defense identification zone (ADIZ) over the East China Sea in November 2013 would be followed by a South China Sea ADIZ. Although the United States and Japan refused to recognize it and continued military flights through the zone without notifying Chinese controllers, both governments advised their commercial airlines to observe the Chinese flight rules. China's longer-range strategic thrust is to exclude the United States as a great-power actor in what China sees as its natural sphere of interest, turning the semi-enclosed SCS into a Chinese lake bordered by Southeast Asian states reordered in a twenty-first-century version of the traditional Confucian sovereign–vassal relationship.

The US posture is clear. It takes no position on the legal merits of individual claims to sovereignty, but in February 2014, for the first time, an American official explicitly rejected China's nine-dash line as the basis for maritime claims as being inconsistent with UNCLOS.[20] The United States insists that the South China Sea disputes are regional in their impact and should be dealt with in a framework in which the interests of all stakeholders can be addressed. At the 2011 EAS, President Obama succinctly stated the US position that the United States had "a powerful stake in maritime security in general and in the resolution of the South China Sea issue specifically—as a resident Pacific power, as a maritime power, as a trading nation and as a *guarantor of security* in the Asia Pacific" (emphasis added).[21] The Chinese position is uncompromising: that in disputes in the South China Sea "outside forces [i.e., the United States] should not get involved under any excuse."[22] The tactic is to isolate the maritime ASEAN states in political-economic-military asymmetric bilateral negotiating relationships as China uses force to secure and police its claimed territorial and maritime rights within the nine-dash line.

What the strategic and tactical impact of the US "pivot" might mean for the ASEAN countries whose maritime jurisdictions have been placed at risk by China is being tested by the Philippines. The Philippines is a relatively soft target for China's creeping maritime imperialism. Its naval assets are few and overmatched. China has tried to isolate Manila from its ASEAN partners, threatening that to support the Philippines would damage ASEAN's friendly relations with China. Manila has been heartened in its resistance to Chinese bullying by political and material backing from the United States. As noted in chapter 2, the United States has given Manila assurances about the US–Philippines MDT. The April 2013 US–Philippines Enhanced Defense Cooperation Agreement will lead to a higher regional US military profile. China has warned that a "troublemaking" Philippines—backed by the United States—will be emboldened to recklessly confront China, which will make a peaceful resolution more difficult, if not impossible, and intensify regional tensions.[23] However, the United States has not specifically stated that the MDT extends to the Kalayaan claim or contested waters. What the United States might or might not do would be consequential, not just for the Philippines but for American "soft" security alignments elsewhere in Southeast Asia. In the "pivot" the United States has burnished old security ties and developed new ones. Vietnam and Indonesia especially have gained new strategic importance in the US power-centered "hub-and-spoke" security network in Southeast Asia. Beijing has accused the United States of promoting a "containment policy" directed against China.

The Political Stakes for ASEAN

The already weakened foundations of the ASEAN Political-Security Community have been further undermined by its institutional inability to fashion a collective position that addresses the issues of the disputes in the South China Sea. The principled basis of the APSC as stated in the Bali Concord II is that the member states "regard their security as fundamentally linked to one another, bound by geographic location, common vision, and objectives." The SCS crisis proves that this is demonstrably false. ASEAN has essentially said to its members facing China in the SCS, "You're on your own." There is no fundamental member state security linkage since there is no common security interest.

The strategic vision from continental Southeast Asia does not look across the South China Sea. The continental states' interest is in doing business with China, not confronting it. Nor have the maritime states been able to shape a common response to the Chinese challenge, even though there is acknowledgment that the nine-dash line has no UNCLOS basis. In a response to China's UN submission, Indonesia pointed out that the so-called nine-dash line "clearly lacks international legal basis and is tantamount to upset the UNCLOS 1982."[24] In similar briefs to the UN, Vietnam and Malaysia raised objections to the Chinese claims. Yet, when the Philippines applied in 2013 to the Permanent Court of Arbitration for an award that, inter alia, would declare China's nine-dash line illegal, no other state would join the Philippines' arbitral suit (discussed below).

In addition to shattering the facade of ASEAN unity and solidarity, ASEAN's lowest-common-denominator approach to the South China Sea disputes has seriously jeopardized its oft-repeated claim of centrality in the region's security architecture, let alone its international political relevancy. This has certainly been the case for the forty years since China seized the Paracels. No matter the Chinese provocations, ASEAN reverts to what has become its default position of dialogues with China for the sake of dialogues at a level of exchange that has not constrained China's actions.

DECLARATION ON THE CONDUCT (DOC)
OF PARTIES IN THE SOUTH CHINA SEA

For more than twenty years, ASEAN's response to China's South China Sea claims has been to engage in diplomatic exchanges with China in a determinedly nonconfrontational manner. It has sought to prevent the jurisdictional and territorial rivalries between some of its members and China from spilling over into the broader regional agenda of ASEAN–China relations.

ASEAN's strategy has been to try to preserve the status quo in the South China Sea without alienating China. The tactic has been to enmesh China in a web of normative and legal commitments that would constrain its unilateralism in changing the status quo by forceful means. China's strategy has been to satisfy ASEAN's quest for dialogue, without binding commitments or retreat from claims to sovereignty and maritime jurisdictions. High on Beijing's list of priorities is to exclude the United States from the dialogue.

ASEAN Declaration on the South China Sea (1992)

China's readiness to use force to establish its rights in the SCS had been signaled in 1974 in the Paracels. It was brought home to Southeast Asia in the Vietnamese–Chinese clash at Johnson Island and Fiery Cross Reef in the Spratlys, followed by the building of fortified positions that posed challenges to Vietnam's and the Philippines' Spratlys occupations. China's publication and expansive interpretation of its 1992 Law on the Territorial Sea and Contiguous Zone of the People's Republic of China heightened concerns about China's ultimate goals.[25] If Beijing were determined to enforce the claims in the law—and as it turned out it was—this promised to embroil all of the ASEAN maritime states in disputes with China. Spurred to a regional response, ASEAN seized the political agenda with its 1992 Declaration on the South China Sea (appendix I). ASEAN did not take a position on the bilateral disputes themselves. At the regional level, the issue for ASEAN was the mode of dispute resolution. The declaration emphasized the necessity to resolve by peaceful means and without resort to force all of the sovereignty and jurisdictional disputes. It prospectively called for the application of the principles embodied in the TAC—to which China was a signatory—as a basis for establishing a code of conduct (COC) in the South China Sea. Although China was not mentioned by name, it was alluded to as a "concerned party" and as such was invited to subscribe to the declaration of principles. Why, if China did not abide by the provisions for peaceful dispute resolution in the TAC—a treaty—it would be any more willing to abide by the principles of a nonbinding declaration or a future COC was not addressed.

The declaration suggested that functional cooperative activities could be undertaken to promote confidence-building measures (CBMs) without prejudicing the sovereignty and jurisdictional problems in areas such as pollution, navigation, piracy, and other transnational issues that have been addressed in other chapters of this book. Indonesia spearheaded the effort to establish parameters for functional cooperation. It initiated and has chaired since 1990 annual and officially nongovernmental Track II "Workshops on Managing Potential Conflict in the South China Sea." The goal has been to find areas of functional cooperation leading to confidence-building measures and habits of cooperation that could eventually produce a political atmosphere conducive to finding solutions to the territorial and jurisdictional disputes.[26] China has participated in the workshops, but with the proviso that it did not discuss matters of sovereignty or territorial jurisdiction. Nor would China allow any multilateral scientific research project that might suggest the legitimacy of international intervention in Chinese sovereign territory and waters. After a quarter of a century, the workshop process has not been able to move from its Track II "talk shop" informality to intergovernmental functional project cooperation, let alone create habits of cooperation that could translate to the political level. Other efforts to promote CBMs include ARF's ISM on marine security and the ASEAN Maritime Forum (chapter 5).

ASEAN members learned from China's 1995 seizure of Mischief Reef from the Philippines how ineffective their 1992 declaration was in reining in Chinese ambitions. It did not slow down China's stone marker–by pillar–by navigation buoy expansion of its physical claim to jurisdiction over the contested land and water. ASEAN continued to press China for a formal commitment to its proposed COC. China did not retreat from its insistence that issues of sovereignty and jurisdiction are not matters for multilateral disposition. China would only accept a text that did not undermine its sovereign claims or close its options in defending its claims. From Beijing's vantage, the threat to peace was the unwillingness of the affected ASEAN states to acknowledge China's sovereign rights in the SCS.

The best that ASEAN could obtain from China was the 2002 nonbinding Declaration on the Conduct of Parties in the South China Sea (appendix II). The DOC stated the parties' commitment to international law, the UNCLOS, and voluntary adherence to the principles of peace, self-restraint, nonuse of force, functional cooperation, and consultation. They agreed to respect freedom of navigation in and overflight above the SCS. They undertook not to escalate disputes and would refrain from actions to change the territorial status quo. The final paragraph of the DOC repeated the 1992 declaration's call for a code of conduct. China's willingness to sign the DOC was on the condition that it was a general and nonbinding expression of intentions and did not reference any specific case such as Mischief Reef. That China did not view the DOC as a real policy constraint has been demonstrated in subsequent years as its growing capabilities have been matched by more aggressive enforcement of its claims.

Importantly for China, in the DOC the signatories undertook to resolve their disputes through "friendly consultations and negotiations by *sovereign states directly concerned* with universally recognized principles of international law including the 1982 Convention on the Law of the Sea" (emphasis added). ASEAN accepted China's consistent position that disputes had to be resolved bilaterally. Neither ASEAN (not a sovereign state) nor nonclaimant states (e.g., the United States) have a role. As for the UNCLOS, China in its reservations when ratifying the covenant specifically stated that it did not accept any of the compulsory procedures entailing binding decisions provided for in Section 2 of Part XV of the Convention with respect to the category of disputes listed in Article 298: delimitation of overlapping territorial seas, EEZs, and continental shelves as well as military activities and enforcement activities.[27] ASEAN, fully aware that China had exempted itself from the application of UNCLOS dispute-resolution mechanisms, still hoped that China would abide by UNCLOS principles.

The DOC was not self-executing. It needed to be implemented. In the meantime, China continued to flaunt its principles and intent. It was not until 2005 that an ASEAN–China Joint Working Group (JWG) on the DOC began consultations on implementation.[28] The draft guidelines for implementation were not ready until 2011. Through March 2014, the JWG had met ten times as it continued to review implementation. Even as China dragged out the DOC process to its advantage, ASEAN pressed China to negotiate the COC. At the Indonesia-hosted 2011 EAS, the South China Sea issues were raised during the "leaders' retreat." Over vigorous Chinese objections, President Yudhoyono ruled that such a discussion was appropriate and important for the EAS. Chinese premier Wen Jiabao directly contradicted the Indonesian president, asserting that the EAS was not the proper forum, adding that the relevant parties, the involved ASEAN states, should do something more conducive for mutual trust and understanding.

ASEAN in Crisis

The July 2012 ASEAN Foreign Ministers' Meeting (AMM) in Phnom Penh, chaired by Cambodian foreign minister Hor Namhong, stripped away any remaining veneer of ASEAN solidarity when, for the first time in the forty-five-year history of ASEAN, no final Chairman's Statement was issued. The foreign ministers of Indonesia, Malaysia, the Philippines, and Vietnam had drafted a summary of the South China Sea discussion in the context of the norms of the DOC which included references to the Scarborough Shoal incident and China's leasing to oil companies exploratory blocks in Vietnam's EEZ. The Cambodian host, advised behind the scenes by Chinese diplomats, objected, echoing China's position that these were bilateral disputes not to be dealt with as an ASEAN matter. Indonesian foreign minister Marty Natalegawa, seconded by his Singaporean and Malaysian counterparts, argued that the final communiqué should express the common concerns of all ASEAN members about the situation in the South China Sea. The issue boiled down to if we cannot defend the DOC, what is the value of a COC? The Cambodian foreign minister, and behind him Prime Minister Hun Sen, was adamant—no reference to Chinese behavior or no final communiqué.[29] The AMM ended in disarray.

Cambodia and China inveighed against certain countries that sought to disturb peaceful relations between China and ASEAN. The Philippines, blamed for the failure of the AMM, officially rebutted the accusation saying the strain being felt by ASEAN was attributable to the failure of AMM's chair. To this point, the undersecretary of the Philippines Department of Foreign Affairs quoted Singapore foreign minister K. Shanmugan as saying the failure was a blow to ASEAN's credibility because "it was unable to deal with something that is happening in our neighborhood and not say something about it," adding, "there is no point in papering over it. There was a consensus among the majority of countries. The role of the Chair in the context is to forge a complete consensus amongst us all. But that did not happen."[30]

Immediately following the AMM breakdown, Foreign Minister Marty undertook a two-day flurry of flights to Manila, Hanoi, Bangkok, Singapore, and back to Phnom Penh to salvage what he could. He was concerned not only with papering over the unprecedented break in ASEAN solidarity, but as well to find a minimum consensus on going forward to COC negotiations with China. Marty was able to get agreement on what became ASEAN's face-saving Statement of ASEAN Foreign Ministers on ASEAN's Six-Point Principles on the South China Sea.[31] In the 20 July 2012 statement, the foreign ministers committed themselves to (1) the full implementation of the DOC, (2) the guidelines for the DOC, (3) the early conclusion of the COC, (4) full respect for international law including UNCLOS, (5) the continued exercise of restraint and nonuse of force, and (6) the peaceful resolution of all disputes in accordance with international law and UNCLOS. Although hailed as a show of Indonesian leadership in ASEAN, the six points, in fact, simply restated the principles of the 2002 DOC, adding nothing new. Manila and Hanoi went along at Marty's behest to save the ministerial meeting and perhaps even ASEAN itself. Point 5 must have been particularly galling. To suggest that the parties *continue* to exercise restraint and nonuse of force simply ignored the Chinese lack of restraint and use of force in the events concerning which the Philippines and Vietnam wanted ASEAN to take official note.

A number of lessons can be drawn from the outcome of the 2012 AMM. It was a clear example of the maritime–continental strategic division in ASEAN. It underlined again how important the role of the ASEAN chair is in controlling the agenda. It also confirmed for any doubters that Cambodia was China's voice and veto in ASEAN. This was demonstrated again at the

November 2012 ASEAN Summit when Cambodia inserted in the draft text of the Chairman's Statement that ASEAN had agreed not to internationalize the SCS territorial disputes. The Philippines protested that there was no consensus, and the reference was omitted. The AMM also showed that the political and security interests of ASEAN's maritime states with respect to China cannot realistically be defended from an ASEAN diplomatic platform. This will be important for post-Yudhoyono governments. For a decade—2004–2014— the two Yudhoyono administrations, first with Foreign Minister Hassan Wirajuda and then Marty Natalegawa, made a major political investment in ASEAN as the cornerstone of Indonesia's foreign policy. In a security environment in which Indonesia's maritime zones are at risk, a new Indonesian government may look to alternatives.

TOWARD A CODE OF CONDUCT
(COC) IN THE SOUTH CHINA SEA

The Philippines Application for Arbitration

Manila, frustrated by ASEAN's inaction, took its SCS case outside of ASEAN. On 22 January 2013, and apparently without consultation with other ASEAN states, the Philippines delivered to the Chinese ambassador a "Notification" and "Statement of Claim" announcing that it had initiated an arbitral proceeding at the Hague, Netherlands–based Permanent Court of Arbitration (PCA). It requested an arbitral tribunal to clearly establish the sovereign rights and jurisdictions of the Philippines over its maritime entitlements in the West Philippine Sea [South China Sea].[32] This was based on the UNCLOS dispute-resolution mechanisms of Article 287, "Choice of Procedure," and Annex VII, "Arbitration." The Philippines is challenging the validity of China's nine-dash-line claim to almost all of the South China Sea including the West Philippine Sea and calling for China to desist from unlawful activities that violate the sovereign rights and jurisdictions of the Philippines based on the UNCLOS. Manila's show of resoluteness greatly angered China and discomforted continental ASEAN states because it rocked the Chinese boat. There was also concern, particularly from Indonesia, that a Beijing backlash might jeopardize a COC negotiation.

On 15 February 2013, China vehemently rejected the Philippines' initiative, returning the "Notification." Beijing accused Manila of trying to steal Chinese sovereignty and claimed that the maritime disputes are not covered by the UNCLOS. China refused to participate in the PCA process having, as noted above, exempted itself from the UNCLOS dispute-resolution provisions. China's refusal to participate has not prevented the process from moving forward. UNCLOS Annex VII, Article 9, stipulates that if one of the parties does not appear or fails to defend its case, the other party can request the Tribunal to continue and to make its award. In April 2013, a five-member arbitral panel had been appointed. Rules of procedure were adopted, and on 30 March 2014 the Philippines submitted a ten-volume, four-thousand-page "Memorial" laying out the Philippines' case for the jurisdiction of the Arbitral Tribunal and the merits of the Philippines' claim.[33] If the panel takes jurisdiction and in fact makes an award, there is no expectation that China will take cognizance of any opinion that might be rendered. If it turns out only to be a moral victory, it would lay bare to the international community China's disregard for international law, UNCLOS, and its DOC pledges.

COC Consultations

Indonesia's frustration at the lack of progress in formulating the COC has been expressed in uncharacteristically blunt words by President Yudhoyono, who said in August 2012, "Things do not necessarily have to be this slow," adding, "We need to send a strong signal to the world that the future of the South China Sea is predictable, manageable, and optimistic."[34] Marty himself has worried that events are outpacing progress and that the DOC might become a dead letter. Time is on China's side. To ASEAN entreaties for an early conclusion of the COC, the stock Beijing reply is that a COC could be concluded "when the time is ripe," with no indication of a calendar.

With the DOC implementation guidelines finally in place in 2011, an ASEAN senior officials' working group completed a draft of proposed elements for a COC, which was adopted by the foreign ministers at the July 2012 AMM.[35] The adoption of the "elements" by the AMM was overshadowed by the contretemps over the Chairman's Statement. The consensus on the "elements" was a partial diplomatic victory for Vietnam and the Philippines, which had insisted that an ASEAN consensus on the COC had to be reached before having China involved. Taking the initiative, Foreign Minister Marty promised to flesh out the "elements" package with a "nonpaper" that became the Zero Draft Regional Code of Conduct in the South China Sea.[36] This was presented for discussion to his ministerial colleagues on the sidelines of the October 2012 UNGA session. The document was rooted in the DOC, the "elements," and the six-point principles, all of which China would have no problem verbally accepting but behaviorally rejecting. Some prescriptive articles, however, would be unlikely to get China's acquiescence, for example, respect for EEZs and continental shelves and refraining from military exercises, military surveillance, and other provocative actions. In the Zero Draft, Marty tried to reconcile the concerns of Vietnam and the Philippines but at the same time provide a basis for consensus building with China.

Chinese foreign minister Wang Yi, visiting Jakarta in early May 2013, agreed to talks with ASEAN on a COC. At an August 2013 special China–ASEAN Foreign Ministers' Meeting in Beijing commemorating the tenth anniversary of the China–ASEAN Strategic Partnership, it was announced that the DOC JWG would begin consultations on the COC under the framework of the DOC.[37] Three weeks prior to that, Wang Yi, ending a six-day Southeast Asian visit, gave a press conference in Hanoi during which he outlined the Chinese parameters for moving the COC process forward under the framework of implementing the DOC.[38] Wang Yi made four points. First, talk of a quick consensus was unreasonable, unrealistic, and not serious. The formulation of a COC is a "process of sophisticated and complicated coordination." In other words, while ASEAN may have a draft of a COC and want early conclusion to the process, China will start from scratch. Second, consensus has to be reached as broadly as possible and keeping in mind the comfort level of all parties. "Wills of individual countries or a few countries should not be imposed on other countries." The unstated reference is to Vietnam and the Philippines. Third, interference has to be eliminated "to create the necessary conditions and atmosphere, not going the opposite way." The implied "interference" is of course the American claim to be a regional stakeholder and supporter of ASEAN's push for a COC. Fourth, the road map to a COC should be formulated through consultations in a step-by-step approach. The top priority is implementation of the DOC, not its replacement. China views the COC as subordinate to the DOC, part of its implementing process. ASEAN had conceived the COC as a superior instrument, exchanging the voluntary expressions of the DOC with binding legal engagements to which China could be held accountable.

The linking of the DOC implementation to the COC suggests that if the consultations in the JWG become a future negotiation of the COC, its scope will not be broadened to cover the issues at the heart of the current insecurities. The ASEAN–China JWG had its first meeting on the COC in China in September 2013. In what was described as "healthy discussions," it was agreed that the COC process would move step by step to reach consensus through consultation.[39] At the March 2014 JWG meeting in Thailand, the COC discussion focused on areas of convergence and commonalities as a basis for drawing up terms of reference for an Eminent Persons and Expert Group or other mechanisms to support the consultations.[40] Thailand, as ASEAN's coordinator of ASEAN–China relations, echoing Wang Yi, has indicated that the COC drafting process has no time frame and will be cautious and step by step.[41] At the same time, China continues to alter the status quo. In May 2014, it moved an oil rig into position in the disputed zone off the Vietnamese coast, drove off Vietnamese coast guard ships, and belligerently threatened to punish Vietnam if it should try to interfere.[42]

Even if at some future point a nonbinding, nonenforceable consensus-based Code of Conduct for Parties in the South China Sea should be reached, it is doubtful that it will significantly alter Chinese behavior. At no point in its dealings with ASEAN and ASEAN states has China compromised the claims of sovereignty and jurisdiction that are the source of the conflict. Nor has China yielded in its refusal to apply the prescribed UNCLOS instruments to adjudicate or arbitrate its bilateral disputes. China consistently claims it is committed to peaceful resolution of disputes, but what that means, having rejected legal and diplomatic modes of dispute resolution, is for the weaker party to surrender. The history of China's diplomacy in South China Sea competition is one of declarations of cooperation followed by unilateral acts revising the status quo followed by new declarations of cooperation.

If the prospect of a COC that will in fact restrain China seems so remote, why has ASEAN fastened on to the process with such tenacity for so long with no real progress? ASEAN had to give some kind of security blanket to Manila and Hanoi, no matter how flimsy, if any semblance of community solidarity were to be maintained. To simply abandon the frontline states would accelerate the polarization of ASEAN in the China–US great-power competition. One of the goals is to keep China engaged in a dialogue, but that means not to challenge China on specific cases in dispute. For some ASEAN observers, there is a sense that dialogue for the sake of dialogue postpones the inevitable. Faced with the geostrategic realities of the Southeast Asia–China relationship, it can be asked, "What are the alternatives?"

There are some indicators that the negotiating climate may be changing. After the initial shock of the Philippines filing for arbitration, it is recognized that a legal win for Manila is a win for all ASEAN SCS stakeholders, legally undermining as it would China's claimed jurisdictions. The Philippines has succeeded in connecting with Vietnam and Malaysia in tripartite "claimants meetings" to cooperate in resisting China's nine-dash line.[43] Brunei was originally included but was a no-show. Malaysia's willingness to become actively engaged with other claimants in 2014 reflects a changed appreciation of the seriousness of repeated Chinese naval incursions, illegal fishing, and harassment of supply vessels to offshore oil platforms.[44] In 2014, Indonesia's position seems to be moving from one of "strategic ambiguity" to "strategic uncertainty" and on toward "strategic concern."

Foreign Minister Marty has tried to keep open a possible mediating role for Indonesia between China and the ASEAN claimants, but from China's point of view, there is nothing to be mediated. Nor has Marty's point-man position on pressing for an early conclusion to the COC been rewarded by Chinese concessions. What the Indonesian foreign ministry has treated as a diplomatic problem is being viewed by the military as a potential strategic threat. The

March 2014 acknowledgment of Chinese penetration into the EEZ north of the Natuna Islands was noted above. A senior Ministry of Defense official has asserted that Chinese claims have a large impact on the security of Natuna waters.[45] Indonesia has deployed more naval assets to the area. In developing the 2014 "Komodo" multilateral naval exercise in Natuna waters, the planners indicated that one of its goals was to "pay attention to the aggressive stance of the Chinese government by entering the Natuna area."[46]

Whether or not the comments from military sources reflect a policy change is a matter of debate.[47] From Marty's vantage point, there has been no change in Indonesian policy: there is no territorial dispute with China; Indonesia is not a claimant state in the South China Sea; and Indonesia does not accept the nine-dash line and has asked for a formal explanation from China of its legal basis and background. This does not address Chinese encroachments in Indonesia's EEZ. While China's naval and fishery activities in Indonesian waters have stirred concern, the future anxiety is for the nine-dash-line overlap of the East Natuna gas block, one of the largest in the world, with an estimated forty-six Tcfs of recoverable natural gas.[48] To challenge China on the EEZ overlap would change Indonesia's SCS negotiating status—from a neutral, possible mediator, to a disputant state. If nothing else, the comments by senior Indonesian military officers are a public manifestation of discord on China between the military and the foreign ministry.[49]

Foreign Minister Marty has doggedly pursued the attainment of the Code of Conduct as the best way to defend Indonesia's national interests in the South China Sea: the EEZ, freedom of navigation, ASEAN unity, and ASEAN centrality between China and the United States. The step-by-step approach with no timetable for conclusion means that Marty's successor(s) will inherit the COC process. It also means that every year elapsed makes the COC less relevant to the real situation in the SCS. The question is, will future Indonesian governments be willing to make such a policy investment with little probability of practical impact?

PROSPECTS FOR JOINT
DEVELOPMENT AGREEMENTS (JDAs)

It seems clear that China is not going to scale back its South China Sea claims nor cease its activities to enforce these claims. China's violations of the TAC and DOC, and probable violations of a future COC, may have international diplomatic and political costs for China, but the rewards of demonstrating Chinese dominion would be large, strategically and materially. In the words of the Indonesian scholar/diplomat who conceived the workshop process, "It is basically a scramble for resources."[50] Real national interests and relative power are in the foreground of this scramble, while UNCLOS and ASEAN norms are relegated to a rhetorical background. As China's energy requirements grow, the search for settlement becomes even more urgent for concerned Southeast Asian states. Realistically and pragmatically, this means that ASEAN claimants will have to find a framework that does not depend upon defending sovereign claims by simply invoking UNCLOS articles. The solution most often discussed is to put aside sovereign claims and to agree to cooperate in exploration and exploitation of resources in disputed areas through joint development agreements (JDAs) in which issues of sovereignty are shelved as benefits are shared.[51]

As noted in chapter 5, a model JDA exists in the Gulf of Thailand where Malaysia and Thailand are exploiting natural gas fields under their 2,800-square-mile (7,250 sq km) overlap. A 1979 MOU on joint exploration and exploitation led to the creation in 1991 of the Malaysia–Thailand Joint Authority (MTJA) operating on a 50-50 cost–benefits basis. In 2009, Malaysia and Brunei resolved two outstanding boundary and maritime disputes by linking the maritime dispute to a settlement of outstanding issues over the Limbang salient, a piece of Sarawak that separates the two parts of Brunei. This was followed in 2012 by an agreement to jointly develop in a "commercial arrangement" two oil and gas blocks off the Borneo coast. A key to a JDA is the quality of the political relationship between the contracting parties.

From the 1990s China has proposed joint development in disputed waters. A central issue for drafting a JDA is the delimitation of its boundary, that is, the limits of the two parties' jurisdictional claims and demarcation of the overlap. The bases for delimitation of maritime zones and continental shelves are set out in UNCLOS. If a country accepted China's claimed limits as set by the nine-dash line, it would mean ceding to China potential resources. Even if the JDA were phrased to protect the basic claims to sovereignty and jurisdiction, it would give political credibility to the nine-dash line as a basis for negotiations. Any government that entered such an unequal arrangement would have to be prepared to expect protest and nationalist backlash.

During President Gloria Macapagal-Arroyo's administration, the Philippines was willing to explore possibilities of future joint development projects with China. In September 2004, she oversaw the signing in China of a three-year Agreement on Joint Marine Seismic Undertaking in Certain Areas of the South China Sea (JMSU), to take effect in July 2005. It was ostensibly not a government agreement. It was between the China National Offshore Oil Corporation and the Philippines National Oil Corporation. Such an undertaking could only be in anticipation of joint exploration and development. At that point, the governments would have to draft a JDA delimiting its area.

The other ASEAN claimants were stunned. The Philippines had been the primary mover for coordinated ASEAN efforts to maintain the status quo in the region, yet it had cut a deal with China without consultation. Vietnam accused the Philippines of violating the DOC. However, it only took six months for the reality of the Sino-Philippine accord to bring Vietnam on board. In March 2005, the bilateral seismic survey became tripartite when Vietnam's state-owned PetroVietnam joined the JMSU in what Arroyo hailed as "a diplomatic breakthrough for peace and security in the region."[52] Chinese president Hu Jintao, visiting Manila shortly after the signing, said that China and the Philippines "have taken the lead in the groundbreaking joint development in the South China Sea."[53]

There were hidden costs for the Philippines in the agreement. In January 2008, details of the scope of the vague "certain areas of the South China Sea" that the Philippines agreed to explore jointly were made public.[54] The nearly fifty-eight-thousand-square-mile (143,000 sq km) JMSU zone included more than nine thousand square miles (24,000 sq km) of indisputably Philippine continental shelf that had never been claimed by China or Vietnam. After blindsiding ASEAN, the Arroyo government now was charged by angry politicians and editorialists with not only relinquishing its Spratly claims but selling out the country's sovereignty. In return for giving China the deal, it was alleged that China promised $8 billion in loans and grants, thus adding to the scandals engulfing the Arroyo administration over its dealings with China.[55] The controversy erupted just as the Philippine Congress was readying a measure to confirm that the Philippines' national territory included Kalayaan; this despite China's warning that it would hurt friendly relations and mutually beneficial cooperation.[56] As it turned out, the JMSU did not lead to any production agreements and was not renewed at expiry in 2008.

A proposed JDA in the Spratlys was at the center of President Aquino's 2011 proposal for an ASEAN–China Zone of Peace, Freedom, Friendship, and Cooperation (ZoPFFC) in the South China Sea. The zone would be created by segregating the nondisputed areas from the disputed. In the disputed areas—the Spratlys—a demilitarized enclave would be created as a joint cooperation area for development and conservation. As Aquino put it, "What is ours is ours, and with what is disputed, we can work towards joint cooperation."[57] For ASEAN and China, the ZoPFFC was a nonstarter. Only Vietnam was interested, with President Truong Tan Sang promising to support it during his October 2011 visit to Manila.[58]

It was Aquino's intention to put the ZoPFFC on the agenda of the ASEAN–China Summit and the EAS. China's vigorous opposition to even discussing the matter with ASEAN reflected its consistent position that disputes were bilateral and ASEAN multilateralism was not appropriate. Furthermore, as a practical matter, the ZoPFFC's segregation of disputed–nondisputed areas had an assumption that the nondisputed areas included the UNCLOS-delimited maritime zones, which would have erased the nine-dash line. ASEAN was reluctant to endorse the proposal because it would directly challenge China. Indonesia's foreign minister Marty was particularly concerned that making the ZoPFFC an ASEAN matter could be a spoiler for the COC negotiation.[59] With no backing from ASEAN, Manila shelved the initiative.

Economic logic and China's strategic advantage might argue that for the Southeast Asian states whose maritime zones are at risk, joint development is better than continued confrontation. President Xi Jinping and Premier Li Keqiang continue to offer prospects for maritime cooperation and joint development in Southeast Asia, but with no compromise on claims or dispute resolution. China would be the aggregate economic winner in a China + 1 process. China would be a political winner, too, by eliminating an irritant in its relations in Southeast Asia. The Southeast Asian states would not be losers, however. Joint development would be better than no development in an atmosphere of intimidating threat scaring off investment, concessionaires, and contractors. As China's force capability grows, there is even a future possibility of Chinese seizure of territory à la Scarborough Shoal as it enforces its sovereignty and jurisdiction. Looking at the issues at play in the South China Sea, Ralf Emmers came to the conclusion that the economic logic of cooperation could not prevail, "making the joint development of resources an unlikely scenario in the years to come."[60] China's decision to position a militarily protected oil rig in Vietnam's EEZ in May 2014, noted above, may indicate that Beijing no longer feels it necessary to dangle a carrot of joint development.

The Philippines and Vietnam have been left exposed by their community partners. At the May 2014 ASEAN Summit, hosted by Myanmar, both President Benigno Aquino and Prime Minister Nguyen Tan Dung called for a strong ASEAN position on the security threats in the SCS. The Chinese countered that the Philippines and Vietnam were attempting to harm friendship and cooperation between China and ASEAN.[61] China prevailed. The day before the summit, the ASEAN foreign ministers issued a "statement on current developments in the South China Sea" that expressed concern, without mentioning countries, about unspecified ongoing developments in the South China Sea. They repeated once more the formulas of the DOC and the Six Principles with respect to international law, peaceful resolution, restraint, nonuse of force, and the need for an early conclusion of the COC.[62] The summit's Chairman's Statement, wary of upsetting China, was more of the same. Rather than ASEAN solidarity, ASEAN neutrality is the collective response.

NOTES

1. United Nations, *The Law of the Sea, Official Text of the United Nations Convention on the Law of the Sea with Annexes and Index* (New York: United Nations, 1983).

2. UNCLOS, Articles 3, 57, and 76.

3. Communication by China to the Secretary General of the UN with Reference to the Joint Submission by Malaysia and Vietnam, accessed at http://www.un.org/Depts/los/clcs_new/submissions_files/mysvnm33_09/chn_2009re_mys_vnm_e.pdf.

4. "Loss of James Shoal Could Wipe Out State's EEZ," *Borneo Post Online*, 5 February 2014, accessed at http://www.theborneopost.com/2014/02/05/loss-of-james-shoal.

5. "Daring Show of Force by PLA Navy," *South China Morning Post* (Hong Kong), 27 March 2013.

6. Hancox and Prescott list 147 named features; see David Hancox and Victor Prescott, *A Geographical Description of the Spratly Islands and an Account of Hydrographic Surveys amongst Those Islands*, vol. 1, no. 6, *Maritime Briefings* (Durham, UK: Durham University International Boundaries Research Unit, 1995).

7. Rommel C. Banlaoi, "Renewed Tensions and Continuing Maritime Security Dilemma in the South China Sea: A Philippine Perspective," in *The South China Sea: Cooperation for Regional Security and Development*, ed. Tran Truong Thuy (Hanoi: Diplomatic Academy of Vietnam, 2010).

8. The English-language text of the law was accessed at http://vietnamnews.vn/politics-laws/228456/the-law-of-the-sea-of-viet-nam.html.

9. Foreign Ministry Spokesperson Hong Lei's Regular Press Conference, 21 June 2012, accessed at http://www.fmprc.gov.cn/mfa_eng, link "Press and Media Service," then "Regular Press Conference."

10. Foreign Ministry Spokesperson Hong Lei's Regular Press Conference, 31 March 2014, accessed at http://www.fmprc.gov.cn/mfa_eng, link "Press and Media Service," then "Regular Press Conference."

11. Marius Gjetnes, "The Spratlys: Are They Rocks or Islands?" *Ocean Development & International Law* 32, no. 2 (2001): 191–204; Robert W. Smith, "Maritime Delimitation in the South China Sea: Potentiality and Challenges," *Ocean Development & International Law* 41, no. 3 (2010): 214–36.

12. China's UNCLOS ratification understandings can be accessed at http://www.un.org/depts/los/convention_agreements/convention_declarations.htm.

13. The text of the law can be accessed at http://www.un.org/Depts/los/LEGISLATIONANDTREATIES/PDFFILES/CHN_1992_Law.pdf.

14. The statistical data on South China Sea energy resources are those given by the US Energy Information Administration of the Department of Energy, updated to 7 February 2013 and accessed at http://www.eia.gov/countries/analysisbriefs/South_China_Sea/south_china_sea.pdf.

15. "Indonesia's Military Flexes Muscle as S. China Sea Dispute Looms," *Jakarta Globe*, 13 March 2014.

16. As quoted in "Oil Majors Avoid Philippine Bids for China-Claimed Sea Blocks," Bloomberg News, 31 July 2012, accessed at http://www.bloomberg.com/news/2012-07-31/Philippines-to-offer-offshore-oil-blocks-in-china-claimed-areas .html.

17. Scott Bentley, "Mapping the Nine-Dash Line: Recent Incidents Involving Indonesia in the South China Sea," *Strategist* (Australian Strategic Policy Institute Blog), 29 October 2013, accessed at http://www.aspistrategist.org.au.

18. Carlyle A. Thayer, "China: Hainan Province Authorities Escalate Fishing Disputes," *Thayer Consultancy Background Brief*, 9 January 2014, accessed at http://www.iacspsea.com/wp-content/uploads/2014/01/Thayer-China-Hainan-Province -Authorities-Escalate-Fishing-Disputes.pdf.

19. The dates and nature of the incidents are listed in Ronald O'Rourke, *Maritime Territorial and Exclusive Economic Zone (EEZ) Disputes Involving China: Issues for Congress* (Washington, DC: Congressional Research Service, April 2014), 4–5, accessed at http://www.fas.org/sgp/crs/row/R42784.pdf.

20. "Maritime Disputes in Southeast Asia," testimony of Daniel R. Russell, assistant secretary of state for Asia and the Pacific, before the House Committee on Foreign Affairs, Sub-Committee on Asia and the Pacific, 5 February 2014.

21. The citation is from a "Background Briefing by a Senior Administration Official on the President's Meetings at ASEAN and the East Asia Summit," accessed at http://www.whitehouse.gov/the-press-office/2011/11/19/background-briefing-senior -administration-official-presidents-meetings-a.

22. "Full Text of Chinese Premier Wen's Statement at 14th China ASEAN Summit," accessed at http://news.xinhuanet.com/english2010/china/2011-11/18/c_131255936 .htm.

23. "Commentary: Emboldened Manila May Upset U.S. Rebalancing to Asia," accessed at http://news.xinhuanet.com/english/world/2014-04/28/c_133294852.htm.

24. Indonesia's communication to the UN on the matter can be accessed at http://www.un.org/Depts/los/clcs_new/submissions_files/mysvnm33_09/idn_2010re _mys_vnm_e.pdf.

25. The English-language text of the Chinese Territorial Sea Law can be accessed at http://www.un.org/Depts/los/LEGISLATIONANDTREATIES/PDFFILES/ CHN_1992_Law.pdf.

26. "South China Sea: Contribution of 2nd Track Diplomacy/Workshop Process to Progressive Development of Regional Peace and Security" is a history of the first twenty years of the workshop by its Indonesian founder, Dr. Hasjim Djalal, accessed at http://carlospromulo.org/wp-content/uploads/2009/12/Hasjim-Djalal.pdf.

27. See note 12 supra.

28. The terms of reference for the ASEAN—China Joint Working Group can be accessed at http://www.asean.org/news/item/terms-of-reference-of-the-asean-china -joint-working-group-on-the-implementation-of-the-declaration-on-the-conduct-of -parties-in-the-south-china-sea.

29. The discussion of the 2011 AMM draws on publications by Australian analyst Carlyle A. Thayer, who had access to participant notes: Carlyle A. Thayer, "Behind the Scenes of ASEAN's Breakdown." *Asia Times Online*, 27 July 2012, accessed

at http://www.atimes.com/atimes/Southeast_Asia/NG27Ae03.html; and Carlyle A. Thayer, "ASEAN, China and the Code of Conduct in the South China Sea," *SAIS Review* 33, no. 2 (2013): 75–84.

30. Undersecretary Erlindo F. Basilio, "Why There Was No ASEAN Joint Communiqué," accessed at http://www.gov.ph/2012/07/18/why-there-was-no-asean-joint -communique.

31. Indonesian Ministry of Foreign Affairs, "Six Point Principles, ASEAN's Consensus on South China Sea," accessed at http://www.kemlu.go.id/Pages/News .aspx?IDP=5717&I=en.

32. The "Notification and Statement" of claim can be accessed at the UNCLOS link on the home page of the Philippines Department of Foreign Affairs, accessed at http://www.dfa.gov.ph. This also includes the briefing and Q & A by Secretary of Foreign Affairs Albert Del Rosario announcing the Philippines' démarche.

33. Secretary Del Rosario's statement on the submission of the Memorial to the arbitral procedure can be accessed at http://www.dfa.gov.ph/index.php/2013-06-27 -21-50-36/unclos.

34. As quoted in "We Need Ocean Code of Conduct, Yudhoyono Says," *South China Morning Post* (Hong Kong), 14 August 2012.

35. The content of the four-page document has been published in Carlyle A. Thayer, "ASEAN's Code of Conduct (Unofficial)," *Thayer Consultancy Background Brief*, 11 July 2012, accessed at http://www.scribd.com/doc/211788387/Thayer -Commentary-100913.

36. The content of the "Zero Draft" has been summarized and analyzed by Mark Valencia, "What the 'Zero Draft' Code of Conduct for the South China Sea Says (and Doesn't Say)," accessed at http://www.globalasia.org/Issue/ArticleDetail/43/what -the-zero-draft-code-of-conduct-for-the-south-china-sea-says-and-doesnt-say.html; and Carlyle A. Thayer, "South China Sea in Regional Politics: Indonesia's Efforts to Forge ASEAN Unity on a Code of Conduct," accessed at http://www.csis.org/files/ attachments/130606_Thayer_ConferencePaper.pdf.

37. PRC Ministry of Foreign Affairs, "Special China–ASEAN Foreign Ministers Meeting Held in Beijing," 29 August 2013, accessed at http://gr.china-embassy.org/ eng/zgyw/t1072011.htm.

38. PRC Ministry of Foreign Affairs, "Foreign Minister Wang Yi on Process of 'Code of Conduct in the South China Sea,'" accessed at http://www.fmprc.gov.cn/ mfa_eng/wjb_663304/wjbz_663308/activities_663312/t1064869.shtml.

39. PRC Ministry of Foreign Affairs, "The Sixth Senior Officials Meeting and Ninth Joint Working Group Meeting on Implementation of the 'Declaration on Conduct of Parties in the South China Sea' Are Held in Suzhou," 15 September 2013, accessed at http://www.fmprc.gov.cn/mfa_eng/zxxx_662805/t1079289.shtml.

40. Press release, Ministry of Foreign Affairs of the Kingdom of Thailand, "The 10th ASEAN–China Joint Working Group on the Implementation of the Declaration on the Conduct of Parties in the South China Sea (JWG on DOC)," 19 March 2014, accessed at http://www.mfa.go.th/main/en/media-center/14/44171-The-10th -ASEAN-China-Joint-Working-Group-on-the-Im.html.

41. Director General of ASEAN Affairs Department, Thailand's Ministry of Foreign Affairs, as quoted in "No Timeframe for South China Sea Code of Conduct: Thai ASEAN Affairs Official," Xinhuanet, 21 March 2014, accessed at http://english .peopledaily.com.cn/90777/8604812.html.

42. "Chinese Media Threatens Vietnam with a 'Lesson It Deserves' over Oil Rig," *South China Morning Post* (Hong Kong), 8 May 2014.

43. "4 ASEAN West PHL Sea Claimants to Meet in Manila to Discuss Disputes," accessed at http://www.gmanetwork.com/news/story/283306/news/national/4-asean -west-phl-sea-claimants-to-meet-in-manila-to-discuss-disputes.

44. Prashnth Parameswara, "Malaysia Walks Tightrope on China and South China Sea," Jamestown Foundation China Brief 14, no. 2 (20 March 2014), accessed at http://www.jamestown.org/single/?tx_ttnews%5Btt_news%5D=42127&tx _ttnews%5BbackPid%5D=7&cHash=368543df7bdcbdf7185d593e23ba0b45%23 .Uyx4J8cxWyA#.U-ptdfkweSo.

45. "China Includes Part of Natuna Waters in Its Map," accessed at http://www .antaranews.com/en/news/93178/china-includes-part-of-natuna-waters-in-its-map.

46. "Batam to Host Komodo Naval Joint Exercise," *Jakarta Post*, 15 June 2013.

47. Ann Marie Murphy, "The End of Strategic Ambiguity: Indonesia Formally Announces Its Dispute with China in the South China Sea," *PacNet* 26 (1 April 2014); Evan A. Laksmana, "Why There Is No 'New Maritime Dispute' between Indonesia and China," *Strategist* (Australian Strategic Policy Institute Blog), April 2014, accessed at http://www.aspistrategist.org.au/why-there-is-no-new-maritime -dispute-between-indonesia-and-china.

48. Ristian Atriandi Supriyanyo, "Indonesia's South China Sea Dilemma: Between Neutrality and Self-Interest," *RSIS Commentary*, no. 126/2012 (12 July 2012), accessed at http://www.rsis.edu.sg/wp-content/uploads/2014/07/RSIS12620122.pdf.

49. The point is made by Greta Nabbk-Keller, "Is Indonesia Shifting Its South China Sea Policy?" *Interpreter* (16 April 2014), accessed at http://www.lowyinter preter.org/post/2014/04/16/Indonesia-Natuna-shift-south-china-sea-policy.aspx.

50. Hasjim Djalal, "South China Sea Island Disputes," *The Raffles Bulletin of Zoology* (2000), suppl. 8 (*The Biodiversity of the South China Sea*), accessed at http:// lkcnhm.nus.edu.sg/rbz/biblio/s8/s08rbz009-021.pdf.

51. Various cooperative schemes are discussed in Mark J. Valencia, Jon M. Van Dyke, and Noel Ludwig, *Sharing the Resources of the South China Sea* (Honolulu: University of Hawaii Press, 1999).

52. As quoted in Luz Baguioro, "Three Nations Sign Pact for Joint Spratlys Survey," *Straits Times* (Singapore), 15 March 2005.

53. As quoted in Aurea Calica, "GMA, Hu Vow to Turn South China Sea into 'Area of Cooperation,'" *Philippine Star* (Manila), 29 March 2005.

54. Barry Wain, "Manila's Bungle in the South China Sea," *Far Eastern Economic Review* 171, no. 1 (January/February 2008): 45–48.

55. For a review of the scandals, see "Happy Birthday GMA, Hope You Spend the Rest of Your Days behind Bars," editorial, *Philippines News* (Manila), 7 April 2014, accessed at http://www.philnews.com/2014/14a.htm.

56. "Spratly Issue Worries China, Saying It Could Spoil Relations," *Manila Times*, 13 March 2008.

57. An analysis of the ZoPFFC plan based on the Department of Foreign Affairs "paper" on it can be found in Rommel C. Banlaoi, "Philippine Solution to the South China Sea Problem: More Problems, Less Solutions," accessed at http://academia .edu/1463826/Philippine_Solution_to_the_South_China_Sea_Problem_More_Prob lems_Less_Solutions.

58. "Manila, Hanoi Forge Cooperation in South China Sea," Reuters, 26 October 2011, accessed at http://www.reuters.com/article/2011/10/26/us-philippines-vietnam -idUSTRE79P2WA20111026.

59. For a discussion of ASEAN's treatment of the ZoPFFC proposal, see Ian Storey, "Intra-ASEAN Dynamics and the South China Sea Dispute: Implications for the DoC/CoC Process and the ZoPFFC Proposal" (paper presented at the Third International Workshop on "The South China Sea: Cooperation for Regional Security and Development," Hanoi, 3–5 November 2011), accessed at http://www.nghiencuubi endong.vn/en/conferences-and-seminars-/the-third-international-workshop-in-south -china-sea/640-intra-asean-dynamics-and-the-south-china-sea-dispute-implications -for-the-doccoc-process-and-the-zopffc-proposal-by-ian-storey.

60. Ralf Emmers, "Resource Management in the South China Sea: An Unlikely Scenario" (paper presented at NICCS South China Sea Conference, 6–7 December 2012), accessed at http://www.nanhai.org.cn/include_lc/upload/Upload Files/2013129100941408.pdf.

61. "S. China Sea Issue Not Problem between China, ASEAN," accessed at http:// english.peopledaily.com.cn/90883/8623664.html.

62. "ASEAN Foreign Ministers' Statement on the Current Developments in the South China Sea," 10 May 2014, accessed at http://www.asean.org/news/asean -foreign-ministers-statement-on-current-developments-in-the-south-china-sea.

SUGGESTIONS FOR FURTHER READING

Robert D. Kaplan, *Asia's Cauldron: The South China Sea and the End of a Stable Pacific* (New York: Random House, 2014) is a geopolitical analysis of what is at stake in the conflict. *China's Maritime Disputes in the East and South China Seas* contains the 2013 hearings of the US–China Economic and Security Review Commission. The transcript is available as a PDF at http:// origin.www.uscc.gov/sites/default/files/transcripts/USCC%20Hearing%20 Transcript%20-%20April%204%202013.pdf. A particular emphasis on the US role is given in IISS authors Sarah Raine and Christiane Le Mière, *Regional Disorder: The South China Sea Disputes* (London: IISS, 2013). Even though China is not represented at the PCA arbitration of the Philippines claim, there is a Chinese perspective which is detailed in Stefan Talmon and Bing Bing Jia, *The South China Sea Arbitration: A Chinese Perspective*

(Oxford: Hart Publishing, 2014), and Sam Bateman and Ralf Emmers, eds., *Security and International Politics in the South China Sea: Towards a Cooperative Management Regime* (New York: Routledge, 2012). The South China Sea dispute is the special focus of *Contemporary Southeast Asia* 33, no. 3 (December 2011).

Chapter Seven

Terrorism and Transnational Crime in Southeast Asia

Traditional threats to state sovereignty, territorial integrity, and jurisdictional claims were examined in chapters 5 and 6. Another category of threat originates from nonstate actors whose activities have no boundaries in terms of the international system but which affect relations between states. This chapter will focus on two such manifestations of transnational threat in contemporary Southeast Asia: terrorism and transnational crime. The challenge for the state actors individually and together in ASEAN has been to develop mechanisms to meet this new order of threat for which the national compartments of sovereignty and exclusive jurisdiction can be obstacles to effective countermeasures.

TERRORISM

After the destruction of New York's World Trade Center on 11 September 2001, Washington announced that Southeast Asia was a second front in a global war on terror. Southeast Asian leaders enlisted in that war with varying degrees of enthusiasm. The joint struggle against an elusive terrorist enemy meant that, after more than a quarter of a century, security again was the United States' greatest regional concern. The difference was that the American war in Indochina had visible state-based Cold War enemies (chapter 3). The protagonists of terror are linked in a shadowy network of groups and individuals articulating a virulent Wahhabist brand of radical Islam and deliberately directing deadly force against innocent civilians (box 7.1). The American connection of the "war on terror" to the invasions of Iraq and Afghanistan did not lead to an expansion of the security consensus on terrorism in Southeast Asia; just the opposite. Malaysia and Indonesia expressly

Box 7.1.   Wahhabism

Wahhabism is the primary religious stream inspiring Islamic terrorists. It is a fundamentalist Sunni Islamic movement that aggressively seeks to restore Islam to its original seventh-century purity of belief and practice as set forth in the Koran and the authoritative statements of the Prophet Mohammad (hadith) as handed down by tradition. The Wahhabi ideological origins are in the teachings by revered religious scholar Ibn Abd al Wahab (1703–1792) to the Bedouins of the Arabian Peninsula. It is the religion of contemporary Saudi Arabia, which has been accused of propagating it through the funding of Muslim institutions in other Muslim countries. Although of historically different origins, Wahhabism and Salafiyya, another conservative Islamic revival movement, have similar puritanical goals. With a pan-Islamic dynamic, Wahhabists insist on the strict enforcement of Islamic law in a community where there is no boundary between the state and religion. Although violence or holy war (jihad) is not necessarily intrinsic to Wahhabism, its morphing in the form of contemporary terrorism had its roots in the resistance war against the Soviet Union in Afghanistan. Thousands of Muslim volunteer fighters (mujahideen) were radicalized in mosques and schools funded by Saudi Arabia.

opposed the war in Iraq. Only traditional security partners, the Philippines, Thailand, and Singapore, supported the United States. All, however, continued cooperation in regional counterterrorism.

The support for counterterrorism from Southeast Asian leaders was not based on American perceptions of national interests but their own interests. The terrorists were a threat to their own national institutions and pluralist ideologies. In the local context, the grievances are not just those of Islamic puritans but also reflect social and ethnic inequalities. For the United States, the war against al-Qaeda and its allies was global. For Southeast Asians, it was localized. The antagonists were domestic radical Islamists and separatists. That which linked the Southeast Asian states' counterterrorist campaigns to each other and to the United States was the transboundary networking of terrorists with links to al-Qaeda.

In confronting the terrorists' holy war (jihad), leaders in Muslim-majority countries like Indonesia and Malaysia or those with large Muslim minorities like Thailand and the Philippines are fully aware of public sensitivities. Although accused by the radicals of joining the American "war against Islam," the domestic counterterrorists explicitly rejected an identification of terrorism with religion. In the words of a 2002 ASEAN Summit declaration, "We deplore the tendency in some quarters to identify terrorism with particular religions or ethnic groups."[1] It is politically understood that what ASEAN calls "terrorist elements" are in fact Islamist extremists. The identification of terrorism with acts rather than actors and assigning causation in general terms to social and economic circumstances rather than ideology and political goals is an effort to neutralize negative reactions in the Muslim community.

The Regional Response

Terrorist groups' organizational, recruitment, and financial scope is transnational. The linked terrorist networks do not recognize state boundaries. Effective countermeasures require international cooperation. At their November 2001 ASEAN Summit, the ASEAN heads of government adopted an ASEAN Declaration on Joint Action to Counter Terrorism. They expressed their commitment to combat terrorism, adding that cooperative joint practical counterterrorism measures should "be in line with specific circumstances in the region and in each member country." In August 2002, the United States and ASEAN issued a Joint Declaration to Combat International Terrorism that included the usual commitments to greater information flow, intelligence sharing, and capacity building. A similar undertaking came out of the January 2003 ASEAN–EU Ministerial Meeting.

In practical terms the regional cooperative measures suggested were not new but efforts to strengthen the capacity of the existing bilateral and regional frameworks for fighting transnational crime. The leaders emphasized that the United Nations should play the major role at the international level and urged all ASEAN states to accede to the twelve major international conventions on terrorism. The importance of the UN and international law is a theme that appeared in subsequent ASEAN statements and reflected regional uneasiness about the United States as a "global policeman."

The ASEAN Regional Forum (ARF) put terrorism on its agenda in 2002 when it adopted a Statement on Measures against Terrorist Financing and set up an Inter-Sessional Meeting on Counter-terrorism and Transnational Crime (ISM-CTTC) which first met in March 2003. There is also an ARF expert working group on crime and terrorism. Terrorism has become an item in the ASEAN + 3 dialogues. On a broader scale of participation, Indonesia and Australia cohosted the February 2004 Bali Ministerial Meeting on Counter-Terrorism, which brought together ASEAN and China, the EU, Fiji, France, Russia, South Korea, Timor-Leste, the United Kingdom, and the United States. The participants basically reaffirmed the existing commitments to combat terrorism.

As a follow-up to the Bali meeting, the ministers established an ad hoc working group of senior legal officials to study the adequacy of existing regional legal frameworks for combating terrorism. In 2004, eight ASEAN countries (not including Thailand and Myanmar) agreed to a Treaty on Mutual Legal Assistance in Criminal Matters, which previously had been a matter of a varying mix of bilateral arrangements. The treaty specifically stated, however, that it did not apply to extradition, which has long been a sensitive issue in ASEAN. In January 2007, the ASEAN Summit gave their counterterrorism cooperation a legal underpinning with the signing of the ASEAN Convention on Counter-terrorism. Up to then ASEAN had been the only major geopolitical global region without a legally binding agreement on terrorism.[2] Although hailed as a breakthrough, it created no new instrumentalities, being essentially a codification of the developing pattern of legal and enforcement-assistance measures. Missing from it was a guarantee of extradition.

As part of capacity building, new regional institutions have been set up to provide legal and law enforcement training and networking facilities. Malaysia established the Southeast Asia Regional Center for Counter-Terrorism (SEARCCT) to develop and organize capacity building programs. Since it opened its doors in July 2003 through June 2012, 3,038 individuals had passed through ninety-six training courses and workshops.[3] The United States had discussed such a regional institution with Malaysia, but Malaysian opposition to the US role in the Middle East prevented any formal American partnership. The United States has, however, been the major provider of training resources. An Indonesia–Australia Jakarta Center for Law Enforcement Cooperation (JCLEC) was established in 2004 as a resource for Southeast Asia in the fight against terrorism. The training base is the Indonesian Police Academy in Semarang. In 2013, 2,249 participants passed through eighty-one training programs.[4] In September 2011, on American initiative, a thirty-nation Global Counterterrorism Forum (GCTF) was launched, headed by foreign ministers.[5] Indonesia is the only Southeast Asian state among the founder members. Indonesia and Australia cochair the GCTF's Southeast Asia Capacity Building Working Group in which there is participation by relevant officials from throughout the region.

Under the symbolic and rhetorical expressions of ASEAN's will to combat terrorism and cooperate in capacity building, the real struggle is at the national level where the acts of terrorism take place. Since 2001, when terrorism jumped to the top of security priorities, the level of domestic threat in Southeast Asia has been lowered, but not eliminated. A regional climate of consultative confidence does not mean that the guard has been let down. Where the threat has been most critical, in Indonesia and the Philippines, robust security partnerships have been important in enhancing counterterrorism capabilities.[6]

Indonesia and the Jema'ah Islamiyah (Islamic Community)

On 12 October 2002 two bomb attacks at tourist bars on the island of Bali killed nearly two hundred innocents, many of them young Australians. What made the Bali attack singular was not just the number of casualties but the fact that the investigation clearly demonstrated the connection between radical Islamists of the Jema'ah Islamiyah (JI) and al-Qaeda. The JI was placed on the American list of foreign terrorist organizations (FTOs).[7] The global "war on terror" had come to Indonesia, something even President Megawati could not deny.

The JI

The Bali bombings exposed the JI as Indonesia's principal terrorist enemy. Its roots go back to the failed 1950s West Java Darul Islam (DI) revolt against the new pluralist Indonesian state. The DI's goal of an Islamic state stayed alive as the ideological underpinning of JI. Rhetorical militancy was accompanied in the late 1970s and early 1980s by occasional acts of violence and terrorism. One of the most prominent radical teachers at that time was Abu Bakar Ba'asjir, who had a transnational goal of the establishment of a new caliphate uniting under one political-religious ruler all Muslims in Southeast Asia. Forceful countermeasures by the Suharto government scattered the militants. A number went to jail, and others, including Ba'asjir, fled into exile, many to Malaysia. It was in Malaysia in the mid-1990s that the JI was established and connected with local jihadist groups.

In the post-Suharto period of democratization, Ba'asjir and other JI members returned to Indonesia to take up the struggle. A widespread network of JI cells was developed with al-Qaeda connections. Ba'asjir emerged as JI's spiritual leader and leading voice of an Islamist agenda for Indonesia.[8] JI's link to al-Qaeda was forged by the Southeast Asian mujahideen (soldiers of Islam) who joined the resistance to the Soviet Union's invasion and occupation of Afghanistan from 1979 to 1989. Under the sway of the Taliban, Southeast Asian mujahideen received training and indoctrination in al-Qaeda training camps. Returning to Southeast Asia with new lethal skill sets and radical incentive, the JI veterans became the terrorist backbone of regional Islamic fundamentalism with ties to radical Muslim groups throughout Southeast Asia. It was through the JI that al-Qaeda established its foothold in Southeast Asia.[9] From the strategic point of view, the al-Qaeda link raised the JI's sights from the struggle for Islam in Southeast Asia to the global struggle of Islam against the West in general and the United States in particular.

Indonesian Counterterrorism

In the months following 9/11, Indonesia had resisted American, Australian, Malaysian, and Singaporean pressure—based on good intelligence—to act against the JI. Known JI plotters were not arrested, including Hambali (aka Riduan Ismudin), JI's underground operational leader and Southeast Asia's most wanted terrorist. Hambali was finally arrested in Thailand in 2004 and turned over to the United States for imprisonment in Guantanamo, Cuba. Good police work, with foreign expert forensic analysis and intelligence, wrapped up the JI cell that carried out the Bali bombings. Three of the bombers were tried and sentenced to death in 2003 and executed in 2008. Other plotters are serving long jail sentences. Abu Bakar Ba'asjir was tried and convicted of treason in the Bali bombings, but the conviction was overturned on appeal. He was rearrested for conspiracy in the Bali bombings, found guilty, and served twenty-five months of a thirty-month sentence. His conspiracy conviction was overturned in 2006, effectively clearing him of any involvement in the terrorist attack.

In East Indonesia, JI-influenced groups poured gasoline on the fire of sectarian and ethnic violence that caused thousands of lives to be lost and half a million internally displaced people. In August 2003, a suicide bombing attack at a Marriott hotel in Jakarta killed eleven. In September 2004, a truck bomb outside the Australian embassy killed eleven and wounded two hundred innocent Indonesians. In October 2005, three suicide bombers killed twenty people in attacks on restaurants in Bali. The electoral mandate given to President Susilo Bambang Yudhoyono in 2004 opened a political window for a stronger counterterrorism campaign in Indonesia. With Western intelligence, training, and technical skills well in the background and enhanced Indonesian capabilities in the forefront, the Yudhoyono government moved decisively against the terrorists. In January 2006, the United States ended all restrictions on security assistance to Indonesia that had been imposed because of Indonesia's record in East Timor. Since then a bilateral security relationship has resumed with a priority on counterterrorism. Indonesia's normalization of security relations with Australia in the 2006 Lombok Treaty provided additional access to counterterrorist security assistance.

Good intelligence and aggressive policing, especially an elite antiterrorist paramilitary unit, Densus 88, effectively dismantled JI's command structures, isolating the cells from leadership. In an effort to regroup, the scattered terrorists set up a secret training camp in Aceh Province. This was raided by Indonesian security forces in 2010. Many senior militant leaders were killed or captured, and the intelligence from the raid led to more than two hundred arrests. Fugitives fleeing the camp are still at large and plotting.[10] In 2011, Abu Bakar Ba'asjir was found guilty of mobilizing and financing the militant groups that had set up the Aceh camp and sentenced to fifteen years in jail. The link between the cleric and the militants was through an organization called Jema'ah Anshorut Tauhid (Partisans of the Oneness of God), or JAT. Ba'asjir had founded JAT in 2008 as JI was driven underground. JAT was placed on the American FTO list in 2012. Although no victory has been declared, there has not been a major terrorist incident in Indonesia since the October 2005 Bali attacks. Vigilance is still high since, although weakened, scattered, and with diminished influence, the diehard militants still have a capacity to strike back.

The Philippines and the Abu Sayyaf Group (ASG)

The ASG ("Bearer of the Sword") is a band of Islamic extremists based in the Sulu Archipelago but operating in Mindanao as well. The ASG takes advantage of the general environment of insecurity in southern regions of the Philippines. The professed goal is the creation of an Islamic state. The ASG's first terrorist attack was the killing of two American evangelists in 1991. Its most notorious attack was the sinking of *Superferry 14* in Manila Bay in 2004, killing over one hundred passengers and crew. The ASG was placed on the American FTO list in 1997. The ASG's links to the JI and al-Qaeda made it a major target of the war on terror. The ASG and ASG-connected MILF units have provided training facilities for JI terrorists from Indonesia. The American war on terror and the Philippines' war on Muslim separatism in its south converged in the campaign against the ASG.[11]

The ASG's founder was Abdurajak Janjalani, who brought back from Afghanistan a virulent Wahhabist ideology.[12] Janjalani was killed in a 1998 shootout. His younger brother, Khadaffi Janjalani, succeeded him. He was killed in 2006. His successor, Abu Sulamein, was shot to death in a firefight with the army in January 2007. Despite leadership losses, the ASG regroups and fights back. In July 2007, a clash between the ASG and Philippine marines left fourteen marines dead. Ten of the recovered bodies were beheaded. Over the years, the ASG has financed itself by banditry, piracy, extortion, and kidnappings for ransom. The ASG strength at the end of 2012 was estimated at two hundred to four hundred fighters, down from its top estimated strength of one thousand. Like its Indonesian counterparts, however, a weakened ASG is still dangerous. It takes only a few terrorists to wreak great havoc. The political threat is that ASG attacks will provoke military retaliations damaging the precarious peace with the MILF (chapter 5).

When President Gloria Macapagal-Arroyo traveled to the United States in November 2001 to celebrate the fiftieth anniversary of the US–Philippines Mutual Defense Treaty (MDT), she and President Bush issued a joint statement in which the two leaders pledged military cooperation to end the terrorist activities of the ASG.[13] They promised a vigorous plan to strengthen the Philippine security forces' capacity to combat terror. The way had been paved by the 1999 Visiting Forces Agreement (VFA) that provided a new legal framework for American military personnel in the Philippines.

The stationing of American Special Forces in the southern Philippines to advise and assist the Armed Forces of the Philippines (AFP) in counterterrorism operations against the ASG has been at the point of the US–Philippines' counterterrorism alliance. This is the only place in Southeast Asia that American forces support counterterrorism measures in the field. They were first deployed in Operation Enduring Freedom as Joint Task Force 510 and, after August 2002, as Joint Special Operation Task Force-Philippines (JSOTF-P) with a force of six hundred US military personnel. The JSOTF-P assisted and advised at the strategic and operational levels in tactics, intelligence, and psychological warfare. The JSOTF-P has been credited with helping the AFP make significant gains against the ASG. Although technically only advisors, the JSOTF-P's role at the battalion and company levels of the AFP sometimes blurs the distinction between advice and operational involvement.[14] Nationalist critics of the government's close security arrangement with the United States accuse it of violating the constitutional ban on foreign bases, troops, or facilities without a treaty ratified by the Philippine Senate. The government's answer is that the US role is legal under the MDT. As noted in chapter 5, it was announced in 2014 that JSOTF-P will be dissolved, although some personnel will remain in an advisory capacity.

The status of the Philippine Communist Party/New People's Army internal war was noted in the section on the Philippines in chapter 2. One of the conditions demanded by the CPP-NPA for the peace negotiations is the removal of its designation as an FTO by the US government.

TRANSNATIONAL CRIME

The United Nations Convention against Transnational Organized Crime (TOC) is the main international instrument in the fight against transnational crime. It was adopted in 2000 and went into force in 2003.[15] Its goal is to promote greater international cooperation against the broadening and expanding criminal syndicates and networks around the world. There is a long list of different activities like drug trafficking, trafficking in persons, trafficking in firearms, smuggling, money laundering, counterfeiting currency, counterfeiting documents, and so on, that meet the definition of transnational organized crime (see box 7.2). All of these kinds of criminal activities take place in

Box 7.2. TOC Definition of Transnational Crime (from Article 3)

A crime is a transnational crime if

- it is committed in more than one state;
- it is committed in one state but a substantial part of its preparation, planning, and direction or control takes place in another state;
- it is committed in one state but involves a criminal group that engages in criminal activities in more than one state;
- it is committed in one state but has substantial effects in another state.

Southeast Asia. Although the primary responsibility for crime fighting rests with the national authorities, the ASEAN states have sought to foster cooperation among themselves and with dialogue partners.

ASEAN's Declaratory Anticrime Regime

The call for cooperation in fighting transnational crime has been on ASEAN's agenda since 1976 when the Bali Concord I urged intensified cooperation in eradicating narcotics trafficking. Since then the ASEAN ministerial meetings and summits regularly appeal for cooperation in transnational crime prevention. The declaratory anticrime ASEAN stance papers over the very slow progress in building cooperative institutions and structures for effective enforcement of existing national laws. Poor national police capabilities, weak judicial systems, and corruption seem to give the edge to the criminals. Another major problem has been an absence of any harmonization of criminal codes and an unwillingness to extradite or render accused nationals to the jurisdictions of another state.

The first ASEAN effort to establish a regional framework for fighting transnational crime was the 1997 ASEAN Declaration on Transnational Crime issued at a meeting of ASEAN interior or home affairs ministers. Besides the usual exhortations for cooperation and coordination, the declaration called for the creation of an ASEAN Ministers' Meeting on Transnational Crime (AMMTC). This is now part of the Political and Security Community. The task of the AMMTC is to coordinate the activities of the relevant working bodies including the ASEAN Senior Officials on Drug Matters (ASOD) and the ASEAN Chiefs of Police Association (ASEANAPOL) as well as other functional areas such as customs and immigration.

A central thread in the effort to enhance regional capabilities has been the insistence on more open communication and intelligence sharing among the national agencies involved in the common fight. ASEAN itself, however, does not have an institutional capability to coordinate or act as a clearinghouse. After a decade of communiqués, declarations, work programs, and other tools to encourage greater cooperation, the AMMTC at its 2007 meeting had what was described as a candid exchange of views on the need for "a more feasible and substantive line of communication amongst our relevant national organs for the expeditious and substantive exchange of intelligence and information."[16] The most successful example of formal information sharing has been the promotion by ASEANAPOL of its electronic database system (e-ADS), which links to Interpol's global database.

The AMMTC has been expanded to the "plus 3" format. The first ASEAN + 3 transnational crime meeting was in January 2004. The following year, the AMMTC + 3 endorsed a work plan, which still remains the agenda of the ministers and their officials. At the 2002 ASEAN + China Summit, China and ASEAN jointly declared cooperation in the field of nontraditional security issues, giving priority to transnational crime. An MOU on a five-year work plan for cooperation between ASEAN and China was adopted in 2004. China pressed ASEAN to institutionalize an AMMTC + China, the first of which took place in 2009, at which time the MOU was renewed. The overlapping and duplications of self-congratulatory items in the communiqués of the AMMTC, the AMMTC + 3, and the AMMTC + China show no inkling of practical measures designed to create transnational capabilities to combat transnational crime, including extradition and rendition.[17]

Piracy

The greatest maritime threat to international trade moving through the Southeast Asian region's waterways is piracy, which was one of the concerns listed in ASEAN's 1997 Declaration on Transnational Crime. The perennial problem of piracy received greater international attention when after 9/11 it was connected to the threat of terrorism.[18] Piracy has been on the ARF's agenda since its June 2003 Statement on Cooperation against Piracy and Other Threats to Maritime Security.[19] Under the ARF umbrella, there is an Inter-Sessional Meeting on Maritime Security as well as a Maritime Security Expert Working Group. Piracy is also an item for the ASEAN Maritime Forum. The straits of Malacca and Singapore, one of the busiest maritime thoroughfares in the world, are particularly vulnerable. More than sixty thousand vessels a year ply the straits carrying more than 40 percent of world trade, including 80 percent of the energy supplies of China, Japan, and South

Korea. Navigation is slow, and ships are confined to designated traffic lanes. The port of Singapore is the world's second largest, after Shanghai, averaging 140,000 vessels on an annual basis. Any incident or event that might impede passage through the straits or threaten the security of Singapore's port would disrupt regional economies and have global consequences for trade.

For piracy-reporting purposes, the International Maritime Board's (IMB) Piracy Reporting Center based in Kuala Lumpur uses a broad definition: "Piracy is an act of boarding or attempt to board any vessel with the intent to commit theft or any other crime and with the intent or capability to use force in the furtherance of that act."[20] This definition does not differentiate between the hit-and-run attacks of armed robbers and the hijacking of vessels. The great majority of the incidents of piracy reported by the IMB are hit-and-run attacks in or close to territorial waters. These are not acts of piracy as defined by UNCLOS, but rather armed robbery against ships.[21] The IMB definition, however, captures the maritime security environment in both the territorial and high seas.

A sudden increase in incidents after 1998 became very worrisome to ship-owners and regional national security managers. The perceived threat of terrorism and piracy was threefold. Terrorists as pirates could seek to generate financial support for their activities through robbery and ransom. Terrorists could hazard or impede navigation by sinking ships, which in the case of oil tankers would cause coastal environmental damage. Finally, there was a threat scenario in which terrorists could use a seized ship as a weapon against regional ports. From 99 reported attacks in Southeast Asia in 1998, the number mounted to 167 in 1999. One driving force for the increase was the impact of the 1997 Asian financial crisis (chapter 8). The numbers continued to rise: 257 in 2000 and 445 in 2003. The incidence of piracy with its possible links to terrorists caused Lloyd's Market Association in 2005 to give the Malacca Strait a war-risk insurance rating. This added to the pressure from China, India, Japan, and the United States, countries with major shipping interests, on the littoral states to tighten their maritime security regimes.

Regional Cooperation Agreement on Combating Piracy and Armed Robbery against Ships (ReCAAP)

Japan took the lead in framing a program for cooperative security.[22] In April 2000, Japan hosted a Conference on Combating Piracy and Armed Robbery against Ships, billed as the first regional conference on the piracy problem. Participants included the ten ASEAN states, Bangladesh, China, Hong Kong, India, Japan, South Korea, and Sri Lanka. In a document called "Asia Anti-Piracy Challenges 2000," the conference agreed to greater cooperation to meet the common threat. A second conference was held in Tokyo in October

2001, the Asia Cooperation Conference on Combating Piracy and Armed Robbery against Ships. After three years of negotiation, the ReCAAP was finalized in November 2004.[23] It went into force in September 2006 for fourteen contracting parties, since increased to nineteen.[24] Two of the most vulnerable states, Indonesia and Malaysia, although promising to cooperate, have withheld their signatures, apparently concerned about the scope of the agreement's coverage of territorial waters.[25]

ReCAAP reinforces existing obligations to take measures to prevent and suppress piracy and armed attacks against ships. Its major innovation was the establishment of an Information Sharing Center (ISC) located in Singapore, which was launched in November 2006. The ISC's purpose is to share information to help improve national responses and enable the development of operational coordination. Jurisdictional and territorial sensitivities that have inhibited operational cooperation are reflected in the agreement. Article 2:4 acknowledges that the agreement does not prejudice the position of any party to disputes concerning territorial sovereignty or the application of the UNCLOS. Article 2:5 states that nothing in the agreement authorizes a party to exercise jurisdiction or perform functions in the territory of another party that are exclusively reserved to the other by its national laws.

Malacca Strait Coordinated Patrols

ReCAAP and other declaratory statements did not provide for an on-the-water surveillance, prevention, and enforcement presence. Malaysia and Indonesia began coordinated patrols in 2002 in their own territorial waters. In July 2004, Singapore joined the coordinated patrols, code-named MALSINDO. Singapore had pressed its partners to accept a proposed US Regional Maritime Security Initiative (RMSI) that would have a special US force join the antiterrorism and antipiracy patrolling. The RMSI was flatly rejected by Malaysia and Indonesia as an encroachment on their sovereignty. Behind the scenes, China did not want the United States to become directly involved in guarding a waterway vital for its oil imports.

In the MALSINDO patrol arrangements, the national units operated independently under their own commands and stayed in their own territorial waters. In September 2005, the MALSINDO countries launched an "Eyes in the Sky" (EiS) project for aerial patrols with missions flown in turn by dedicated aircraft from the three states and which allowed the planes to fly up to three miles into the airspace over each other's territorial waters. In April 2006 the terms of reference and standard operating procedures for the management and coordination of MALSINDO and EiS were brought together in the Malacca Strait Patrols (MSPs). The question of hot pursuit is based on bilateral agreements between Indonesia and Malaysia and Indonesia and Singapore. Thailand had expressed interest since 2005 in joining the coordinated patrol network. Its association was on an ad hoc basis until 2009 when it formalized its involvement in the MSP.

Although continuing to rule out a physical foreign military presence for straits security, Malaysia and Indonesia have called on the user community for assistance in obtaining naval and coast guard assets, technical assistance, and intelligence sharing. The United States, for example, has worked with Indonesia to establish a radar warning system for the Malacca Strait along the Sumatran coast. Both the United States and Japan have donated fast patrol craft dedicated to straits security. In 2007, Japan's coast guard opened an Office of Piracy Countermeasures to expand cooperation with Southeast Asian coast guards. The commitment made by the littoral states to antipiracy cooperation and a real decline in pirate incidents in the straits region led Lloyd's to lift the war-risk rating in August 2006. Lloyd's stated that "evidence has shown that not only has the situation improved within the area but that the measures are long term."[26]

The IMB reported eleven attacks in the Malacca Strait in 2006, a five-year low. There were only seven attacks in 2007. The steady decline in incidents reported in 2007 for all of Southeast Asia including Indonesia and the straits was, according to the IMB, the "cumulative result of increased vigilance and patrolling by the littoral states" as well as precautions taken on board. In December 2013, the MSP countries signed an agreement that, for the first time, provided for joint patrols. This appears to be a tactical adaptation to the 2011–2013 uptick in piracy reports.[27]

IMB data showing the relative success of counterpiracy activities in the Malacca and Singapore straits region do not mean that piracy has been eradicated. In fact, half of the incidents reported worldwide occur in Southeast Asia. Indonesia is the world's leading country for piracy, succeeding Somalia where a major international interdiction effort has reduced attacks from 160 in 2011 and 49 in 2012 to only 7 in 2013. Table 7.1 shows the trends in piracy in Southeast Asia from 2006 to 2013. The high number of attacks in Indonesia reflects in part the porosity and expanse of its archipelago littorals with its many bays, coves, and inlets from which pirates operate and take refuge. Secondly, the sudden spike in 2012–2013 may be a result of the loss of land-based economic opportunities in the recent recession. Very importantly, however, Indonesia lacks maritime capabilities to police its maritime domain. Also, it is clear that criminal activities at sea in many cases have active and passive support from corrupt shore-based civil and police authorities.

Table 7.1. Actual and Attempted Pirate Attacks in Southeast Asia, 2006–2013

Year	2006	2007	2008	2009	2010	2011	2012	2013
Indonesia	50	43	28	15	40	46	81	106
Other SEA	33	27	26	31	29	34	23	22
Total SEA	83	70	54	46	69	80	104	128

Source: IMB, *Piracy and Armed Robbery against Ships,* Annual Reports.

The Sulu and Sulawesi Seas Zone

The focus on the Malacca and Singapore straits is because their security is of vital global interest. It is not, however, the only hotbed of piracy in Southeast Asia. The maritime zone of the Sulu and Sulawesi seas in the triborder area of Malaysia, Indonesia, and the Philippines is a center of criminal activity—piracy; smuggling; trafficking in drugs, people, and weapons; and kidnapping—with connections to terrorism and ethnic insurgency.[28] The maritime triborder zone lies at the center of ASEAN's BIMP-EAGA subregional growth zone (chapter 4). Until greater prevention and enforcement capabilities are created and deployed, the region will remain better known for its criminal and terrorist activity than its commercial prospects. Of particular concern to Indonesia and Malaysia has been the passage by sea of JI terrorists from ASG and MILF training sites in the Philippines to Sulawesi, Kalimantan, and Sabah. The common security interests of the three countries led them to develop a framework for cooperation in border security and combating transnational crime in their territories. They signed a trilateral Agreement on Information Exchange and Establishment of Common Procedures in May 2002.[29] Although bilateral protocols for cooperation may be in place, they do not provide for operational capacity to police the maritime zones.

A 2006 Philippine initiative for a coordinated patrol system similar to that in the Malacca Strait has made no headway. Unsettled maritime borders, contested jurisdictions, and the outstanding issue of sovereignty in Sabah have precluded a triborder operation like the MSP. The obstacle seems to be what one analyst has called a "traditional trust deficit" inhibiting security cooperation.[30] A small step forward came in February 2014 with the signing in Jakarta of a maritime border agreement by the foreign ministers of Indonesia and the Philippines.[31]

Narcotics Production and Trafficking

The production and distribution of illicit drugs has long been recognized as a major criminal activity in Southeast Asia, with socially devastating, economically undermining, and politically corrupting consequences. The two categories of drugs of concern are opiates and methamphetamine-type stimulants. Crystal methamphetamine, known as "ice," is a purer and more addictive form of methamphetamine. Although the principal responsibility for combating the domestic impacts of crime and addiction falls to the national governments, interdicting the trade requires interstate cooperation and international assistance. At the global level, narcotics trade is tracked by the United Nations Office on Drugs and Crime (UNODC). At the national level, capabilities have been boosted by foreign assistance for counternarcotics programs, including support from drug enforcement agents from the US Drug Enforcement Agency (DEA) and the Australian Federal Police (AFP), among others.

The Golden Triangle

Historically, the remote highlands at the heart of continental Southeast Asia where the Myanmar, Laos, and Thailand borders converge have been a major source of the opium from which morphine and then heroin are processed. This has been romantically called the Golden Triangle. On the temperate slopes, opium poppies are cultivated at the nations' margins by poor farmers, many of whom are ethnic minorities. The raw opium is purchased by middlemen, often ethnic Chinese, taken to opium refineries for processing, and then into the Southeast Asian and Chinese international drug markets. Over the years the trade has financed ethnic insurgent armies, warlords, criminal syndicates, and politicians. In the second half of the twentieth century the Golden Triangle was the world's largest source of opium. In the first years of the twenty-first century the cultivation of opium poppies in the Golden Triangle had been reduced by 81 percent, but, as table 7.2 shows, it has suddenly rebounded.[32] Myanmar remains the second-largest opium poppy grower in the world, but its poppy cultivation is less than a third of Afghanistan's. It is estimated that the 2013 opium yield from Myanmar's poppies would be 872 tons, the

Table 7.2.   Golden Triangle Opium Poppy Cultivation in Hectares

Country	1998	2006	2007	2012	2013
Lao PDR	26,800	2,500	1,500	6,800	3,900
Myanmar	130,300	21,500	27,700	51,000	57,800
Thailand	1,486	157	205	209	265
Total	158,586	24,157	29,405	58,009	61,965

Source: UNODC, *Southeast Asia Opium Survey 2013: Lao PDR, Myanmar, Thailand.*

Note: 1 hectare = 2.47 acres

highest figure since UNODC began assessing production. The fact that the overall growth of poppy cultivation in the Golden Triangle and opium yields have dramatically increased since 2006 stems from both heightened demand, particularly from China, and, given the inadequacy of alternatives for impoverished villagers, the economic rewards from growing opium poppies. That an upward trend will continue seems indicated by the fact that current opium production from Myanmar and Laos is unable to meet Chinese demands.[33]

Even as the long war in Southeast Asia against opium and its derivatives has met a reversal, the methamphetamine threat is growing. The center of production is in the ethnic minority states of Myanmar. Drug gangs in their labs along the Myanmar–China and Myanmar–Thailand border are producing hundreds of millions of tablets annually for markets in Thailand, China, India, and onward through distribution by criminal syndicates often linked to Southeast Asian expatriate communities. A major center for drug processing is in an area of Myanmar's Shan State controlled by the United Wa State Army (UWSA), which has unilaterally declared its own Wa State.

The Myanmar counternarcotics program is headed by its Central Committee for Drug Abuse Control (CCDAC). The CCDAC partners with the UNODC in eradication programs which have had donor support from Australia, Japan, and Germany. American support for counternarcotics activity and crop eradication in Myanmar had been limited by the suspension of direct bilateral contributions because of the American sanctions against the junta. There has been indirect US support through UNODC and other multilateral frameworks. The CCDAC has been given new impetus in the changing domestic Myanmar political order. However, the implementation of its crop-eradication strategies has been politically constrained by the government's efforts to accommodate the ethnic minorities' conditions for reintegration into the now democratizing—but still Burmese-dominated—state. Even where there has been a brokered peace, some of the ethnic groups continue to engage in narcotics production and trafficking.[34]

When Secretary of State Hillary Clinton visited Myanmar in December 2011, signaling the reshaping of the US relationship with post-junta Myanmar, she assured the resumption of bilateral counternarcotics cooperation. Nevertheless, the congressionally required FY 2014 annual *Presidential Determination* [PD] *of Major Drug Transit or Illicit Drug Producing Countries* singled out Myanmar, along with Bolivia and Venezuela, as demonstrably failing during the previous twelve months to make substantial efforts to adhere to their obligations under international agreements. Section 706 of the annual Foreign Relations Authorization Act requires the cutoff of US bilateral assistance in such cases unless waived by the president. In PD 2013–2014, President Obama granted Myanmar a national interest waiver because of the progress made in governance, democratization, and human rights as well as the commitment to reform and action on future poppy eradication.[35]

While opium poppy cultivation in Thailand remains at a relatively low and stable level, the flow of methamphetamines in the country has not abated. Successive governments have had highly publicized campaigns against the influx of Myanmar-processed narcotics. Thailand's counternarcotics enforcement assets are not capable of patrolling and monitoring its long and remote borders with Myanmar and Laos. Furthermore, the necessary cross-border coordination with the counternarcotics forces of its neighboring countries is complicated by border histories.

Laos continues to be designated a major drug transit state. Because of its central location and new roads and bridges connecting it to China, Vietnam, and Thailand, Laos will remain an important route for drug traffickers. The converging economic structures of the Greater Mekong Subregion (chapter 4) and the ASEAN Economic Community open new opportunities for narcotics trafficking with enhanced transport infrastructure and looser borders. According to UNODC's executive director, criminal drug trade networks are "positioned to take advantage of this well-intentioned integration process."[36] Of course, the Golden Triangle is not the only location where illicit drugs are produced in Southeast Asia. The second-largest source of methamphetamines in Southeast Asia is the Philippines, where the local "shabu" is fabricated for domestic consumption and trafficking to Indonesia, the Canadian and American west coasts, and Australia.

The Regional Framework for Counternarcotics

The problem of drug abuse and trafficking has been on the ASEAN declaratory agenda since 1976. The commitment to counternarcotics made in the second ASEAN Summit's Bali Concord I was followed quickly in September 1976 by a Declaration of Principles to Combat the Abuse of Narcotic Drugs.[37] To implement the principles, an ASEAN Drug Experts' group produced in 1984 an ASEAN Regional Policy and Strategy in the Prevention and Control of Drug Abuse and Illicit Traffic. The policy and strategy document was significant in that it went beyond the issues of health and social policy. It recognized that narcotics consumption and trafficking were threats to national security and political stability.[38] The experts' group became the ASEAN Senior Officials on Drug Matters (ASOD), tasked with coordinating ASEAN cooperation. In their 1997 Vision 2020 statement, the ASEAN heads of government set a goal of an eventual drug-free ASEAN. This was given programmatic endorsement in the 1998 AMM's Joint Declaration for a Drug-Free ASEAN 2020.[39] Two years later, the 2000 AMM advanced the drug-free target to 2015, coincident with the ASEAN Community.

The goal of a drug-free ASEAN by any date, let alone 2015, is, as are ASEAN's other endeavors, aspirational. Achievement will depend on the uneven capabilities of its member states. This will require political will by leaders of member states as well as support from donor nations and agencies. ASEAN efforts are closely linked through a 2002 memorandum of agreement to cooperation with UNODC. This has been very important programmatically for bilateral cooperation between ASEAN members and dialogue partners in winning financial and technical support for national drug prevention, drug abuse, and drug enforcement activities. A symbolic demonstration of cooperation with its major partners was the Bangkok Political Declaration in Pursuit of a Drug-Free ASEAN 2015 that was issued by an October 2002 international conference on a drug-free ASEAN sponsored by ASEAN and UNODC.

The most structured effort at multilateralism is the ASEAN and China Cooperative Operations in Response to Dangerous Drugs (ACCORD) adopted in October 2000. The work plan for the ACCORD was revised at a 2005 second ACCORD conference in Beijing with priority given to the growing ATS problem. The 2005 meeting also endorsed an initiative for regional joint action against ATS-related crimes including trafficking. It proposed greater cooperation among enforcement agencies. Its plan of action is linked to UNODC's regional strategic programs. An examination of the level of regional cooperation actually reached through the ACCORD process shows that it falls short of its goals. Rather than an action-oriented grouping, it is another example of an ASEAN + China consultative mechanism tied to the annual meeting of the ASOD-supported workshops and experts' groups. Ralf Emmers pointed out that after six years, cooperation in the ACCORD framework was primarily national and bilateral. He noted that "policy implementation at a multilateral and collective level has not yet been attained."[40] This remains the case.

The ACCORD has been driven by China as part of Beijing's strategy to combat the influx of drugs to Yunnan and beyond. The Golden Triangle has become China's counternarcotics frontline, the source of 60 to 70 percent of drugs consumed in China. Already by 1993, China had executed an MOU with the LPDR, Myanmar, Thailand, and UNODC on collaborative efforts to control the flow of opiates. In 1995, Cambodia and Vietnam became parties to the MOU, making its cooperative regime GMS-wide. At a May 2013 ministerial meeting of the GMS signatories to the 1993 MOU, the parties reaffirmed and strengthened their commitment to cross-border cooperation in the Nay Pyi Taw Declaration on Drug Control.[41]

China's nontraditional security interest in counternarcotics became more traditional after an October 2011 attack by an alleged drug gang killed thirteen crewmen on Chinese vessels on the Mekong River as it flowed between Thailand and Laos. To bolster security against the lawlessness of the region, China "persuaded" Thailand, Myanmar, and the LPDR to allow so-called joint armed river patrols. The first was in December 2011. The sixteenth patrol was in December 2013 and consisted of one hundred Yunnan border policemen on three patrol boats traveling from their home port in Yunnan to Chiang Saen, Thailand, a 362-mile (512 km) round trip.[42] The patrols are, with the exception of UN peacekeeping, the first Chinese security forces to operate outside of China's borders since its limited invasion of northern Vietnam in 1979 during the Third Indochina War (chapter 3). This seems to be another signal of China's expanded view of its security interests and the willingness to deploy its security forces outside of China to defend its national interests.[43]

Trafficking in Persons (TIP)

Modern-day slavery is trafficking in persons who are forced, defrauded, or coerced into labor or sexual exploitation. What the actual numbers might be of victims of trafficking in Southeast Asia is difficult to know. The only real count is of cases that have entered the national police or justice systems. This would only be the tip of the iceberg. What can be said with confidence is that the numbers are in the tens of thousands. The transnational aspect of TIP does not count persons who are trafficked within their own countries. Sexual exploitation has been the most documented purpose of cross-border trafficking. The abuse, violence, and indignities visited on the victims of the traffickers are a gross violation of human rights. Trafficking also has huge social costs in terms of gender rights, minority rights, child welfare, and public health.[44]

All of the Southeast Asian states are touched to some extent by human trafficking, either as states of origin, transit, or destination, or in the worst cases—Thailand, for example—all three. Southeast Asian states have put in place a variety of antitrafficking national laws and regulations. Antitrafficking is incorporated in ASEAN's 1997 Declaration on Transnational Crime. In addition to ASEAN's declaratory statements, there have been efforts at multilateral cooperation in which Southeast Asian nations, donor countries, and NGOs have been brought together in the common effort to eradicate TIP. The ASEAN commitment is not matched by domestic capabilities and political willingness to enforce antitrafficking laws and regulations.

The global benchmark for assessing the antitrafficking efforts a country is making is the implementation of the legally binding provisions of the UN Protocol to Prevent, Suppress and Punish Trafficking in Persons, Especially Women and Children. Commonly called the Palermo Protocol, this was an optional supplement to the TOC Convention and entered into force in 2003. The Palermo Protocol provided the first globally approved legally binding definition of trafficking in persons (box 7.3).

The Palermo Protocol is particularly important in the attention it gave to victims' rights, calling on the signatories to provide for the physical, psychological, and social recovery of victims of trafficking including shelter, medical care, and counseling. This victims-first approach is in sharp contrast to culturally, politically, and legally unsympathetic Southeast Asian officialdom. The status of Southeast Asian signatures, accessions, and ratifications to the major TIP-related international agreements is documented in table 7.3.

One measure of how successful the Southeast Asian states have been is their ranking in the annual US State Department's *Trafficking in Persons Report* (*TIP Report*) prepared by the Office to Monitor and Combat Trafficking in Persons.[45] The *TIP Report* is mandated by Congress and is based on compliance with the Trafficking Victims Protection Act (TVPA). There are four levels of placement in the 2013 *TIP Report*. Tier 1 lists countries that fully comply with the TVPA's minimum standards for the elimination of trafficking. There is no tier 1 Southeast Asian state. Tier 2, countries not in full compliance but which are making significant efforts to comply, includes Brunei, Indonesia, Laos, the Philippines, Singapore, Timor-Leste, and Vietnam. A tier 2 "watch list" consists of countries that require special scrutiny. Cambodia, Malaysia, Myanmar, and Thailand are on the "watch list." Tier 3 is reserved for countries that do not satisfy the minimum standards and are

---

Box 7.3. International Definition of Trafficking in Persons

Palermo Protocol, Article 3 (a)

Trafficking in persons shall mean the recruitment, transportation, transfer, harboring or receipt of persons, by means of the threat or use of force or other forms of coercion, of abduction, of fraud, of deception, of the abuse of power or of a position of vulnerability or of the giving or receiving of payments or benefits to achieve the consent of a person having control over another person, for the purpose of exploitation. Exploitation shall include at a minimum, the exploitation of the prostitution of others or other forms of sexual exploitation, forced labor or services, slavery or practices similar to slavery, servitude or the removal of organs.

Table 7.3. TIP-Relevant International Conventions

Country	Status of Southeast Asian Signature (S), Ratification (R), or Accession (A)*					
	Palermo Protocol to Suppress & Punish Trafficking in Persons	ILO Convention 182, Elimination of Worst Forms of Child Labor	Optional Protocol to the Convention on the Rights of the Child, on the Sale of Children, Prostitution, and Child Pornography	Optional Protocol to the Convention on the Rights of the Child in Armed Conflict	ILO Convention 29, Forced Labor	ILO Convention 105, Abolition of Forced Labor
Brunei		R	A			
Cambodia	R	R	R	R	R	R
Indonesia	R	R	R	R	R	R
Lao PDR	A	R	A	A	R	
Malaysia	A	R	A		R	
Myanmar	A		A	A	R	
Philippines	R	R	R	R	R	R
Singapore		R		R	R	
Thailand	S	R	A	A	R	R
Timor-Leste	A	R	R	A	R	
Vietnam	A	R	R	R	R	

Source: US Department of State, 2013 Trafficking in Persons Report.

*Treaty adherence is by signature, followed by state ratification. After a treaty comes into force with the minimum number of ratifications, adherence is by accession. There is no difference in international law on the binding legal effect of adherence between ratification and accession.

not making a significant effort to comply. The list is dynamic. Both Malaysia and Myanmar, for example, were once tier 3 countries. Malaysia was promoted to the tier 2 "watch list" in 2011 and Myanmar in 2012. Tier 3 countries are subject by the TVPA to certain foreign security assistance sanctions to be invoked by presidential determination. Sanctions were placed on Myanmar—already under the US human rights sanction regime—but were waived for Malaysia in the national interest of security cooperation with Malaysia.

Although most of the Southeast Asian states are working to enhance their antitrafficking capabilities and are improving their treatment of the victims of trafficking, a reading of the country narratives in the State Department's *TIP Report* shows how far there is to go. The policy problem can be explained as how to convert the normative statements and "soft mechanisms of cooperation" into strengthening the three Ps: prevention, protection, and prosecution.[46] The UNODC, the custodian of the Palermo Protocol, admits that "translating it into reality remains problematic. Very few criminals are convicted and most victims are probably never identified or assisted."[47]

Australian Initiatives

Australia has funded three successive multilateral programs to enhance capabilities in combating trafficking in persons. In 2003–2006, the Asia Regional Cooperation to Prevent People Trafficking (ARCPPT) worked with Cambodia, Laos, Myanmar, and Thailand. Its successor, the Asia Regional Trafficking in Persons Project (ARTIP), 2006–2013, expanded to include Indonesia and the Philippines. It has been succeeded by the Australia–Asia Program to Combat Trafficking in Persons (AAPTIP), a new five-year (2013–2018), $50 million program building on the ARTIP foundation. The long-term Australian support is focused on strengthening the criminal justice response to trafficking with respect to both law enforcement and judiciary.[48]

The COMMIT Process

The Coordinated Mekong Ministerial Initiative against Trafficking (COMMIT) is the first regional instrument that has made a serious effort to institutionalize a multisectoral approach to combat trafficking within the GMS. The COMMIT process began in 2003 with a series of informal discussions and roundtables among GMS government representatives. It was formalized in an MOU signed at the October 2004 first COMMIT Inter-Ministerial Meeting by Cambodia, China, Lao PDR, Myanmar, Thailand, and Vietnam. The coordinating body for COMMIT is the United Nations Inter-Agency Project on Human Trafficking in the Greater Mekong Sub-Region (UNIAP), established in 2000.[49] Box 7.4 identifies the specific forms of trafficking that

Box 7.4.   Trafficking in Persons within the Greater Mekong Subregion

- Trafficking from Cambodia, China, Laos, and Myanmar to Thailand for labor exploitation, including the sex trade
- Trafficking of children from Cambodia to Thailand and Vietnam for begging and, lately, from Vietnam to Cambodia, Laos, and Thailand for the same purpose
- Trafficking of women and girls from Vietnam, Laos, and Myanmar to China for forced marriages and of boys for adoption
- Domestic trafficking of kidnapped children in China for adoption and of women and girls for forced marriages
- Trafficking of women and girls from Vietnam to Cambodia for the sex trade

Source: Susu Thathun, Project Director, UNIAP, accessed at http://www.fmreview.org/text/FMR/25/10.doc.

COMMIT addresses. The COMMIT programs are organized in three-year plans of action with specific project links to other major antitrafficking actors—UN agencies, NGOs, and intergovernmental organizations.

The Bali Process

The Bali Process on People Smuggling, Trafficking in Persons, and Related Transnational Crime broadens the regional consultative framework for collaboration on the illegal movement of people to the Asia-Pacific. It was initiated at the Regional Ministerial Conference on People Smuggling, Trafficking in Persons, and Related Transnational Crimes held in Bali in February 2002.[50] Cochaired by Australia and Indonesia, its stimulus was the flow of people originating in South Asia and the Middle East to Australia through Indonesia. Present at the 2013 Fifth Ministerial Conference on the Bali Process were thirty-five of its forty-four members; three international organizations (the International Organization for Migration [IOM], UNHCR, and UNODC); and ten observer nations and organizations. Structure below the cochairmanship is given to the process by a Steering Committee (Australia, Indonesia, New Zealand, Thailand, UNHCR, and IOM) and a seventeen-member ad hoc group to develop concrete recommendations for regional cooperation on people smuggling and trafficking. The ad hoc group consists of the Steering

Committee and Afghanistan, Bangladesh, India, Malaysia, Maldives, Myanmar, Pakistan, Sri Lanka, Thailand, the UAE, and the United States. The Bali Process was designed to demonstrate political commitment to the common purpose of cooperating in combating trafficking in persons and people smuggling. Its major initiative is a nonbinding Regional Cooperation Framework (RCF) in which member states are encouraged to enter practical arrangements to reduce irregular movement of people in the Asia-Pacific region. To facilitate this, a Regional Support Office (RSO) for the Bali Process was established in February 2008. The Australian–Indonesian cochairs of the Bali Process have concluded—perhaps prematurely—that its contribution to strengthening and facilitating nonbinding and informal cooperation among policy makers and practitioners, international organizations, and NGOs made it a model for regional cooperation against human trafficking in the Asia-Pacific region and beyond.[51]

Indonesia–Australia Relations and the New Boat People

Australia has long been a destination for refugees and asylum seekers. In recent years, however, the staggering increase in the inflow of illegal migrants has challenged Australia's policy and relations with Indonesia. Since 2009 there has been a sharp increase in arrivals as thousands of illegal migrants, the majority from South and Southwest Asia, have attempted to reach Australia on vessels of varying seaworthiness passing through or originating in Indonesia (table 7.4).

Successive Australian governments have been conflicted as they sought to balance their international obligations toward refugees with the enforcement of immigration laws. A driving force was the domestic electoral impact of a polarizing public opinion. Priority is given to interception at sea. The vessels are taken to Australian-administered Christmas Island, located in the Indian Ocean 236 miles (380 km) south of Java. This is the site of an overcrowded immigration detention center where the arrivals are processed for disposition of their refugee or asylum claims. At the end of 2013 there were more than 2,500 men, women, and children interned there. Human rights groups have severely criticized the practices and conditions in the Christmas Island center. Australia has tried to reduce the Christmas Island burden by outsourcing the boat people to detention centers on Manus Island in Papua New Guinea and in the tiny island state of Nauru. In 2014, Cambodia was approached as another possible detention site. In anticipation of a coming election, in July 2013 Labor prime minister Kevin Rudd announced that anyone arriving by boat without a visa would be sent to the offshore centers for processing for resettlement and would be barred from settling in Australia regardless of their refugee or asylum status.

Table 7.4. Refugee Boat Arrivals in Australia, 2009–2013

	Number of Boats	Crew	Number of People (Excludes Crew)
2009	60	41	2,725
2010	134	345	6,555
2011	69	168	4,565
2012	278	392	17,204
2013	300	644	20,587
Total	841	1,590	51,636

Source: Australia Parliamentary Research Paper, 23 January 2014.

For more than a decade, Australia has tried, so far unsuccessfully, to convince Malaysia and Indonesia to share the illegal immigrant burden in a regional framework, since it is from their shores that the people smugglers are sailing. In bilateral and multilateral settings, Australia has sought commitments of action against the syndicates behind the lucrative people-smuggling enterprises. In August 2013 Indonesia hosted a Special Conference on the Irregular Movement of People. Thirteen countries of origin, transit, and destination pledged in the conference's Jakarta Declaration to take coordinated joint actions in the fields of prevention, early detection, protection, and prosecution to address irregular movement of persons, but in a diplomatic nonspecific and nonbinding way.[52]

With a win in Australia's September 2013 election, Prime Minister Tony Abbott, who campaigned on the slogan "Stop the Boats," has taken a harder line on boat people. In an operation called "Sovereign Borders," the navy has been deployed to turn back or tow back to Indonesian waters boats carrying refugees and migrants. In some cases, the passengers were placed in lifeboats, pointed to the Indonesian coast, and their ships sunk. Although the intercepting Australian vessels operated outside of Indonesia's twelve-mile territorial sea, there were numerous "inadvertent" breaches of the border. As could be expected, Operation Sovereign Borders displeased Jakarta. It denounced Australia's violation of refugee conventions, warning that Australian unilateralism could damage relations as it risked cooperation and trust between the countries. What the Indonesian foreign minister called Australia's slippery slope in the boat people problem, together with Indonesian anger over new revelations of Australian espionage, threatens the Indonesian–Australian agreement on a six-point "road map" to restoration of normal bilateral relations (chapter 2).[53]

The claim that the Bali Process is a model for regional cooperation has already been noted. The inability of the Indonesian and Australian cochairs to fashion a working bilateral framework to address people smuggling suggests the political difficulty in translating the model into an operational mode. The real solution will come only when the push factors in the countries of origin become less intense.

NOTES

1. A compilation of ASEAN declarations, joint declarations, and statements on combating transnational crime and terrorism was published in 2012 and can be accessed at http://www.asean.org/resources/publications/asean-publications/item/asean-documents-on-combatting-transnational-crime-and-terrorism.

2. For a discussion of the modeling for an ASEAN counterterrorism treaty, see Gregory Rose and Diana Nestorovska, "Toward an ASEAN Counter-Terrorism Treaty," *Singapore Year Book of International Law* 9 (2005): 157–89.

3. The SEARCCT website is http://www.searcct.gov.my. The 2012 figure on individuals passing through SEARCCT programs was given by the Malaysian permanent representative to the UN in a statement on an agenda item concerning UN global counterterrorism strategy, accessed at http://www.searcct.gov.my/news -events/speeches-collections?id=72.

4. The JCLEC website is http://www.jclec.com.

5. The GCTF website is http://thegctf.org.

6. Since 2004 the US Department of State has published an annual *Country Report on Terrorism* (*CRT*) with information compiled by the National Counterterrorism Center (NCTC). This is released at the end of April for the previous year. The CRTs can be accessed at http://www.state.gov/j/ct/rls/crt.

7. The FTO list can be accessed at http://www.state.gov/j/ct/rls/other/des/123085 .htm.

8. The most detailed analyses of the Jema'ah Islamiyah have been done by Sidney Jones for the International Crisis Group. Beginning with "Violence and Radical Islam" (October 2001), she and her colleagues have produced a series of studies that rival or even surpass the intelligence production of Western embassies or of Indonesia's own state intelligence agencies. They can be accessed through the Indonesia country link at http://www.crisisgroup.org.

9. For a survey of the JI and its links, see Greg Barton, *Struggle in Indonesia: Jemaah Islamiyah and the Soul of Islam* (Sydney, Australia: University of New South Wales Press, 2004).

10. International Crisis Group, "How Indonesian Extremists Regroup," *Asia Report* 228 (16 July 2012).

11. Rommel C. Banlaoi, "The Role of Philippine-American Relations in the Global Campaign against Terrorism: Implications for Regional Security," *Contemporary Southeast Asia* 24, no. 2 (August 2002): 294–312.

12. For a brief history of the ASG, see Zack Fellman, *The Abu Sayaff Group*, Case Study Number 5 (Center for Strategic and International Studies, Aqam Futures Project, November 2012), accessed at http://csis.org/files/publication/111128_Fell man_ASG_AQAMCaseStudy5.pdf.

13. Office of the Press Secretary, "Joint Statement between the United States of America and the Republic of the Philippines," 20 November 2001, accessed at http://www.gpo.gov/fdsys/pkg/pdf/WCPD=2001-11-26-Pg1697.pdf.

14. For an assessment of the JSOTF-P role, see Mark Munson, "Has Operation Enduring Freedom–Philippines Been a Success?" *Small Wars Journal* 9, no. 4 (April 2013), accessed at http://www.smallwarsjournal.com/jrnl/art/has-operation-enduring-freedom-Philippines-been-a-success.

15. The text of the TOC Convention can be accessed at http://www.unodc.org/pdf/crime/a_res_55/res5525e.pdf.

16. "Joint Communiqué of the Sixth ASEAN Ministerial Meeting on Transnational Crime (AMMTC)," 6 November 2007, accessed at http://nyen.xmu.edu.cn/Article/ShowArticle.asp?ArticleID=1179.

17. AMMTC statements and communiqués can be accessed at the AMMTC link on the ASEAN Political-Security Community page at http://www.asean.org.

18. Adam J. Young and Mark J. Valencia, "Conflation of Piracy and Terrorism in Southeast Asia: Rectitude and Utility," *Contemporary Southeast Asia* 25, no. 2 (August 2003): 269–83.

19. The ARF statement on piracy can be accessed at http://aseanregionalforum.asean.org/library/arf-chairmans-statements-and-reports/172.html.

20. The IMB was founded by the International Chamber of Commerce Commercial Crimes Services in 1981 to be the focal point for the fight against maritime crime. The website can be accessed at http://www.iccwbo.org. Piracy statistics are from the annual piracy reports of the IMB's Piracy Reporting Center established in Kuala Lumpur in 1992. It offers weekly, quarterly, and annual reports on worldwide piracy.

21. For discussions of the application of the UNCLOS definition of piracy in Southeast Asia, see Zou Keyuan, "Implementing the United Nations Convention on the Law of the Sea in East Asia: Issues and Trends," *Singapore Year Book of International Law* 9 (2005): 45–49. The inadequacy of the legal definitions of piracy for policy makers is examined by Dana Dillon, "Maritime Piracy: Defining the Problem," *SAIS Review of International Affairs* 25, no.1 (2005): 155–64.

22. John F. Bradford, "Japanese Anti-Piracy Initiatives in Southeast Asia," *Contemporary Southeast Asia* 26, no. 3 (December 2004): 480–505.

23. The text of the ReCAAP can be accessed at http://www.recaap.org.

24. The ReCAAP contracting parties are Australia, Bangladesh, Brunei, Cambodia, China, Denmark, India, Japan, South Korea, Laos, Myanmar, the Netherlands, Norway, the Philippines, Singapore, Sri Lanka, Thailand, the United Kingdom, and Vietnam.

25. Yoichiro Sato, *Southeast Asian Receptiveness to Japanese Maritime Security Cooperation* (Honolulu: Asia-Pacific Center for Strategic Studies, September 2003), 3, posted at http://www.apcss.org.

26. As cited in "Market Removes Malacca Strait from List," accessed at http://www.lloyds.com/news-and-insight/news-and-features/archive/2006/08/market_re moves_malacca_straits_from_the_list.

27. "Joint Patrols to Take on Malacca Pirates," *Bangkok Post*, 13 December 2013.

28. A concise overview of the threats in the triborder region is Ian Storey, "The Triborder Sea Area: Maritime Southeast Asia's Ungoverned Space," accessed at http://www.jamestown.org/single/?tx_ttnews%5Btt_news%5D=4465.

29. The text of the agreement can be accessed at http://www.asean.org/ar chive/17346.pdf.

30. Ristian Atriandi Supriyanto, "The Sabah Incursion: Gaps in Regional Maritime Security," *RSIS Commentary*, no. 063/2013 (15 April 2013), accessed at http://www.eurasiareview.com/20042013-the-sabah-incursion-gaps-in-regional-maritime -security-analysis.

31. "RI, Philippines Set to Sign Boundary Agreement," *Jakarta Post*, 25 February 2014.

32. The statistics on opium in this section are drawn from the United Nations Office on Drugs and Crime (UNODC), *World Drug Report 2013*, and UNODC's *Southeast Asia Opium Survey 2013: Lao PDR, Myanmar*. Both can be accessed at http://www.unodc.org.

33. UNODC, *Southeast Asia Opium Survey 2013*, 11.

34. US Department of State, *2014 International Narcotics Control and Strategy Report* (INCSR), vol. 1, *Drug and Chemical Control*, 120.

35. The text of the PD and the justification for the waiver can be found at pp. 7–13 in the INCSR of note 34.

36. Yury Fedotov, foreword to UNODC, *Southeast Asia Opium Survey 2013*.

37. Accessed at http://www.asean.org/communities/asean-political-security -community/item/asean-declaration-of-principles-to-combat-the-abuse-of-narcotics -drugs-manila-26-june-1976.

38. For the development of ASEAN's policy framework, see http://www.asean .org/communities/asean-political-security-community/item/cooperation-on-drugs -and-narcotics-overview.

39. The text of the declaration can be accessed at http://www.asean.org/communi ties/asean-political-security-community/item/joint-declaration-for-a-drug-free-asean.

40. Ralf Emmers, "International Regime Building in ASEAN: Cooperation against the Illicit Trafficking and Abuse of Drugs," *Contemporary Southeast Asia* 29, no. 3 (December 2007): 518.

41. The declaration can be accessed at http://www.unodc.org/documents/south eastasiaandpacific/2013/05/mou/NAY_PYI_TAW_DECLARATION_EDITED.pdf.

42. Hu Yongqi, "Patrols Bring Security to Mekong River," *China Daily*, 17 December 2013.

43. Xiaobo Su, "China's Antidrug Policies in Southeast Asia's Golden Triangle," East–West Center, *Asia Pacific Bulletin* 234 (26 September 2013), accessed at http://www.eastwestcenter.org/publications/chinas-antidrug-policies-in-southeast -asia%E2%80%99s-golden-triangle.

44. For a general overview of the problem, see UNODC, *Global Report on Trafficking in Persons* (February 2009), accessed at http://www.unodc.org/documents/Global_Report_on_TIP.pdf.

45. *TIP Reports* can be accessed at http://www.state.gov/j/tip/rls/tiprpt.

46. Ralf Emmers, Beth Greener-Barcham, and Nicholas Thomas, "Institutional Arrangements to Counter Human Trafficking in the Asia Pacific," *Contemporary Southeast Asia* 28, no. 3 (December 2006): 505.

47. The quote is from the UNODC website at http://www.unodc.org/unodc/en/human-trafficking/index.html.

48. Australian Agency for International Development, "Australia–Asia Program to Combat Trafficking in Persons: Project Design Document," accessed at http://aid.dfat.gov.au/Publications/Documents/aaptip-design-framework.pdf.

49. The UNIAP website is http://www.no-trafficking.org.

50. The Bali Process website can be accessed at http://www.baliprocess.net.

51. "The Bali Process: A Model for Regional Cooperation in the Fight against Human Trafficking," accessed at the Bali Process website's documentation link.

52. The text of the Jakarta Declaration on Addressing Irregular Movements of Persons can be accessed at http://www.unhcr.org/5214ae709.pdf.

53. "Media Conference with Indonesian Foreign Minister Marty Natalegawa," 5 December 2013, accessed at http://foreignminister.gov.au/transcripts/Pages/2013/jb_tr_131205.aspx?ministerid=4.

SUGGESTIONS FOR FURTHER READING

There is a growing and often sensational body of literature on terrorism in Southeast Asia. A representative sample includes Justin V. Hastings, *No Man's Land: Globalization, Territory, and Clandestine Groups in Southeast Asia* (Ithaca, NY: Cornell University Press, 2010); Gregory Abuza, *Militant Islam in Southeast Asia: Crucible of Terror* (Boulder, CO: Lynne Rienner, 2003); Rohan Gunaratna, *Inside Al Qaeda: Global Network of Terror* (New York: Columbia University Press, 2002); Mike Millard, *Jihad in Paradise: Islam and Politics in Southeast Asia* (Armonk, NY: M. E. Sharpe, 2004); Kumar Ramakrishna and See Seng Tan, eds., *After Bali: The Threat of Terrorism in Southeast Asia* (Singapore: Institute of Defence and Strategic Studies and World Scientific Publishing, 2003); Paul J. Smith, ed., *Terrorism and Violence in Southeast Asia: Transnational Challenges to States and Regional Stability* (Armonk, NY: M. E. Sharpe, 2005).

A sample of studies of various aspects of transnational crime would include Allen Dupont, *East Asia Imperiled: Transnational Challenges to Security* (Cambridge, UK: Cambridge University Press, 2005); James O. Finckenauer and Ko-lin Chin, *Asian Transnational Organized Crime* (Hauppauge,

NY: Nova Scientific Publishers, 2006); Bertil Lintner, *Blood: The Criminal Underworld of Asia* (London: Palgrave Macmillan, 2003); Sallie Yea, ed., *Human Trafficking in Southeast Asia* (New York: Routledge, 2014); Derek Johnson and Mark Valencia, *Piracy in Southeast Asia: Status, Issues, and Response* (Singapore: Institute of Southeast Asian Studies, 2005); Adam J. Young, *Contemporary Maritime Piracy in Southeast Asia: History, Causes, and Remedies* (Singapore: Institute of Southeast Asian Studies, 2007). For narcotics, see Ko Li-chin, *The Golden Triangle: Inside Southeast Asia's Drug Trade* (Ithaca, NY: Cornell University Press, 2009), and the classic study of the historical drug trade in the Golden Triangle, Alfred A. McCoy, *The Politics of Heroin in Southeast Asia* (New York: Harper & Row, 1972).

Chapter Eight

Southeast Asia in the Regional and International Economies

An important goal of all the new states of Southeast Asia was to promote economic growth. The question was how to break out of dependency in an international exchange relationship in which exported low-cost primary commodities came back as higher-cost, value-added manufactured goods. The term "neocolonialism" captured the market inequalities that existed between the new states of Southeast Asia and the West and Japan. Their answer was economic development, which came to mean industrialization.

The Southeast Asian states first adopted an industrialization strategy of import substitution which would allow them to close the exchange gap. The problem was that the domestic markets were not large enough to support industrialization platforms for real economic growth based only on import substitution. Economic development came only when capital was invested in growth strategies of export-led industrialization. The policy problem for Southeast Asia has been how to maintain and defend its access to and share of international trade and investment, particularly with a rising Chinese economic tiger prowling the same markets as the would-be Southeast Asian tiger cubs. The answer was to try to build a bigger production and market platform through ASEAN's regional economic integration.

INTRA-ASEAN REGIONALISM: FROM COMPETITION TO COOPERATION

The goal of the ASEAN Economic Community, to be launched in 2015, is to establish ASEAN as a single market and production base, thus strengthening its competitiveness in the global economy. The AEC has been an incremental project, building on programs and agreements that have been in place for years. One critic put it quite bluntly: "The Southeast Asian nations had over 30 years to build an 'ASEAN house,' and they have squandered the opportunity. Had ASEAN evolved along the lines envisioned by its founders, it would not have displayed the disarray with which its members confronted the rise of China."[1] This ignores the reality of the founders' clear design based on sovereignty, noninterference, and consensus. Furthermore, for the first thirty years the stewards of the founders' vision were foreign ministers, and politics was in charge. Finally, it should be pointed out, the drive for closer cooperation and integration was not internally generated but was a response to the external challenges of regional and global economic forces.

The Initial Steps

In ASEAN's early years, the foreign minister drivers of ASEAN gave little priority to matters of real economic cooperation. The members' national economic development plans were competitive rather than complementary. The search for access to economic assistance, investment, and markets was viewed as a zero-sum game. Initial efforts to reconcile national self-interest and regional cooperation were disappointing and concrete achievement elusive.

The UN Blueprint

The first proposals to give economic policy flesh to the bare bones of the Bangkok Declaration came in the recommendations of a UN team of economists commissioned in 1969 by the ASEAN foreign ministers. Their work was completed in 1972 and their blueprint adopted in principle by the governments at the 1976 Bali Summit.[2] The strategy called for industrialization based on market sharing and resource pooling. This was the genesis of the ill-fated ASEAN Industrial Projects (AIPs) scheme.[3] Only two of the proposed five projects came onstream, and these had already been slated as national projects. There was a proposal for a system of "complementarity agreements" in the ASEAN Industrial Complementation (AIC) scheme, through which specified manufacturing activities were to be horizontally integrated across state boundaries. The automotive industry was chosen as an appropriate industry for initial regionalization. This was quickly derailed by Malaysia's decision to build its own automobile, the Proton Saga, with Japan's Mitsubishi Corporation. An ASEAN Industrial Joint Venture (AIJV) initiative was started in 1983. The AIJVs were private undertakings from the ASEAN region (but with non-ASEAN equity participation) that would be given a 50 percent tariff preference in intra-ASEAN trading (raised to 75 percent in 1986). The AIJV concept got off to a slow start and quickly bogged down in

ASEAN and national bureaucratic mazes where "the merits of the AIJVs are not well perceived in all capital cities in ASEAN."[4]

The ASEAN Task Force

As national jealousies and overlapping bureaucracies stymied progress, criticism of ASEAN's slow pace toward functional cooperation mounted. The ASEAN Chamber of Commerce and Industry (ASEAN CCI) reviewed ASEAN's performance in 1981 and found it wanting, describing a "decrescendo" since the Bali Summit.[5] In response to the critics, the foreign ministers commissioned an ASEAN Task Force on ASEAN Cooperation. The mandate was to appraise ASEAN's progress, identify policy measures that would maximize the attainment of ASEAN's objectives, and define new directions for cooperation. The task force reported its recommendations to the 1983 AMM, which then parceled them out to various committees for consideration. This set the stage for the relative indifference of the foreign ministers at the 1984 AMM, when they endorsed the effort in principle, accepted some politically easy recommendations, and then consigned the meat of the report to "further study," a limbo from which it was never resurrected.

The report's recommendations did not deviate significantly from the UN blueprint strategy. The report emphasized that ASEAN regionalism had no supranational objectives—that its aim was cooperation, not integration. What was troublesome to the task force—and put it at odds with the foreign ministers—was the degree of vigor to be applied to cooperation. In the words of the report, "Behind all aspects of cooperation lies the political will to cooperate. . . . Regional interests are usually accorded priority only if they coincide with or promote national interest."[6] As one observer noted, cooperation that demanded sacrifices from the members could not flourish given the differing national outlooks and priorities.[7] These outlooks and priorities were embedded in competitive national development plans taking place behind high tariff and nontariff barriers (NTBs) to protect national markets. A particular bogey for Indonesia and Malaysia was vibrant and open-to-the-world Singapore.

The Preferential Trade Arrangements (PTAs)

The UN blueprint also called for market sharing as a means of liberalizing and expanding intra-ASEAN trade. The initial effort was the 1977 Preferential Trade Arrangement (PTA). This mechanism called for negotiations on a bilateral or multilateral basis of an ASEAN margin of tariff preference that would apply on a most-favored-nation basis to all ASEAN states.[8] In implementing the PTA, protracted negotiations over goods to be included and excluded had the effect of seriously limiting its trade significance. By the

1986 Manila ASEAN Summit, only 5 percent of items offered under the PTA were actively traded. How minimal the impact was is suggested by the fact that PTA-traded goods accounted for just 2 percent of intra-ASEAN trade, which itself was only 17 percent of ASEAN total trade.[9]

Philippine president Corazon Aquino opened the 1986 AMM in Manila by scolding the foreign ministers for lack of progress in economic cooperation. "After 19 years of existence," she said, "ASEAN should already be evaluating the impact of regional economic cooperation instead of endlessly discussing how to get it off the ground."[10] While the foreign ministers concentrated their attention on the diplomacy of the Third Indochina War (chapter 3), their economic ministerial counterparts had a new focus centered on moving from PTA arrangements to an ASEAN Free Trade Area (AFTA), with ultimately the goal of an ASEAN common market. Under the sponsorship of the ASEAN CCI, a "Group of 14"—a veritable who's who of ASEAN economic and financial brainpower—began to chart a course toward economic integration, offering concrete recommendations to foster the organizational process. The Group of Fourteen's 1987 final report made trade liberalization the highest priority for ASEAN.[11] Other studies followed in increasing volume and influence. By the end of the 1980s, the practical policy aspects of free trade dominated the ASEAN official, academic, and business dialogue. The breakthrough was the decoupling of the idea of ASEAN free trade from the goal of an ASEAN common market. This was necessary if Indonesia were to be brought on board.

The ASEAN Free Trade Area (AFTA)

The January 1992 Singapore summit meeting, only the fourth in twenty-five years, was the first opportunity for ASEAN member nations to respond collectively to the dramatic restructuring of the regional international environment. The Third Indochina War had been officially closed. Cold War imperatives no longer dominated ASEAN's policy plate. Not since the 1976 Bali Summit had expectations been so high for the prospect of a purposeful and progressive redirection of ASEAN. A sense of urgency was felt as the European Common Market and the North American Free Trade Agreement (NAFTA) changed ASEAN perceptions of global market access. To lead ASEAN to the pledged higher economic plane, the leaders signed a Framework Agreement on Enhancing ASEAN Economic Cooperation.[12] Called a landmark in ASEAN's history, the way forward was the establishment of an ASEAN Free Trade Area to be phased in over a period of fifteen years (2008).

Up until the 2003 Bali Summit with its proposed AEC, AFTA was the economic cement of ASEAN, no matter how weak when compared to the political cement of the Third Indochina War. The implementing mechanism for AFTA was a system of Common Effective Preferential Tariffs (CEPT) that would progressively lower tariffs on intra-ASEAN trade in goods to 0 to 5 percent (box 8.1). The CEPT scheme went into effect on 1 January 1993, on a schedule to be realized by 2003, with tariff cuts on both "fast" and "normal" tracks.[13] The Philippines had circulated the draft of a comprehensive ASEAN Treaty of Economic Cooperation that included not only goods but services, capital, and labor. This was quickly shunted aside. AFTA did not affect the ASEAN member states' external bilateral or multilateral trading relations. Each member state maintained its own national tariff regime and trade regulations for non-ASEAN trading partners.

AFTA was initially hedged with conditions, qualifications, and escape clauses, such as an ASEAN-minus-X formula that would allow nonparticipation in specific circumstances. The loopholes reflected consensual accommodation of national domestic protectionist demands. Like the PTA, AFTA had lengthy exclusion lists in three categories. A "temporary" category protected certain domestic producers. A "sensitive" category protected the political lightning rods of raw agricultural products, especially rice. A "general" category was based on national security, health, morals, historic importance, and other internationally recognized criteria. Only about 1 percent of all ASEAN tariff lines fell in the general exclusion category. The temporary and sensitive categories for exclusions had time limits, after which they would be included in the CEPT scheme.

In 1995, the target tariff level of 0 to 5 percent for the ASEAN 6 was advanced from 2008 to 2003, and then again in 1998 to 2002. The late-entering CLMV countries were given longer deadlines: 2006 for Vietnam, 2008 for Laos and Myanmar, and 2010 for Cambodia. The CEPT agreement was

Box 8.1. CEPT

The implementing mechanism of the ASEAN Free Trade Area was the common effective preferential tariff (CEPT). This was a tariff preferential to ASEAN members applied to goods identified for inclusion in the CEPT scheme and meeting rules of ASEAN origin. Local content was defined as "substantial transformation" in terms of value added of at least 40 percent of ASEAN content. The CEPT scheme covered all manufactured products including capital goods and processed agricultural goods. Excluded were goods placed in "temporary" or "sensitive" categories which were to be phased into the CEPT tariff lines over time.

amended in January 2003 by a protocol that set a target for elimination of all intra-ASEAN import duties by 2010 for the ASEAN 6 and 2015 for the CLMV countries. In 2010 the CEPT-AFTA agreement was superseded by the ASEAN Goods in Trade Agreement (AGITA), which enhanced the original agreement by consolidating the existing commitments on trade in goods. When the AGITA came into force, the ASEAN 6 was essentially a free trade area with 99.2 percent of its excluded items at 0 percent tariff. The CLMV had 69 percent of its excluded tariff lines at 0 percent tariff.

ASEAN statistics show that intra-ASEAN trade has grown but as a share of its total trade remains at about 25 percent, up from the 19 percent before AFTA (table 8.1). The CLMV share of intra-ASEAN trade is 10 percent or less, and of that, Vietnam has by far the largest part.

The ASEAN states also worked to create more comprehensive programs of cooperation in other sectors of the regional economy, what has been called "AFTA-plus." The services sector is a large and expanding component of GDP in ASEAN countries. In 1995, the ASEAN economic ministers signed the ASEAN Framework Agreement on Services (AFAS) under which measures for intraregional liberalization of trade in services would be negotiated.[14] The goal is to provide national treatment for services suppliers among ASEAN countries. A 2003 protocol to the AFAS applied the ASEAN-minus-X formula, allowing the liberalization of specific services without having to extend the benefit to nonparticipating countries.

In order to stimulate the flow of investment within ASEAN, an ASEAN Investment Area (AIA) was endorsed at the 1995 ASEAN Summit. The AIA agreement covered manufacturing, agriculture, mining, forestry, and fishery sectors and services incidental to those sectors. The AIA called for opening up these sectors to foreign investment and national treatment to foreign investors. Temporary exclusions in the manufacturing sector ended for the ASEAN 6 and Myanmar in 2003 and for Vietnam, the LPDR, and Cambodia in 2010. Temporary exclusions in the other sectors ended for the ASEAN 6 plus Cambodia in 2010 and for Vietnam in 2013, and were scheduled to end for the LPDR and Myanmar in 2015. The AIA ministers began the task of widening the scope of the AIA to cover investments in services in 2003. The ASEAN-minus-X formula again was applied. The original AIA framework was superseded in 2012 by the ASEAN Comprehensive Investment Agreement (ACIA), which greatly expanded both the scope and protections offered in a liberalized investment regime for ASEAN and ASEAN-based foreign investors.[15]

The regional commitment to cooperative measures promoting economic growth did not address the problem of regionally harmonizing, first five and then ten, different economic systems with their mix of state and private

Table 8.1.   Intra-ASEAN Trade as a Percentage of World Trade (WT), 2006–2012 (US$ Millions)

Year	2006	2007	2008	2009	2010	2011	2012
Intra-ASEAN	352,774	401,820	470,112	376,177	518,805	598,242	602,048
ASEAN WT	1,494,805	1,610,787	1,897,127	1,538,878	2,045,731	2,388,592	2,474,424
ASEAN % WT	25.1	24.9	24.7	24.4	25.3	25.0	24.3

Sources: ASEAN Statistical Yearbook 2012, table V.1 "ASEAN Total Trade, Intra-ASEAN and Extra-ASEAN Trade 2006–2011" and ASEAN Trade Statistics 2012, table 20, accessed at http://www.asean.org/news/item/external-trade-statistics-3.

enterprise, different banking systems, different regulatory structures and procedures, different tax systems, and different judicial systems, all items that would have to be tackled in a truly integrative process. There are also the structural distortions and disincentives of corruption, lack of transparency, and cronyism.

THE CRASH OF '97

The end of a decade of rapid growth by Southeast Asia's "little tigers" came in the financial crisis of 1997–1998. In Southeast Asia, it started with an assault on the Thai currency, the baht, which had been pegged to a basket of currencies dominated by the US dollar. The mid-decade decision by the United States and Japan to let the dollar appreciate against Japan's yen and China's 1994 devaluation of its yuan against the dollar left Thailand's and other ASEAN countries' exports at a competitive disadvantage and their currencies overvalued. In the growth years, awash with capital, abundant liquidity had been invested in excess productive capacity, real estate, and other speculative ventures. In 1997, as Thai current account deficits widened and the baht weakened, the Thai central bank gave up on efforts to defend the baht.

On 2 July 1997, without warning to its ASEAN partners, the Thai central bank abandoned the dollar peg and allowed the baht to float. Within two months it had lost 38 percent of its value. This triggered a regional financial shockwave revealing the structural sand on which Southeast Asian bubble economies had been built. The collapse starkly exposed the inadequacies and institutional weaknesses that had been concealed by high economic growth rates. The cumulative impact of currency speculation, nonperforming loans, massive debt, crony capitalism, weak or nonexistent regulatory safeguards, and corruption left a trail of institutional and political wreckage in the banking and finance sectors. Thailand, Malaysia, and Indonesia were particularly hard hit, but the impact was felt throughout the region as investment plummeted, liquidity dried up, and confidence failed. Growing economies contracted as output fell and growth rates dropped dramatically and even turned negative. By 1998, Thailand and Indonesia were in deep economic depressions.

The Global Response

The immediate task facing the afflicted countries was recapitalization and restoring investor confidence. The International Monetary Fund took the lead in managing the international response, coordinating rescue operations by multilateral funding agencies and bilateral assistance packages.[16] The total pledged for Thailand was $17.2 billion and for Indonesia $49.7 billion. Japan was the largest single donor with $4 billion for the Thai package and $5 billion for the Indonesian rescue. Singapore also made $5 billion available for Indonesia. The United States did not participate in the Thailand package. This was a strategic error since it left the impression of America not caring for its historical ally. As the financial contagion spread, the United States did not repeat the Thai mistake, pledging as a "second line of defense" $3 billion for the Indonesian package. Thailand finished paying back its IMF debt in 2003 and Indonesia in 2006.

The IMF-organized support programs were contingent on the imposition of an IMF financial regime of structural reform, adherence to macroeconomic fundamentals, and budgetary austerity—the so-called Washington consensus. For Southeast Asian economic nationalists, the IMF conditions were viewed as a kind of economic Pax Americana. Jakarta was told that the United States would not support Indonesia if it did not accept the IMF terms. Malaysia refused to submit to the rigors of an IMF package, with Prime Minister Mahathir blaming the crisis on Western capitalists who wanted to take over Asia's distressed economies. Malaysia adopted capital controls and other domestic measures to salvage financial stability.

The Regional Response: The Chiang Mai Initiative (CMI)

The financial crisis showed that the countries of Southeast Asia were ill prepared to manage the volatile flows of global capital coursing through the region. The ASEAN 6 recognized that they could not construct a financial self-protection framework simply from their own resources. Wary of the IMF, they turned instead to the wider East Asian region for cooperation. This was the genesis of the ASEAN + 3. The leaders of China, Japan, and South Korea were invited to attend the 1997 Kuala Lumpur ASEAN Summit. When repeated the next year at a summit in Hanoi, China proposed regular meetings between the countries' finance and monetary officials. The emergent ASEAN + 3 framework for East Asian cooperation was institutionalized in the first Joint Statement on East Asian Cooperation at the 1999 Manila Summit.[17]

One of the first fruits of the new regional relationship was the Chiang Mai Initiative (CMI). Meeting on the sidelines of the May 2000 ADB meeting in Chiang Mai, Thailand, the finance ministers of the ASEAN + 3 announced the CMI, the central feature of which established an ASEAN + 3 currencies swap arrangement (box 8.2).[18] This built on and expanded the 1977 ASEAN Currency Swap Agreement, which with only a $200 million facility available was too small to meet the challenges posed by the global economy. Designed

Box 8.2.   Currency Swap Agreement

For a country facing immediate current account liquidity problems, a currency swap agreement allows that country to exchange its local currency for foreign currency—often the US dollar—with a country party to the agreement's central bank or monetary authority currency reserves. It is designed for short-term support, with the exchange to be reversed at a future date. In the agreement there is a maximum swap commitment and maximum swap line.

to alleviate balance-of-payments difficulties, the CMI provided for a network of bilateral swap agreements for short-term currency exchanges between ASEAN central banks and their East Asian counterpart institutions. The original CMI facility was $78 billion, increased to $120 billion in 2008, and again to $240 billion in 2012. In 2009, the CMI became the CMIM (Chiang Mai Initiative Multilateralization), replacing the existing swap networks with a single contractual agreement. The financial commitments to the CMIM are divided 20 percent–80 percent ($48 billion and $192 billion) between ASEAN and its East Asian partners. The tiered economic relationships within ASEAN are reflected in its countries' commitment (table 8.2).

Table 8.2.   CMIM Financial Commitments (US$ Billions)

Country	Contribution	Percent
China*	76.8	32
Japan	76.8	32
South Korea	38.4	16
Plus 3 Total	*192*	*80*
Indonesia	9.104	3.793
Malaysia	9.104	3.793
Singapore	9.104	3.793
Thailand	9.104	3.793
Philippines	9.104	3.793
Vietnam	2.00	0.833
Cambodia	0.24	0.100
Myanmar	0.12	0.050
Brunei	0.06	0.025
Lao PDR	0.06	0.025
ASEAN Total	*48*	*20*
Total	*240*	*100*

Source: ASEAN +3 Macroeconomic Research Office (AMRO).

*Includes Hong Kong Monetary Authority.

The idea of a self-managed currency pooling arrangement suggests a de facto Asian Monetary Fund (AMF) outside the oversight and discipline of the IMF. In fact, Japan had proposed in September 1997 a $100 billion AMF.[19] This was viewed as a thinly veiled effort to evade the conditionality of IMF assistance. The scheme was given the cold shoulder by the World Bank, the IMF, the EU, and the United States. One of the objections to an AMF was the potential moral hazard posed by access to pooled reserves without effective structures for monitoring and surveillance of the requesting country's financial health and practices as well as the absence of conditionality. Surveillance had been high on the agenda of the IMF-sponsored Manila Framework group of fourteen Pacific-region finance and central bank deputies who began meeting in November 1997 to promote a new framework to enhance regional financial stability.[20]

In 1999 ASEAN established an ASEAN Surveillance Process to exchange information on financial developments and provide an early warning system.[21] ASEAN surveillance had many shortcomings. It was "informal and simple," and its peer review took place in the context of the ASEAN way. In the CMIM, the ASEAN process has been replaced by the ASEAN + 3 Macroeconomic Research Office (AMRO), which monitors and analyzes regional economics to contribute to detection of risk and recommend remedial action. The governance of the CMIM has been expanded to include ASEAN + 3 central bank governors as well as the finance ministers. The CMIM is a supplement to the IMF, not a substitute. The linkage is that a country wishing to draw on the CMIM facility can only get up to 30 percent of its drawing rights without having in place an IMF standby agreement, which is subject to IMF surveillance and conditionality. Whether the CMIM can build the capacity to act autonomously as an AMF seems to depend on two factors: the development of AMRO and the politics of the China–Japan economic relationship. There has been no financial crisis yet to test the workings of the CMIM.

By 1999 the ASEAN states had weathered the worst of the crisis and with international assistance began to regain the lost economic ground, but progress was slow and depended more on global demand and interest rates than national policies in ASEAN countries, let alone ASEAN mechanisms. As a result of the financial crisis and as part of the recovery progress, the ASEAN leaders resolved to hasten and deepen their economic cooperation. This was the thrust of the Bali Concord II. The idea was to put all of the economies in the same boat, rather than every ASEAN country for itself. The fragility of ASEAN's integrative thrust was illustrated in November 2006 when Thailand's central bank suddenly imposed capital controls to limit investment inflows that were putting upward pressure on the baht. This was done unilaterally, without consultation with Thailand's ASEAN partners. The

Thai stock market nosedived, and markets elsewhere in the region plunged as investors lost confidence. The contagion of the 1997 crash sprang to mind. The Thai finance minister defended the move in terms of national interest. "A small nation like ourselves," he said, "if we don't protect ourselves, who else will protect us?"[22] He certainly did not expect ASEAN and the CMI to protect Thailand.

PATTERNS OF ASEAN TRADE AND INVESTMENT

The driving force of ASEAN cooperation has been the desire to expand trade and attract investment. The financial crisis of 1997–1998 was a temporary setback. The structural and macroeconomic policy adjustments in the national economies of those countries most severely affected have been strengthened. Their export platforms and AFTA-plus have enhanced the region's investment climate. In one sense, closer intra-ASEAN economic cooperation was an adjustment to emerging global trading blocs. In terms of directions of trade, there was no significant diversion of trade from ASEAN's principal external markets. There was concern, however, about the future growth of those markets and investment opportunities.

AFTA also was the beginning of an adjustment to emerging competition with China in trade and the diversion to China of foreign direct investment (FDI). The gloomiest forecasts had China moving up the manufacturing ladder to mid- and high levels of technology, leading to the deindustrialization of Southeast Asia. This bleak scenario would have Southeast Asia reverting to square one as a primary product–exporting region serving rising China's demand for resources. An alternative vision had Southeast Asia reorienting its trade from the United States and Europe to be integrated into a Chinese economy with its growing markets and income. In either case, the outcome portended a decoupling of Southeast Asia from its Western partners, leaving it as a Chinese economic hinterland. These alarmist projections did not take into account measures that Southeast Asian states can take—and are taking— to sustain their growth. Nor are these projections supported by an empirical base that can demonstrate that such an outcome is inevitable or that China's rise is necessarily sustainable at its current rate of ascent.

Trade Patterns

Table 8.3 shows ASEAN merchandise trade and share of trade, including intra-ASEAN, with the region's ten most important trading partners in 2012. The top four external trading partners accounted for more than 41 percent of

ASEAN trade. Of these, China has the greatest share. China surpassed the United States in 2008 and Japan in 2009. There is nothing in the trade data that would suggest as yet a trade diversion to China indicative of any impending decoupling of ASEAN members' economies from their traditional major trade partners. The aggregate share of trade held by Japan, the EU, and the United States was 29.3 percent of the ASEAN total, much more than double China's 12.9 percent. The rapid expansion of two-way China–ASEAN trade does suggest that China's share of ASEAN trade will continue to increase in the future, barring major market slowdowns. Table 8.4 compares the value of ASEAN trade in 2007 and 2012 and the percentage change. On an annual basis, since 2009 the growth rate has averaged 21.6 percent. It can be expected that the 2013 trade figures will show China's trade share increasing and the value approaching $4 billion, which would be a more than 25 percent annual increase. The stated ASEAN–China trade targets are $5 billion in 2015 and $1 trillion in 2020.[23] China's position as the single most important trading partner for ASEAN will not be challenged, but for ASEAN this does

Table 8.3.   Top Ten ASEAN Trade Partners, 2012 (US$ Millions)

Country	Trade Value*			% Share of Trade		
	Export	*Import*	*Total*	*Export*	*Import*	*Total*
Intra-						
ASEAN	323,855.0	278,193.2	602,048.2	25.8	22.8	24.3
China	141,892.0	177,592.8	319,484.8	11.3	14.5	12.9
Japan	126,507.0	136,376.8	262,883.7	10.1	11.2	10.6
EU-28	124,891.7	117,707.2	242,598.9	10.0	9.6	9.8
United						
States	108,035.7	91,991.5	200,027.2	8.6	7.5	8.1
South						
Korea	55,030.3	75,999.8	131,030.1	4.4	6.2	5.3
Taiwan	35,219.2	61,032.7	96,251.9	2.8	5.0	3.9
Hong Kong	80,507.1	14,235.3	94,742.4	6.4	1.2	3.8
India	44,055.4	27,760.3	71,815.8	3.5	2.3	2.9
Australia	45,724.3	23,774.8	69,499.1	3.6	1.9	2.8
Total top						
10	*1,085,717.7*	*1,004,664.5*	*2,090,382.1*	*86.5*	*82.2*	*84.4*
Others	168,863.0	217,182.3	386,045.3	13.5	17.8	15.6
Total						
ASEAN						
trade	*1,254,580.7*	*1,221,846.8*	*2,476,427.4*	*100.0*	*100.0*	*100.0*

Source: ASEAN Trade Statistics 2012, table 20, accessed December 2013 at http://www.asean.org/news/ item/external-trade-statistics-3.

*In some cases the export + import total may be off by rounding to the nearest 0.1 or 0.0.

**Table 8.4.   Top Four ASEAN External Trade Partners' Trade Value
Growth, 2007–2012 (US$ Millions)**

Partner	2007	2012	% Change
China*	171,117.7	319,484.8	86.7
EU	187,571.8	242,598.0	29.5
Japan	173,060.0	262,887.3	49.6
United States	179,968.0	200,027.2	11.1

Sources: ASEAN Statistical Yearbook 2012, Table V.12. ASEAN Trade Statistics 2012, table 20, accessed at http://www.asean.org/news/item/external-trade-statistics-3.

*Does not include Hong Kong.

not devalue its other important trade partners. China's robust trade growth in ASEAN is underpinned by a number of factors. Chinese exporters bring to Southeast Asia the same kind of product competitiveness that China has demonstrated around the world since its entry into the WTO in 2001. More important, however, has been the phasing in of a free trade agreement between China and ASEAN as well as bilateral agreements with some ASEAN countries; but the low-hanging fruit has been plucked. Then there is a factor of the ties of local ethnic Chinese businesses to China.[24]

ASEAN data presented in the aggregate as in tables 8.3 and 8.4 do not reflect the real patterns of trade in the region. Table 8.5 shows ASEAN trade in 2011 on a country basis. Singapore accounts for a third of the total, and adding Indonesia, Malaysia, and Thailand, 85 percent of ASEAN trade is accounted for. The CLMV countries' share of ASEAN trade is less than 10 percent, most of which is Vietnam's, which now exceeds the Philippines. The relative economic importance of the countries within ASEAN has been factored into China's strategy of "rebalancing" its relations in the region with new emphasis on Thailand, Malaysia, and Indonesia.[25] Singapore has a special role in ASEAN trade as an entrepôt. As noted in chapter 6, Singapore is the world's second-largest container port. As a transshipment point, it handles goods being imported from other ASEAN countries for reexportation or goods being reexported from Singapore to other ASEAN countries. Malaysia and Indonesia have tried to challenge this with container-handling port facilities in, respectively, Johor and Batam.

Investment Patterns

The productive capabilities of the market economies of Southeast Asia require access to capital from international financial institutions like the World Bank and the ADB and foreign direct investment. World Bank and ADB lending has been important for infrastructure development in Southeast Asia.

Table 8.5.   ASEAN Trade by Country, 2011 (US$ Millions)

Country	Total Trade	% ASEAN Trade
Brunei	14,822.3	0.6
Cambodia	12,844.1	0.5
Indonesia	380,932.3	16.0
Lao PDR	3,955.9	0.2
Malaysia	415,721.9	17.4
Myanmar	14,925.1	0.6
Philippines	111,751.6	4.6
Singapore	775,152.6	32.5
Thailand	458,904.4	19.3
Vietnam	199,582.1	8.3
Total	*2,388,592.3*	*100*

Source: *ASEAN Statistical Yearbook 2012*, table V.2.

Their aggregate lending patterns were shown in tables 2.3 and 2.4. FDI has played a critical role in the industrial development propelling GDP growth rates in Southeast Asia. A stable and peaceful regional international environment is seen as a requisite of a favorable investment climate. Table 8.6 shows the 2010–2012 cumulative top ten sources of FDI inflow in ASEAN with percentage share of total inflow.

ASEAN's early concerns that a rising China was sucking up FDI that would otherwise go to ASEAN are not supported by investment patterns. The continued attractiveness of reduced costs of labor-intensive manufacturing, resource harvesting, and infrastructure projects, as well as the offshoring of production facilities by Japanese, European, and North American transnational corporations, indicates that Southeast Asia remains a "bright spot for FDI."[26] There is not a zero-sum competition with China since the investment platforms are different. The threat to investment comes from uncertain legal frameworks and corruption as well as human rights issues, for example, labor conditions in the garment industry in Cambodia or indigenous rights and the mining industry in Indonesia's Papua.

Like the aggregate ASEAN trade data, aggregate ASEAN FDI inflow statistics do not indicate the pattern of inflows. Table 8.7 shows the total ASEAN FDI inflow from 2004 to 2011 by country and its percentage of the total. Four countries—Indonesia, Malaysia, Singapore, and Thailand—accounted for 86 percent of the FDI inflow. If Vietnam is added in, the five-country percentage is 95 percent. It is increasingly difficult to continue to justify classifying Vietnam with the other CLMV countries as being on a second tier of ASEAN. Vietnam outperforms the Philippines. It can be expected that there will be future divergences from the investment pattern of the last few

Table 8.6.   Top Ten Sources of FDI Inflow in ASEAN, 2010–2012 Cumulative with Percentage Share (US$ Millions)

Country/Region	2010–2012 Value	% of Total Inflow
EU	71,047.5	22.3
Intra-ASEAN	53,494.9	16.8
Japan	46,894.1	14.7
United States	25,666.4	8.1
China	14,210.4	4.5
Hong Kong	10,470.9	3.3
South Korea	8,377.6	2.6
Australia	6,935.1	2.2
Taiwan	6,001.9	1.9
India	4,314.5	1.4
Total top 10	*247,413.3*	*77.7*
Others	71,070.6	22.3
Total ASEAN inflow	*318,483.9*	*100*

Source: ASEAN FDI Statistics, database, 30 October 2013, table 27, accessed at http://www.asean.org/images/resources/2014/Jan/StatisticsUpdate28Jan/Table%2027/pdf.

years. Two factors are in play. First, the long crisis of political stability in Thailand, without resolution in sight, risks new investment as well as capital outflow, with investors looking for less risk in Vietnam, Malaysia, and Indonesia.[27] Second, the emergence in Myanmar of new investment opportunities is proving attractive, despite the inadequacies of infrastructure, with estimates that FDI will have tripled at the end of fiscal year 2014.[28]

It is obvious that Singapore, with a third of the ASEAN region's trade in goods and receiving more than half of ASEAN's FDI inflow, stands out statistically. This can be placed in the broader context of other factors that make Singapore ASEAN's leader in the global economy. As a global financial center, it ranks fourth, behind London, New York, and Hong Kong.[29] Singapore's IT readiness has been ranked second in the world since 2010.[30] In addition to its busy port, Singapore's Changi Airport is the busiest international hub in Southeast Asia, carrying fifty-four million passengers in 2013.[31] In overall economic competitiveness, Singapore ranks second only to Switzerland.[32] All in all, in the regional and international economies Singapore punches far above its population and territorial weight. In aggregating data for ASEAN, it's Singapore and all the others. Singapore's success is a source of envy and rivalry for its regional neighbors. It is not clear how Singapore's desire to be the economic hub of Southeast Asia will fit within the framework of the AEC. Economic nationalists in Malaysia and Indonesia fear that a disproportionate share of the projected benefits of greater openness and integration in the region's economy will accrue to Singapore.

Table 8.7. FDI Inflow to ASEAN Countries and Percentage of Total Cumulative, 2004–2011 (US$ Millions)

Country	FDI Inflow 2004–2011	% Total FDI Inflow
Brunei	3,724.4	0.7
Cambodia	4,891.6	0.9
Indonesia	69,280.0	13.0
Lao PDR	1,735.3	0.3
Malaysia	53,108.6	10.0
Myanmar	4,018.6	0.7
Philippines	14,445.8	2.7
Singapore	270,794.4	51.0
Thailand	64,982.5	12.2
Vietnam	45,378.9	8.5
ASEAN total	*532,360.2*	*100*

Source: *ASEAN Statistical Yearbook 2012*, table VI.9.

ECONOMIC REGIONALISM BEYOND AFTA

AFTA and its corollary AFAS and AIA services and investment liberalization programs have helped the ASEAN nations' economic growth through expanded and deeper intra-ASEAN integration. Similar patterns of cooperation and structures for integration have been pursued by ASEAN countries with their major extraregional economic partners. Since recovery from the Crash of '97, there has been a rush for bilateral and regional free trade agreements (FTAs and RTAs). This has been led by ASEAN's economic winners as they seek even greater market access to the wider East Asian and global markets. They have been prompted by uncertainties in the global trade and investment climate. The promise of liberalization of trade through the processes of the WTO has faded. The Doha round of WTO negotiations that began in 2001 has sunk in the quagmire of agriculture and global North–South recriminations. At the same time that global negotiations for trade liberalization have broken down, ASEAN sees the politics of protectionism in Europe and North America as a threat to trade expansion. To secure their economic futures, the ASEAN nations have moved forward on national and regional trade agendas. Outside of AFTA, the member countries are free to manage their own national trade relations, and through ASEAN they can engage collectively. The bargains they reach collectively do not exclude better bargains reached bilaterally.

The proliferation of FTAs and RTAs has provoked debate about their economic costs and benefits. On one side, it is warned that the trade-diverting results and overlapping rules in a patchwork pattern of competitive FTAs and

RTAs will make liberalization in the global framework of the WTO or the proposed East Asian and Pacific region frameworks discussed below harder to achieve in the future.[33] Alternatively, it has been argued that the growing networks of FTAs and RTAs are necessary building blocks—not needing consensus among 151 nations—to global trade liberalization. The spread of FTAs, with their built-in trade preferences, will provide incentives for the hesitant to catch up. The term "competitive liberalization" was coined to describe this process.[34]

ASEAN's "Noodle Bowl" of FTAs

Since 2002, ASEAN states have collectively signed or are negotiating six RTAs. In the same period individual ASEAN states have entered into, are negotiating, or have proposed more than sixty bilateral or other multilateral FTAs (table 8.8). Singapore has set the pace, followed by Thailand and Malaysia. By 2014, Singapore had concluded twenty bilateral or multilateral FTAs with thirty-one trading partners, with another five under negotiation, making it the most trade networked of the ASEAN countries. The FTAs have different scopes and depths. The most comprehensive—and the most difficult to negotiate—cover trade in goods, services, investment, government procurement, intellectual property rights, and other nontrade items. These are sometimes called "WTO-plus" agreements. Just a glance at table 8.8 shows the lack of participation beyond the ASEAN RTAs of the CLMV countries. Excepting Vietnam, a late entry, this is because of their relative economic insignificance in the region's trade and investment patterns (tables 8.5 and 8.6). This feature of ASEAN's tiering has led to warnings that the weaker economies will be marginalized and disadvantaged as the "winners" win more. This also has implications for ASEAN solidarity.

Southeast Asia is also a good example of the "spaghetti bowl" effect, translated to Asia as "noodle bowl," of multiple free trade arrangements.[35] The term describes the lack of uniformity in the differing complex rules of trade from one FTA to another, making trade more expensive for business and in the end costing more for the consumer. If, as economists argue, the opening of the floodgate of FTAs will in fact negatively impact global liberalization of trade and even ASEAN economic integration, why do the political leaders pursue it? In part, because even if the hodgepodge of bilateral and regional FTAs is second best when compared to a WTO framework, it is politically attainable in the lifetime of a government.[36] More directly to the political point, there is fear of being left out of the scramble. Prime Minister Thaksin put it bluntly when defending the proposed Thailand–US FTA. Fearing the competition from Singapore and Malaysia for US markets, he argued that "as

Table 8.8.   Southeast Asia's Noodle Bowl of FTAs

Signed	Negotiating	Proposed
ASEAN–Australia/NZ ASEAN–China ASEAN–India ASEAN–Japan ASEAN–ROK		ASEAN–Hong Kong ASEAN–Pakistan ASEAN–GCC[+]
Brunei–Japan Brunei–Trans-Pacific SEP[‡]		Brunei–Pakistan Brunei–US
Indonesia–Japan	Indonesia–Australia Indonesia–EFTA* Indonesia–ROK	Indonesia–Chile Indonesia–US
Lao PDR–Thailand		
Malaysia–Australia Malaysia–Chile Malaysia–India Malaysia–Japan Malaysia–New Zealand Malaysia–Pakistan	Malaysia–EFTA* Malaysia–EU Malaysia–US	Malaysia–ROK Malaysia–Syria Malaysia–Turkey
Philippines–Japan		Philippines–EFTA* Philippines–US
Singapore–Australia Singapore–China Singapore–Costa Rica Singapore–EFTA* Singapore–EU Singapore–GCC[+] Singapore–India Singapore–Japan Singapore–Jordan Singapore–New Zealand Singapore–Panama Singapore–Peru Singapore–ROK Singapore–Trans-Pacific SEP[‡] Singapore–US	Singapore–Canada Singapore–Mexico Singapore–Pakistan Singapore–Ukraine	
Thailand–Australia Thailand–China Thailand–India Thailand–Japan Thailand–Peru Thailand–New Zealand	Thailand–Chile Thailand–EFTA* Thailand–US	Thailand–Canada
Vietnam–Japan	Vietnam–EFTA* Vietnam–EU Vietnam–ROK	

Sources: ADB Asia Regional Integration Center: Free Trade Agreements, accessed at http://www.aric.adb
.org/fra-all; Bilaterals.com, accessed at http://www.bilaterals.com; Singapore FTA, accessed at http://
www.fta.gov.sg/fg_fta.asp.

*EFTA–European Free Trade Association (Iceland, Liechtenstein, Norway, and Switzerland).

[+]GCC–Gulf Cooperation Council (Bahrain, Kuwait, Qatar, Oman, Saudi Arabia, and the United Arab Emirates).

[‡]Trans-Pacific SEP–Trans-Pacific Strategic Economic Partnership (Brunei, New Zealand, Chile, and Singapore).

other countries pursue their own deals . . . we need to move now, before we have no more room to move."[37]

All of the ASEAN countries are part of the group's RTAs with Australia/ New Zealand, China, India, Japan, and South Korea. In a number of cases, an ASEAN country has a separate bilateral FTA with the external partner as well as the RTA. The RTAs are negotiated at a lowest-common-denominator consensus level, which means that the bilateral FTA can be of a higher quality in terms of coverage and conditions.

China–ASEAN Free Trade Agreement (CAFTA)

The blossoming of ASEAN–China trade depicted in table 8.4 can be linked to the staged implementation of ASEAN's first RTA. When fully implemented in 2015, the CAFTA will encompass the world's largest market, with more than 1.8 billion potential consumers. Pushed hard by China, which wanted to open Southeast Asian markets to competitive Chinese agricultural products and manufactures, ASEAN agreed in 2002 to an ASEAN–China Comprehensive Economic Cooperation Framework Agreement, which first led in 2004 to an agreement on trade in goods. The trade deal, effective July 2005, provided for an "early harvest" group of items for immediate tariff reductions and "normal" and "sensitive" tracks for liberalization of trade to zero tariffs for the ASEAN 6 in 2010 and the CLMV countries in 2015. By 2015 more than eight thousand product categories will be at a zero tariff. Tariffs on 97 percent of the products classified in the normal track have been eliminated on schedule by the ASEAN 6.

The initial trade strategy was front-loaded with the products that would generate the quickest benefits. For China, this meant flooding Southeast Asian markets with goods from Chinese agricultural and manufacturing sectors that were more competitive than Southeast Asia's. This was particularly true in Myanmar, Laos, Cambodia, and Thailand's northern provinces, which have been inundated with Chinese goods in a kind of legal dumping. Trade became part of the wider Chinese strategy of integrating continental Southeast Asian markets and resources into the development of its southwest Yunnan Province. As China and the ASEAN 6 closed in on the 2010 target date for full implementation of the scheme, protectionist urges kicked in, particularly in Indonesia, and the detailed negotiations went very slowly.

The 2002 RTA framework agreement was comprehensive in scope. In addition to the 2004 merchandise agreement, ASEAN and China have agreed to liberalize trade in services and investments. A trade-in-services agreement went into effect in July 2007 with a package of commitments and was followed by a second package of commitments in November 2011. An investment agreement was finalized in August 2009. Differential treatment and flexibility were offered to the CLMV countries. In October 2013, it was announced that China and ASEAN would begin negotiations to upgrade the CAFTA to enhance further trade facilitation and investment cooperation.[38] Parallel with increasing trade and investment has been the growing use of Chinese currency, the yuan or renminbi (RMB), for trade settlement rather than the US dollar.

Japan–ASEAN Economic Partnership Agreement (EPA)

Japan negotiated its first-ever bilateral FTA, called an Economic Partnership Agreement (EPA), with Singapore in 2002. Since then Japan has negotiated six other EPAs with ASEAN countries: Malaysia (2006), the Philippines (2006), Brunei (2007), Indonesia (2007), Thailand (2007), and Vietnam (2009). Japan's free trade strategy as ASEAN's second-largest export market was to build a network of bilateral FTAs in which the economic asymmetry between Japan and an ASEAN country would be a negotiating plus. Rather than a "stringing together" of bilateral pacts, as the ASEAN secretary general put it, ASEAN wanted a regionwide agreement with Japan.

The signing of the CAFTA moved Japan to begin negotiations for an ASEAN RTA. A framework agreement for a regional EPA was established in 2003. Negotiations for a comprehensive EPA began in 2005. It was originally expected that the agreement would be concluded in 2009, but the 2006 ASEAN–South Korea agreement (discussed below) speeded up the process. After eleven rounds of negotiations, the basic agreement was reached in November 2007, and on 14 April 2008 the last ASEAN state signed off on it. The Japan–ASEAN EPA was ASEAN's first comprehensive free trade agreement covering not only merchandise trade but the services and investment sectors, which have been negotiated separately in the other RTAs in place. Under the pact, over ten years, Japan will have removed tariffs on 90 percent of imports from ASEAN, and the ASEAN 6 will have phased out tariffs on 90 percent of their imports from Japan, including consumer electronics and autos. As in its bilateral FTAs, Japan continues to protect its agricultural sector including rice, beef, and dairy products. The CLMV countries have been given fifteen to eighteen years to comply fully.

South Korea

South Korea used its 2005 bilateral FTA with Singapore as a bridge to Southeast Asia. It crossed that bridge with the ASEAN–Republic of Korea Framework Agreement on Comprehensive Economic Cooperation in 2006. This led to the ASEAN–Korea Free Trade Agreement (AKFTA) covering goods that was signed in May 2006 and went into effect in July 2006. It was realized for the ASEAN 6 in 2010. The CLMV countries have until 2016–2018 to finalize their tariff reductions. An agreement on trade in services was signed in November 2007, and an investment agreement was reached in 2009. The agreement on goods was an ASEAN-minus-one pact because Thailand refused to sign. The Thais protested South Korea's exclusion of Thai agricultural products, particularly rice, from the FTA cuts. Bilateral talks between Bangkok and Seoul resulted in an April 2008 compromise which permitted Thailand to have a slower schedule in reducing tariffs on imports from Korea of certain sensitive products. In addition to its Singapore bilateral, Seoul is negotiating or proposing bilaterals with Indonesia, Malaysia, and Vietnam.

Australia and New Zealand (AANZFTA)

Since 1983, Australia and New Zealand have traded within their own bilateral free trade area in the Australia–New Zealand Closer Economic Relations (CER) agreement. In the context of the CER, Australia and New Zealand were treated as a unit in the negotiations for an ASEAN–CER or AANZFTA. Negotiations began in 2005 for a comprehensive FTA. It had been hoped that negotiations could be concluded by the end of 2008, but, as a high-value FTA, progress was slow on issues of market access, rules of origin, and intellectual property rights. The New Zealand trade minister, comparing the AANZFTA negotiation with ASEAN's China, Japan, and South Korean agreements, stated that the latter had "generally been at a lower level of ambition."[39] The agreement was signed in February 2009 and came into force in January 2012.

India (AIFTA)

India hopes to position itself as a fourth major-power actor in Southeast Asia, putting itself on the same regional footing as China. This includes an Indian RTA with ASEAN, for which a framework agreement was reached in 2003. At the 2005 ASEAN–India Summit, the ASEAN side noted that the negotiations had not moved forward as expeditiously as hoped. A proposed implementation date was moved back from January 2006 to January 2007. The major difficulty has been Indian restrictions on major agricultural exports from ASEAN to India. The crucial item has been palm oil, which is Malaysia's and Indonesia's largest export item to India. In July 2006, ASEAN suspended negotiations with India. An Indian special envoy was sent to ASEAN to revive the talks. ASEAN agreed, but with the proviso that India had to make more concessions. The bargaining gaps narrowed through negotiations in 2007 as India brought its exclusion list down from 1,400 items to 489, close enough to ASEAN's target of 400.

It was hoped that the agreement could be signed in April 2008, but the palm oil issue still was a sticking point. India would not accept Indonesia's terms for a compromise formula that would decrease Indian market access to Indonesia to make up for continued high tariffs on palm oil. After six years, a final, but hedged, trade in goods (TIG) agreement was signed in August 2009 and went into effect in 2010. In the AIFTA, a substantial number of tariff lines will be reduced to zero by December 2016, with the Philippines and the CLMV countries given two to three years of additional time. Separate negotiations for FTAs in trade in services and investment have gone on since the implementation of the TIG agreement. It was hoped that they would be finalized by July 2014.

The lengthy and tough negotiations for an ASEAN–India RTA stand in sharp contrast to the CAFTA. India's political and economic weight does not tip the balance in Southeast Asia the way China's does. Also, ASEAN has been on a learning curve in its RTA negotiations as it seeks to harmonize the differing interests of its members in tiered implementation formulas and in evaluating the costs and benefits of concessions. Part of the learning curve is that they may have given too much away in the first fruits of the CAFTA.

European Union

The EU and ASEAN agreed to begin negotiations for a comprehensive trade pact in May 2007, following a feasibility study showing benefits for both sides. From the EU side, an ASEAN trade agreement was an acknowledgment of the breakdown of the Doha round of WTO negotiations and of the growing number of FTAs in Southeast Asia by the EU's global economic competitors. In its turn, ASEAN was anxious to strike a deal in advance of possible EU–China and EU–India trade agreements. The goal was ambitious in its wide-ranging scope and depth. It was soon clear, however, that the harmonizing of interests of ten ASEAN countries and twenty-five (now twenty-eight) EU countries was far more difficult than in earlier ASEAN RTAs. A major stumbling block was the unwillingness of some EU states to include Myanmar. By the fourth round of negotiations in April 2008, the ASEAN position on topics such as intellectual property, rules of origin, services, and investment had become defensive with only Singapore pushing for greater liberalization. After the seventh round in 2009, "both sides agreed to take a pause in the negotiations in order to reflect on the format of future negotiation."[40]

In a new European format, the focus turned toward engaging a smaller group of ASEAN countries in negotiations for bilateral FTAs. Negotiations with Singapore and Malaysia were launched in 2010. The EU and Singapore reached an agreement in September 2013. The Malaysia negotiation has not ended. Thailand was added to the EU's wish list by FTA negotiations that began in March 2013. The EU is also exploring the possibility of a comprehensive economic partnership agreement with Indonesia. From Brussels's long-range vantage, the bilateral agreements could be the building blocks for consolidation in a future regional agreement, if even on an ASEAN-minus-X basis.

The United States

The Singapore–US FTA, which went into force in January 2004, is the model for US trade negotiation strategy in the Southeast Asian region. It is a leading-edge, high-quality WTO-plus instrument that expanded market access in goods, services, investment, government procurement, and trade-related intellectual property rights (TRIPS). It was groundbreaking in its environmental protections and guarantees of labor rights. The scope of the US–Singapore FTA is more comprehensive than any other FTA or RTA signed or proposed by ASEAN or its members. As noted in chapter 3, the United States and ASEAN had signed a regional Trade and Investment Framework Agreement (TIFA) in August 2006 as part of the ASEAN–US Enhanced Partnership. A TIFA is an initial step toward an FTA. The resistance to the Washington non-trade agenda, TRIPS and labor for example, would seem to make reaching a US–ASEAN RTA unlikely. The United States has a bilateral TIFA with every ASEAN country except Laos. The US trade relationship with the LPDR is based on a bilateral trade agreement that is not yet fully implemented. Laos only joined the WTO in 2013. The Myanmar TIFA was signed in Washington in March 2013. After long years of US economic sanctions, the TIFA signified the resumption of normal relations.

Washington's insistence on non-trade-related provisions in comprehensive FTAs reached a dead end in negotiations with Thailand and Malaysia. Negotiations for a Thailand–US FTA, which began in 2004, were subject to protests by various Thai social and labor groups. Negotiations were suspended as a consequence of the 2006 Thai coup which drove Prime Minister Thaksin Shinawatra from office. The Thai condition for restarting negotiations has been to start from scratch. The United States launched FTA negotiations with Malaysia in March 2006. Transparency, reciprocal access to government contracts, TRIPS, and Malaysia's preference system for ethnic Malays were among the sticking points. They were suspended in January 2008, ostensibly in protest against American support of Israeli policies in Gaza. After a year's delay, a new round began, but the Malaysian side was in no rush to resolve the outstanding issues and the negotiations were suspended indefinitely in 2009.

President George W. Bush's administration pressed its trade agenda on the basis of Trade Promotion Authority (TPA) legislation. With the TPA, the president could put a trade agreement on a "fast track" to Congress, which had to vote it up or down without amendment within ninety days. This gave US negotiating partners confidence that an agreement with the United States would not be subject to future renegotiation because of congressional interventions. The TPA expired in June 2007.

There are other multilateral FTA frameworks engaging ASEAN countries. Brunei and Singapore are joined with New Zealand and Chile in the Trans-Pacific Strategic Economic Partnership (TP-SEP), better known as the P4. Implemented in 2006, it built on the existing Singapore–New Zealand bilateral FTA. The P4 provided for a three-step phasing out of tariffs by 2015. In 2008, the P4 became a "plus 3" with Australia, Peru, and Vietnam joining. In chapter 4, it was noted that Myanmar and Thailand are part of the BIM-STEC. A framework agreement for a BIMSTEC FTA was concluded in 2006 with a proposed 2017 date for full implementation. Little progress has been made, however. Indonesia and Malaysia participated in the 2010 Preferential Tariff Agreement of the Eight Developing Countries (D-8) grouping that was formed in 1997. The other D-8 members are Bangladesh, Egypt, Iran, Nigeria, Pakistan, and Turkey. Malaysia has ratified the OIC's preferential tariff system (TPS-OIC). Indonesia has signed the framework agreement but has not ratified it.

ECONOMIC REGIONALISM
BEYOND ASEAN: DUELING DESIGNS

Even as the ASEAN states' AFTA-plus economic architecture and their network of FTAs and RTAs were phasing in, important external partners were proposing wider frameworks for regional and interregional economic cooperation and integration. This would require new political and economic adjustments for ASEAN's members. In October 2013, an ADB assessment of the impact of ASEAN's proliferating RTAs concluded that they "have done little to promote regional economic integration or integration with the wider Asian or global economy."[41] Described as "weak" and "trade light," they did not address the abundant nontrade barriers that impede the flow of goods, services, and investment. In other words, they are low-quality agreements.

As the WTO's global trade talks sputtered, political and economic attention focused on regional frameworks within which trade liberalization could be achieved. For the Southeast Asian states, the issue has been defining the region within which they could gain the most benefits and least costs of trade liberalization but still maintain their claim to ASEAN's centrality. A major question has been whether the Pacific Ocean unites a region of Pacific Rim countries or whether it divides the Americas from a more natural East Asian region. The geopolitical overtones at first glance seem obvious in terms of US–China rivalry, but to phrase the matter simply in terms of inclusion or exclusion of one or the other from competing economic frameworks is too simple.

APEC and the Free Trade Area of Asia and the Pacific (FTAAP)

The first concrete example of the realization of a trans-Pacific region was the establishment of the Asia-Pacific Economic Cooperation (APEC) forum in November 1989. APEC is an intergovernmental grouping of economies to promote economic cooperation and trade facilitation among Pacific Rim countries. ASEAN resisted the initial appeals for Pacific regionalism, largely because of Indonesian and Malaysian reservations. The concern was that the ASEAN members' voices would be muted and their influence diluted and diminished in a broader grouping dominated by Japan and the United States. Nevertheless, when it became apparent that the ASEAN countries' major Pacific trading partners were going forward with the scheme, the ASEAN 6 joined Australia, Canada, Japan, New Zealand, South Korea, and the United States at the founding APEC ministerial meeting. The exigencies of the international economy, pressure from domestic economic interests, and diplomacy overcame ASEAN reluctance. Added to these factors was ASEAN's desire not to be left out.

APEC's membership has expanded to twenty-one economies. In 1991, China, Hong Kong, and Taiwan (an economy, not a state) were admitted. This was followed by Mexico and Papua New Guinea (1993); Chile (1994); and Peru, Russia, and Vietnam in 1998. A ten-year moratorium on new members was put in place in 1997, which was extended in 2007 to 2010. The moratorium was an effort to keep the membership from becoming too large to make meaningful decisions and retain its relevance. In 2010 the moratorium was not renewed, and the APEC leaders agreed to review future membership. ASEAN would like Cambodia, Laos, and Myanmar to be members, and India is the only EAS member excluded.

Malaysia's Prime Minister Mahathir refuted the conceptual underpinnings of APEC, which sought to unite like-minded Pacific Rim countries in pursuit of WTO-compliant trade liberalization. He expressed the view that East Asian economies had to defend themselves against Europe and North America, rather than join them. This was the anti-APEC posture that led him in December 1990 to propose—without consultation with his ASEAN counterparts—the formation of an East Asia Economic Group (EAEG).[42] In its original iteration, the EAEG was to be an economic bloc that could negotiate as a unit on issues of international trade. Although any real leverage it might have depended on Japan's inclusion, Mahathir denied that the EAEG would be a yen bloc.

The United States lobbied vigorously against the EAEG. In a letter to the Japanese foreign minister, Secretary of State James Baker warned that it would "divide the Pacific in half."[43] This has been a consistent US position on exclusive East Asian arrangements. In ASEAN, guided by Indonesian president Suharto—who had been insulted by Mahathir's unilateralism—the EAEG was downgraded to an ad hoc East Asia Economic Caucus (EAEC) as a "noninstitutional entity." Mahathir may have had the last laugh, however, when in referring to the ASEAN + 3 in 2003, he said, "We would be very happy if we stopped hiding behind this spurious title and called ourselves the East Asia Economic Group."[44]

President Bill Clinton hosted the first APEC leaders' meeting in November 1993 on Blake Island, Washington. Mahathir conspicuously boycotted the meeting. The next year, President Suharto hosted the second of what became annual APEC summits in Bogor, Indonesia. Suharto's up-front support of the APEC process was a rebuff to Mahathir, who had to choose whether to cause a major breach in ASEAN by staying away or swallow his pride and take part—which he did. The nonbinding Bogor Declaration was APEC's signature undertaking.[45] In it, the leaders resolved to liberalize trade and investment in the Asia-Pacific region with the goal of free and open trade by 2010 for the developed economies and by 2020 for the developing economies. It was viewed as an endorsement of American liberal international economic policy.

In Southeast Asia, the APEC program of trade and investment liberalization seemed like a larger American-driven Pacific regionalist overlay of AFTA. Unlike ASEAN-centered extraregional engagements, however, ASEAN was not in control of the APEC agenda. ASEAN's strategy was twofold. First, through AFTA-plus structures it moved to stay ahead of APEC. Second, from within APEC, the ASEAN 6, with Malaysia at the point, resisted efforts to move APEC from loose consultative structures to institution building that might give binding effect to its decisions.

APEC accepts that high-quality FTAs and RTAs have an important role in trade liberalization in the APEC region. At the same time it has studied the benefits and policy implications of an APEC region–integrating Free Trade Area of Asia and the Pacific. The FTAAP became a part of the APEC agenda when it was urged by President Bush at the 2006 Hanoi APEC leaders' meeting. The Hanoi Declaration recognized the difficulties of negotiating such an instrument but instructed APEC officials to begin a feasibility study of an FTAAP as a long-term proposition.[46] At their 2007 Sydney, Australia, meeting, the APEC leaders declared that through a range of practical and incremental steps, they will examine the options and prospects for an FTAAP. Priority has been given to looking at the convergence and divergence of the existing FTAs and RTAs among members. The all-things-being-equal economic answer seems simple: disentangle the noodles by consolidating the multiple arrangements into a single uniform regional arrangement, what APEC calls "docking and merging" FTAs and RTAs between and among APEC members in a next-generation FTAAP.[47] This would be an inclusive instrument bringing all APEC parties into one—WTO compliant—trade, services, and investment regime. However, it will not be economists doing the disentangling; it will be politicians. There will have to be a demonstrable coincidence of econometric modeling and political appreciation of national interests.

The East Asia Free Trade Area (EAFTA) and the Comprehensive Economic Partnership in East Asia (CEPEA)

An alternative model for unraveling the East Asian "noodle bowl" is not to start from the inclusiveness of an FTAAP, but the exclusivity of the ASEAN + 3 grouping which now encompasses nearly every area of functional cooperation. In 2003, the ASEAN + 3 Summit endorsed the proposal of the East Asia Study Group for a future East Asia Free Trade Area (EAFTA). Such an FTA would solidify Chinese dominance in the ASEAN + 3 processes. Unlike an FTAAP, it would be another element in Beijing's strategy to exclude the United States from the regional international architecture. In 2005, a joint expert group spearheaded by China launched a feasibility study of an EAFTA. The expert group reported back in August 2006, claiming that the benefits of an EAFTA would exceed those of AFTA, the ASEAN RTAs, or any other bilateral or subregional arrangement.[48] It would make East Asia more competitive internationally. The experts called for comprehensive WTO-plus trade, services, and investment agreements, taking as reference points the existing FTAs. They left open the possibility of extending the EAFTA at the "appropriate time" to other countries with which ASEAN was negotiating RTAs. The report was taken under advisement, and in 2007 a second-phase sector-by-sector study led by South Korea got underway.

The expert group's reference to an "appropriate time" for expansion of an EAFTA was a response to the Japan-promoted Comprehensive Economic Partnership in East Asia (CEPEA) that would include all of the participants in the EAS at that time: ASEAN 10, Australia, China, India, Japan, New Zealand, and South Korea. Japan's initiative was widely viewed as an attempt to dilute China's influence in an ASEAN + 3 setting. In accepting the EAFTA report at the January 2007 ASEAN + 3 Summit, the Chairman's Statement added, "We should continue to examine other possible FTA configurations such as the East Asia Summit."[49] Econometric modeling showed that a CEPEA would yield the largest gains to East Asia with relatively small losses to nonmembers through trade diversion. An EAFTA would be less beneficial than a CEPEA but would still provide more benefits than any of the existing ASEAN FTAs and RTAs.[50] There is also the question of what impact an EAFTA would have for the ASEAN states on their extraregional trade relations. The ASEAN 6 would not want preferential arrangements in a closed regional framework to jeopardize their access to Europe or the United States. The United States strongly opposes an EAFTA based on closed regionalism rather than the open regionalism of APEC.

Lurking in the background for Southeast Asia is the negotiation of a China–Japan–South Korea trilateral FTA. It had been discussed over time, but negotiations were only formally announced in May 2012, with a fourth round of negotiations taking place in March 2014. A CJKFTA would link ASEAN's three most important East Asian economic partners in a minus-ASEAN framework. The economic diplomacy of the CJKFTA, however, seems overtaken by the political/military issues in China's and Korea's bilateral relations with Japan.

The Trans-Pacific Strategic Economic Partnership (TPP)

While still embracing the long-term goal of the FTAAP, President Obama tried to give APEC's Pacific regionalism credibility through a building-block approach. At the 2009 Yokohama APEC Summit, he launched the TPP together with P4 members Australia, Brunei, Chile, New Zealand, Peru, Singapore, and Vietnam. The original eight have been joined by Canada, Japan, Malaysia, and Mexico, the twelve accounting for 40 percent of global GNP and a third of world trade. The goal is to fashion a high-quality comprehensive agreement that would set the standard for the future expansion of TPP membership. From the TPP's American vantage point, this is the road to the FTAAP. From the American side as well, the TPP comprehends an economic dimension of the Obama administration's "pivot."

The Philippines has already knocked at the door. Thailand has expressed interest, but its beleaguered government is incapable of making any major decisions, particularly since the May 2014 military coup. Indonesia is cautiously weighing its priorities in terms of existing trade relations. Jakarta is aware, however, that two export competitors, Malaysia and Vietnam, have joined the TPP negotiation. Japan's decision in 2013 to take part in the TPP was important. As the second-largest economy in East Asia, it gave the TPP greater economic heft and helped lessen the imbalance in the TPP between the United States and the other members. Japan's decision was perhaps based as much on political considerations as economic. In the strategic tension in East Asia, joining the TPP would be an affirmation of close Japan–US ties. When Japan signaled its intention to join the negotiating process, the prime minister at the time, Naoto Kan, told his future partners that Japan would "put everything on the table."[51]

At the 2011 APEC Summit in Honolulu, the TPP leaders announced that they had achieved a framework for the negotiation of the agreement. It would include non-trade-related provisions with respect to environmental protection, government procurement, TRIPS, and labor—the American model.[52] The negotiations have been slow. An October 2013 deadline for completion was extended to the December twentieth round, but a twenty-first round was held in February 2014, with an indefinite number of rounds probably to follow. Under the banner of a twenty-first-century trade agreement, the usual issues of trade negotiations persist: market access, protectionist carve-outs, exclusions, and the details of the non-trade-related items. Japan did not put it all on the table, insisting on protecting domestic agriculture and closing its automobile market from US competition. The same issues that doomed the US–Malaysia bilateral negotiation are sticking points in the TPP negotiation. President Obama had hoped to conclude the Japan negotiation during his April 2014 trip to Asia, but Prime Minister Abe had yet to overcome the resistance of the politically powerful agricultural interest groups. In Malaysia, Prime Minister Najib told President Obama that the country was not ready to finalize the TPP because of domestic sensitivities.

There is awareness that even if a final agreement is reached—which would require American concessions—before a new American president is elected in 2016, the lack of a TPA fast track jeopardizes the entire enterprise. President Obama has strongly supported a bill introduced in Congress in January 2014 that would restore the TPA, but it does not enjoy the support of the congressional leadership necessary for its enactment.

The Regional Comprehensive Economic Partnership (RCEP)

At the 2011 Bali ASEAN Summit, the leaders reconciled China's and Japan's competing visions of the EAFTA and the CEPEA by adopting the ASEAN Framework for Regional Comprehensive Economic Partnership.[53] The negotiating principles were approved by the ASEAN economic ministers in August 2012.[54] The sixteen negotiating partners are the ASEAN 10 plus Australia, China, Japan, India, New Zealand, and South Korea—the EAS minus Russia and the United States. ASEAN's centrality is specifically acknowledged. Indonesia chairs the RCEP Negotiating Committee. The first negotiating round was in May 2013 with the fourth in April 2014. Completion is hoped for in 2015. If completed, it would be the world's largest trading bloc.

The goal is a comprehensive trade agreement covering goods, services, and investment with broader and deeper engagements and improvements over the existing ASEAN +1 FTAs. However, according to the guiding principles and objectives of the negotiations, the existing ASEAN + 1 FTAs and the bilateral FTAs among the participants would remain in effect, and *no provision in the RCEP would detract from them* (emphasis added). This does not untangle the FTA noodle bowl. As conceived, rather than harmonizing and unifying the plethora of divergent trade, investment, and services agreements, the RCEP seems to add a new layer on top of the noodles. This is a deliberate recognition of the economic disparities between the ASEAN 10 and the external six and the disparities within ASEAN itself. A key word used in discussing the RCEP is "flexibility." This suggests that final agreement will be of low quality with limited trade liberalization, that is, similar to the existing regional FTAs. One ADB economist has warned that the negotiation for the RCEP could be "a race to the bottom."[55]

Great attention has been paid to the relationship between the TPP and the RCEP. They have often been portrayed as driven by great-power rivalry, with China excluded from the TPP and the United States excluded from the RCEP, driving a wedge down the Pacific. This would not be by the rules of the two frameworks. Eight of the participants in the RCEP negotiations are also participants in the TPP negotiations. Both the TPP and the RCEP explicitly provide for future accessions by countries that accept the terms of the agreements. The devil is in the details of the terms of accession. The question is whether they would have to be fully agreement compliant immediately or whether there could be flexibility and phasing in. Without time to adjust, China, as well as Indonesia and India, would be reluctant to step into a US–dominated WTO-plus framework.[56] For the United States there would be little incentive, other than geopolitics, to accede to a low-quality RCEP, let alone whether Congress would approve it.

There is another view that would see the TPP and RCEP as complementary frameworks for trade expansion and facilitation in the Asia-Pacific region. Membership in one or the other, or in both, does not exclude bilateral trade relationships including FTAs with nonmembers. Singapore is a good example of what might be called the "more the merrier" approach to trade relations. Furthermore, there is the question of whether either framework can be realized in the form in which it has been presented. A successful completion of the RCEP assumes that the political bitterness that permeates China–Japan and ROK–Japan bilateral relationships can be overcome in the RCEP. China seems to be hedging its bet on the RCEP by its pressure on ASEAN, noted earlier, to upgrade the CAFTA. As for the TPP, without fast-tracking, which seems unlikely, Congress will be free to plaster it with amendments requiring new negotiations. In both cases, what might emerge are new sets of bilateral and more limited multilateral FTAs, adding to the noodle bowl.

ASEAN's Outlook

Even as negotiations for a higher stage of East Asian or East Asia and Pacific economic integration are going on, the ASEAN states will continue the implementation of their present agreements in the framework of the AEC and AFTA. What the impact of either the TPP or the RCEP on AFTA might be is unclear. Would AFTA become redundant, and if so, would some of the AEC cement be weakened? ASEAN states will have to consider the costs to ASEAN solidarity and identity if member states are absorbed into wider integrative frameworks. Their view of economic relations with China, Japan, and the United States would be viewed through other than an ASEAN lens. Despite ASEAN's insistence on centrality, the differential rewards of enhanced trade will go to those states that have already benefited the most from the existing patterns of trade. This is the concern that has been expressed about the TPP effectively splitting ASEAN for the rewards of greater market access outside of AFTA or an RCEP.

The AEC has special political importance for the ASEAN Community project since some of its units are the only ones in ASEAN that can be identified as being part of an integrative process as already existing programs are accelerated and upgraded. There remains a great deal of work to be accomplished before its targets are reached, certainly not by 2015, or even 2020. The goal of an ASEAN single market and production base is aspirational, with no realistic timeline.

NOTES

1. Walden Bello, "China and Southeast Asia: Emerging Problems in an Economic Relationship," *Focus on the Global South*, 26 December 2006, accessed at http://www.focusweb.org/china-and-southeast-asia-emerging-problems-in-an-economic-relationship.html.

2. United Nations, "Economic Cooperation among Member Countries of the Association of Southeast Asian Nations, Report of a United Nations Team," *Journal of Development Planning* 7 (1974).

3. For ASEAN's early industrialization strategies see Marjorie L. Suriyamognkol, *Politics of ASEAN Economic Cooperation* (Singapore: Oxford University Press, 1988).

4. Hamzah Sendut, as quoted in the *Indonesia Times*, 8 August 1986.

5. ASEAN CCI, *Review of ASEAN Development* (Hong Kong: ASEAN CCI, November 1981).

6. The sixty-six-page *Report of the ASEAN Task Force to the ASEAN Ministerial Meeting* was never released as an official ASEAN document. Copies were available through ASEAN national secretariats. There was a press release on the *Recommendations of the ASEAN Task Force in the Seventeenth ASEAN Ministerial Meeting*, Jakarta, 9–10 July 1984. No record of the ASEAN Task Force exists on the official ASEAN website.

7. Susumu Awanohara, "Much Ado about Nothing," *Far Eastern Economic Review*, 24 May 1986, 66.

8. The details of the PTA can be accessed at http://www.nus.edu.sg/pdf/1977%20Agreement%20Preferential%20Tariff%29Arrangements-pdf.

9. The data are drawn from Ooi Guat Tin, "ASEAN Preferential Trading Arrangements: An Assessment," and Gerald Tan, "ASEAN Preferential Trading Arrangements: An Overview," both in *ASEAN at the Crossroads*, ed. Noordin Sopiee, Chew Lay See, and Lim Siang Jin (Kuala Lumpur: Institute of Strategic and International Studies, 1989).

10. Corazon Aquino, "Time Is Well Past for Talking," *Diplomatic Post* (Manila), July–September 1986, 8.

11. ASEAN CCI, *The Way Forward: Report of the Group of Fourteen on ASEAN Economic Cooperation and Integration* (Kuala Lumpur: Institute of Strategic and International Studies, 1987).

12. The Framework Agreement can be accessed through the AFTA agreements and declarations link at http://asean.org/communities/asean-economic-community/category/asean-trade-in-goods-agreement.

13. The CEPT Agreement can be accessed at the same site as in note 12 above.

14. The AFAS Framework Agreement can be accessed at http://www.asean .org/communities/asean-economic-community/item/asean-framework-agreement-on -services.

15. The ACIA can be accessed at http://www.asean.org/communities/asean -economic-community/category/agreements-declarations-7.

16. The IMF program is outlined in "Recovery from the Asian Crisis and the Role of the IMF," *IMF Issue Brief*, June 2000, accessed at http://www.imf.org/external/np/exr/facts/asia.htm.

17. The statement can be accessed at http://www.asean.org/news/item/joint-state ment-on-east-asian-cooperation-28-november-1999.

18. "Joint Ministerial Statement of the ASEAN + 3 Finance Ministers," accessed at http://www.mof.go.jp/english/international_policy/convention/asean_plus_3.

19. Masahiro Kawai, "From the Chiang Mai Initiative to an Asian Monetary Fund" (ADB Institute Paper, April 2010), accessed at http://www.aric.adb.org/grs/papers/kawai%205.pdf.

20. The fourteen parties represented were Australia, Brunei, Canada, China, Hong Kong, Indonesia, Japan, South Korea, Malaysia, New Zealand, the Philippines, Singapore, Thailand, and the United States. In addition to the IMF, representatives of

the World Bank and the Asian Development Bank participated. A link to all of the meetings of the Manila Framework can be accessed at http://www.mof.go.jp/english/international_policy/financial_cooperation_in_asia/manila_framework/index.html.

21. ADB, "ASEAN Surveillance Process (ASP)," accessed at http://aric.adb.org/initiative/asean-surveillence-process.

22. "Thai Finance Minister Says Capital Controls Were Bid to Save the Country," *Star* (Penang), 24 December 2006.

23. Xinhuanet, "China, ASEAN Aim to Boost Trade to 1 Trl USD by 2020," accessed at http://www.xinhuanet.com/English/china/2013-/10/10/c_125503861.htm.

24. Amy Chang, "Beijing and the Chinese Diaspora in Southeast Asia: To Serve the People," *NBR Special Report* 43 (National Bureau of Asian Research, June 2013).

25. Kavi Chongkittavorn, "China's Rebalancing Strategies to Asean," *Nation* (Bangkok), 13 October 2013.

26. UNCTAD, *World Investment Report 2013*, 45, accessed at http://unctad.org/en/publicationslibrary/wir2013_en.pdf.

27. "Thailand Economy 'Sick Man of Southeast Asia,'" *Nation* (Bangkok), 26 March 2014.

28. "Foreign Investment in Myanmar Triples," *Bangkok Post*, 1 March 2014.

29. As listed by the Qatar Financial Centre-sponsored *Global Financial Centres Index* 115 (March 2014), accessed at http://www.longfinance.net/news/long-finance-blogs/the-pamphleteers/905-sustainable-competitiveness-of-financial-centers.html.

30. As reported in the World Economic Forum's *Global Information Technology Rankings*, accessed at http://www.weforum.org/issues/global-information-technology.

31. The airport data are from the Airports Council International, Annual Traffic Data, accessed at http://www.aci.aero/Data-Centre/Annual-Traffic-Data/Passengers/2013-final.

32. As reported in the World Economic Forum's Global Competitiveness Index Ranking, accessed at http://www.weforum.org/issues/global-competitiveness.

33. Bernard K. Gordon, "Asia's Trade Blocs Imperil the WTO," *Far Eastern Economic Review* 168, no. 10 (November 2005): 5–10.

34. C. Fred Bergsten, "Competitive Liberalization and Global Free Trade: A Vision of the Early 21st Century" (Working Paper 96-15, Peterson Institute of International Economics, 1996), accessed at http://www.piie.com/publications/wp/wp.cfm?ResearchID=171.

35. The now popular description of the growing number of FTAs as a "spaghetti bowl" was first used by Jagdish Bhagwati, "U.S. Trade Policy: The Infatuation with Free Trade Areas," in *The Dangerous Drift to Preferential Trade Agreements*, ed. Jagdish Bhagwati and Anne O. Krueger (Washington, DC: AEI Press, 1995), 1–18.

36. This is the argument made by Barry Desker, "In Defence of FTAs: From Purity to Pragmatism in East Asia," *Pacific Review* 17, no. 1 (March 2004): 3–26.

37. As quoted in Tony Allison, "Thailand, US Inch Ahead on Trade Accord," *Asia Times*, 14 January 2006, accessed at http://www.atimes.com/atimes/Southeast_Asia/HA14Ae01.html.

38. "China, ASEAN to Upgrade Their FTA," *China Daily*, 25 October 2013, accessed at http://usa.chinadaily.com.cn/business/2013-10/25/content_17060136.htm.

39. New Zealand Trade Minister Phil Goff, as quoted in *China View*, 23 April 2008, accessed at http://www.chinaview.net.

40. European Commission, "Free Trade Agreements" page, accessed at http://www.ec.europa.eu/enterprise/policies/international/facilitating-trade/free-trade/index_en.htm.

41. ADB, *ASEAN Economic Integration Monitor*, October 2013, 41, accessed at http://www.adb.org/sites/default/files/pub/2013/aeim-oct-2013.pdf.

42. On the origins of the EAEG and Mahathir's intentions, see Linda Low, "The East Asia Economic Grouping," *Pacific Review* 4, no. 4 (1991): 375–82.

43. As quoted by Shim Jae Hoon and Robert Delf, "Bloc Politics: APEC Meeting Clouded by Fears of Regionalism," *Far Eastern Economic Review*, 18 November 1991, 26.

44. As quoted in "ASEAN Plus-3 Should Be Called East Asia Economic Group," *Asian Economic News*, 11 April 2003.

45. The Bogor Declaration can be accessed at http://www.apec.org/Meeting-Papers/Leaders-Declarations/1994/1994_aelm.aspx.

46. The declarations of APEC leaders' meetings can be accessed at http://www.apec.org.

47. APEC, "Free Trade Agreements and Regional Trade Agreements," accessed at http://www.apec.org/Groups/Other-Groups/FTA_RTA.aspx.

48. *Towards an East Asia FTA: Modality and Road Map. A Report by the Joint Expert Group for a Feasibility Study on EAFTA*, accessed at http://www.thaifta.com/thaifta/Portals/0/eafta_report.pdf.

49. "Chairman's Statement of the Tenth ASEAN Plus Three Summit," Cebu, Philippines, 14 January 2007, accessed at http://www.aseansec.org/19315.htm.

50. Masahiro Kawai and Ganeshan Wignaraja, "EAFTA or CEPEA: Which Way Forward?" *ASEAN Economic Bulletin* 12, no. 2 (2008): 113–38.

51. As cited in "Bold or Plain Reckless," *Economist*, 5 February 2011, 51.

52. An outline of the proposed agreement can be accessed at http://www.ustr.gov.

53. The "framework" can be accessed at http://www.asean.org/news/item/asean-framework-for-regional-comprehensive-economic-partnership.

54. The "Guiding Principles and Objectives," accessed at http://www10.iadb.org/intal/intalcdi/PE/CM%202013/11581.pdf.

55. Jayant Menon, "The Challenge Facing Asia's Regional Comprehensive Economic Partnership," *East Asia Forum*, 23 June 2013, accessed at http://www.eastasiaforum.org/2013/06/23/the-challenge-facing-asias-regional-comprehensive-economic-partnership.

56. Peter Drysdale, "China Economic Containment and the TPP," *East Asia Forum*, 12 December 2011, accessed at http://www.eastasiaforum.org/2011/12/12/china-economic-containment-and-the-tpp.

SUGGESTIONS FOR FURTHER READING

The ADB publishes a semiannual *Asian Economic Integration Monitor* that reviews regional economic cooperation and integration. A PDF download is free and can be accessed at http://www.adb.org/publications/series/ asian-economic-integration-monitor. Giovanni Campannelli and Masahiro Kawai, eds., *The Political Economy of Asian Regionalism* (Tokyo/Heidelberg: Asian Development Bank Institute and Springer, 2014); T. J. Pemple, *The Politics of the Asian Economic Crisis* (Ithaca, NY: Cornell University Press, 1999); Stephan Haggard, *The Political Economy of the Asian Financial Crisis* (Washington, DC: Institute of International Economics, 2010); Ippe Yamazawa, *Asia-Pacific Economic Cooperation: New Agenda in Its Third Decade* (Singapore: ISEAS, 2011); Christopher Findlay, *ASEAN and Regional Free Trade Agreements* (New York: Routledge, 2014); Sanchita Basu Das, Jayant Menon, Rodolfo Severino, and Omka Lai Shrestha, eds., *The ASEAN Economic Community: A Work in Progress* (Singapore: ISEAS, 2013) [a free PDF download is available at http://www.adb.org/publications/ asean-economic-community-work-progress]; Peter A. Petri and Michael G. Plummer, *ASEAN Centrality and the ASEAN–US Economic Relationship* (Honolulu: East–West Center, 2014); Eul-Soo Pang, *The U.S.–Singapore Free Trade Agreement: An American Perspective on Power, Trade and Security in the Asia Pacific* (Singapore: ISEAS, 2011); C. L. Lim, Deborah K. Elms, and Patrick Low, eds., *The Trans-Pacific Partnership: A Quest for a Twenty-First Century Trade Agreement* (New York: Cambridge University Press, 2012).

Chapter Nine

Human Security in Southeast Asian International Relations

The introduction of the concept of human security as an international relations category reflects a paradigm shift from the state to the individual. Human security is a condition in which individuals are safe in their economic and societal circumstances in a setting of equality and justice. The discussion of how human security fits into international relations often is so diffuse that it leads critics to pass it off as a feel-good semantic catchall. It is more accurate to view it as a topical umbrella under which a variety of policies and programs, domestic and international, addressing specific issue areas affecting an individual's welfare and status, can be systematically interrelated in a holistic way. The emergence of human security as an object of international attention can be traced back to the 1994 United Nations Development Program's report on *New Dimensions of Human Security*.[1] The twin goals were epitomized as *freedom from want* and *freedom from fear*. As the dialogue about human security developed, two major emphases gained currency. Freedom from want was conceived of in terms of a broad human needs–based approach. Freedom from fear became more narrowly focused on political defense of human rights in the state.

HUMAN NEEDS AND HUMAN SECURITY

For the 1994 UNDP report, the primary threats to human security were economic and social: poverty, disease, employment, displacement, education, environment, gender inequality, and so forth. The UN secretary general's Commission on Human Security 2003 report, titled *Human Security Now: Protecting and Empowering People*, equated human security with sustainable development.[2] At this level of generalization, it is difficult to frame policy terms for the international community beyond already well-established programs of development and humanitarian assistance by UN agencies, donor governments, and NGOs. One effort to make human security more concrete was the adoption at the UN's Millennium Summit in 2000 of eight Millennium Development Goals (MDG) with a target date for achievement of 2015 (box 9.1).

In Southeast Asia, MDG progress is regionally facilitated by the cooperation of the UNDP, ESCAP, and ADB. The MDG have been incorporated in each ASEAN state's national development programs. MDG progress is evaluated in annual UNDP MDG reports. The 2012–2013 *Asia-Pacific Regional Country Report* judged the Southeast Asian subregion as making the greatest progress, being an early achiever on twelve of the indicators, on track on two, and slow in only six. The Philippines and Timor-Leste were outliers, having a high number of indicators showing slow or no progress and even regression.[3] As the 2015 MDG terminal date approached, attention turned toward a post-2015 "transformative" development agenda. To stimulate the global discussion, in July 2012, UN secretary general Ban Ki-moon appointed a twenty-seven-member High-Level Panel of Eminent Persons to provide recommendations on the development framework beyond 2015. Indonesia's president Yudhoyono cochaired the panel. The Indonesian president submitted the panel's report to the secretary general on 30 May 2013.[4] Yudhoyono's appointment was viewed as recognition of Indonesia's commitment to and achievements in implementing the MDG targets.

Box 9.1.   Millennium Development Goals

The UN Millennium Summit in September 2000 adopted the Millennium Declaration in which leaders pledged a new global partnership to reduce extreme poverty with time-bound targets and a deadline of 2015. The eight Millennium Development Goals (MDG) are as follows:

• eliminate extreme hunger and poverty;
• achieve universal primary education;
• promote gender equality and empower women;
• reduce child mortality;
• improve maternal health;
• combat HIV/AIDS, malaria, and other diseases;
• ensure environmental sustainability; and
• develop a global partnership for development.

Another measure of human security can be found in the UNDP's Human Development Index (HDI). This is a composite measure of indicators along three dimensions: life expectancy, educational attainment, and command of resources needed for a decent living. Table 9.1 locates the Southeast Asian countries in the HDI ranking of 186 countries in the UNDP's HD categories: very high HD, high HD, medium HD, and low HD.

The achievement of human security developmental goals depends not only on the ability to mobilize internal and international resources but on how those resources are utilized. This raises the issue of governance, that is, the way in which authority in the state is exercised. The goal of freedom from want requires more than just resources; it requires good governance. For human security to be achieved, governments should have both the will and capacity to promote social and economic policies in the interest of the public good and implement those policies fairly and uniformly, inclusive of all elements of the population. It is an article of faith in the West that good government is democratic government and that human security requires civil society participation. Yet, for Southeast Asia, an outcome-oriented view of good governance in terms of satisfying needs is independent of types of political systems and institutional structures, since, according to a key ADB proposition, none of them can claim to have any comparative advantage from the point of view of governance.[5] Authoritarian Singapore's place on the HDI index and communist Vietnam's MDG achievement record are cases in point. The intervening variable between resource availability and human security, at least in terms of freedom from want, is not necessarily democracy.

The issue of corruption is perhaps the most internationally visible test of the assumed requisites of good governance such as rule of law, accountability, and transparency. Corruption encourages inefficiencies in the allocation of scare economic and social resources intended for the public good. As corruption eats away at government budgets, assistance packages, and regulatory

Table 9.1. Southeast Asian HDI Rankings (Total Number of Ranked Countries: 186)

Very High	High	Medium	Low
Singapore 18	Malaysia 64	Thailand 103	Myanmar 149
Brunei 30		Philippines 114	
		Indonesia 121	
		Vietnam 127	
		Timor-Leste 134	
		Cambodia 138	
		Lao PDR 138	

Source: UNDP *Human Development Report 2012–2013.*

structures, the programmatic basis for human security is undermined. While no country in Southeast Asia is free of corruption, there is a spread as shown by Transparency International's composite public sector Corruption Perceptions Index (CPI) measuring 177 countries on a scale of one to one hundred. Southeast Asia's results are shown in table 9.2.

The problem of corruption forces tough choices for the international donor community that underwrites important programs and projects to enhance human security in the region. This is starkly presented in Cambodia, by most measures the most corrupt Southeast Asian nation. The Hun Sen government has been unwilling to attack the corruption that is siphoning off funds, plundering natural resources, and trampling on human rights. Reform has not taken place despite the pleas and threats of the international donor community. ODA continues to flow, essentially without conditions. The West's double dilemma is that to punish Cambodia by cutting off or lowering assistance levels would reduce or end programs designed to enhance human security. It would be devastating to the NGOs that act as agents for programs and are dependent on external grants for funding. It would also deepen Cambodia's reliance on China, which does not contribute to human security in Cambodia.

REFUGEES

One population class whose human security is at particular risk is refugees who flee their homelands because of war, ethnic oppression, or other threats

Table 9.2.   Transparency International Corruption Perception Index, 2013

Country	Score	Rank
Singapore	86	5
Brunei	60	38
Malaysia	50	53
Philippines	36	94
Thailand	35	102
Indonesia	32	114
Vietnam	31	116
Timor-Leste	30	119
Lao PDR	26	149
Myanmar	21	157
Cambodia	20	160

Source: Transparency International, accessed at http://www.transparency.org/policy_research/survey_indices/cpi.

Note: Southeast Asian Scores (1–100) and Global Ranking (186 Countries).

to their human security. Their presence in the countries of first asylum can be viewed by the international community as a humanitarian and human rights problem. Governments of first asylum, however, often view refugees as economic, social, cultural, and political burdens with consequent policies of expulsion and threat of forced repatriation.

The International and Regional Frameworks

The Office of the United Nations High Commissioner for Refugees (UNHCR) is the principal international agency responsible for coordinating protection for refugees and working in tandem with national governments and NGOs. The international legal base for the protection of refugees is the 1951 Geneva Convention Relating to the Status of Refugees, which responded to the post–World War II European refugee crisis. The 1967 Protocol to the Convention extended the geographic and temporal jurisdiction, giving it universal coverage.[6] In Southeast Asia, only the Philippines and Timor-Leste have acceded to the Convention and Protocol.[7] Nevertheless, the law and norms of the Convention are the framework of the UNHCR's activities on behalf of refugees in Southeast Asia, sometimes against state resistance. The mid-2013 UNHCR census of refugees in Southeast Asia understates the problem since only refugees recognized officially either by the UNHCR or national authorities are included (table 9.3).[8]

There is no ASEAN agreement on refugees. Most of the countries of the region do not have legislation regulating the rights of refugees and asylum seekers, leaving it up to immigration authorities or the police. Without

Table 9.3.   UNHCR Mid-2013 Southeast Asia Refugees Statistical Snapshot

Country	Refugees From	Refugees In	IDP*
Brunei	1	0	0
Cambodia	13,807	69	0
Indonesia	15,168	2,078	0
Laos	7,835	0	0
Malaysia	505	91,398	0
Myanmar	415,373	0	632,000
Philippines	747	142	16,905
Singapore	66	3	0
Thailand	214	82,460	0
Timor-Leste	—	—	—
Vietnam	314,195	0	0
Total	*767,911*	*176,150*	*648,905*

Source: http://unhcr.org/pages/4b17be9b6.htm.

*Internally displaced persons.

national systems, the general policy is to treat them as illegal immigrants subject to detention, expulsion, and involuntary repatriation. The UNHCR becomes the in-country advocate for protection and rights of refugees. In some cases this is in collaboration with domestic civil society organizations. Complementing the UNHCR, the intergovernmental International Organization for Migration (IOM) humanitarian mission's scope is not just migrants but includes refugees and internally displaced persons.[9] In Southeast Asia, Brunei, Malaysia, and Singapore are not IOM members, and Indonesia is an observer state.

Although, as discussed in chapter 7, the Bali Process has its roots in the trafficking of so-called boat people from South and Southwest Asia through Southeast Asia to Australia, it also comprises refugee movements in Southeast Asia. Both the UNHCR and IOM are participants in the Bali Process, which underlines the duties of governments to ensure the protection of refugees and their legal rights. This would include access to consistent assessment procedures and durable solutions including voluntary repatriation, resettlement within or outside the region, and, where possible, in-country settlement.

Southeast Asian Refugee Communities

The Legacies of the Indochina Wars

The first major test for the UNHCR in Southeast Asia followed the 1975 communist victories in Vietnam, Cambodia, and Laos. Southeast Asia was flooded with Indochinese refugees across Laotian and Cambodian land borders and large numbers of boat people from Vietnam, many of them Sino-Vietnamese. Thousands of Hmong, an ethnic minority in Laos who had sided with the United States in the war, crossed the Mekong into northeast Thailand. Thousands of Cambodians pushed into neighboring Thai provinces to escape the Khmer Rouge's killing fields. By 1978, UNHCR camps housed 150,000 Cambodians. The number doubled after the 1978 Vietnamese invasion (chapter 5).

The ASEAN countries of first asylum agreed to establish transit sites where the UNHCR could register and process refugees for third-country resettlement. They barred in-country resettlement and insisted on guarantees that they would not be left with a residual problem of illegal immigrants.[10] The United States has admitted 1.3 million Indochinese refugees. Australia, Canada, France, and Great Britain also took in significant numbers of refugees.

A "residual problem" existed in Thailand. Even after the resettlement of the initial wave of Hmong—in the United States more than one hundred thousand—many remained in camps. In addition to those who were not eligible for third-country resettlement, new arrivals continued to be treated by the UNHCR as refugees. The Thai government claimed they were illegal economic migrants. Over UNHCR protest, Thai prime minister Abhisit's final solution in December 2009 was to forcibly repatriate the last 4,371 Hmong men, women, and children for a "better life" in a Lao government resettlement zone. The resettlement zone was closed to international verification of proper treatment. The United States denounced the Thai act as "a serious violation of international humanitarian principles."[11]

In Vietnam's highlands, ethnic minorities collectively known as Montagnards (highlanders) collided with the Vietnamese government as it consolidated its authority over the Montagnards' traditional homelands. Many of the Montagnards were Christian and had allied themselves with France and the United States in the first two Indochina Wars. They protested incoming Vietnamese settlers occupying ancestral land, suppressing indigenous cultures, and closing churches. To escape government repression, two thousand of them fled across the border into Cambodia in 2001 where they were gathered in two UNHCR camps. A tripartite Cambodia–UNHCR–Vietnam agreement on voluntary repatriation was reached in 2002. Because Vietnam would not allow the UNHCR to monitor the process, the UNHCR withdrew from the agreement. The camps were closed, and forced repatriation followed. At the end of 2003, Cambodia's treatment of the Montagnards was labeled by the UN human rights envoy in Cambodia a clear violation of the refugee convention.[12]

Because of international pressure and especially Hanoi's desire to normalize trade relations with the United States, a new tripartite agreement was reached in January 2005 allowing the UNHCR to participate again in programs of voluntary repatriation and processing of those eligible for third-country resettlement. Vietnam accepted UNHCR missions to Vietnam's Central Highlands to monitor the returnees. The largest group resettled, more than nine hundred, went to the United States. In 2007, the senior US official responsible for refugees indicated that both Cambodia and Vietnam had lived up to their commitments on the treatment of the refugees. The camps were closed in 2011.

Myanmar: Flight from the Junta

Even as the Indochinese refugee population in Thailand declined, during the reign of Myanmar's military junta a flood of cross-border refugees from Myanmar sought refuge and asylum in Thailand and Malaysia. At any one time there were more than 140,000 of them in nine Thai-administered camps along the border. The largest number was from ethnic minority groups that were targets of brutal military campaigns. A smaller group was composed of political refugees and anti-junta dissidents. The Thai government allowed the UNHCR to work with the ethnic minorities in the border camps but did not process claims by urban-settled Myanmarese political dissidents seeking asylum. UNHCR's third-country resettlement program for the Myanmar refugees began in January 2005. The United States received the largest number, sixty-two thousand through 2012 when the program ended. There is cautious hope that the changed political circumstances in Myanmar—a democratizing government and a search for peace with the ethnic minorities—will lead to prospects for voluntary return of the refugees in the border camps.

Myanmar: The Plight of the Rohingya

The Rohingya are a Muslim minority people living in western Myanmar's Rakhine State (formerly Arakan). Numbering an estimated 800,000 to 1.3 million, the Rohingya are not only religiously different from the majority Buddhist population but are also ethnically related to the Bengalis of Bangladesh. Under British colonial rule, the Rohingya were considered nationals but were deprived of citizenship by the junta in 1982. Stateless, the Rohingya became victims of government and popular political, social, and economic discrimination. The long-simmering tensions in Rakhine erupted in violence in 2012, pitting Rohingya against Rakhine Burmese who were backed by Myanmar security forces. The viciousness of the suppression and atrocities against the relatively defenseless Rohingya led thousands to flee, becoming either internally displaced or boat people heading toward Thailand, Malaysia, and Indonesia. Refugees landing on the Thai coast were treated harshly and pushed back to sea to try to reach Malaysia or Indonesia.

As the plight of the Rohingya gained regional and global attention, Myanmar's government clung stubbornly to its claim that the Rohingya were illegal immigrants. As far as the Rohingya IDPs were concerned, Nay Pyi Taw's position was that the UNHCR had three choices: repatriation to Bangladesh (firmly rejected by Dacca), build larger UNHCR camps to house them, or resettle them in third countries. This was contrary to international sentiment as espoused by the UN secretary general, the OIC, and ASEAN, which called for humanitarianism and reconciliation, which as a first step would require the grant of citizenship to the Rohingya. As external pressure on Myanmar to make concessions increased, a domestic backlash led to attacks on Muslims elsewhere in Myanmar, fanned by Buddhist monks. Up to that point, Myanmar's Muslim ASEAN partners had cast the Rohingya problem in terms of the ASEAN Charter and universal humanitarian values. But, with the widening of the Buddhist–Muslim divide, Indonesia's president Yudhoyono warned that unless Myanmar addressed Buddhist-led violence against Muslims it could cause problems with Muslims in the region.[13] The Rohingya question threatened Myanmar's democratization. Even as conditions worsened for the Rohingya, Myanmar, chairing ASEAN in 2014, would not allow a challenge to its handling of the Rohingya issue, once again undercutting ASEAN's moral authority.

Malaysia's Hard Line

Malaysia has the largest number of refugees in Southeast Asia, 90 percent of them from Myanmar. UNHCR protection of refugees is limited in a Malaysian political and economic environment that equates refugees with the thousands of illegal migrant workers in the country. As such they are subject to arrest, detention, and deportation. Even UNHCR-registered refugees are subject to harassment, arrest, and deportation. Malaysia fears that if it should abide by international standards, it would be swamped by refugees. A new refugee problem could emerge if the internal war in Thailand's southern Malay provinces should escalate.

Indonesia: West Papuans, East Timorese, and Boat People

At the beginning of 2013, there were still eight thousand West Papuan refugees from Indonesia's Papuan provinces receiving UNHCR protection and support in camps on Papua New Guinea's border with Indonesia. This number does not include refugees outside of UNHCR administration dependent on volunteer humanitarian assistance. The establishment of the camps dates from the mid-1980s. In 2013, pressed by the unprecedented demand for its services globally, the UNHCR turned over responsibility for the welfare of the West Papuans to the PNG government. Third-country resettlement does not seem to be an option. Port Moresby is aware that security on the border depends on the refugee sites not being used as sanctuaries for the Free Papua Movement (OPM) (chapter 5).

The assault on the population by Indonesian army-backed militias following the 1999 East Timor independence vote sent tens of thousands of East Timorese westward into adjoining Indonesian West Timor (chapter 2). INTERFET's intervention forced pro-Indonesia militias to flee to the same regions. The UNHCR began operations in West Timor in October 1999 to provide humanitarian relief in the refugee camps and began an ultimately successful voluntary repatriation program that saw 220,000 refugees return to Timor-Leste. The UNHCR closed out its operation in West Timor in December 2005. The agency continued to work in Timor-Leste to deal with the upwards of 150,000 IDPs following the internal political violence in 2006 (chapter 2), closing the office in July 2012.

As was discussed in chapter 7, for more than a decade, Indonesia has been a major transit point for refugees and asylum seekers trying to reach Australia. The refugee issue for Indonesia is with those individuals or groups who become stranded in Indonesia. If the Australian policy of turning back refugee vessels to Indonesia is rigorously enforced, it will increase the Indonesian refugee count. In the absence of a regional solution, their disposition is a matter of Indonesia–UNHCR relations. Indonesia is not a party to the global conventions and does not have a national refugee system. The government has authorized the UNHCR to carry out its mandate in Indonesia. At the end of 2013, the UNHCR-Jakarta had registered 7,111 asylum seekers, mainly from Afghanistan, Iran, and Myanmar, and 3,206 refugees, mainly from Afghanistan, Myanmar, Somalia, and Sri Lanka.[14] While waiting for the UNHCR process to work, the refugees/asylum seekers are held in detention centers whose conditions have been criticized by human rights groups. Of the options available for the registered refugees and those denied asylum—third-country resettlement, voluntary repatriation, or in-country settlement—resettlement to a third country is the only realistic solution, since Indonesia prohibits recognized refugees from taking up residence. The wait for resettlement can be long and futile given the clamor for resettlement by the millions of refugees around the world.

The Uighurs: Caught between China and the UNHCR

The Uighurs are a Central Asian Muslim ethnic group who were once a majority in what is now China's Xinjiang Province. Like the Tibetans, they see their culture and political identity threatened by the migration of Han Chinese and Beijing's heavy-handed, discriminatory rule. Uighur protests have led to violent ethnic clashes and in some cases terrorist acts against the Chinese state. As groups of asylum-seeking Uighurs have surfaced in Southeast Asia, the Southeast Asian governments have been torn between the UNHCR's and NGO human rights groups' insistence that their rights as asylum seekers be observed and China's demand that they be deported and repatriated where they face an uncertain future of harassment, imprisonment, and even execution.

In December 2009, Cambodia forcefully took twenty Uighurs from a UNHCR processing site and delivered them to a waiting Chinese military transport in Phnom Penh. This took place the day before China announced a $1.2 billion economic assistance grant to Cambodia. Malaysia has twice deported Uighurs to China, eleven in 2011 and six in 2013, even as the UNHCR was reviewing their asylum claims. Thailand's Muslim south has become a kind of way station used by people smugglers of Uighurs on their way to Turkey. In the first three months of 2014, Thai authorities had detained more than four hundred. Human Rights Watch and other advocacy groups urged the government, which had allowed Chinese officials and the UNHCR access to the detained Uighurs, not to force them back to China.

MIGRANT LABOR

In 2012, the International Labor Organization (ILO) reported that there were 105.5 million migrant workers in the world.[15] Of that number 30.7 million were Asian. In Southeast Asia, the Philippines and Indonesia are the largest suppliers of overseas labor. In 2012 more than two million overseas Filipino workers (OFWs) were deployed. Nearly 90 percent of the OFWs are in the Arab Gulf states. In Southeast Asia, Singapore and Malaysia host tens of thousands of OFWs.[16] Indonesian migrant workers number more than 1.3 million. Abbreviated as TKI (Tenaga Kerja Indonesia), over 50 percent are concentrated in Malaysia and Singapore. In Thailand, 90 percent of the migrant labor force is from Myanmar, of which the great majority are illegal and subject to the worst forms of exploitation. Remittances from the overseas labor force are an important contribution to the domestic economies. In 2012, Filipino OFWs sent home $24 billion.

The global framework for the protection of overseas migrant workers is the 1990 International Convention on the Protection of the Rights of All Migrant Workers and Members of Their Families that entered into force in 2003.[17] As of January 2014, the Southeast Asian parties to the convention were Indonesia, the Philippines, and Timor-Leste. Unlike refugees, migrant workers as a class do not have a UN international bureaucracy committed to their welfare and protection. There is a UN special rapporteur on the human rights of migrants whose mandate covers all countries, not just the parties to the migrant convention. The major multilateral intergovernmental body that monitors migrants' movement is the IOM.

It was not until 2007 that ASEAN addressed the question of migrant labor, a previously taboo subject because of political sensitivities. It adopted an ASEAN Declaration on the Protection and Promotion of the Rights of Migrant Workers that called for the development of an ASEAN instrument for the protection of migrant labor.[18] ASEAN's sudden attention to the issue may be connected to the fact that the Philippines was the summit chair. The task of drafting an "instrument" has proved daunting. Indonesia and the Philippines presented a "zero draft" in 2009 and were stonewalled by Malaysia. Two issues have divided the labor-exporting countries and the importing countries: whether the "instrument" should cover undocumented workers as well as documented, and whether it should be a binding "agreement" or nonbinding "framework." After seven years the senior officials of the ASEAN Labor Ministers' Meeting (ALMM) are still working to prepare a consensus "instrument" ready for the 2015 inauguration of the ASEAN Community.

Even if migrant protection is institutionalized in an ASEAN framework, real protection will continue to be based on national policies and bilateral diplomacy between labor-exporting and labor-importing countries. The question is how the country of origin's interest in the protection of its citizens can be reconciled with the country of destination's policies, laws, and internal regulations. In the best cases, this is managed through bilateral agreements covering contract laborers who arrive documented and with work permits for fixed periods. Thailand has agreements with Cambodia, Laos, Myanmar, and Malaysia. Malaysia has agreements with Indonesia, the Philippines, and Thailand. The agreements, however, do not guarantee protection to undocumented labor, either arriving directly or overstaying permits.

In terms of intra-ASEAN relations, the issue of protection of Indonesian workers in Malaysia has been a major irritant in an already touchy bilateral relationship. The largest deployment of Indonesian overseas workers is to Malaysia. In 2012, 50 percent of the 1.5 million documented foreign workers in Malaysia were Indonesian. Added to this are the estimated more than a million illegal Indonesians. The most politically sensitive group of workers has been Indonesian women domestic servants. Often lured by unscrupulous recruiters, they have been targets of exploitation and abuse. The Malaysian government has historically looked the other way. Responding to public and parliamentary anger about the treatment of the estimated three hundred thousand maids in Malaysia, the Indonesian government banned sending domestic workers to Malaysia in June 2009. Cambodia and Myanmar had also applied bans on exporting domestic maids to Malaysia.

The Indonesian ban was lifted in 2011 after a new MOU was negotiated that theoretically provided better working conditions and protection. Continuing reports of exploitation, imprisonment, withholding of wages, and rape of TKIs led to a domestic political backlash against President Yudhoyono, accusing him of being weak in dealing with Malaysia. The chairwoman of the parliamentary commission on labor charged that the government's failure to protect Indonesian migrant workers was "because the government just wants the money generated by the TKIs, but remains indifferent when the TKIs are tortured, raped, and abused."[19] Foreign Minister Marty has acknowledged the evident link between national issues and external issues in the problem of protection of nationals, reemphasizing Indonesia's focus on prevention, early detection, and protection.[20] Indonesia has announced a policy of phasing in the ending of sending live-in maids abroad by 2017.

The Indonesian maids are legal but unprotected by Malaysia's national labor laws. Undocumented workers are treated as illegal immigrants. The Malaysian government has tough laws to detain and expel illegal workers. The government has in the past used the volunteer vigilante group RELA (Ikatan Relawan Rakyat [People's Volunteer Corps]) to hunt down and detain suspected undocumented laborers. RELA has been accused by international and domestic human rights organizations of systematic murder, battery, and rape as a tactic. The law was changed in 2012, no longer allowing RELA to carry out its own raids or to use firearms except in self-defense.[21] A new round of Malaysian sweeps against illegal labor began in September 2013 and again in January 2014, aimed at arresting and deporting four hundred thousand illegal immigrants. Among the national groups affected, the Indonesians are the largest, followed by Myanmarese. Even if Malaysia should sign the international convention or if a consensual basis for an ASEAN instrument should emerge, the bilateral issues and their political implications would continue to exist.

DISASTERS AND DISEASE

Southeast Asia is a region where large numbers of its population live under geophysical and health threats inherent in the Southeast Asian natural environment. In emergency conditions, the human needs that go beyond the capabilities of a state or that are transboundary in impact require international responses. While responses may have long-term political overtones, the causes are nonpolitical, which makes such cooperation possible.

Humanitarian Relief

The modern states of Southeast Asia continue the region's history of experiencing natural disaster: typhoons, flooding, earthquakes, mudslides, and volcanic eruptions. The governments do not have the human, financial, communications, and logistics capabilities and infrastructure to respond fully from their own resources to large-scale disaster. Bilateral and coordinated multilateral external assistance involving national governments, UN agencies, and NGOs has a vital role to play. Nowhere was this more fully demonstrated than in the response to the earthquake and tsunami of 2004.

On 26 December 2004, off the coast of Indonesia's Aceh Province on the island of Sumatra, a magnitude 9 deep-sea earthquake in the Indian Ocean triggered a devastating tsunami washing the Indian Ocean littoral. The tsunami caused immense loss of life and massive destruction. More than a quarter of a million people died, over 110,000 in Aceh alone. Hundreds of thousands were displaced. Peninsular Thailand's west coast was hard hit, with more than six thousand persons dead or missing and important tourist centers badly damaged. More than two million people were left in desperate straits. The countries affected were overwhelmed by the pressing immediate needs and future tasks of reconstruction and rehabilitation. The international community faced an unprecedented challenge. The response was the mobilization of the largest international humanitarian rescue and relief operation since World War II.

Among the first responders were US fleet elements diverted to Aceh. In all, thirteen ships and thousands of sailors spearheaded the immediate relief effort. Utilizing staging facilities in Thailand and Singapore, the American "soft power" deployment was the backbone of the logistical operations that supported the arriving disaster and relief teams from ASEAN and around the world. By the end of 2007, the third anniversary of the tsunami, governments, individuals, and corporations had pledged more than $13 billion for tsunami recovery. To keep the tsunami victims in the spotlight, UN secretary general Kofi Annan named former American president Bill Clinton as the UN special envoy for tsunami recovery. Clinton chaired the Global Consortium for Tsunami Recovery. For ASEAN, the tsunami experience was a prompt to the grouping to provide a regional framework for proactive and coordinated response to major natural disasters. In July 2005, the leaders signed the ASEAN Agreement on Disaster Management and Emergency Response (AADMER) under the oversight of the Socio-Cultural Community's ASEAN Ministerial Meeting on Disaster Management (AMMDM). In the framework of the AADMER, an ASEAN Coordinating Center for Humanitarian Assistance on Disaster Management (AHA Center) has been established as a regional hub to coordinate ASEAN's disaster relief. The AHA's coordinator is ASEAN's secretary general.

The first test for the AADMER came in the May 2008 Cyclone Nargis, which devastated Myanmar's Irrawaddy Delta region. More than 140,000 died or went missing as the tidal surge drove twenty-five miles (40 km) inland over the low-lying rice basket of Myanmar. More than a million people were made homeless. The severity of the disaster rivaled that of the tsunami. What made the response to Cyclone Nargis different from that of the tsunami was Myanmar's ruling junta's initial resistance to foreign assistance. In a paranoid fashion, the junta saw an influx of aid givers as a threat to their rule. The storm struck on 2 May. It was not until 9 May that an overwhelmed government began to receive food, medicine, and basic supplies—but no foreign aid workers. At the urging of the ASEAN secretary general, an ASEAN Emergency Response Team under the AADMER umbrella began surveying the situation. On May 19, an emergency ASEAN foreign ministers' meeting convinced the junta to allow admission of ASEAN aid workers. Finally, on 23 May, the government grudgingly allowed the admission of international aid workers. How much human misery the three-week delay caused for the 1.5 million people at risk in the delta cannot, of course, be measured. It speaks, however, to the indifference of Myanmar's military rulers to the suffering of their people. The ASEAN presence in Myanmar was structured as the ASEAN Humanitarian Task Force for the Victims of Cyclone Nargis, headed by Secretary General Surin. The broader, international oversight was from the Tripartite Core Group of ASEAN, Myanmar, and the UN.[22]

Disaster relief has become a functional area for potential cooperation within ASEAN-centered dialogue platforms. As noted in chapter 5, there are intersessional meetings (ISMs) on disaster relief in the ARF and an expert working group in the ADMM-Plus with an agenda including disaster relief. At the topmost level of the dialogue process, the EAS has listed disaster management as one of its six priority areas. As a practical matter, in-the-field support for disaster relief depends on the capabilities of the responding agencies. ASEAN has been criticized for its slow reaction to the human havoc reaped by the November 2013 Typhoon Haiyan in the Philippines.[23] It was most visible in the quick trip to the Philippine city of Tacloban by Secretary General Minh in his capacity as coordinator of the AHA. He symbolically delivered two thousand "family kits" to survivors. In the emergency, however, it was American naval assets that overcame the logistical logjam, a capability that no ASEAN country could match.

Pandemic Disease

The eradication of epidemic disease is built into the MDG and is an important element of human security. This component has been called "biosecurity." Southeast Asia is located in what one epidemiologist has called "ground zero" of new epidemics.[24] Recurrent epidemics take a toll not only on the populations but on economic growth and development, particularly as disease impacts men and women in the most productive years of their lives. Prevention, monitoring, and treatment stress already overburdened health infrastructures even as the mobility of people within and between nations makes containment more difficult. Because disease knows no boundaries, through the ASEAN Health Ministers' Meetings, ASEAN has sought to be proactive in seeking to contain infectious diseases.

SARS

The regional vulnerabilities to such biothreats were demonstrated in 2003 with the spread from China to Southeast Asia of severe acute respiratory syndrome

(SARS). The spread of the disease was addressed at an emergency ASEAN summit meeting in April 2003 where the heads of government mandated a comprehensive regional response. Although the actual job of fighting the disease fell to the public health officials of the individual states, coordination was carried out by the health ministers of the ASEAN + 3. The international effort was coordinated by the World Health Organization (WHO). Over eight thousand cases were documented by WHO, with a mortality rate of 9 percent. The economic costs of SARS in East Asia were put at $18 billion in nominal GDP terms and overall costs of $60 billion by the ADB.[25] The ASEAN health ministers declared ASEAN to be SARS-free in June 2003, claiming to be the first to make a regionwide response to the epidemic. One important lesson learned from SARS as an emergent disease was the need for transparency. China's attempt to hide the original occurrence delayed WHO's response.

Avian Flu

From 2004 to 2008, a new pandemic threatened the populations and economies of Asia and beyond. It is a particularly virulent form of the H5N1 strain of avian influenza. It begins in infected domestic and wild fowl and is passed from infected birds to humans. It has a high mortality rate. The only treatment is the patented drug Tamiflu. In 2013, a spreading, drug-resistant strain of avian flu, H7N9, was diagnosed in China, which posed a significant risk of cross-border transmission. The great fear—a global one, not just Southeast Asian—is that eventually an avian flu virus will mutate for human-to-human transmission rather than just bird-to-human. The disease is contained by removing its source, which means quarantining and culling infected flocks of domestic fowl. The public health systems in Southeast Asia have a limited capacity to respond to a pandemic and depend on international cooperation and support. The affected Southeast Asian governments, in cooperation with WHO and donor nations, erected surveillance and response mechanisms at both national and regional levels. The WHO had a Regional Influenza Preparedness Plan, and ASEAN drafted a Regional Framework for Control and Eradication of Highly Pathogenic Avian Influenza (HPAI). In three international donor conferences between January 2006 and December 2007, $3 billion was pledged to combat avian flu worldwide. The United States is the single largest donor with a pledge total of $629 million. Emphasis on the prevention of avian flu has become a staple of the final communiqués of ASEAN leaders' meetings, ASEAN-pluses, and the EAS.

HIV/AIDS

The WHO reported that in 2010, 3.5 million adults and children in Southeast Asia were living with HIV/AIDS. The toll is greatest in the population aged fifteen to forty-nine, with a high rate of transmission from injected drugs and unprotected commercial sex. The highest numbers of reported cases are in Thailand (490,000) and Indonesia (380,000). Indonesia has the most rapid increase in the number of new cases. UNAIDS, the United Nations HIV/AIDS program, has designated the spread of the disease as the greatest threat to development and security facing the ASEAN nations.[26] An ASEAN Task Force on AIDS (ATFOA) to coordinate regional policies was established in 1993. A series of multisectoral ASEAN work programs has sought to connect officials, scientists, NGOs, and external donors in a joint effort to identify strategies for prevention, care, and treatment.

An important problem has been access to antiretroviral treatment which is expensive. The need to combat HIV/AIDS has challenged Western pharmaceutical licensing practices and patent protection from generics, raising serious international intellectual property rights (IPR) questions. Thailand took the lead in 2007 by issuing compulsory licenses for the production of generic versions of two American-patented HIV/AIDS drugs and threatened to break cancer and heart disease patents if the prices were not voluntarily reduced. The United States in return placed Thailand on the US Trade Representative's "priority watch list." The issue is the interpretation of the Doha Declaration on the TRIPS Agreement. Thai public health officials insist that the TRIPS Agreement does not and should not prevent governments from taking measures to protect public health, including the right to grant compulsory licenses.[27]

During the reign of the Myanmar junta, the spread of infectious diseases including HIV/AIDS was beyond the ability of the country to control. The sealing off of the country from international public health resources only accelerated a soaring rise in cases. Concern both for the human security of Myanmar's population and the threat of infectious diseases being carried by refugees led to adding HIV/AIDS to draft UNSC resolutions condemning Myanmar's threat to regional peace and security. Aung San Suu Kyi made the prevalence of HIV/AIDS in Myanmar a focus of her campaign for democracy. As an advocate, she was named the UNAIDS goodwill ambassador in 2012 and launched the UNAIDS World AIDS Day "Zero Discrimination" program.

HUMAN RIGHTS AND HUMAN SECURITY

The place of human rights in the contemporary international system was first enunciated in the 1945 Preamble to the Charter of the United Nations, reaffirming faith in fundamental human rights, in the dignity and worth of the human person, and the equal rights of men and women. This was given substance in the UNGA's 1948 Universal Declaration of Human Rights, which became the foundation of the UN system's international human rights regime. By accepting membership in the UN, the countries of Southeast Asia accepted its obligations, including human rights and freedoms. Although not a treaty, the declaration has been accepted in principle as the measure of what the charter requires. Today, more than one hundred treaties and other international instruments flow from the constituting base of the UN Charter and Declaration. The core agreements are shown in box 9.2. The UN's normative regulative framework is the standard by which a government's treatment of its own people is measured by UN agencies, other governments, and human rights NGOs. Although human rights are routinely breached around the world, no government willingly acknowledges itself a rights violator. The pattern of the Southeast Asian states' formal legal acceptance of the international rights regime is uneven. There is no ASEAN consensus on regionalization of the global norms. Table 9.4 shows the status of the ASEAN states signing, acceding to, or ratifying the core agreements giving instrumental effect to human rights.

Balancing the call for respect for human rights, Article 2 of the UN Charter states that a principle of the UN is "sovereign equality," which means that the UN has no authority to intervene in matters essentially within the domestic jurisdiction of a member. The tension between the international goal of

---

Box 9.2. Core International Human Rights Treaties

- Covenant on Economic, Social, and Cultural Rights (CESCR)
- Covenant on Civil and Political Rights (CCPR)
- Convention on the Elimination of All Forms of Racial Discrimination (CERD)
- Convention on the Elimination of All Forms of Discrimination against Women (CEDAW)
- Convention against Torture and Other Cruel, Inhuman or Degrading Treatment or Punishment (CAT)
- Convention on the Rights of the Child (CRC)
- International Convention on the Protection of the Rights of All Migrant Workers and Members of Their Families (CRMW)
- International Convention for the Protection of All Persons from Enforced Disappearances (not yet in force)
- Convention of the Rights of Persons with Disabilities (not yet in force)

Table 9.4.   Status of Southeast Asian Accession, Ratification, and Signature to Core International Rights Conventions in Force

Country	CESCR	CCPR	CERD	CEDAW	CAT	CRC	CRMW
Brunei				A		A	
Cambodia	A	A	R	R	A	A	S
Indonesia	A	A	A	R	R	R	S
Laos	R	S	R	R		A	
Malaysia				A		A	
Myanmar				A	A	A	
Philippines	R	R	R	R	A	R	R
Singapore				A		A	
Thailand		A	A	A	A	A	
Timor-Leste	A	A	A	A	A	A	A
Vietnam	A	A	A	R		R	

Source: UNHRC Treaty Body Basis.

Key: A = accession, R = ratification, S = signature only, blank = no action.

protecting human rights and the domestic authority of a sovereign state has been the constant thread in dialogue between defenders of rights and alleged violators. This tension is replicated at the Southeast Asian regional level in ASEAN's inability to reconcile the ASEAN Charter's claimed commitment to the norms of democracy and human rights with its insistence on state sovereignty and noninterference.

At the international level, the Geneva-based United Nations Human Rights Council (UNHRC) is the principal intergovernmental body tasked with examining, monitoring, and reporting on human rights conditions both in specific countries and on broad themes such as women's rights or freedom of expression. The forty-seven state members are elected by the General Assembly by direct majority vote for candidates drawn from five regional membership groups. The Asia-Pacific group has thirteen seats, three of which are currently held by ASEAN states (expiry of term in parentheses): Indonesia (2014), the Philippines (2014), and Vietnam (2016). A country's human rights record is not a criterion for membership. The Council's reports and resolutions are subject to coalition and regional bloc political and diplomatic maneuvering, depending on the issues or countries being evaluated.

The High Commissioner for Human Rights (UNHCHR) is the principal human rights officer. Neither the UNHRC nor the UNHCHR has enforcement authority. They can only recommend actions to governments. In extraordinary cases "special procedures" can be mandated for human rights oversight in particular countries of concern. Two mandates exist in Southeast

Asia. A special rapporteur on the situation of human rights in Cambodia was established in 1993 and extended in 2011. A special rapporteur on the situation of human rights in Myanmar was established in 1992 and extended in 2013.

Beginning in 2006, the UNHRC instituted a Universal Periodic Review (UPR), a process which in five-year cycles reviews the human rights record of every UN member and makes recommendations for improvement. Although state driven, opportunities are given for documentary or verbal input from civil society stakeholders. The first cycle was concluded in 2011, and the 2012–2016 cycle is underway. Secretary General Ban Ki-moon claimed that the UPR has "great potential to promote and protect human rights in the darkest corners of the world."[28] Cambodia is one of those dark corners. When it came up for its second UPR review in January 2013 it had largely ignored the recommendations made in its first review, leading six NGOs to assert that "rather than improving, the human rights situation in Cambodia has deteriorated since 2009."[29] By 2016 all ASEAN countries will have had two UPR rounds. It is doubtful that any alterations in state behavior where human rights issues exist will stem from state peer review.

Unburdened by the diplomacy of UN consensus seeking, the United States and the EU have greater effective influence in promoting the international human rights agenda in Southeast Asia. This is because they do have enforcement mechanisms including sanctions and contingent conditions for aid and trade. The official lead in the United States comes from the Department of State's Bureau of Democracy, Rights, and Labor (DRL). The DRL compiles an annual report on the status of democracy and rights in 194 countries of the world as well as an *International Religious Freedom Report*.[30] As official statements of the US government, the reports provoke angry reactions from countries accused of rights violations. The congressionally mandated rights reports provide ammunition to international rights advocacy groups and domestic rights NGOs in offending countries. Congress's control over the budgets for US foreign operations is also a lever on human rights. Congressional interest in a robust American stance on human rights is also expressed in its independent oversight over American policy through investigations, hearings, and legislation. Congress's bipartisan Tom Lantos Human Rights Commission gives rights NGOs direct access to policy shapers.[31] Myanmar, Indonesia, and Vietnam have been high on congressional agendas.

The NGO component in the international rights networks is very important. Rights INGOs have been active investigators of rights infringements, marshaling public opinion and embarrassing governments. Two of the most influential and credible are Amnesty International and Human Rights Watch.[32] Other groupings are country, case, or issue specific. At the Southeast

Asian domestic level, NGOs struggle against hostile government agencies and largely passive publics. The local NGOs exist enmeshed in restrictive regulative and legal constraints. Governments use domestic NGOs' connections to INGOs as proof that they are witting agents of foreign powers. Arrests and imprisonment of rights workers by the more authoritarian regimes are not uncommon.

ASEAN AND HUMAN RIGHTS

Despite the UN rights system's claim to universality, there is no unified view on human rights either globally or in Southeast Asia. To many Southeast Asian elites, the West's emphasis on civil and political rights in a democratic framework is the expression of a particular historical and cultural process in economically developed societies. According to ASEAN leaders, the West's preoccupation with political rights ignores economic, social, and cultural rights that are of paramount importance for the full realization of human dignity and individual achievement. The Western and Asian views were compromised, if not reconciled, at the 1993 United Nations Vienna World Conference on Human Rights. The Vienna Declaration stated that "while the significance of national and regional particularities and various historical, cultural and religious backgrounds must be borne in mind," nevertheless "it is the duty of states, regardless of their political, economic and cultural systems, to promote and protect all human rights and freedoms."[33] As for economic development, it was agreed that "while development facilitates the enjoyment of all human rights, the lack of development may not be invoked to justify the abridgement of internationally recognized human rights." The legal context of national sovereignty and noninterference in domestic affairs was not challenged.

Shortly after the Vienna Conference, the six-member ASEAN reaffirmed its commitment to human rights and freedoms by agreeing that ASEAN should consider the establishment of an appropriate mechanism on human rights. There the matter rested for a decade and a half. It was argued by ASEAN officials that a precondition for an ASEAN human rights body was the establishment of national human rights commissions in each ASEAN state. Until 2012, national human rights agencies existed in only four ASEAN countries: the Philippines (1987), Indonesia (1993), Malaysia (1999), and Thailand (1999). They collaborated in the Southeast Asia NHRIs [National Human Rights Institutions] Forum (SEANF). Timor-Leste's Provider for Human Rights and Justice joined SEANF in 2010, followed by the Myanmar National Human Rights Commission in 2012. As rights watchdogs, the national commissions are relatively toothless, with little investigative and no juridical power. They can only advise and recommend to other agencies of their governments. They can also supply country information for the UPR process.

In drafting the ASEAN Charter (chapter 4), two converging policy demands forced attention to the need for some kind of regional human rights regime. The first was civil society demands that human rights be institutionalized in the new charter. The second was the increasing embarrassment to ASEAN of its failure to respond to the shame that Myanmar had brought upon the members. Indonesia's foreign minister Hassan Wirajuda promised that human rights would be part of the charter. It rhetorically committed the group to adhere to the principles of democracy, the rule of law and good governance, and respect and protection of human rights and fundamental freedoms. While member states could find a consensus on a statement of principles, the underlying tension was in how to translate the principles into effective policy. The CLMV countries opposed any human rights compliance mechanism.

Article 14 of the ASEAN Charter compromised on the immediate issue. It stated that "in conformity with the purposes and principles of the ASEAN Charter relating to the promotion and protection of human rights and fundamental freedoms, ASEAN shall establish an ASEAN human rights body." The timing and terms of reference for this "body," however, were not specified. This was to be determined at a future date by the ASEAN foreign ministers.

The ministers wrestled for two years on how to deliver on the promise of "promotion and protection of human rights."[34] The outcome was the establishment in 2009 of the ASEAN Intergovernmental Commission on Human Rights (AICHR) charged with "promoting," but not "protecting," human rights. It is bureaucratically situated in the ASEAN Political and Security Community under the purview of the foreign ministers. The AICHR has no power to investigate complaints or to review the rights records of member states. It is highly unlikely that the existence of the AICHR will substantially alter the human rights practices of the undemocratic ASEAN states.

The AICHR's only achievement to date has been the drafting of an ASEAN Human Rights Declaration (AHRD), adopted at the November 2012 ASEAN Summit. The Vienna compromise is embedded in the AHRD (Principle 7): "The realization of human rights must be considered in the regional and national context bearing in mind the different political, economic, legal, social, cultural, historical, and religious backgrounds."[35] To further ensure that the AHRD was innocuous in terms of realistically changing the ASEAN human rights status quo, Principle 40 states, "Nothing in the Declaration may be interpreted as implying for any State, group or person any right to perform any act aimed at undermining the purposes and principles of ASEAN." While ASEAN may trumpet the AHRD as proof of commitment to human rights, the international rights community views it differently, seeing it as undermining international human rights standards and justifying continuing violations.[36] There is little doubt that the human rights situation in Southeast Asia has not been ameliorated by the existence of the AICHR or its AHRD. In some cases it has even worsened. Nor is there any basis to assert that the ASEAN rights regime had anything to do with prompting democratic change in Myanmar.

Accountability for Crimes against Humanity

The international community, by the Rome Statute of the International Criminal Court (ICC), has created a mechanism to bring perpetrators of genocide, war crimes, and crimes against humanity to account.[37] The ICC, located in the Hague, the Netherlands, is a court of last resort, having jurisdiction only if national court systems fail. The court was established in 2002 after sixty state ratifications and now has 122 parties to it. Only three Southeast Asian states have acceded to the ICC: Cambodia and Timor-Leste in 2002 and the Philippines in 2011. The Indonesian parliament's refusal to ratify is connected to human rights violations in East Timor and Papua linked to retired generals Wiranto and Prabowo, both now in politics. This is even though all prospective parties are assured that the court's jurisdiction would not be retroactive.

The Southeast Asian states also had to take into account the United States' consistent opposition to the court, fearing it could put at risk American officials and military in conflict zones. Using robust diplomacy backed by economic and security assistance, the United States has negotiated more than one hundred bilateral immunity agreements (BIAs), sometimes called Article 98 agreements. In them the signatory agrees not to surrender Americans to the jurisdiction of the court. In Southeast Asia, the United States has BIAs with Brunei (unconfirmed), Cambodia, Laos, the Philippines, Singapore, Thailand, and Timor-Leste.[38] There are two cases in Southeast Asia that would have been prime candidates for the jurisdiction of the ICC if it had existed, but in which closure was sought in ad hoc frameworks: the Khmer Rouge trials in Cambodia and the Timor–Indonesia reconciliation process.

Cambodia and the Khmer Rouge

An estimated 1.7 million Cambodians died from disease, starvation, and mass murder during the Khmer Rouge (KR) rule between 1975 and the Vietnamese invasion that ousted them in 1978 (chapter 3). Despite the reluctance and obstruction of Cambodian prime minister Hun Sen, the international donors who underwrite Cambodia's budget insisted that the aging leadership of the KR be held accountable for their crimes against humanity. Negotiations with the UN for a tribunal began in 1997. The sticking point was who is in charge, Cambodia or the UN. Hun Sen feared that a truly independent trial would open old wounds as well as put his and his associates' own Khmer Rouge past under scrutiny. China backed Cambodian intransigence. An independent trial could throw light on China's own role as the Khmer Rouge's patron during the era of the killing fields. Cambodia's ASEAN partners, especially Myanmar and Indonesia, were also uneasy about a UN-supervised trial because of the precedent it might set for the region.

Even though genocide is an international crime, Cambodia, clinging to the principle of sovereignty, demanded that any trial be in a Cambodian court and based on Cambodian law. The UN and donor nations were distrustful that such a court in a notoriously weak and corrupt judicial system would meet minimum international standards of justice and procedure. They demanded international participation. Lengthy and acrimonious negotiations led to a compromise agreement in March 2003 on the establishment of Extraordinary Chambers in the Courts of Cambodia (ECCC).[39] The ECCC consisted of two courts: a trial court of three Cambodian and two foreign judges and a supreme court of four Cambodians and three foreigners. Decisions had to have the support of at least one international judge. The bench was not sworn in until July 2006, in part because of a dispute over funding, with Cambodia insisting that the international community must pay the entire estimated $56.3 million cost. By 2013 the costs swelled to $210 million, with Japan, the United States, Australia, and Germany being the largest donors.

The ECCC was structured for failure, beset by serial budget crises, corruption, poor cooperation by the Cambodian judges, and political interference attempting to limit the competency of the courts and its docket. In seven years there were only five indictments. Pol Pot, the KR leader, died in 1988. Ieng Sary, eighty-eight, died in 2013 during his trial. Ieng Thirith, eighty-one, Ieng Sary's wife, was found mentally incompetent for trial. Khieu Samphan's (eighty-two) and Nuon Chea's (eighty-seven) trials ended in December 2013, with verdicts in August 2014 of guilty of crimes against humanity and sentences of life imprisonment. The only other conviction, in 2010, was that of Kaing Guek Ev (alias Duch) (seventy-one), the warden of the notorious Tuol Sleng prison. Although other indictments were prepared, Hun Sen stated firmly that there will be no more trials. Judgments about the court itself have been harsh, for example, "if you had wanted to devise a court that wouldn't work, you would be hard put to find a better model," and "therapeutic legalism run amok."[40]

Indonesia and the East Timor Trials

As was discussed in chapter 3, following the 1999 East Timor independence plebiscite, Indonesian army-backed militias went on an organized campaign of destruction and violence against the civilian population. This was what prompted international intervention. The crimes against humanity have been fully documented in the 2005 report by Timor-Leste's Commission for Reception, Truth, and Reconciliation (CAVR).[41] In a September 1999 special session, the UNCHR voted to investigate the affair. No Asian member voted in favor. UN secretary general Kofi Annan appointed an International Commission of Inquiry. The commission reported back to him in January 2000, finding patterns of gross violations of human rights and breaches of humanitarian law by the Indonesian army and its sponsored militias. The commission recommended the establishment of an international human rights tribunal to hold the perpetrators accountable.[42] Parallel to the UN inquiry, the Indonesian National Human Rights Commission (KOMNASHAM) formed its own Commission to Investigate Violations of Human Rights in East Timor. Its conclusions were very similar to those of the UNCHR's commission. Unlike the situation in Cambodia, Indonesia was not pressured to accept an international tribunal. There was concern that Indonesia's fragile post-Suharto democratization process would be put at risk if nationalist passions were unleashed and the Indonesian military closed ranks and withdrew support from the government.

Indonesia insisted that national law would be the basis for finalizing the human rights issues with respect to East Timor. President Megawati created an Ad Hoc Human Rights Court in January 2002. Only eighteen indictments came down for civilian and military personnel who had been on the ground in East Timor, and none for senior leadership up the chain of command. By the end of a weak and legally flawed pro forma prosecution, there were only six convictions, all of which were reversed on appeal. Even though no international tribunal was formed, the human rights situation in East Timor remained on the UNCHR's agenda. At the 2003 meeting, the chairperson's statement expressed disappointment over the process and outcome of Indonesia's ad hoc rights tribunal but, in a victory for Indonesian diplomacy, agreed to drop the issue from future agendas.

In Timor-Leste itself, UNMISET's Serious Crimes Unit aided Timor-Leste's prosecutorial authorities who issued 380 indictments, of which 270 were for individuals in Indonesia. General Wiranto and six other senior officers were charged with crimes against humanity. There was no possibility, however, that Indonesia would extradite anyone charged. Recognizing that good relations with Indonesia was Timor-Leste's paramount interest, President Xanana Gusmão hastened to reassure Jakarta that Dili had no intention of letting the issue of human rights abuses and crimes against humanity disrupt the development of stable, cooperative, and friendly bilateral relations.

Unrelenting international pressure prompted the formation in January 2005 of a United Nations three-member Commission of Experts to review the prosecution of serious crimes in East Timor in 1999. The commission's July 2005 report found that the Indonesian prosecutions were "manifestly inadequate" and showed "an evident lack of political will to prosecute." Furthermore, the commission said the ad hoc court itself did not present a "credible judicial forum." The experts recommended that, if Indonesia did not take steps to review the prosecutions and hold those responsible accountable, then the Security Council should create an ad hoc international court for East Timor in a third country.[43] This, of course, would be subject to China's veto.

Indonesia and Timor-Leste refused to cooperate with the Commission of Experts and tried to preempt it by establishing in March 2005 their own binational Commission on Truth and Friendship (CTF). Supposedly modeled on South Africa's Truth and Reconciliation Commission, the ten-member—five from each country—CTF had no judicial or subpoena power. Its mandate was to establish the truth regarding human rights violations in the wake of the 1999 vote and make recommendations to heal the wounds and foster reconciliation, but not to prosecute or punish. The UN Committee of Experts claimed that the CTF's terms of reference "contradicted international standards on denial of impunity for serious crimes" and noted the absence of any mechanism to compel truth. Secretary General Ban Ki-moon instructed United Nations officials not to cooperate with the CTF because the UN could not be seen as endorsing crimes against humanity.

The CTF missed August 2007 and January 2008 deadlines for presenting its report. According to the Indonesian side, the process of finding a consensus that was unbiased and fair for both Indonesia and East Timor was tough.[44] The CTF finally handed over its report to President Yudhoyono and his Timor-Leste counterpart, José Ramos Horta, in Bali in July 2008. To the surprise of rights NGO skeptics, the report, titled *Per Memoriam Ad Spem* (Through Memory to Hope), confirmed the CAVR's report and the findings of the international inquiries.[45] The report made it clear that the Indonesian military, government, police, and militias bear institutional responsibilities for gross human rights violations against the civilian population of East Timor. It attributed this to the culture and policies of Indonesia's security sectors. The CTF made a number of recommendations to further reconciliation and friendship, but the most important ones that would have explicitly and implicitly forced Indonesia to acknowledge responsibility have been pigeonholed by the two governments.

ASEAN's Human Rights Dilemma

Even a casual perusal of the annual US State Department's *Human Rights Report* shows that every Southeast Asian state has a blemished human rights record. In this chapter and preceding chapters, attention has been called to the poor rights records in the CLMV states, democratizing Indonesia's unwillingness to address rights abuse in Papua and religious discrimination, and the human rights issues in South Thailand. We could add Malaysia, which has long been a target of human rights activists because of the use of government instruments, including a punitive Internal Security Act (ISA), to stifle political opposition. In the Philippines, extrajudicial killings still plague the political environment. For the victims, each case of abuse is special, but it is only in cases of gross and systematic patterns of denial of rights as government policy that human rights concerns become issues in the way governments treat one another in their international relations. While human rights NGOs and advocacy groups may become energized by their agendas, governments prioritize their policy attention and deployment of political and economic capabilities in terms of perceptions of national interest. Governments in liberal democracies assess the priorities of traditional political, economic, and security interests in their dealings with rights-violating states in Southeast Asia.

Within ASEAN, despite the pledges of the ASEAN Charter, human rights have not had priority in the intra-ASEAN relations of the members. This is justified in terms of ASEAN respect for the principles of sovereignty and noninterference as well as the political interest in solidarity. There have been cases, however, when ASEAN has had to confront the dilemma of balancing its stance of noninterference against the negative spillover of egregious behavior by a member state damaging ASEAN's international credibility.

Myanmar

Since the Myanmar armed forces' (Tatmadaw) crushing of democracy in 1988, Myanmar had been ruled by a Tatmadaw junta until 2011, first as the State Law and Order Restoration Council (SLORC), and then, from 1997, as the State Peace and Development Council (SPDC). The junta's s misrule devastated the economy and shattered society. In Asia it could only be compared to North Korea in the human insecurity of its citizens in terms of both needs and rights. Thousands of supporters of the 1988 election-winning National League for Democracy (NLD) were imprisoned or fled into exile. The NLD's iconic leader, Daw Aung San Suu Kyi, suffered years of house arrest. In successive Tatmadaw campaigns against ethnic insurgents, the genocidal abuse of women and children was well documented. The junta was routinely condemned internationally. The Myanmar case, like those of other outrageously egregious human rights violators, tested the limits of what the international community can or is willing to do to force change.

For more than two decades Myanmar fended off international demands for change. It was supported in the UN and other international fora by its ASEAN partners and China. The United States was in the forefront of the campaign to mobilize the international community against the junta so as to isolate it from sources of material and diplomatic support. Beginning in 1997, American presidents put in place an ever-stricter economic sanctions regime, denying Myanmar access to American markets and investment. The United States was joined by the EU, Canada, Australia, Japan, and South Korea, among others. Even with sanctions, the junta had ample access to investments and goods, particularly through ASEAN, China, and India.

ASEAN's offered alternative to sanctions was "constructive engagement," that is, continued association with Myanmar that would through example and suasion lead the junta to modify its behavior and recognize that its own best interests would be served through liberalization. "Constructive engagement," noted in chapter 4, was a justification for admitting Myanmar to ASEAN in 1997. Rather than Myanmar accommodating ASEAN's entreaties for political adaptation, ASEAN, now tarred by the Myanmar brush, had to defend Myanmar's membership.

The UN had been directly involved in the diplomacy of human rights in Myanmar since 1992, when the UNCHR's first of four special rapporteurs on the human rights situation in Myanmar was appointed. In 2000, in addition to the UNCHR special rapporteur, Secretary General Kofi Annan appointed his own special envoy to try to move the diplomacy along. The junta treated the UN envoys with scorn and largely ignored their conclusions. The UNGA, voting on the resolutions drafted in its Third Committee (Social, Humanitarian, and Cultural), repeatedly expressed grave concern at ongoing systematic violations of human rights and fundamental freedoms and called on the government to release all political prisoners, lift all restraints on free political activity, cease suppression of ethnic minorities, and allow all parties to participate in a political transition process with a clear timetable to democracy. In the Third Committee drafting and the final UNGA vote, for years ASEAN consistently voted with Myanmar against the resolution; that is, until 2007. In the Security Council, US and British efforts to have the situation in Myanmar deemed a threat to peace and security were consistently blocked by the double veto of Russia and China. The junta seemed secure in its impunity, telling Ibrahim Gambari, Secretary General Ban Ki-moon's special envoy on Myanmar, in 2007 that "Myanmar will not bow to outside pressure. It will never allow any outside interference to infringe on the sovereignty of the state."[46]

The junta had tried to mollify its ASEAN partners by announcing at the end of August 2003 a vague "road map" that would lead Myanmar on the path to a new constitution and future elections. Neither the constitutional process nor the planned elections included the NLD or Suu Kyi. The junta continued to reject efforts from the UN and ASEAN to mediate a dialogue between the regime and Suu Kyi. Bilateral efforts by non-CLMV ASEAN leaders to engage on issues of democracy were coldly rejected. ASEAN as an organization saw its international standing jeopardized by Myanmar's presence. In December 2007, Singapore invited Special Envoy Gambari to give an informal briefing on the situation in Myanmar to the third EAS meeting. While Gambari was in flight to Singapore, Myanmar prime minister Thein Sein, insisting that this was an unacceptable intrusion into Myanmar's domestic affairs, demanded that the briefing be canceled. It was. The planned first US–ASEAN leaders' meeting in 2007, commemorating thirty years of US–ASEAN partnership, was canceled because President George W. Bush would not dignify the presence of the leader of what his secretary of state, Condoleezza Rice, called "an outpost of tyranny." UN secretary general Ban Ki-moon appealed to ASEAN for special cooperation in dealing with Myanmar because ASEAN had a special political responsibility in promoting democracy there.

The year 2007 was a crucial turning point in reshaping Myanmar's diplomatic environment. The key event was the September so-called Saffron Revolution and the junta's shockingly brutal crackdown on demonstrations by Buddhist monks and their supporters, generating a new wave of international political revulsion against the junta. This spurred the UNHRC, in a special October session, to adopt a resolution deploring violent repression in Myanmar and calling for the release of all political detainees and the lifting of all restraints on freedoms. This was a consensus statement of the forty-seven-member body, which included Indonesia, Malaysia, the Philippines, China, and India.[47] Two months later, the cracks that were beginning to open in ASEAN's lock-step support of Myanmar widened when, in the UNGA voting on the annual Myanmar resolution (A/RES/62-222), Malaysia and the CLMV countries were the only Southeast Asian nations that voted against it.

In the Security Council a consensus statement was hammered out at a political level general enough to satisfy permanent members China and Russia and nonpermanent member Indonesia. As read out on 11 October by the UNSC's president, it deplored the use of violence against peaceful demonstrators, called for the release of all political detainees, and stressed the need for all parties to work together for a peaceful solution.[48] This was followed up by a Security Council consensus press statement on Myanmar in January 2008, affirming the objectives of the Council's October statement and "regretting the slow rate of progress so far towards meeting those objectives."[49]

Secretary General Ban Ki-moon warned Myanmar that the international community was running out of patience, saying the junta had to stop inflicting suffering on its own people and embrace democracy.[50] He broadened support for his "good offices" mandate by convening an informal fourteen-nation group of "Friends of Myanmar" that included the SC Permanent Five, Indonesia, Singapore, Thailand, Vietnam, Australia, India, Japan, Portugal, and Norway. A separate group known as the Focus Group on Myanmar also emerged in 2007, made up of China, India, Indonesia, Myanmar, and the UN.

It was becoming clear that China's position was evolving. Beijing did not want to become part of the Myanmar problem in the view of the non-CLMV ASEAN states. As the United States, Great Britain, and other Western liberal democracies ratcheted up pressure on Myanmar and ASEAN, China claimed that it would provide constructive assistance toward the junta's efforts to realize national reconciliation and democratic progress. With ASEAN, and now China, nipping at its heels, the junta, following its road map, approved a new constitution and elections in 2010. The constitution guaranteed continuing Tatmadaw dominance, and the elections excluded the NLD. Then came the intervening variable of Cyclone Nargis (discussed above), which demonstrated isolation from the economic and social realities of the country.

It is still premature to make a definitive assessment of the relative weight of the decisive factors in the mix of motives that led to unexpected democratization of the 2011 government following the elections (chapter 2). Perhaps it was a combination of sanctions, ASEAN importunities, Chinese back-channeling advice, awareness in the Tatmadaw that the country was falling behind, and popular discontent, among others. Even if the road map ultimately led to a different political destination than anyone expected, it does not mean that Myanmar does not still have serious humanitarian and human rights issues of ASEAN and international concern. Two in particular have already been discussed: the problem of the Rohingya and the military campaigns against ethnic minorities. The issues of human rights pose a problem for Aung San Suu Kyi as she transitions from opposition figure to possible presidential candidate. To the dismay of international rights advocates, their heroine has been silent on the issues, recognizing that to take up the Rohingya cause would be politically unpopular.

Indonesia, ASEAN, and East Timor

Throughout the Suharto government's rule, its real achievements were tarnished by the authoritarian nature of its political system and record of human rights violations beginning in the bloody aftermath of the 1965 coup and transfer of power from Sukarno. Despite a crescendo of allegations and complaints from global human rights organizations, Indonesia's geostrategic importance during the Cold War and its pivotal role in Southeast Asia politically insulated it. As has been noted at several points, from 1976 the question of East Timor was always in the background of Indonesia's bilateral relations. Until 1999, Western policy toward Indonesia remained one of "constructive engagement," which meant regime support. The international situation for Indonesia changed after the 1999 East Timor referendum and the Indonesian army–inspired violence that followed.

The ASEAN states, in a spirit of solidarity, had resolutely backed Indonesia's governance in East Timor to the very end, no matter the international opprobrium attached to it. The situation in East Timor was never part of ASEAN's discourse. Even as the UN was preparing to intervene to halt the anarchic reign of terror in the province, ASEAN leaders were still muttering the ASEAN mantra of noninterference. It was only when, under duress, Jakarta grudgingly gave nominal permission for INTERFET to enter East Timor that ASEAN began consulting on a possible role, not wishing to be simply on the sidelines as international actors intervened to guarantee peace and stability in ASEAN's domain. The ASEAN foreign ministers had an informal meeting in New Zealand at the September 1999 APEC meeting. After that, Thai foreign minister Surin Pitsuwan, the ASEAN chair, traveled to Jakarta to solicit Indonesian president Habibie's approval for participation by the ASEAN states in the East Timor peacekeeping operation. Only then, with Indonesian acquiescence, did ASEAN military units join the INTERFET forces.[51] They were national contributions under the UN flag. The ASEAN flag did not fly in East Timor.

The Philippines

The case of the popular uprising called the "people's power" revolution against President Ferdinand Marcos's attempts to steal the February 1986 snap election showed that ASEAN's principle of nonintervention in the domestic political affairs of member states is ambiguous. Through the years of the Marcos dictatorship in the Philippines, the ASEAN governments had remained largely unconcerned by the destruction of democracy and human rights abuses of the regime. However, as the popular challenge to Marcos led by Corazon Aquino, widow of the murdered democratic standard-bearer Benigno "Ninoy" Aquino, gathered momentum, the implications for possible spillover effects could not be ignored. The ASEAN elite realistically accepted the fact that peaceful succession with all its policy unknowns was preferable to a Marcos attempt to retain power at all costs, which could prove regionally destabilizing.

In an unprecedented departure from previous norms of intra-ASEAN behavior, the ASEAN foreign ministers coordinated a joint statement on the situation that was released simultaneously in their respective capitals on 23 February 1986.[52] Warning that the critical situation in the Philippines portended bloodshed and civil war, widespread carnage, and political turmoil, the ASEAN ministers called on the parties to restore national unity and solidarity, hoping that all Filipino leaders would join efforts to bring about a peaceful solution to the crisis. It was with a sense of relief that ASEAN capitals welcomed the departure of Marcos for Honolulu exile and congratulated Corazon Aquino on the successful struggle of the Philippine people.

Thailand

The kind of intervention made by ASEAN in the Philippine political crisis described above was repeated in December 2013 as legitimate authority was crumbling in Thailand. The possibility of a civil war or military coup in the heart of ASEAN challenged ASEAN's political integrity, threatening to spoil the rollout of the ASEAN Community. Prompted by Thai foreign minister Surapong Tovichakchaiku, the ASEAN foreign ministers issued a joint statement emphasizing that "political stability in Thailand is essential to achieving a peaceful, stable, and prosperous ASEAN Community," and calling on all parties to resolve their internal conflict in a peaceful and democratic manner.[53] A second foreign ministers' appeal, on 11 May, called for a peaceful resolution and respect for democracy.[54] Eleven days later, 22 May, a Thai military coup destroyed democracy in Thailand and left the ASEAN Community with an even greater democracy deficit. Leaders in Jakarta and Manila expressed dismay. President Yudhoyono urged ASEAN to take a stance on the Thai coup in the interests of democracy.[55] ASEAN did not take notice.

NOTES

1. The UNDP 1994 report can be accessed at http://hdr.undp.org/sites/default/files/reports/255/hdr_1994_en_complete_nostats.pdf.

2. The Commission's report can be accessed at http://www.unocha.org/humansecurity/chs/finalreport.

3. The Asia-Pacific MDG report of 2012–2013 can be accessed at http://asia-pacific.undp.org/content/rbap/en/home/library/mdg/asia-pacific-mdg-2012-2013.html.

4. The report, titled "A New Global Partnership: Eradicate Poverty and Transform Economies through Sustainable Development," can be accessed at http://www.un.org/sg/management/pdf/HLP_P2015_Report.pdf.

5. Asian Development Bank, "Governance: Sound Development Management" (ADB Policy Paper, Manila, 1995).

6. The convention can be accessed at http://www.unhcr.org/3b66c2aa10.html.

7. Although the UN Treaty Collections database lists Cambodia as a participant, the signatures to both, 15 October 1992, were during UNTAC's governance, not the 1993 restored Kingdom of Cambodia.

8. The UNHCR breaks down its populations of concern into four categories: refugees, asylum seekers, stateless, and others of concern. The table only reflects the first category of recognized refugees. The difference between a refugee and an asylum seeker is that an asylum seeker is someone who says that he or she is not a refugee but whose claim to asylum status has not yet been determined by a national asylum system. A grant of asylum gives different legal protections than those of a refugee. For practical purposes, until asylum has been granted, the applicant is protected as a refugee.

9. The IOM's website is http://www.iom.int.

10. For details, see http://www.asean.org/communities/asean-political-security -community/item/joint-press-statement-the-special-asean-foreign-ministers-meeting -on-indochinese-refugees-bangkok-13-january-1979.

11. US State Department press statement, 27 December 2009, accessed at http:// www.state.gov/r/pa/prs/ps/2009/dec/134096.htm.

12. Report of Special Representative of the Secretary General for Human Rights in Cambodia Peter Leupracht, "The Human Rights Situation in Cambodia," 19 December 2003, Human Rights Council document E/CN.4/2004/105, p. 17.

13. "Yudhoyono Urges Myanmar to Act on Violence against Muslims," *Today* (Singapore), 24 April 2013.

14. The UNHCR figures were accessed at http://www.unhcr.org/532afe986.html.

15. ILO, "Trends and Outlook for Labour Migration in Asia," accessed at http:// www.adbi.org/files/2013.01.23.cpp.sess1.2.baruah.labour.migration.asia.pdf.

16. Data on the OFW is from the Philippines Overseas Employment Agency (http://www.poea.gov.ph).

17. *UN Treaty Series*, vol. 2220, p. 3, Doc.A/Res/45/158.

18. The declaration can be accessed at http://www.asean.org/communities/asean -political-security-community/item/asean-declaration-on-the-protection-and-promo tion-of-the-rights-of-migrant-workers-3.

19. As quoted in "Malaysia Back in Crosshairs," *Jakarta Globe*, 16 November 2012.

20. "Annual Press Statement Minister for Foreign Affairs Republic of Indonesia R. M. Marty M. Natalegawa," 7 January 2014, accessed at http://www.kemlu.go.id.

21. Vanitha Nadaraj, "Reinventing ReLa: Malaysia's Volunteer Cops Moving with the Times," *Establishment Post* (Singapore), 27 November 2013, accessed at http://www.establishmentpost.com/reinventing-rela-malaysias-volunteer-corps-mov ing-times.

22. For an overview of ASEAN's response to Cyclone Nargis, see Yves-Kim Creach and Lilianne Fan, "ASEAN's Role in the Cyclone Nargis Response: Implications, Lessons and Opportunities," *Humanitarian Exchange Magazine* 41 (December 2008), accessed at http://www.odihpn.org/humanitarian-exchange-magazine/ issue-41. For the organizational format of the ASEAN-led response, view the slideshow at http://www.slideshare.net/GRFDavos/cyclone-nargis-and-asean-promoting -a-regional-mechanism-in-disaster-management.

23. "With Typhoon Haiyan, ASEAN Suffers Katrina Moment," *Bangkok Post*, 23 November 2013.

24. Ann Marie Kimball, "When the Flu Comes: Political and Economic Risks of Pandemic Disease in Asia," in *Trade, Interdependence, and Security*, ed. Ashley J. Tellis and Michael Wills (Seattle: National Bureau of Asian Research, 2006), 365.

25. ADB, "Assessing the Impact and Cost of SARS in Developing Asia," *ASEAN Development Outlook 2003 Update* (Manila: ADB, 2003), 75.

26. Peter Piot, in a report to the ASEAN heads of government at the ASEAN Second Special Session on HIV and AIDS at the Twelfth ASEAN Summit, January 2007.

27. In 2001 the WTO adopted a Special Ministerial Declaration on Trade-Related Aspects of Intellectual Property Rights (TRIPS), attempting to clarify its application to the needs of public health.

28. As cited on the main page of the UPR website, accessed at http://www.ohchr .org/en/hrbodies/upr/pages/uprmain.aspx. Documentation by country can be accessed at this URL.

29. Juliette de Rivero, general director of Human Rights Watch, as quoted in "Cambodia: UN Should Condemn Rights Onslaught," accessed at http://www.hrw .org/news/2014/01/27/Cambodia-should-condemn-rights-onslaught.

30. The bureau can be accessed at http://www.state.gov/g/drl with links to its various activities including the annual human and religious rights reports.

31. The bipartisan commission, institutionalized in 2011 as a US House of Representatives entity, developed out of the Congressional Human Rights Caucus of which Tom Lantos, who died in 2008, was a founding cochair.

32. Amnesty International can be accessed at http://www.amnesty.org and Human Rights Watch at http://www.hrw.org.

33. The Vienna Declaration and Programme of Action can be accessed at http:// www.ohchr.org/en/professionalinterest/pages/vienna.aspx.

34. In his efforts to have an effective human rights agency in ASEAN, former foreign minister Hassan has said, "I was alone"; interview with the author in Jakarta, 22 April 2013.

35. The AHRD can be accessed at http://www.asean.org/news/asean-statement -communiques/item/asean-human-rights-declaration.

36. Human Rights Watch, "Civil Society Denounces Adoption of Flawed ASEAN Human Rights Declaration," accessed at http://www.hrw.org/news/2012/11/19/civil -society-denounces-adoption-flawed-asean-human-rights-declaration.

37. The Rome Statute and details on the ICC can be accessed at http://www.icc -cpi.int.

38. The list is from the Coalition for the International Criminal Court, accessed at http://www.law.georgetown.edu/library/research/guides/article_98.cfm.

39. The ECCC's website is http://www.eccc.gov.kh.

40. As quoted in "Khmer Rouge Trial Nears End, with Tarnished Legacy," accessed at http://www.csmonitor.com/World/Asia-Pacific/2013/1030/Khmer-Rouge -trial-nears-end-with-tarnished-legacy.

41. CAVR is the abbreviation of the Portuguese name of the commission: Comissão de Acolhimento, Verdade e Reconciliação de Timor-Leste. The report,

titled "Chega" (in Portuguese, "No More"), can be read at http://www.cavr.timorleste
.org.

42. "Report of the International Commission of Inquiry on East Timor," accessed
at http://www.ohchr.org/Documents/Countries/COITimorLeste.pdf.

43. The report can be accessed at http://www.etan.org/etanpdf/pdf3/N0542617
.pdf.

44. "Indonesia—Timor-Leste Truth Commission Seeks Consensus," *Jakarta Post,*
26 March 2008.

45. The 371-page report can be accessed at http://www.cja.org/downloads/Per
Memoriam-Ad-Spem-Final-Reeport-of-the-Commission-of-Truth-and-Friendship
-IndonesiaTimor-Leste.pdf.

46. As quoted in "Myanmar Rejects UN Envoy's Bid for 3-Way Talks," *Straits
Times* (Singapore), 7 November 2007.

47. HRC RES S-5/1 can be accessed at http://www.burmalibrary.org/docs5/SRM
-HRC-8-12-en.pdf.

48. "Statement by the President of the Security Council," S/PRST/2007/37, 11 October 2007, accessed at http://daccess-dds-ny.un.org/doc/UNDOC/GEN/N07/538/30/
PDF/N0753830.pdf?OpenElement.

49. Security Council SC/9228, "Security Council Press Statement on Myanmar,"
16 January 2008, accessed at http://www.un.org/News/Press/docs/2008/sc9228.doc
.htm.

50. "Ban Ki-moon of UN warns Myanmar," *International Herald Tribune,* 10
December 2007.

51. Thailand and the Philippines made battalion-size force contributions. A Singapore infantry platoon was included in the New Zealand (composite) battalion. A small
number of Malaysian-language assistants were attached to the Jordanian battalion.
The peacekeeping force structure is summarized in Michael G. Smith, *Peacekeeping
in East Timor: The Path to Independence* (Boulder, CO: Lynne Rienner, 2001), 124.

52. "ASEAN Joint Statement on the Situation in the Philippines," 23 February
1986, accessed at http://www.aseansec.org/4997/.htm.

53. "Statement on Current Developments in the Kingdom of Thailand," accessed
at http://www.asean.org/news/asean-statement-communiques/item/statement-on-cur
rent-developments-in-the-kingdom-of-thailand.

54. "ASEAN Foreign Ministers' Statement on the Developments in Thailand," 11
May 2014, accessed at http://www.asean.org/news/asean-statements-communiques/
item/foreign-ministers-statement-on-developments-in-thailand.

55. As reported by Antara News, accessed at http://www.antaranews.com/en/
news/94188/asean-must-address-coup-in-thailand-yudhoyono.

SUGGESTIONS FOR FURTHER READING

For general discussions of policy and practices, see Yukiko Nishikawa, *Human Security in Southeast Asia* (New York: Routledge, 2012) and Sorpong

Peou, ed., *Human Security in East Asia: Challenges for Collaborative Action* (New York: Routledge, 2009). For the MDG, see Malcolm Langford, Andy Sumner, and Alicia Ely Yamin, eds., *The Millennium Development Goals and Human Rights: Past, Present, and Future* (New York: Cambridge University Press, 2013). For the tsunami and Cyclone Nargis, see Emma Larkin, *Everything Is Broken: A Tale of Catastrophe in Burma* (New York: Penguin, 2010) and Patrick Daly, R. Michael Feener, and Anthony Reid, eds., *From the Ground Up: Perspectives on Post-Tsunami and Post-Conflict Aceh* (Singapore: ISEAS, 2012).

For human rights and specific cases, see Hsien-Li Tan, *The ASEAN Intergovernmental Commission on Human Rights: Institutionalizing Human Rights in Southeast Asia* (New York: Cambridge University Press, 2011); Jesper Bengtsson, *Aung San Suu Kyi: A Biography* (Washington, DC: Potomac Books, 2012); Ben Kiernan, *Genocide and Resistance in Southeast Asia: Documentation, Denial, and Justice in Cambodia and East Timor* (Piscataway, NJ: Transaction Publishers, 2007); Geoffrey Robinson, *"If You Leave Us Here We Will Die": How Genocide Was Stopped in East Timor* (Princeton, NJ: Princeton University Press, 2009).

Chapter Ten

Environmental Issues in International Relations in Southeast Asia

When ASEAN looked to the twenty-first century in its 1997 Vision 2020, it envisioned a "clean and green" Southeast Asia with fully implemented mechanisms ensuring the protection of the region's environment, the sustainability of its natural resources, and a high quality of life for its populations. The record to date in terms of actions and enforcement has not been particularly impressive at either the regional or national level. ASEAN has no authority to intervene to safeguard the environment or to hold nations accountable for transboundary environmental damage and pollution.

The choices made by national governments in the name of economic development have led to accelerating patterns of misuse and inefficient use of resources in Southeast Asia with little attention to sustainability. The cumulative impact of environmental misuse can lead to environmental insecurity, that is, "the inability of the environment to sustain ecological and human value systems."[1] Topping today's global environmental agenda is the challenge of climate change and human contribution to it in the form of greenhouse gas (GHG) emissions. All of the scientific data on the impact of climate change show that Southeast Asia is among the most vulnerable areas that are expected to be severely affected. Prospective cyclical weather change, sea level rise, coastal flooding, water stress, ecosystem destruction, and imperiled agriculture and natural resources threaten economies, societies, and cultural stability in Southeast Asia.

Even though it is recognized that regional cooperation will be necessary to address the issues raised by climate change and environmental degradation, there is little sense of urgency or common purpose in ASEAN. While the definition of environmental impacts is scientific, policy choices and disagreements with respect to those impacts are political. It has been asserted that "no other issue in the [Southeast Asia] region's domestic, interregional, and international affairs" has so swiftly assumed prominence "as the emergence of an increasingly politicized ecological awareness."[2] The policy question is how to reconcile the demand for development with responsible environmental practices.

THE ENVIRONMENTAL POLICY SETTING

Safeguarding the environment is no longer viewed as a matter of sovereign jurisdiction. The normative framework within which international environmental concerns are embedded is framed in the Rio Declaration on Environment and Development adopted by the 1992 United Nations Conference on Environment and Development—better known as the Earth Summit (box 10.1).[3] While accepting the traditional rule that states have the sovereign right to exploit their own resources, the Rio Declaration quickly added that states

Box 10.1.   Rio Principles 2–4

Principle 2

States have, in accordance with the Charter of the United Nations and the principles of international law, the sovereign right to exploit their own resources pursuant to their own environmental and developmental policies, and the responsibility to ensure that activities within their jurisdiction or control do not cause damage to the environment of other States or areas beyond the limits of national jurisdiction.

Principle 3

The right to development must be fulfilled so as to equitably meet developmental and environmental needs of present and future generations.

Principle 4

In order to achieve sustainable development, environmental protection shall contribute an integral part of the development process and cannot be considered in isolation from it.

also have the responsibility to ensure that their activities do not cause damage to the environments beyond their borders.

At the global level of the diplomacy of environmentalism and climate change, the Southeast Asian nations are contributing participants, parties to the 1994 UN Framework Convention on Climate Change (UNFCCC) and to the 1997 Kyoto Protocol to the UNFCCC. Indonesia took the spotlight in 2007 as host in Bali of the thirteenth Conference of the Parties to the UNFCCC. The leaders of the ASEAN states jointly endorsed the UNFCCC process and goals. The rhetorical commitment at the global level has yet to be fully translated into action at the national level, where, with few exceptions, legal and enforcement mechanisms are weak and often embedded in patterns of political corruption.

In the United Nations system, the United Nations Environmental Program (UNEP) is the point agency linking the UN to national states for technical and financial support for programmatic implementation. In the Southeast Asia subregion, UNEP works with national environmental ministries as well as ASEAN, the Mekong River Commission, and the GMS Sub-region Economic Cooperation Program. Every five years UNEP collaborates with ESCAP, UNDP, and the ADB in staging the Asia-Pacific Ministerial Conference on Environment and Development.

The developed Western nations, using their economic leverage, try to persuade and pressure Southeast Asian states to cease destructive environmental practices. They routinely attach environmental requirements as conditions for trade, investment, economic assistance, and project funding. The developed countries are the major equity holders in the World Bank and the ADB, and both banks now make environmental assessments and risk a major part of their approval process for project funding. The linking of environmental issues to trade and finance is decried by Southeast Asian economic nationalists as a form of discriminatory protectionism, and the efforts to influence domestic policy are viewed as a new kind of imperialism. The environmental conditionality of Western aid and investment is in sharp contrast to China's environmental unconditionality.

In determining international environmental policy, Western policy makers and parliaments are informed not only by their own scientific experts but also, politically perhaps even more important, by an assertive and powerful global INGO community that seeks to influence environmental policy and actions. Many of the long-established advocacy organizations have status and credibility with their official counterparts. In Southeast Asia, the INGOs provide support and assistance to linked national domestic environmental NGOs. In Thailand, the Philippines, Indonesia, and Malaysia, where political settings have allowed civil society development, the NGOs are recognized stakeholders. In Cambodia and Laos, environmental activists face great risk, including murder and disappearance, in efforts to slow or halt authoritarian governments' developmental juggernaut.

THE ASEAN FRAMEWORK

Environmental issues first appeared on ASEAN's bureaucratic agenda in 1977. Assisted by the UNEP, an ASEAN Expert Group on the Environment developed a five-year ASEAN Sub-regional Environment Program (ASEP). Three ASEPs were succeeded in 1992 by a five-year Strategic Plan of Action on the Environment (SPAE), 1993–1998, and again for 1999–2004. At the 2003 Bali ASEAN Summit, future ASEAN regional activities were placed in the context of building the ASEAN communities. The first ASEAN Ministerial Meeting on the Environment (AMME) took place in Manila in 1981. In their Manila Declaration on the ASEAN Environment, the ministers expressed their awareness that the ASEAN nations faced common environmental problems and the need "to ensure the protection of the ASEAN environment and the sustainability of its natural resources so that it can sustain the highest possible quality of life for the people of the ASEAN countries."[4] This goal had a place in ASEAN's 1997 Vision 2020, the 1998 Hanoi Plan of Action, and the 2004 Vientiane Action Programme (VAP) that detailed the community-building process. The AMME stipulated that the drafters of the VAP should formulate concrete and realistic strategies, but the VAP was framed in the generalizations of ASEAN-speak, promoting cooperation and enhancing coordination.

The AMME meets formally every three years followed by an AMME + 3, with informal ministerial meetings in between. Routine oversight of the machinery of ASEAN environmental concerns is delegated to the ASEAN Senior Officials on the Environment (ASOEN). The ASOEN is supported by seven ASEAN Working Groups: on Multilateral Environmental Agreements (AWGMEA), Coastal and Marine Environment (AWGCME), Environmental Education (AWGEE), Environmentally Sustainable Cities (AWGESC), Natural Resources and Biodiversity (AWGNRB), Water Resources Management (AWGWRM), and, established in 2010, the AWG on Climate Change (AWGCC). The AWGs' programs are heavily reliant on foreign-donornation funding. Not only does this put in place financial constraints, but it also raises issues of matching ASEAN's priorities to the donors'.

ASEAN's leaders set forth their concern about climate change in the 2010 ASEAN Summit's Leaders' Statement on Joint Response to Climate Change. The 2011 AMME implemented the leaders' guidance with an ASEAN Action Plan on Joint Response to Climate Change (AAP-JRCC) that was endorsed by the leaders at their 2012 summit. The AAP-JRCC is mandated to be at the center of an ASEAN Climate Change Initiative (ACCI). In the framework of the ACCI, the AWGCC will serve as the "implementing body" of the AAP-JRCC.

Since the 1981 Manila Declaration, there have been at least twenty-eight leaders' or ministerial declarations, resolutions, and statements on the environment and climate change, most of them containing the same language about the issues. The bureaucratic shuffle has produced a plethora of overlapping strategies, programs, and projects with a Pandora's box of acronyms. The many strategies and programs of the AWGs are directed in vague ways to promote, enhance, share knowledge and best practices, and so forth. The missing words are to "initiate" and "manage." There is no ASEAN agreement on the environment or climate change that would provide binding targets and markers of real progress in meeting the acknowledged challenges. There is no instrumental ASEAN role that connects to tangible and quantifiable outcomes in the halting or mitigating of regional environmental degradation. The achievement of ASEAN's goals depends on the commitment, the political will, and the capabilities of the individual national governments. No matter how well intentioned or scientifically valid planning at the ASEAN level might be, at the implementing state level, political decisions are made in the context of balancing near-term economic gain against long-run environmental costs.

DEFORESTATION

The environmental issue in Southeast Asia that has the greatest global impact is the loss of forest cover with its implications in terms of climate change and loss of biodiversity. Although Southeast Asia contains only 5 percent of the world's forests, 25 percent of global deforestation is taking place there. Global deforestation is the cause of 20 percent of GHG emissions. In Southeast Asia, according to a 2007 World Bank–sponsored study, Indonesia had become the world's third-largest GHG emitter, behind only the United States and China.[5] Indonesia emits 59 percent of Southeast Asia's total GHGs, and 85 percent of that comes from deforestation, land use change, and burning peatland. Forests disappear because of logging (legal and illegal) and conversion to settled agricultural cultivation including palm oil plantations.

Global and Regional Responses

Deforestation has been an important element in global conferences and actions with respect to the environment, sustainable development, and climate change, beginning with the Rio Earth Summit's statement on Principles for a Global Consensus on the Management, Conservation, and Sustainable Development of All Types of Forests. Within the UN system, successive fora for the development of forest policy have been developed: the Intergovernmental Panel on Forests (IPF), the Intergovernmental Forum on Forests (IFF), and, in 2000, the current UN Forest Forum (UNFF) with universal membership. There is no global treaty or convention on forest management.

Under the auspices of the United Nations Conference on Trade and Development (UNCTAD), in 1983 a binding International Tropical Timber Agreement (ITTA) was negotiated that entered into force in 1985. It brought together timber-producing countries and the consuming nations led by the United States, Japan, and the EU. A new ITTA came into force in 2011. The ITTA provides a treaty basis for consultation and cooperation on issues relative to the management of the international timber economy. The International Tropical Timber Organization (ITTO) was established to facilitate the achievement of the treaty's goals, which give equal weight to trade and conservation. Indonesia, Malaysia, Cambodia, Myanmar, and the Philippines are the Southeast Asian producer-members of the ITTO. The long-term objective is to have all tropical timber entering international trade come from sustainably managed sources. In Southeast Asia, this goal has been endorsed by the ministerial meeting of the ASEAN Ministers of Agriculture and Forestry (AMMAF). The international agreements do not cover the growing domestic consumption of timber in timber-producing nations.

Regional cooperation in combating illegal logging was the subject of the 2001 East Asian Ministerial Conference on Forest Law Enforcement and Governance (FLEG) that brought together on Indonesia's island of Bali timber-producing and consuming countries as well as environmental NGOs. The FLEG meeting resulted in a Bali Declaration in which the parties committed to intensified national and international efforts to combat illegal logging and trade in illegal wood products.[6] Although nonbinding, the Bali FLEG declaration is considered a watershed in promoting cooperation among the stakeholders. It is credited with inspiring governments in Europe, Australia, and the United States to take action against illegal logging. The EU, United States, and Australia require that all imported timber and timber products have third-party certification that they have been legally harvested. In 2013, after a six-year negotiation, Indonesia became the first Asian country to conclude a FLEG-trade voluntary partnership agreement with the EU. Within ASEAN, the AMMAF has oversight of the FLEG process and coordination of relevant agency cooperation. In 2007, with its ASEAN Statement on Strengthening Forest Law Enforcement and Governance, the AMMAF began the progress of developing an ASEAN FLEG collective mechanism.[7] The first result was a 2008–2015 Work Plan for Strengthening FLEG in ASEAN.

The UN global initiative on Reducing Emissions from Deforestation and Forest Degradation (REDD) was launched in 2008. It is a collaborative effort involving the FAO, UNDP, and UNEP. REDD+ programmatically goes beyond deforestation to include conservation, sustainable management, and enhancement of forest carbon stocks. REDD programs operate by supporting national programs in partner countries. The Southeast Asian partner countries are Cambodia, Indonesia, Malaysia, Myanmar, the Philippines, and Vietnam. REDD is funded by Denmark, the EU, Japan, Luxembourg, Norway, and Spain, which have contributed $172 million, nearly 100 percent of which is program-directed to the partner countries.

The Southeast Asian Toll

Fragile ecosystems in Southeast Asia already have been destroyed. Thailand, the Philippines, and Vietnam have essentially lost their productive forests. The greatest demand is from China, which has transformed the world's raw wood trade. China has the second-largest wood-manufacturing sector in the world and is the largest trader in tropical hardwoods. Half of the tropical logs traded globally go to China. China banned domestic logging in 1998 and has avariciously turned to Southeast Asia for supply—legal or otherwise. China's timber policy has been described by one environmental NGO as "exporting deforestation."[8] Myanmar's forests, like other components of Myanmar's resource base, have become adjuncts to China's rise. It is estimated that over a million tons a year of illegally logged Myanmar timber are delivered to China.[9] The Chinese approach is epitomized in a quote from a Chinese timber trader: "When you cross the [Yunnan] border to the Myanmar side, you can see the mountains that no longer have any trees on them. Soon all the trees will be cut. Without the trees there will only be mountains. So, we will look into mining them."[10]

Former timber exporters Thailand, Vietnam, and Malaysia have also emerged as major markets for illegal timber imports from their ASEAN partners Laos and Cambodia. The last thing that logging operators in those countries are concerned about is environmental damage and sustainability. Rampant logging to satisfy Asian markets is destroying Cambodia's forest cover. According to the NGO Global Witness, illegal logging "is part of a massive asset-stripping for the benefit of a small kleptocratic elite" that includes Prime Minister Hun Sen's family.[11] Laos, caught between timber-starved Thailand and Vietnam, is seeing its forests illegally felled to supply its neighbors. The LPDR officially prohibits the export of logs, but the British NGO Environmental Investigation Agency and the Indonesian-based NGO Telapak documented the hundreds of thousands of cubic meters of logs delivered to Thailand and Vietnam annually.[12] Vietnam has become the world's fourth-largest exporter of finished wood products, but half of its raw wood supply is illegally cut, with Laos being the major source.[13] As Lao forests follow in the wake of Cambodian, Thai, and Vietnamese forests—with Myanmar's forest endowment under heavy Chinese pressure—the largest remaining tropical forests in Southeast Asia are in East Malaysia's Sabah and Sarawak states and Indonesia's Kalimantan and Papuan provinces.

Although the export of logs is banned in Malaysia, its booming domestic construction industry has a thirst for timber. With peninsular Malaysia planted over in palm oil, new plantations are being cleared in Sabah and Sarawak. Forest loss in East Malaysia is proceeding steadily. Government-controlled cutting in East Malaysia's forests has not satisfied Malaysian domestic demand or Malaysian brokers for illegal export to China and Vietnam. Indonesia's porous Kalimantan borders with the East Malaysia states are regularly violated by illegal loggers. Indonesia has protested to the Malaysian government, but Malaysian officials are loath to admit that Malaysian logging companies are complicit in the trade since many of the larger ones are politically connected. Stewarded by the World Wide Fund for Nature (WWF [formerly the World Wildlife Fund]), a trilateral "Heart of Borneo" scheme involving Brunei, Malaysia, and Indonesia was launched in 2007 to conserve eighty-five thousand square miles (220,000 sq km) of transboundary tropical forests. The problem will be—as it is in national conservation and preservation areas—how to keep the would-be trespassers at bay.

Indonesia, with the second-largest tropical forests in the world—Brazil's are the largest—has the world's highest rate of deforestation. Data from new high-resolution global mapping tracking forest loss from 2000 to 2012 show that Indonesia's annual rate of loss between 2002 and 2003 was about 10,000 square kilometers (3,861 sq mi) per year, doubling to 20,000 square kilometers (7,722 sq mi) between 2011 and 2012.[14] The Indonesian Forest Ministry quickly denied the scientific data, insisting that the researchers miscalculated since their figures did not agree with the ministry's, which showed a loss of 450,000 hectares (4,500 sq km or 1,737.7 sq mi) a year.[15] The new figures, however, seem to confirm the high rates of forest loss documented by environmental NGOs. According to Forest Watch Indonesia, between 2000 and 2009 Indonesia lost 15.2 million hectares (152,000 sq km or 58,685 sq mi) of forest at an average annual rate of 1.5 million hectares (15,000 sq km or 5,791 sq mi).[16] Greenpeace's forest program in Indonesia records for the period 2009–2011 a forest loss of 1.245 million hectares (12,450 sq km or 4,807 sq mi).[17] As the rate of forest loss drops in Brazil, Indonesia's rises. If the unsustainable rate of deforestation continues, the result would be the loss of all of Indonesia's productive forests within two decades.

A number of factors contribute to the rate of forest loss. First, there is an unabated domestic and foreign demand for the timber. Logging concessions continue to be given. The military and the police are in the logging business. Illegal logging is uncontrolled, with as much as 80 percent of Indonesian log exports being illegal and with the cost to Indonesia placed at $3.2 billion a year. It is argued that administrative decentralization as part of Indonesia's democratization has led to increased logging, both legal and illegal. There are 34 provinces and 497 districts to which authority has been devolved. Resource decisions at the district levels are often made without consideration of national law or social and environmental consequences.[18] Trying to explain Indonesia's dismal performance in preventing illegal logging, the forest minister told a group of NGOs and representatives of donor nations that he had limited power since 85 percent of decision making was held by local governments.[19]

In a dramatic domestic response to the problem of climate change, in 2009 President Yudhoyono pledged to reduce Indonesia's GHG emissions by 26 percent by 2020. A major component of his plan was a two-year moratorium, beginning in 2011, on new permits to log in primary forests or to convert peatland. This was a key element of a $1 billion REDD+ agreement with Norway. The moratorium set aside two hundred thousand hectares (772 sq mi or 2,000 sq km) of virgin forest and peatland. Existing concessions remained intact. Mapping of the covered land was delayed as economic interests negotiated the bureaucratic application of the moratorium. Outside of the protected forests, conversion to palm oil plantations continues to be permitted. The Norwegian environment minister has acknowledged that the moratorium would not be sufficient to meet the GHG reduction pledged for 2020. The disbursement of the Norwegian funds was performance related, and by the end of 2013 only a small amount of the aid had been paid out. Nevertheless, Yudhoyono extended the moratorium for two more years.

The pronouncements and international engagements at the presidential level about forest policy face the reality of the pushback of politically strong logging and palm oil interests together with the lack of commitment to the REDD+ goals by a very corrupt forest ministry. Indonesia's Corruption Eradication Commission (KPK) has cited Indonesia's forest sector as "a source of unlimited corruption."[20] As important as corruption might be, a lack of capacity of the government to implement policy in one of the most decentralized countries in the world is an important driver of deforestation. Although the Indonesian government consistently promises reform, the best available NGO data demonstrate that even if policy reforms were to be successful, Indonesia will still follow the path of Thailand, the Philippines, and the other countries of Southeast Asia where the tipping point has been passed.

THE "HAZE"

The "haze" is the ASEAN euphemism for airborne smoke pollution caused by uncontrolled forest and peatbed fires. The frequency of occurrence and extent of fires in Indonesia's Sumatran and Kalimantan provinces make Indonesia the primary source of environmental assaults on its ASEAN neighbors. It is the single most important transboundary environmental issue affecting Indonesia's relations with its neighbors. Indonesia's policy commitment to haze abatement is undermined by weak enforcement, administrative decentralization, and corruption. Nor can Indonesia effectively mobilize the human, logistical, and technical resources to fight the widespread fires in remote areas.

The haze became a serious Indonesian foreign policy problem and part of the regional international agenda in 1997 when it blanketed nearly two million square miles (5 million sq km) for seven months, endangering public health and causing economic loss of more than $9 billion.[21] Thick haze is encountered annually. In 2013, the haze level approached that of the 1997 disaster, prompting new rounds of recriminations by downwind states. To Singapore's 2013 demand that Indonesia take urgent and definitive action to tackle the problem, Indonesia's coordinating minister for people's welfare retorted that "Singapore should not be behaving as a child and making all this noise."[22]

While the affected states have bilaterally expressed continuing anger, frustration, distress, and concern, at the regional level through ASEAN they have sought a framework to urge and assist Indonesian efforts to meet the haze challenge. The 1995 ASEAN Cooperation Plan on Transboundary Pollution was the platform for the 1997 ASEAN Regional Haze Action Plan. Within ASEAN, a Subregional Ministerial Steering Committee on Transboundary Haze Pollution made up of Indonesia, Brunei, Malaysia, Singapore, and Thailand oversees action plans and working groups focused on prevention, monitoring, and mitigation of the haze. In 1999 the ministers announced their consensus on a regionwide zero-burn policy—but leaving enforcement to Indonesia.

The 2002 ASEAN Agreement on Transboundary Haze Pollution is the treaty framework for ASEAN's collaborative dealings with the haze problem.[23] Hailed by UNEP as a potential model for tackling transboundary issues worldwide, the agreement came into force in November 2003. An annual conference of the parties to the treaty (COP) is included in the AMME. After more than a decade, Indonesia—the source of the haze—is the only ASEAN state that has failed to ratify the agreement, which aggravates its ASEAN partners' unhappiness with Jakarta's response to regional concerns. Even though President Yudhoyono and his foreign minister have continually assured their ASEAN counterparts that they are pushing for ratification, the Indonesian parliament has not shared their urgency and has remained unmoved by regional demands for action.

Implicit in the ASEAN approach has been an assumption—so far not validated—that Indonesia will be willing and able to improve its domestic capabilities to prevent and control the fires. At the fifteenth meeting of the steering committee in July 2013, while the fires roared on in Indonesia, the ministers wrangled over the details of a Singapore-proposed joint haze monitoring system (HMS) based on digitized maps of concessions which would identify through satellite monitoring culpable fire starters. Indonesia reluctantly accepted the HMS, and it was adopted at the October 2013 ASEAN Summit. Even as the fires in Riau again blanketed the straits region in early 2014, Singapore's foreign minister complained that some parties (not naming Indonesia) were not implementing the agreement, thus affecting ASEAN's credibility.[24]

Indonesia's response to what its neighbors view as an economic and public health crisis illustrates again that in the ASEAN setting it is individual state behavior—not ASEAN consensus—that ultimately determines outcomes. An early assessment of ASEAN's role in resolving the haze problem concluded that efforts at the regional level while "leading to a proliferation of meetings and plans have produced little of consequence."[25] After a decade and a half of ASEAN efforts, we can only endorse a 2012 conclusion that ASEAN haze initiatives' "outcomes have been largely ineffective in providing long-term workable solutions for the haze."[26] The haze issue throws into sharp relief the issues of environmental politics within ASEAN even as the challenges of climate change intensify. In this respect, one Malaysian analyst warned that Southeast Asia could be "unsettled by the prospect of a friendly power [Indonesia] being a source of the region's future problems."[27]

THE SOUTH CHINA SEA

In chapter 6, the political and strategic issues that have made the South China Sea a zone of conflict were discussed. It is also a zone of environmental threat and degradation in which the political crisis has impeded international cooperation to address functionally the environmental challenges.

Ninety percent of the SCS's circumference is rimmed by low-lying, thickly populated urban centers and agricultural land now at risk from the rising sea levels caused by climate change. On the land margins of the SCS, spreading urbanization and industrialization have produced a flood of toxic effluent. In the tidal zones, the coastal mangrove forests whose rich biodiversity is important for the marine food chain are being converted to fish and prawn farms at a rapid rate. Thailand has lost more than half of its mangrove forests since 1975; Indonesia, 70 percent; and the Philippines, 75 percent. Oil sludge and ballast discharge foul the water's surface. The SCS has been described as "a sink for regional environmental pollution."[28] In its waters, once-abundant fish stocks are rapidly being depleted. In a 1998 introduction to a comprehensive analysis of the SCS's environmental ills, the director of UNEP's SCS project wrote, "Countries bordering the South China Sea have exploited the coastal resources far beyond their capacities and . . . without some intervention now they will be destroyed forever."[29] The need for cooperation will become more urgent if the number of gas and oil exploration and production platforms in the SCS increases either unilaterally or through joint development areas. The region is unprepared to handle a major disaster like the 2010 BP *Deepwater Horizon* spill in the Gulf of Mexico.

Regional Response

The environmental health of the SCS requires transboundary adaptive and conservation strategies based on multilateral cooperation. This does exist at the level of technical and scientific exchange but is still lacking at the political level. The ASEAN Socio-Cultural Community Blueprint, Section D.7, is titled "Promoting the Sustainable Use of Coastal and Marine Environment." The task of the AWGCME is to implement the actions to support this strategic objective. Like the other AWGs, its mission is to promote and enhance cooperation and collaboration as appropriate to the member states' differing needs and existing institutional, financial, and human capacities, which means little more than workshops, task forces, and bureaucratic exchanges.

The environmental challenges in the SCS have been an agenda item for the ASEAN Maritime Forum (AMF), but as was noted in chapter 6 the AMF process has been driven by the geopolitical regional tensions that impede functional cooperation in low-politics areas of concern. The UNEP has been an important agent in focusing on regional cooperation at the scientific level. One regional program is directed through its Bangkok-based Coordinating Body on the Seas of East Asia (COBSEA).[30] The original Action Plan for the Protection and Development of the Marine Environment and Coastal Areas of the East Asian Sea Region was approved in 1981 and involved the original five ASEAN countries. In 1994, the East Asian Action Plan was expanded to cover Southeast Asia's Cambodia and Vietnam as well as China, South Korea, and Australia. In the absence of any regional legal convention on the SCS, COBSEA promotes national compliance with existing environmental treaties based on member countries' "goodwill." It is, however, much more of a question of political will and capability than goodwill.

From 2002 to 2008, UNEP's Global Environment Facility (UNEP-GEF) funded the Reversing Environmental Degradation Trends in the South China Sea and Gulf of Thailand project. The participants were Cambodia, China, Indonesia, Malaysia, the Philippines, Thailand, and Vietnam. The three priority concerns were habitat loss and degradation, fisheries exploitation, and land-based pollution. Regional working groups and task forces were formed and demonstration sites established. The outcome of the project was a proposed Strategic Action Program for the South China Sea.[31] Among the obstacles facing intergovernmental cooperation identified by drafters of the action plan were lack of a global and regional perspective, lack of respect for and recognition of regional expertise among the leaders, and lack of a regional political consensus.

The Partnership in Environmental Management of the Seas of East Asia (PEMSEA) is the coordinating implementing agency for the Sustainable Development Strategy of the Seas of East Asia (SDS-SEA). The SDS-SEA was initiated by PEMSEA and was developed in collaboration with relevant UN agencies and NGOs in association with state agencies of twelve littoral states. It was formally adopted in the 2002 Putrajaya Declaration of Regional Cooperation for the Sustainable Development of the Seas of East Asia. This was signed at the ministerial level by eight ASEAN states (excluding Laos and Myanmar), China, Japan, and North and South Korea.[32]

As noted in chapter 6, the Indonesia-led Workshops on Managing Potential Conflict in the South China Sea search for CBMs has addressed a number of the environmental threats to the South China Sea. The workshop process has been unable to translate its Track II intellectual exchanges into Track I intergovernmental collaborative regional planning and management programs. The sticking point is the same as in all regionalist SCS initiatives. China is unwilling to go beyond scientific and technical discussions to commit to activities that from Beijing's vantage could be seen as compromising or challenging Chinese sovereign jurisdictional claims over the SCS.

In a discussion of governance in the South China Sea, David Rosenberg identified among the multiple state and nonstate stakeholders what he called three "movements": a resource control movement, a conservation movement, and a security movement.[33] The issues of resource control center on the establishment, fixing, and defending of maritime jurisdictions. The issues of security center on international freedom of access to and through the SCS. The conservation "movement" addresses the mitigation of environmental damage and sustainability of resources. As was discussed in chapter 6, government stakeholders are focused on control and security. It will not be until the conflicts of national interests involved in the control and security realms are resolved or put aside that regional intergovernmental cooperative structures can emerge to meet the challenges perceived in the conservation "movement." Current policy trends indicate that greater policy divergence rather than convergence of the "movements" can be expected.

Fisheries

The critical status of the SCS's fisheries has become an issue in regional food security. Southeast Asia's fisheries are a source of 22 percent of protein in Southeast Asian diets and an important export industry. Fish stocks are being depleted by pollution and uncontrolled overfishing, not just by nationally permitted fishing but by illegal, unreported, and unregulated (IUU) fishing. Thousands of fishing boats are taking smaller catches and using undiscriminating methods. The state-backed Chinese fishing fleet is the largest in the region, deploying factory ships and support vessels. The maintenance of sustainable fish stocks will require cooperative efforts by the maritime states. The global framework for this is the 1982 UNCLOS, Part V on the EEZ, Articles 63 and 64 on management of fish stocks. After a series of conferences, a 1995 Agreement was reached on implementing the UNCLOS provisions on conservation and management of straddling fish stocks and highly migratory fish stocks. The agreement came into force in December 2001. Indonesia is the only ASEAN state that has both signed and ratified it. The Philippines and China have signed but not ratified. Japan and South Korea have signed and ratified. As is the case with other treaties and agreements, the problem is compliance.

At the regional level, the Southeast Asian Fisheries Development Center (SEAFDEC), established in 1967, promotes the development and management of sustainable fisheries. Its membership is the ASEAN countries and Japan, which supports its trust fund. From its inception, SEAFDEC has cooperated with ASEAN, and in 2007 a formal ASEAN–SEAFDEC Strategic Partnership was established. The primary link is the ASEAN Sectoral Working Group on Fisheries (ASWGFi). The common goal is collective regional development and management of sustainable fisheries. The aspiration is documented in the usual ASEAN array of resolutions, statements, and plans of action.

As fish stocks decline, competition and conflict for access to fishery resources increase. The UNCLOS, Article 56, gives maritime states sovereign rights for the purpose of exploring, exploiting, conserving, and managing their EEZs' living or nonliving resources (table 10.1). National efforts to protect and conserve EEZ fish resources through permitting, catch limits, and bans have not been matched by surveillance and patrol capabilities necessary for effective enforcement. Furthermore, as noted in chapter 5, there are many gaps and overlaps in the delimitation of EEZs. Poaching in another country's EEZ is common in Southeast Asia as flagged, falsely flagged, and unflagged vessels venture farther from their national waters in search of catch. It is estimated that the cost to Indonesia of IUU fishing in its vast EEZ is $3.1 to $5.2 billion a year.[34] Although the problem of IUU fishing is discussed in the various ASEAN and ASEAN-related fora, there is no ASEAN action to curtail it even though individual ASEAN countries claim to be committed to eliminating it. According to Indonesia's permanent representative to ASEAN, IUU fishing is a "sensitive" issue to the ASEAN countries that are home to the illegal fishermen.[35] The worst offenders are vessels from Thailand, Vietnam, and Malaysia.

Encounters between an IUU fishing vessel and a national fisheries enforcement ship are not simply a policing matter but can have political and diplomatic consequences. In August 2010, for example, an unarmed Indonesian fishery patrol boat apprehended a Malaysian IUU fishing boat in claimed Indonesian waters. An armed Malaysian patrol boat, after firing warning shots, seized the Indonesian patrol boat and arrested the onboard Indonesian Fishery and Maritime Affairs officers. In March 2014, two Indonesian fishery

Table 10.1.   Southeast Asia's EEZs

Country	Sq Mi	Sq Km
Brunei	9,817	25,427
Cambodia	18,466	47,827
Indonesia (East)	1,396,660	3,617,349
Indonesia (West)	936,694	2,426,028
Indonesia Total	*2,333,354*	*6,043,377*
Malaysia Pen (E)	51,341	132,973
Malaysia Pen (W)	26,543	68,747
Malaysia Sabah	34,602	89,618
Malaysia Sarawak	60,207	155,938
Malaysia Total	*172,693*	*447,276*
Myanmar*	204,349	520,262
Philippines	874,785	2,265,684
Singapore	318	823
Thailand	118,288	306,365
Timor-Leste*	29,828	77,256
Vietnam	539,114	1,396,299

Source: Pew Charitable Trust Sea Around Us Project, http://www.seaaroundus.org.

*Myanmar and Timor-Leste do not have South China Sea EEZs.

officers were killed while trying to arrest a Thai IUU vessel. The Indonesian response was to ban all Thai fishing in its EEZ, idling five hundred Thai fishing boats. Indonesia has been affected by China's claim to Indonesian EEZ fisheries inside China's nine-dash line. On two occasions in 2010, with guns trained, a Chinese maritime enforcement cutter forced an Indonesian patrol vessel to release Chinese fishing boats apprehended in Indonesia's EEZ north of its Natuna Islands. Similarly, in March 2013, an Indonesian patrol vessel boarded a Chinese fishing boat in Indonesia's EEZ and arrested nine crewmen. A Chinese cutter arrived on scene and threateningly demanded the release of the prisoners. The Indonesian captain acquiesced in consideration of the safety of his crew.[36]

What has been hypothesized as possible "fishing wars" according to one analyst has placed the fishermen in a precarious position of being viewed as "agents of their home governments and pawns in the maritime policies of their respective states."[37] The politicization and securitization of fishery issues have made it more difficult to develop multilateral framework measures for conservation and sustainability. It is worth noting that the 2002 Declaration of Conduct (DOC), discussed in chapter 6, has no direct reference to fisheries.

RIVERS, DAMS, AND ECOSYSTEMS

One of the most intensely debated issues in the dialogue between development and the environment is the adverse environmental, social, and economic impacts of large or mega-dams. The damming of free-flowing rivers has been an important element in economic development strategies in Southeast Asia. Large multipurpose dams are utilized for hydroelectric power generation and water impoundment for irrigation and flood control. It has been only in recent years that the cost-benefit analysis of dam building and river development has been calculated in other than financial terms. The damming of a river has enormous impact on its ecosystem and the life of the people who depend on it for their livelihood. The natural flood cycle along a dammed river is interrupted. Behind the dam, forests give way to reservoirs. Biodiversity is negatively affected. Villagers are displaced. Fisheries are disrupted and decline. The changed downstream flow leads to new patterns of erosion and river-carried nutrients. The balance of nature that took thousands of years to emerge is altered. China has been very active in dam building in Southeast Asia. China hopes to reduce by 15 percent electrical generation by fossil fuel by 2020. A significant part of the hydropower will be imported from Chinese-built dams in Myanmar, Laos, and Cambodia.

On the initiative of the World Bank, in 1998 the World Commission on Dams (WCD) was tasked with addressing the controversial issues associated with large dams and issued its report in November 2000.[38] The empirical basis was a comparative survey of 125 representative large dams around the world—twelve in Southeast Asia—and eight detailed case studies.[39] The WCD's Southeast Asia case study was Thailand's Pak Mun dam which sits three miles upstream from the Mun River's confluence with the Mekong River. From its conception in the early 1980s to its completion in 1994 and its operations today, it has been a source of controversy and protest. The WCD's conclusion about the Pak Mun dam was that if all of the benefits and costs had been adequately assessed, the project as it stands would not have been built. The Electrical Generating Authority of Thailand (EGAT) and the Thai government rejected the report.

The WCD's report provided new criteria for the evaluation, building, operation, and decommissioning of dams. The criteria are recommendations, not mandates, and have largely been ignored by dam-building states in Asia. INGOs like the International Rivers Network (IRN) and Rivers Watch East and Southeast Asia (RWESEA) see the WCD recommendations as the benchmark against which to measure environmentally and human rights–destructive damming.

Sarawak Dams

In the 1990s, Malaysia's Bakun dam project was another poster child of anti–large dam protest. Located on the Balui River in a remote area of Sarawak's rain forest, the 2,400-megawatt-capacity dam began generating operations in 2011. Standing at 679 feet (207 m), it is the highest dam in Southeast Asia. Its reservoir is an expanse of 270 square miles (700 sq km), flooding logged-over forest and forcibly displacing ten thousand indigenous people to miserable resettlement facilities. At the 1996 symbolic rock-blasting ceremony inaugurating construction, Prime Minister Mahathir told the audience, "Malaysia wants to develop and I say to the so-called environmentalists: Mind your own business."[40] Although perhaps expressed more diplomatically, Mahathir's attitude that development comes first and environment second is widely shared by leadership in Southeast Asia. The original plan was for 90 percent of Bakun dam's electricity to be delivered to West Malaysia by undersea cable, but this was abandoned for technical and cost considerations. It now operates at less than capacity in a Sarawak with surplus energy. While perhaps a white elephant without benefits outweighing its economic, human, and environmental costs, the Bakun dam stands out as one of Transparency International's "Monuments of Corruption."[41]

A total of twelve Sarawak dams are on the drawing boards, with six scheduled for completion by 2020. The dams are part of the Sarawak Corridor of Renewable Energy (SCORE) initiative and add to existing excess generating capacity, flooding more land and displacing more indigenous groups. The building spree will generate profits for the Chinese state-owned construction companies and their local political backers. The Australian firm Hydro Tasmania's consultancy business, Entura, had been a consultant to Sarawak Energy's dam-building projects and provided technical oversight. A storm of Australian NGO and parliamentary criticism in defense of indigenous rights in Sarawak led the company to announce that it would be leaving Sarawak at the end of 2013.[42]

The Myitsone Dam

In Myanmar, the September 2011 suspension of China Power International's Myitsone dam project was hailed as a triumph for civil society and environmentalism. Under a 2006 agreement between the Chinese state company and the ruling military junta, the $3.6 billion project will rise at the confluence of the two northern rivers that form the headwaters of the Ayeyawady (Irrawaddy) River in the "cradle of Burmese civilization" and the heartland of the Kachin ethnic group. The government's thirty-year plan was for sixty-four hydropower projects. The leaked CPI in-house environmental impact statement on the Myitsone dam concluded that more study of downstream effects was necessary and that the dam as planned was too large. It was ignored. The Myitsone dam is supposed to be the uppermost of a seven-dam cascade from which 90 percent of the electricity generated will go to China. Domestic and international environmental NGOs campaigned against it as well as nationalist opponents of Chinese penetration of Myanmar. The issue was taken up by the NLD's Aung San Suu Kyi.

President Thein Sein announced the suspension of the project in September 2011 in a letter to parliament in which he stated, "As our government is elected by the people, it is to respect the people's will. We have the responsibility to address public concerns in all seriousness. So construction of Myitsone dam will be suspended in the time of our government."[43] The duration of the suspension, given as "in the time of our government," suggests that at the maximum this would mean until a new president is sworn in after the 2015 elections; at the minimum, until Thein Sein might be replaced before an election. Although hailed as a win for democracy, the suspension of the project was also related to the high degree of insecurity at the dam site where it was in the sights of the Kachin Independence Organization (KIO). The future of the dam has become part of the KIO–Myanmar government peace process.[44]

The last line of Thein Sein's announcement was that "coordination would be made with the neighboring friendly nation, the People's Republic of China, to accept the agreements regarding the project without undermining cordial relations." Beijing reacted with diplomatic propriety in the hope that this was only a temporary setback. Uncertainty about post-junta China–Myanmar relations did lead to a drop in Chinese investment. Myanmar's priority in China's ASEAN foreign policy has been downgraded as measured by official visits. Looking to the future, China has made cautious outreach to the opposition but really is in a quandary about engaging with Aung San Su Kyi and her global role in Asian democratization.[45]

The Salween River Basin

The Salween River, known in China as the Nu Jiang, runs nearly 1,750 miles (2,800 km) and is the region's longest free-flowing river. Rising on the Tibetan Plateau, its course takes it through China's Yunnan Province into Myanmar, and in its lower reach it borders Thailand before reaching the Andaman Sea's Gulf of Martaban. On Nu's upper reach, China had a plan for thirteen hydropower dams. Construction of the first dam was scheduled to begin in 2004. In an unprecedented move, in April 2004 Chinese prime minister Wen Jiabao put the project on hold and called for a full review of the Nu River hydro projects. Shortly before Wen left office in March 2013, the plans for the dams were revived—scaled back to five. There has been no release of any environmental impact statement.

In 1989, Myanmar and Thailand established a working group to promote and coordinate the development of hydropower projects in the Salween Basin. A 2005 MOU between the Myanmar junta and Bangkok called for five dams, to which a sixth has been added. One dam, the Tasang, at 748 feet (228 meters) would be Southeast Asia's highest, exceeding the Bakun dam. The sites are located in areas of ethnic insurgency, and the work has been limited to clearing and site preparation. The Myanmar military has ruthlessly displaced thousands of local residents. The prospect of a general peace with the minority groupings has led the Thai, Chinese, and Burmese investors to urge the Thein Sein government to pick up the pace of construction, which, when completed, would have a fifteen-thousand-megawatt capacity to be delivered mainly to China.[46]

Damming the Mekong River

Along its more than three-thousand-mile (4,800 km) course, once it drops from the Tibetan Plateau and through the gorges of Yunnan, the Mekong

River with its tributaries is the life's blood of the Mekong Basin's sixty million inhabitants. Its fisheries are a major source of protein. In its navigable stretches, it is a commercial and market artery. Its flood-borne deposits of nutrient-rich silt and irrigation water are critical to the region's agriculture. Life along the river is geared to its annual cycle of high and low water. In Cambodia the Mekong flood reverses the flow of the Tonle Sap, filling the "Great Lake," Cambodia's rice and fish basket. In Vietnam, it is the river's flow through its multiple mouths into the South China Sea that keeps back salt water intrusion into the delta's rice fields. The eight-hundred-thousand-square-mile (207 million sq km) drainage basin is larger than France or Texas. Even though the river flows through six sovereign states, geophysically it is a hydrological unit. All upstream water-management projects, whether for flood control, irrigation, or hydroelectric generation, cause alterations in the flow of the river through diversion, canalization, or damming. Any change in the river's rate and volume of flow affects the balance of the ecosystem and pattern of life along the Mekong.

Over the past two decades more than a hundred large dams have been in various stages of completion, construction, or planning on the Mekong and its tributaries in the name of economic development. This has produced conflicts of interest in two politically sensitive issue areas: the different needs of upstream and downstream countries and the social and environmental costs of development. Unlike the rivers of Sarawak or Myanmar's Ayeyawady, the Mekong is a transboundary river. Upstream–downstream issues are central to the international politics of the development of the Mekong Basin. The question is whether a regional framework for coordination and planning can emerge for the exploitation and utilization of the hydropower potential of the basin's rivers that will reconcile the conflicting economic and political interests as well as satisfy the demands for environmental and social safeguards.

The Mekong River Commission

There is only one international treaty governing freshwater international watercourses, the 1997 United Nations Convention on the Law of Non-Navigational Uses of International Watercourses. Its two major principles are (1) "equal and reasonable use" and (2) "obligation not to cause significant harm to neighbors."[47] The terms "equal," "reasonable," and "significant" were not defined, left to the affected states to negotiate. None of the Mekong's riparian states is party to the convention, although its existence does provide a normative base from which to view states' activities affecting the Mekong.

The first institutional effort at comprehensive development planning in the Mekong Basin was the 1957 UN-sponsored Mekong Committee. The original committee was made up of Thailand, Cambodia, and South Vietnam. After the Indochina wars, in 1995 Cambodia, Laos, Thailand, and Vietnam signed an Agreement on Cooperation for the Sustainable Development of the Mekong River Basin.[48] A new Mekong River Commission (MRC) was set up to be the implementing agency, with its headquarters first in Bangkok and now split between Vientiane and Phnom Penh. The MRC's mission is to "promote and coordinate sustainable management and development of water and related resources" for the benefit of the riparian countries. The governing body of the intergovernmental MRC is its Joint Council made up of ministers of environment or water resources of the four countries. Decisions by the council must be unanimous. Where unanimity does not exist, the issue concerned can be referred to leaders of the governments. Although called the Mekong Commission, it is the lower Mekong that is covered by the 1995 agreement. Myanmar and China are not parties to the agreement. Since 1996 the MRC has had an informal link to the upstream countries in an annual dialogue, but the dialogue partners are not bound by the agreement or decisions of the Joint Council. In 2010 the first MRC Summit took place with the heads of the MRC governments and the Myanmar foreign minister and China's vice foreign minister. According to its convener, Thai prime minister Abhisit, the summit underscored the urgency of comprehensive cooperation between the countries of the upper and lower Mekong.

The MRC has scientific and technical programs on all aspects of the river. These programs are supported by development partners. In 2012, there were sixteen, of which Australia, Belgium, Finland, and Switzerland were the largest donors. It is the impact of hydropower dams, however, that figures in the international politics of the river's governance. While dams on the Mekong's tributaries can have negative ecological and social impacts, a major concern in the last decade has been proposals for construction of up to twelve run-of-the-river mainstream Mekong River dams. According to the MRC's 2003 Procedures for Notification, Prior Consultation and Agreement (PNPCA), a proposed mainstream dam must undergo a prior consultation that would allow the other member riparians to discuss and evaluate the impact of the dam on their own uses of water or other effects. Tributary dams only require MRC notification. In 2010, the MRC commissioned a Strategic Environmental Assessment of mainstream hydropower damming which reported in October 2010.[49] The conclusion was that one or more mainstream dams could have profound implications for the sustainable development of the Mekong Basin and irreversibly affect the lives and livelihoods of its population. The main recommendation was to defer decision making about mainstream dams for ten years while more complete studies could be made and the feasibility of alternatives to run-of-the-river dams could be studied. In boldface type the report said, "The Mekong mainstream should never be used as a test case for proving or improving hydropower technologies."

China's Upstream Threat

In its insatiable quest for energy China has embarked on an ambitious dam-building program on the upper Mekong—known in China as the Lancang River. Since 1996, five mega-dams have been completed, and in 2013 another eight were under construction, with up to twenty-three more planned. The Lancang cascade of mainstream dams is being built without assessment or consultation with the downstream Southeast Asian nations. China has made it absolutely clear that it will not allow its industrial development and shift to non-fossil fuel to slow down to appease environmentalists or downstream concerns. China has scorned the WCD process as not applicable to China's economic growth needs and an unwarranted intrusion into China's internal affairs. As a nonmember of the MRC, China is not bound by the consultative commitments of PNPCA.

When the full complex of dams is completed, perhaps in a quarter of a century, China's hydraulic mastery of its reaches of the river means its decisions on opening and closure of sluices and gates can give it control over the river's water level to its Vietnam delta outlets to the sea. The environmental consequence of China's unilateralism for the lives and livelihood of the people who live along the Mekong is a matter of great concern. The flow of nutrients vital to agriculture is affected. The migratory patterns of fish are disturbed. A Thai official at an MRC workshop has charged that the existing Chinese dams have "already destroyed the river's ecosystem."[50] At the least, as one study is headlined, "China's Lancang Dams Endanger Millions both Upstream and Downstream."[51]

It is not just dam building on the Lancang/Mekong that troubles the downstream inhabitants. China is widening and deepening the river by blasting rapids and dredging so that even in the dry season five-hundred-ton vessels can commercially navigate from Yunnan to river ports in northern Thailand and Laos. Ultimately, up to one hundred rapids are set for demolition. Environmental officials in Laos, Thailand, and Cambodia have repeatedly warned of the damage to the Mekong ecosystem that is being caused by the navigation project. Upstream migration of fish species for spawning will be impeded as well as downstream changes in water flow as the elimination of the rapids causes stronger currents and greater riverbank erosion. The river projects fit into a plan for an integrated GMS transportation system—roads, rail, and river—linking continental Southeast Asia to southwest China (chapter 4).

China's unilateralism on the Mekong can be compared to its actions in the South China Sea (chapter 6). On questions of what are internationally shared resources, China is unwilling to accept the principle of shared responsibilities. China will not be held to a riparian consensus on consultation and cooperation on transboundary matters. Describing China's role on the river as "trickle-down hegemony," one analyst has concluded that "China has by and large pursued its own interests without regard for how these actions will affect its downstream neighbors."[52]

The Laos "Battery" of Southeast Asia

With its numerous Mekong tributaries, Laos is envisioned as a future hydroelectric "battery" at the center of a Southeast Asian power grid supplying electricity to energy-thirsty China, Thailand, and Vietnam. It is argued by proponents of hydropower development in Laos that the export of electricity will be for the foreseeable future the main economic resource available to the government for the achievement of its development goals. Dam building in Laos has come under the same environmental and social scrutiny as dam building elsewhere in Southeast Asia. Just as the Bakun and Pak Mun dams became earlier iconic symbols of mega-dam activity, in the last decade the Nam Theun 2 dam was the focus in Laos. Originally proposed in the early 1990s, heavy opposition from environmentalists caused the World Bank to delay a loan decision. The economic crisis intervened, but the plan went back on track in July 2003 when the Thai cabinet approved an EGAT twenty-five-year purchasing power agreement, giving the green light to the Lao government and the developing consortium to go ahead. The dam, the largest in Laos, went on line in December 2010.

The new symbol of Laos's indifference to the security of the Mekong ecosystem is its decision to build a mainstream dam at Xayaburi, north of Vientiane, the first of a proposed five-dam cascade. Vigorously opposed by Thailand, Cambodia, and Vietnam, it was agreed in 2011 as a result of the PNPCA consultation process that more studies were necessary. Vietnam argued that no mainstream dam should be approved until 2020. The consensus was quickly broken, however, when suspended work on the Xayaburi dam was resumed. In March 2014, Laos reported that the dam was nearly 30 percent completed.

With a thumb in the MRC eye, in 2013 Laos announced that it was going to dam the Don Sahong channel of the Mekong, north of the Cambodian border, claiming that it was not mainstream. Over the strong objections of its MRC partners, Vientiane insisted that only notification, not PNPCA prior consultation, was required. However, at a January 2014 MRC meeting the issue was elevated to the Joint Council and, if no unanimity emerges there, ultimately to the heads of state. There was dismay, therefore, that the second MRC Summit in April 2014 did not address the issue. The summit's results left the

MRC with, as one critic put it, "a sense of malaise, a lack of leadership and papering-over of deep divisions on dam-building."[53] Not to be left out of the rush to harness the river, Cambodia's own ambitious dam-building program now includes plans for two mainstream dams at Stung Treng and Sambor.

The MRC is suffering a crisis of legitimacy and relevancy as the number of planned midstream Mekong dams increases, with more to come. China, Cambodia, and Laos have demonstrated that power production has priority over people and their environment. Vietnam is the most directly at risk from the multiple mainstream dams on the Mekong which will magnify effects of climate change that already threaten its delta regions.

NOTES

1. Khairulmaini Osman Salleh, "Climate Insecurity in Southeast Asia: Designing Policies to Reduce Vulnerabilities," in *Climate Change, Hydropolitics, and Transboundary Resources*, ed. David Michel and Amit Pandya (Washington, DC: Stimson Center, 2009), 33, accessed at http://www.stimson.org/books-reports/troubled -waters-climate-change-hydropolitics-and-resources.

2. James Clad and Aurora Medina Siy, "The Emergence of Ecological Issues in Southeast Asia," in *Southeast Asia in the New World Order: The Political Economy of a Dynamic Region*, ed. David Wurfel and Bruce Burton (New York: St. Martin's, 1996), 52.

3. The Rio Declaration can be accessed at http://www.unep.org/Documents/De fault.asp?DocumentID=78&ArticleID=1163.

4. Links to all of the declarations and statements can be accessed through the resources tab at http://www.evironmentasean.org/documentation.

5. "Indonesia and Climate Change: Current Status and Policies," accessed at http://sitesources.worldbank.org/INTINDONESIA/Resources/Environment/Climat eChange_Full_En.pdf.

6. The text of the Bali FLEG declaration can be accessed at http://siteresources .worldbank.org/INTINDONESIA/FLEG/20171550/EAP-FLEGjan03.pdf.

7. The "Statement" can be accessed at http://www.asean.org/communities/ asean-economic-community/item/asean-statement-on-strengthening-forest-law-en forcement-and-governance-fleg.

8. Environmental Investigative Agency, *Appetite for Destruction: China's Trade in Illegal Timber* (November 2012), accessed at http://www.eia-international.org/ appetite-for-destruction-chinas-trade-in-illegal-timber.

9. "China Accused over Burma Forests," BBC News, 18 October 2005.

10. EIA, *Appetite for Destruction*, 12.

11. "Group Says Illegal Logging Benefits Ruling Class in Cambodia," *International Herald Tribune*, 1 June 2007.

12. "Illegal Logging Hits Laos Forests," *Nation* (Bangkok), 1 April 2004; "Illegal Logs from Laos Fuel Mekong Region's Furniture Industry," *Straits Times* (Singapore), 22 March 2008.

13. "Laos Forests Feeding Vietnam Industry, Group Says," *Straits Times* (Singapore), 28 July 2011.

14. M. C. Hansen et al., "High-Resolution Global Maps of 21st Century Forest Cover Loss," *Science* 342, no. 6160 (15 November 2013): 850–53.

15. The figures were given by the secretary general of Indonesia's Forest Ministry as reported in "Map Shows Deforestation in Indonesia Is World's Fastest," *Jakarta Post*, 8 November 2013.

16. Forest Watch Indonesia, *Portret Keadaan Hutan Indonesia Periode 2000–2009* (Jakarta: FWI, 2011).

17. Greenpeace, "Certifying Destruction," September 2013, PDF accessed at http://www.greenpeace.org.

18. Ida Aju Pradnya Resosudarmo, "Shifting Power to the Periphery: The Impact of Decentralization on Forests and Forest People," in *Local Power and Politics in Indonesia: Decentralization & Democracy*, ed. Edward Aspinall and Greg Fealy (Singapore: ISEAS, 2003), 230–45.

19. As reported in "Indonesia Extends Logging Moratorium to Protect Rainforests," *Financial Times*, 15 May 2013.

20. "Corruption Allegations Cloud the Indonesia–Norway Billion Dollar Deal," accessed at http://www.redd-monitor.org/2010/09/21/corruption-allegations-cloud -the-indonesia-norway-billion-dollar-deal.

21. David Glover and Timothy Jessup, eds., *Indonesia's Fire and Haze: The Cost of Catastrophe* (Singapore: ISEAS, 1999).

22. "Indonesia Chides Singapore over Reactions on Haze Situation," Channel News Asia, 21 June 2013, accessed at http://www.channelnewsasia.com/news/speci alreports/mh370/news/indonesia-chides/717798.html.

23. The agreement can be accessed at http://haze.asean.org/?page_id=185.

24. "ASEAN Members Slow in Adopting Haze Monitoring System: Shanmugam," accessed at http://www.channelnewsasia.com/news/specialreports/mh370/news/ asean-members-slow-in/957922.html.

25. James Cotton, "The 'Haze' over Southeast Asia: Challenging the ASEAN Mode of Regional Engagement," *Pacific Affairs* 72, no. 3 (Fall 1999): 351.

26. Helen Mohamad Varkkey, "The ASEAN Way and Haze Mitigation Efforts," *Journal of International Studies* (Malaysia) 8 (2012): 89, accessed at http://www .academia.edu/2458600.

27. Yang Razali Kassim, "The Haze and ASEAN: Environmental Politics, Diplomacy and Stability," *RSIS Commentary* 121/2013 (July 2013), accessed at http:// www.eu-asiacentre.eu/pub_details.php?pub_id=106.

28. David Rosenberg, "Environmental Pollution around the South China Sea: Developing a Regional Response," *Contemporary Southeast Asia* 21, no. 1 (April 1999): 142.

29. East Asian Seas Regional Coordinating Unit, *Transboundary Diagnostic Analysis for the South China Sea*, EAS/CRU Technical Report No. 14, accessed

at http://www.unepscs.org/remository/Download/14_-_South_China_Sea_Project_Knowledge_Documents.html.

30. The COBSEA website is http://www.cobsea.org.

31. Documents can be accessed through links at http://www.unepscs.org.

32. The Putrajaya Declaration and other documents can be accessed through the publications link at http://www.pemsea.org.

33. David Rosenberg, "Governing the South China Sea: From Freedom of the Seas to Ocean Enclosure Movements," *Harvard Asia Quarterly* 12, nos. 3–4 (Winter 2012): 4–12.

34. The low figure is from the Indonesian Ministry of Maritime Affairs and Fisheries and the high figure from an industry group, the People's Coalition for Fisheries, accessed at http://www.aseannews.net/illegal-fishing-costs-indonesia-3-billion-dollars-a-year.

35. Ambassador I Gede Ngurah Swajaya, as quoted in "A Lot More Talk by ASEAN than Action," accessed at http://www.aseannews.net/a-lot-more-talk-by-asean-than-action.

36. Scott Bentley, "Mapping the Nine-Dash Line: Recent Incidents Involving Indonesia in the South China Sea," *Strategist* (Australia), 29 October 2013, accessed at http://www.aspistrategist.org.au.

37. Lucio Blanco Pitlo, "Fishing Wars: Competition for South China Sea's Fishery Resources," International Relations and Security Network (10 July 2013), accessed at http://isnblog.ethz.ch/security/fishing-wars-competition-for-south-china-seas-fishery-resources.

38. World Commission on Dams, *Dams and Development: A New Framework for Decision Making* (London: Earthscan, 2000). It is also available as a PDF file at http://www.unep.org/dams/wcd.

39. The Southeast Asian dams were, in Indonesia, the Seguling; in Malaysia, the Muda and Semeyih; in the Philippines, the Magat and Pantabangan; in Thailand, the Bhumibol, Lam Pao, Pak Mun, and Sirindhorn; and in Vietnam, the Nui Coc and Ea Yu dams.

40. "Mahathir Slams Critics of Dam Project," *Straits Times* (Singapore), 17 March 1996.

41. So labeled in Transparency International's "Global Corruption Report 2005," accessed at http://www.transparency.org/whatwedo/pub/global_corruption_report_2005_corruption_in_construction_and_post_conflict.

42. "Hydro Tasmania to Withdraw from Sarawak Dam Building Program," Environment News Service, 5 December 2012, accessed at http://www.ens-newswire.com/2012/12/05/hydro-tasmania-to-withdraw-from-sarawak-dam-building-program.

43. The text of the letter can be accessed at http://www.president-office.gov.mm/en/?q=briefing-room/statements-and-releases/2011/09/30/id-230.

44. David Dapice, "China and Yunnan Economic Relations with Myanmar and Kachin State: Powering the Peace Process," accessed at http://ash.harvard.edu/extensions/ash/docs/chinayunna.pdf.

45. For an overview of China's Myanmar rethink, see Yun Sun, "China Adapts to a New Myanmar Reality," *Asia Times*, 23 December 2013, accessed at http://atimes.com/atimes/Southeast_Asia/SEA-04-231213.html.

46. For the Salween dams, see the links at http://www.internationalrivers.org/campaigns/salween-dams.

47. For the convention, see http://legal.un.org/avl/ha/clnuiw/clnuiw.html.

48. For documents and details, see the Mekong River Commission's website at http://www.mrcmekong.org.

49. *Strategic Environmental Assessment of Hydropower on the Mekong Main Stream*, accessed at http://www.mrcmekong.org/assets/Publications/Consultations/SEA-Hydropower/SEA-FR-summary-13oct.pdf.

50. "Thailand Opposes Lower Mekong Dams," *Bangkok Post*, 1 July 2010.

51. Kaori Ohsawa et al., *Lancang-Mekong: A River of Controversy* (Berkeley, CA: International Rivers Network, 2003).

52 Alex Liebman, "Trickle-Down Hegemony? China's 'Peaceful Rise' and Dam Building on the Mekong," *Contemporary Southeast Asia* 27, no. 2 (August 2005): 281.

53. Tom Fawthrop, "Mekong Summit Struggles to Halt Devastating Dams," *The Diplomat* (Tokyo), 9 April 2014, accessed at http://thediplomat.com/2014/04/mekong-summit-struggles-to-halt-devastating-dams.

SUGGESTIONS FOR FURTHER READING

Peter Boomgaard, *Southeast Asia: An Environmental History* (Santa Barbara, CA: ABC-CLIO, 2007); Victor T. King, *Environmental Challenges in Southeast Asia* (New York: Routledge, 2013); James Fahn, *A Land on Fire: Environmental Consequences of the Southeast Asian Boom* (Boulder, CO: Westview Press, 2003); Lorraine Elliott and Mely Caballero-Anthony, eds., *Human Security and Climate Change in Southeast Asia* (New York: Routledge, 2013); Henriette Litta, *Regimes in Southeast Asia: An Analysis of Environmental Cooperation* (Wiesbaden: Springer, 2012); Sarinanda Singh, *Natural Potency and Political Power: Forests and State Authority in Contemporary Laos* (Honolulu: University of Hawaii Press, 2012); Paruedee Nguitragool, *Environmental Cooperation in Southeast Asia: ASEAN's Regime for Trans-boundary Haze Pollution* (New York: Routledge, 2011); Ian Charles Campbell, *The Mekong: Biophysical Environment of an International River Basin* (New York: Routledge, 2013); François Molle, Tira Foran, and Mira Kokonan, eds., *Contested Waterscapes in the Mekong Region: Hydropower, Livelihoods and Governance* (Singapore: ISEAS, 2010); Jim Glassiman, *Bounding the Mekong: The Asian Development Bank, China, and Thailand* (Honolulu: University of Hawaii Press, 2010).

Chapter Eleven

Conclusion: Nation-States, ASEAN, and Autonomy

The substance of international relations in Southeast Asia consists of transactions based on a complex array of broad national interests pursued by the state and nonstate actors in the region. In discussing regional international relations, policy makers and academics tend to first look at issues in interest areas that focus on security in the basic sense of defense of sovereignty, territorial integrity, and populations. Traditional security interests are singularly important as providing the political framework for states to exist and function in an international system regulated by interstate relations. A fixation on security, however, gives only a partial glimpse of the full range of interests that informs the agendas being pursued by the actors. The chapters in this book have attempted to show the scope of traditional and nontraditional interests that are in play and the kinds of policies that have been chosen to further those interests as well as the clash of interest priorities.

THE STATE AS ACTOR

The starting point for this study has been the state as the primary international actor. While acknowledging the intellectual richness of international relations theory, by centering attention on the state actor and national interests, one almost perforce arrives at a realist perspective. The emergence of ASEAN as a protoinstitutional fixture in the region's international relations has in recent years and academic quarters, particularly in Southeast Asia itself, skewed inquiry away from the state to the role of a hypothesized ASEAN actor. An ASEAN-centered approach to analysis, however, tends to blur the fact that the Southeast Asian nation-states have conceded no sovereignty, supranational authority, or capabilities to ASEAN that could regulate, limit, or prohibit independent action by any member state. ASEAN has neither the political qualities nor the power to act independently of its ten controlling member states. In the ASEAN context, the state's claim to sovereignty, as we have repeatedly seen, is affirmatively formulated as the principle of non-interference. We have underlined the fact that firm adherence to the founding principles of ASEAN sets sensitive political limits to the effectiveness of ASEAN's cooperative arrangements.

In the regional Southeast Asian international setting, as in the global nation-state system, it is the national decision makers—the state's policy elite—who set the priorities of national interests to be pursued and make the choice of policy tools as related to the vitality of the state's interests. These decisions not only involve rational ends–means, risks–rewards calculations, but also have a nonrational affective ideational underpinning of nationalism. The potent identity for Southeast Asian policy makers is their national identity, not an attachment to an abstract ASEAN identity which has no local markers. As has been pointed out in several of the preceding chapters, nationalisms in Southeast Asia are not necessarily secular but can reflect deeper emotions than simply the state, for example, ethnicity, religion, and historical grievances. When nationalist passions are aroused, the task of peaceful resolution of disputes becomes more difficult. One cannot fully understand the nationalist framework of the Preah Vihear dispute without an appreciation of long-standing historical animosities in the Thailand–Cambodia bilateral relationship. Similarly, Singapore's ofttime testy relationships with its Malaysian and Indonesian neighbors cannot be fully explicated without understanding how Singapore's success as an ethnic Chinese state leads to resentments in Jakarta and Kuala Lumpur. Even states with similar ethnicity and religion such as Malaysia and Indonesia can have their relationships disturbed by competitive nationalisms, with each feeling culturally superior to the other.

The foreign policy tools that are utilized in Southeast Asia are those of traditional statecraft, from diplomacy and suasion to coercion. The argument that has been made here is that it is the member states' policy outputs that determine the course of ASEAN, not the other way around. The policy makers' choices are limited by the state's capability to act to support its interests in the international environment. That capability is the manifestation of power, which is relative to the power of other states and to the issue areas in which it is wielded. Nowhere is the gap between interest and relative capability more clear in Southeast Asia than in the South China Sea conflicts where Vietnam's and the Philippines' national interests have been explicitly defined as defense of their territorial and maritime rights. However, their capabilities are no match for China, either bilaterally or through ineffectual appeals for a regional ASEAN common front. The fact that both Vietnam and China are ruled by supposedly "fraternal" communist parties has no bearing on the conflict—at least from China's side. The Philippines' clear response, and more ambiguously Vietnam's, is that of classic realist state behavior: to seek a balance of power, with the United States as the balancer. The critical decision making for the two Southeast Asian states, and realistically for ASEAN, will take place in Beijing and Washington, not Southeast Asia, and will be based on US and Chinese interests in the totality of their bilateral relations, not just Southeast Asian.

The working out of relations between and among nations in Southeast Asia, while based on real capabilities, takes place in a normative framework that is both universal and regional. It has its origins in international law and the principles of the Charter of the United Nations. These have been augmented and enhanced in the regional setting by formal reference to the Bandung Principles, UNCLOS, the TAC, and other expressions of regional norms and injunctive rules of conduct alluded to in the text: the ASEAN Charter, the AHRD, and the DOC. Despite the almost reflexive invocations of the norms by Southeast Asian foreign ministers and heads of government, they provide no guide to international practice in Southeast Asia and do not replace national interests as independent variables in the decision making of Southeast Asian national elites. They are among the items that have to be factored into policy cost-benefit analyses on a case-by-case basis depending on the issue area and the actors involved. Unless there are measures of censure and enforcement, the deterrent to violation of norms in the Southeast Asian regional subsystem is, as it is in the global system, reciprocity and retaliation, but this too involves calculation of relative power.

Again in Southeast Asia, nowhere is the gap between normative rules governing state behavior and the application of those rules more obvious than in the South China Sea. Chapter 6 detailed the years-long tortuous history of drafting a Code of Conduct in the South China Sea. What the Southeast Asian states understand, but will not openly address, is the fact that every proposed element of the COC already exists in other documents to which China is a party: TAC, DOC, UNCLOS, and other bilateral and multilateral engagements that China has made in the region. The ASEAN proponents of the COC say that it will be different. It will be "binding," a position that China rejects. Even if it were "binding," how would it be enforced? The ASEAN countries so far have been unable or unwilling to confront China in a unified challenge to its refusal to adhere to the norms in place. This is because member states have different national interests that might be put at risk in calling China out. China fully understands that the state, not ASEAN, is the primary actor and insists that all disputes be bilateral, a relationship that for China means might makes right.

Within ASEAN, the greatest gap between norms and application is in the organization's commitment to democracy and promise to promote and protect human rights. Chapters 4 and 9 outlined the diplomatic process through which these elements of democratizing Indonesia's agenda became grudgingly incorporated into the ASEAN textual fabric. It is not that the reluctant states, particularly the CLMV authoritarians, had been persuaded to change their ways, but that they were deferring to Indonesia's critical importance to ASEAN. As state actors in an organization that abides by the rules of sovereignty and noninterference, the CLMV countries could accept the norms on paper to mollify Indonesia but remain free to ignore them. There would be neither censure nor retaliation. ASEAN's consistency in being unable to address the egregious violation of human rights by its member states, most recently in Myanmar against the Rohingya, mocks ASEAN's claim to moral authority by virtue of its charter.

The discussion in chapters 9 and 10 of nontraditional interest areas of international relations in Southeast Asia also showed the primary role of the state. Regardless of global and regional treaties, agreements, or other multilateral undertakings in ASEAN or other formats, actual policy formation and implementation is based on the individual state's decision making and capabilities. A state's action or inaction can be crucial in transboundary environmental issues.

The lack of both Indonesian political will and enforcement capabilities has stalled for more than a decade the prevention and mitigation measures pressed by the signatories of the Haze Pollution Agreement. The Lao PDR's unilateralism in Mekong dam construction poses a greater threat to Vietnam's future security than China's actions in the South China Sea. Despite years of collection of scientific and technical data, multiple workshops, and Track II deliberations, there are no Track I intergovernmental programs through which real resources have been mobilized to address jointly the management and conservation of the SCS's fisheries.

WHERE DOES ASEAN FIT IN?

An important theme of the book is that ASEAN is only a piece of the pattern of international relations in Southeast Asia. We do not pretend to have looked at all of the pieces but certainly have demonstrated that the processing of international relations in Southeast Asia is not unique to the region because of ASEAN. Despite the protestations of ASEAN cultural reductionists, Southeast Asia is not analytically sui generis. It is a regional setting for a state-based international relations subsystem. ASEAN is an intergovernmental arrangement for the promotion of interstate cooperation in areas of state activity where there is a high degree of complementarity of member states' interests. This covers a large part of what might be called the gristmill of international relations: immigration, transportation, telecommunication, education, and credentialing, to mention only a few of the areas of the sometimes mundane matters that states deal with in their routine interactions. Certainly, in these functional areas of state responsibilities, ASEAN has facilitated in a top-down way the flow of interstate transactions. Facilitation is not integration. The transactions are still those of sovereign nation-states, not a regionalization through an ASEAN institution.

ASEAN has been important in providing a structured forum in which the member states can collectively engage their extraregional interlocutors. The discussion in the book emphasized this aspect of ASEAN. From this vantage, ASEAN can be seen as a diplomatic caucus or concert in which the member states can gain a politically amplified hearing by dialogue partners. In ASEAN + 1, ASEAN + 3, and ASEAN + 10 settings, the grouping has been able to elicit commitments and pledges that might not be as forthcoming on just a bilateral state-to-state basis. But the commitments and pledges are fulfilled in bilateral arrangements.

From the 2003 Bali Concord II to the present, the bureaucratic managers of ASEAN have been busy with action plans and blueprints designed to give policy substance to the conceptual vagueness of the leaders' 1997 Vision 2020. A key question, looking to the future, is whether the formal establishment of the ASEAN Community in December 2015 will change ASEAN's international role, its functions, or the ASEAN way. The realist's answer is no.

To answer the first of the three questions posed at the end of chapter 1: the national leaders have not succeeded in reinventing ASEAN as a more effective collaborative mechanism. An examination of the buildup to the AC shows that there has been no significant alteration in ASEAN's modus operandi or its relationship to the member states. The AC and its three "pillars"—the AEC, ASCC, and APSC—have no institutionalized integral structures independent from the policy will of member states. Nor does it appear that there has been an injection of new policy content that would allow community interests to have priority over national interests. Furthermore, it has no real community political culture that could provide a common ASEAN political platform. In fact, in many respects the significant divergences among the member states that have been pointed out in the preceding chapters have greater impact on "community" policy making than was the case at ASEAN's inception. If anything, ASEAN's expansion has widened the qualitative and quantitative divisions in ASEAN, not closed them.

In short, there is little to distinguish the ASEAN Community from ASEAN, the association. The AC is a bureaucratic reframing of a voluntary association of sovereign states within which efforts are made to find areas of cooperation in the pursuit of shared interests. Where these efforts have been most successful has been in interest areas unrelated to vital national security objectives and in areas that do not negatively affect vested domestic economic or political interests. Public health stands out in this respect, with the response to SARS, HIV/AIDS, and avian flu being examples.

The APSC

For ASEAN's international standing, the most important of the subcommunities is the ASEAN Political-Security Community. The APSC blueprint envisaged ASEAN to be a rules-based community of shared values and norms, a cohesive, peaceful, stable, and resilient region with shared responsibility for comprehensive security. As the discussion has shown, these goals are as remote today as they were in 2003. We have seen that Indonesia's plan for the APSC was eviscerated in the name of consensus.

Democracy and Human Rights

A particular disappointment was ASEAN's collective abandonment of actions—rather than words—in the defense of democracy and human rights. One of the questions raised in chapter 1 was whether the political values gap between ASEAN and the West in these areas of international concern could be narrowed through democratization and regime change in Southeast Asia. What little new democratic space has been won has been matched by democratic erosion elsewhere, especially in Thailand where in May 2014 a democratically elected government was ousted by a military coup. Even where democracy exists, as in Indonesia, it is under constant assault from poor governance, corruption, ethnic violence, and religious sectarianism. The APSC, despite its ASEAN Charter tasking, has not furthered democratization in Southeast Asia. The ASEAN way seems to have no place for democracy. In fact, the ASEAN way has made ASEAN a conservative, illiberal defender through inaction of authoritarianism and human rights violators.

Democracy and human rights are the most politicized items on the nontraditional international relations agenda. There is a perceptual gulf between Southeast Asia and the liberal West. Public advocacy for human rights raises the question of what the best foreign policy approach to encourage change might be: confrontation, constructive engagement, or behind-the-scenes quiet diplomacy. The experience in Southeast Asia suggests that where successes have been achieved, no matter how modest, effective human rights advocacy requires activity in all three policy approaches. The question of human rights in the international relations of Southeast Asia is not one of absolute versus relative or East versus West. It is where and with what priority specific rights issues fit into the national interests of the state actors in their complex networks of bi- and multilateral interactions.

For China, there is little problem in identifying its disinterest in Southeast Asian human rights issues. For China, to support Southeast Asian resistance to US and EU pressure on human rights violations is to defend its own poor human rights record. China, however, unlike Southeast Asian rights violators, has such enormous economic importance to the West that it is relatively immune from sanctions and can ignore the rhetoric. It is much more complicated for the United States. All of the interests involved must be considered in a decision-making milieu where the voices of Congress and advocacy NGOs have weight. The results sometimes seem puzzling to hard-core realists who see US assaults on the rights record of allies and friends as counterproductive in terms of the US–Southeast Asia–China triangle. To political liberals, however, it is necessary as evidence, even if imperfect and inconsistent, of the commitment of the United States to the global cause of human rights.

The APSC's Crisis Management

The ASEAN foreign ministers provide the critical interface between ASEAN and its external partners. As a ministerial group they function in the ASEAN Community at three levels: the AMM, the APSC Community Council, and the Coordinating Council. Wearing their foreign ministers' hats, they operate simultaneously in two different policy realms—ASEAN and national— which at times, as has been pointed out, may be difficult to harmonize, as in the Cambodia–Thailand bilateral relationship or the July 2012 failed AMM. The ASEAN Charter's Article 41 charges the foreign ministers with providing the strategic policy directions for ASEAN external relations, in essence a kind of ten-headed ASEAN "foreign ministry," each minister working from national interest agendas. They are tasked with developing and coordinating common positions and directions to pursue joint actions on the basis of unity and solidarity. This is to be carried out in a way that ensures consistency and coherence in the conduct of ASEAN's external relations.

In intra-ASEAN and external challenges heavily weighted with political, security, and strategic considerations, the APSC's crisis management has had little influence on outcomes. This is the case in the South China Sea conflicts discussed in detail in chapter 6, but that is only the latest example of ASEAN's inability to develop common positions in support of regional peace, stability, nonuse of force, and peaceful resolution of disputes. In cases where the foreign ministers have conflicting views of national interest, the prescribed course of a consistent, coherent, joint action on the basis of unity and solidarity has not emerged. But this too is part of the ASEAN way. The Bali Concord II which laid out the framework for the APSC, recognized the sovereign right of the individual countries to pursue their individual foreign policies and defense arrangements, and the Vientiane Action Programme for the APSC specifically eschewed a joint ASEAN foreign policy.

The success or failure of particular programs, units, or structures embraced in the AEC and the ASCC does not really affect the integrity of ASEAN the organization or its international credibility. They seem to have a momentum that does not depend on the high politics of the APSC. A failed APSC, however, would seriously damage the international credibility of ASEAN. Its workings provide the political cement for the organization's international facade. The cement is weakening, and cracks are appearing. The APSC is being critically tested in its handling of the South China Sea conflicts. Chapter 6 alluded to the Bali Concord II's foundational premise of the APSC, that the member states "regard their security as fundamentally linked to one another, bound by geographic location, common vision, and objectives." The history of disputes and conflicts involving ASEAN states has shown, however, that there is no common fundamental security linkage. Security in ASEAN is divisible by ten. A threat to one is not a threat to all. President Yudhoyono, in his October 2009 second inaugural address, characterized Indonesia's foreign policy as being one of "a thousand friends and zero enemies." He was describing "a strategic environment in which no country perceives Indonesia as an enemy and there is no country that Indonesia considers an enemy."[1] It is doubtful that either the Philippines or Vietnam could say the same. This is neither their strategic environment nor necessarily the future strategic environment of other South China Sea littoral states as China's ambitions are translated by force into reality.

At a number of points in the text we have referenced the fact that rather than being bound together by geography, as the Bali Concord II would have it, there is a deepening strategic interest divide between continental Southeast Asia and maritime Southeast Asia. The 2014 Thai military coup punctuates the collapse of democracy at the GMS's center. It is possible that national interest tied to China in the GMS could rival in the future the continental states' interests in ASEAN. It has already led to stalemate in the APSC's crisis management, preventing specific references to China's actions in the SCS or endorsing the littoral states' position that the nine-dash line is illegal. We have noted the ASEAN foreign ministers' May 2014 statement in response to the appeals for ASEAN intervention by Vietnam and the Philippines regarding China's newest provocative intrusions in the states' respective EEZs. Although the foreign ministers expressed concern about the developments that had increased tension, they urged all parties concerned to exercise self-restraint and avoid actions that could undermine peace and stability.[2] Tellingly, this seemed to apportion responsibility for the situation equally between their aggrieved ASEAN partners and China. ASEAN secretary general Le Luong Minh caused a furor when he accused China of violating the DOC and said ASEAN had to get China out of Vietnam's territorial waters.[3] China's foreign ministry spokesman called Le's comments a "Vietnamese provocation" and said that "in advocating a certain country's claim" he was sending the wrong signals on ASEAN's position of not taking sides.[4]

The Issue of ASEAN's Centrality

The institutional and political inability of the APSC—the ASEAN foreign ministers—to act in concert when faced by a strategic crisis raises serious questions about ASEAN's claim to centrality in regional international relations. A corporate goal of ASEAN, citing the ASEAN Charter, Article 14:1, is "to maintain the centrality and proactive role of ASEAN as the primary driving force in its relations and cooperation with external partners in a regional architecture that is open, transparent, and inclusive." This statement is a recurring formula in ASEAN's multilateralism represented in the ARF, the ADMM-Plus, the AMF, and the EAS, as well as underpinning ASEAN + 1, ASEAN + 3, and other ASEAN-plus dialogues. But the real sinews of Southeast Asian states' international relations are their bilateral political and economic ties within the region and especially to external Asian, American, and European powers. The assertion that an ASEAN centrality and proactive role is the "driving force" in regional international relations gives the concept a political content that remains undefined.

What "centrality" in practice seems to mean is the creation of the multiple multilateral fora in which ASEAN member states as a group can interact with external partners in a way that assures that they are not politically marginalized. By engaging the great and not-so-great powers in regular and structured regional platforms for dialogue and diplomatic exchange, ASEAN has gained an international identity independent of the bilateral relations of the member states. It can be argued that in this way ASEAN is fashioning CBMs. Undoubtedly, the regional and extraregional states' interests in and policy commitments to ASEAN have contributed to peace and stability in Southeast Asia. Yet when political and security stakes are high, ASEAN influence on state behavior gives way to national interest and traditional instruments of foreign policy. The South China Sea conflicts suggest that ASEAN is not central, as it accepts China's insistence that the group keep the issue off their multilateral agendas. Faced with the most critical issue facing them, the ASEAN foreign ministers in their APSC hats retreat to the political margins of near irrelevancy in terms of dispute resolution. Nevertheless, Indonesian president Yudhoyono in his plenary session remarks at the May 2013 Twenty-Fourth ASEAN Summit could still argue that "the ASEAN Political-Security Community will enhance the joint capacity to address security challenges."[5]

A Question of Leadership

Alice Ba summed up the issues succinctly, writing that for ASEAN to maintain its influence and claim to centrality, "it will have to demonstrate its own organizational coherence and clarity of leadership."[6] The hoped for clarity of leadership is not going to emerge through the formal annual rotation of the ASEAN chairmanship, with each chair having his own national interest agenda. Also the rule of consensus holds proactive, forward-looking initiatives hostage to the reluctant. Of all the ASEAN states, Indonesia has had the greatest potential for leadership. President Yudhoyono's two foreign ministers, Hassan and Marty, worked to give substance to the promises of the APSC, seeking to transfer Indonesia's experience in democratization to ASEAN and to move the grouping toward a political and strategic coherence necessary to be an effective actor in shaping the regional security environment. In ASEAN, Indonesia is chair only once a decade, and even as chair in 2003 and 2011 its initiatives were blunted by the need for consensual solidarity. Indonesia showed its latent soft-power capabilities within the ASEAN framework when Foreign Minister Marty Natalegawa, with no brief from the Cambodian ASEAN chair, rescued the July 2012 AMM.

Indonesia has gone along with the ASEAN consensus on the South China Sea. With no territorial claims of its own, Jakarta had hoped that it might be able to mediate. Foreign Minister Marty even offered himself in May 2014 as a possible mediator between Vietnam and China. However, a new Indonesian government will be processing the policy implications of the nine-dash line and China's possible maritime claims in Indonesia's EEZ and on its continental shelf. The future government will not have the same ten-year investment in ASEAN solidarity that President Yudhoyono and his two foreign ministers had. Indonesian interests in its maritime zones are analogous to Vietnam's and the Philippines' in their zones. In the latter cases, it is clear that the APSC has rebuffed them. A major question that will confront Indonesia in the APSC is whether an ASEAN consensual position that prioritizes the GMS states' ties to China over the maritime interests of the ASEAN SCS littoral states is in Indonesia's national interests.

This is not the first time the problem of measuring the relative importance of ASEAN solidarity as opposed to national interests has faced Jakarta decision makers. It is part of an ongoing debate in Jakarta about a post-ASEAN or possible ASEAN-plus foreign policy. Rizal Sukma, a well-known Indonesian foreign policy analyst with a realist outlook, complaining that Indonesia puts solidarity with ASEAN above other interests, argued that "Indonesia should free itself from any undeserving obligation to follow the wishes of any state or a grouping of states, including ASEAN, if by doing so we sacrifice our own national interests."[7] In the same realist vein, Jusuf Wanandi, an intellectual leader in the first Indonesian foreign policy think tank, pointed out that ASEAN was only an instrument of Indonesian foreign policy and if the instrument does not do the job of securing national interests, other instruments can be utilized.[8] Indonesia's attitude toward the APSC's political qualities is critical since, as we quoted Dewi Anwar in chapter 2, ASEAN needs Indonesia more than Indonesia needs ASEAN. Whatever centrality ASEAN may claim in regional international relations depends on the centrality of Indonesia in ASEAN.

President Yudhoyono continues to insist that ASEAN is the cornerstone of Indonesia's foreign policy. However, as the image of China's peaceful rise is blurred in Southeast Asia by the reality of its regional great-power ambitions, that cornerstone, in particular the APSC, may not be a firm basis for guaranteeing Indonesia's national security interests. The South China Sea question for Indonesia and its ASEAN partners is magnified by its direct link to the broader strategic challenge of contending Chinese and American interests in Southeast Asia and how the regional states will relate to them. The policy choices made by Yudhoyono's successors will be consequential not just for ASEAN but for the dynamically evolving Southeast Asian strategic environment.

THE SUBORDINATE REGIONAL STATE SYSTEM

A subordinate Southeast Asian regional international system was defined in chapter 1 as one in which the policy autonomy of the regional states is constrained by controlling political and economic forces originating in the dominant global state system, itself driven by the interests of the great powers. Nothing in this study of international relations in Southeast Asia suggests that after more than six decades of independence the basic political structure of the subordinate system has fundamentally changed. What has changed are the kinds of adaptive demands being made on the Southeast Asian states. The bipolarity of the Cold War is being replaced by an emerging new great-power regional bipolarity in which China has replaced the USSR as the countervailing great power. In the new bipolarity, the advantages the United States once held of near political and security hegemony are challenged by China in a way the USSR was not capable of, in particular, a new kind of "big stick" of economic access to China.

As the dynamics of great-power relations in Southeast Asia shift from American preponderance to a great-power relationship based on China's rise and a US "pivot" or "rebalance," a more complex political and security environment for the Southeast Asian states has resulted. In this environment, ASEAN postures itself as nonthreatening to either China or the United States. ASEAN does not want to be forced to take sides. This has led to intra-ASEAN political paralysis when, by not taking sides, it leaves a member state without community support and forces it to go outside of ASEAN for external support: to the UN, international courts, or an ally. The second question at the end of chapter 1 asked if ASEAN can maintain its claim to "centrality" in maneuvering between China and the United States. The answer is that ASEAN is not central to the great-power relationship, which involves economic, political, and strategic stakes that include Southeast Asia, but not as the defining issue area. Furthermore, it is not just a tug of war between China and the United States for influence in the region. At different points in the text we have indicated that other external actors, in particular Japan and India, are significant for the region. Both India and Japan have security as well as economic interests as they project higher regional profiles. Their close ties to the United States include shared democratic values, which still has ideological resonance in Southeast Asia. While the EU is also important, it does not have the proximate presence that the other significant actors have.

For the ASEAN states, economic security is a vital interest that, if not coequal to political security, is still very important. The region's economic and political stability depend on predictable peaceful relations between China and the United States. The Southeast Asian states have attempted to manage their place in the new bipolarity by enmeshing the external powers in a web of bilateral and multilateral economic arrangements and partnerships, many of which were described in chapter 8. In one sense, this can be described as an ASEAN economic hub-and-spoke system in which ASEAN is at the hub of economic spokes running to China, the United States, Japan, and other ASEAN + 1 partners. This is another meaning for ASEAN centrality. Each of the ASEAN states has its own network of bilateral economic relations with China, the United States, and other important trade and investment partners. The hope is that growing regionwide economic interdependencies with both the United States and China will have a political spillover, helping to mediate their regional great-power bilateral relations through a common interest in a stable and peaceful region in which they can pursue their interests in a win-win fashion. Paradoxically, it is through such a web of economic interdependencies that the region seeks greater policy autonomy.

Interdependency is implicit in Indonesia's ideal structuring of its great-power relations in a regional order that is characterized as a "dynamic equilibrium." This is a system in which there is no preponderant power. It would be based on enmeshing all of the state actors in a network of inclusive overlapping and interlocking multilateral structures. The cement would be mutually reinforcing interests through which all countries can gain and prosper. The notion of such a "dynamic equilibrium" seems to have become the ASEAN default position. In such a structure, according to President Yudhoyono, the middle and smaller states, which would not have a foot in either the American or Chinese camp, could contribute to the management of a stable and cooperative relationship between China and the United States on the basis of, in Yudhoyono's phrasing, "morally binding" rules and norms of peace and cooperation, but then, realistically, he added an important caveat: "if adhered to."[9] The operational weakness of the "dynamic equilibrium" model is that it does not explain how we get from here to there.

The "dynamic equilibrium" paradigm rests on assumptions that can be questioned. The first is that economic interests would override the announced political and strategic goals of China, which are to exercise sovereignty and jurisdiction over the South China Sea and exclude the United States as a great power in what China sees as its Southeast Asian sphere of interest. The second is that it assumes that China cannot have it both ways: growing economic relations with ASEAN and salami-slicing ASEAN on land and sea at the same time. China has made it clear that ASEAN's economic interests in the relationship with China would be damaged if it internationalized what China insists are bilateral disputes. On the other hand, ASEAN or individual ASEAN states have not suggested to China that its economic interests in ASEAN might be damaged by aggressive behavior. Finally, it assumes that China has a greater interest in the ASEAN collective than it does in its relations with ASEAN's individual states.

There are few who would not concede that the relative power relationship of the United States and China in Southeast Asia has altered in the past decade. That does not necessarily mean that the United States and China are in a zero-sum power game for influence in Southeast Asia. The changing relationship poses strategic questions for all three involved—the United States, Southeast Asia, and China. Is US great-power dominance a necessary condition for the defense and promotion of US national interests in Southeast Asia? Can Chinese aspirations and interests accommodate a US stake in Southeast Asia's future? If the answer to the first question is yes, and to the second, no, then the future political environment of the region will be marked by tension and insecurities. A third question is what can the Southeast Asian states do themselves to help the Americans and Chinese shape their answers? This relates to the third question asked at the end of chapter 1 about possible outcomes as the struggle for autonomy continues.

In the worst-case scenario, Southeast Asia will be sucked into the vortex of China's rise as part of a China-centric satellite system. This would put an end to any claim of ASEAN's centrality. This conclusion or other variants of a future Chinese paramountcy is highly deterministic. It leaves out of consideration the fact that, with perhaps two exceptions, Southeast Asia has more to lose than gain economically in a closed regional structure centered on China. The China-rules outcome ignores the US great-power role in Southeast Asia which, in addition to the hard power represented by the "pivot," is paralleled by the soft power of democracy and support for the Southeast Asian norms that China flaunts. In the framework of the US political commitment to stay the great-power course in the region, enhanced US military-to-military and security assistance ties to Southeast Asian states give material evidence of the US power presence.

Of course, the credibility of the American security guarantee remains to be tested. Friendly Southeast Asian leaders were not impressed by the US handling of the Russian invasion of Crimea or the refusal to give military assistance to Syrian insurgents. Furthermore, President Obama's April 2014 visits to Malaysia and the Philippines, while reassuring, left questions as to the conditions under which the United States would come to the defense of its friends and allies in the case of Chinese use of force. China was quick to seize on the president's unwillingness to address the issue to tell Southeast Asia, don't depend on the Americans.

Indonesia could have a decisive voice in setting the future course for the region. It is Southeast Asia's largest country with the largest economy and has positioned itself as a middle power. As the preceding chapters have shown, it is unlikely that its basic political and security interests can be promoted through ASEAN. Indonesia has been ambivalent about the American "pivot," and it has been assiduously courted by China to stay neutral on the South China Sea. The Chinese foreign minister called his Indonesian counterpart after the May 2014 ASEAN Summit to complain that Vietnam was damaging ASEAN's relations with China. It would not be unless or until Indonesia disengages from the ASEAN consensus and the concentration on the COC and engages China directly on the real issues of conflict in the South China Sea that its "natural" regional leadership role could come into play. China can limit a Cambodia- and LPDR-led ASEAN consensus, but it could not ignore an Indonesia that had distanced itself from that consensus. This would give greater weight to the Indonesia–Vietnam strategic partnership as the north–south axis of a maritime Southeast Asian grouping of states that might offer a more imposing negotiating platform from which to deal with China as well as linking their security interests. In this kind of regional international environment it would be accepted, as President Obama said in Manila in May

2014, that China with its economy and population would be a dominant actor, but in which security is maintained, not by a "dynamic equilibrium," but by the workings of a balance of power that included the United States and that could be extended to India, Australia, and Japan. Of course, Beijing would call this "containment."

NOTES

1. Accessed at http://www.presidenri.go.id/index.php/pidato/2005/05/19/332 .html.

2. "ASEAN Foreign Ministers' Statement on Developments in the South China Sea," 10 May 2014, accessed at http://www.asean.org/news/asean-statement-commu niques/item/asean-foreign-ministers-statement-on-the-current-developments-in-the -south-china-sea.

3. "China Must Exit Disputed Waters, ASEAN Leader Says," *Wall Street Journal*, 16 May 2014.

4. "China Demands ASEAN Neutrality over South China Sea," *Straits Times* (Singapore), 19 May 2014.

5. As quoted in "ASEAN Security Community Solution for Security Challenges: President Yudhoyono," Antara News, accessed at http://www.antaranews.com/en/ news/93985/asean-security-community-solution-for-security-challenges-president -yudhoyono.

6. Alice D. Ba, *(Re)Negotiating East and Southeast Asia: Region, Regionalism, and the Association of Southeast Asian Nations* (Stanford, CA: Stanford University Press, 2009), 222.

7. As quoted in Barry Desker, "Is Indonesia Outgrowing ASEAN?" *RSIS Commentary*, no. 125/2010 (29 September 2010), accessed at http://www.rsis.edu.sg/ wp-content/uploads/2014/07/RSIS1252010.pdf.

8. Jusuf Wanandi, "Insight: RI's Foreign Policy and the Meaning of ASEAN," *Jakarta Post*, 6 May 2008.

9. President Yudhoyono, keynote speech, IISS Shangri-La Conference, 1 June 2012, accessed at http://presidenri.go.id/index.php/eng/pidato/2012/06/01/1867.html.

Appendix I

Provisions of the 1992 ASEAN Declaration on the South China Sea

1. EMPHASIZE the necessity to resolve all sovereignty and jurisdictional issues pertaining to the South China Sea by peaceful means without resort to use of force;
2. URGE all parties concerned to exercise restraint with the view to creating a positive climate for the eventual resolution of all disputes;
3. RESOLVE, without prejudicing the sovereignty and jurisdiction of countries having direct interests in the area, to explore the possibility of cooperation in the South China Sea relating to the safety of maritime navigation and communication, and protection against pollution of the marine environment, coordination of search and rescue operations, efforts towards combating piracy and armed robbery as well as collaboration against illicit trafficking in drugs;
4. COMMEND all parties to apply the principles contained in the Treaty of Amity and Cooperation in Southeast Asia as the basis for establishing a code of conduct over the South China Sea;
5. INVITE all parties concerned to subscribe to this Declaration of Principles.

Source: http://cil.nus.edu.sg/1992/1992-asean-declaration-on-the-south -china-sea-signed-on-22-july-1992-in-manila-philippines-by-the-foreign -ministers.

Appendix II

Declaration on the Conduct of Parties in the South China Sea

(4 November 2002)

1. The Parties reaffirm their commitment to the purposes and principles of the Charter of the United Nations, the 1982 Convention on the Law of the Sea, the Treaty of Amity and Cooperation in Southeast Asia, the Five Principles of Peaceful Coexistence, and other universally recognized principles of international law which shall serve as the basic norms of state-to-state relations.
2. The Parties are committed to finding ways for building trust and confidence in accordance with the above mentioned principles and on a basis of equality and mutual respect.
3. The Parties reaffirm their respect for and commitment to freedom of navigation in and overflight above the South China Sea as provided for by the universally recognized principles of international law including the 1982 Convention on the Law of the Sea.
4. The Parties concerned undertake to resolve their territorial and jurisdictional disputes by peaceful means, without resorting to threats or use of force, through friendly consultations and negotiations by sovereign states directly concerned in accordance with universally recognized principles of international law, including the 1982 Convention on the Law of the Sea.
5. The Parties undertake to exercise self-restraint in the conduct of activities that would complicate or escalate disputes and affect peace and stability including among others, refraining from action of inhabiting on presently uninhabited islands, reefs, shoals, cays and other features and to handle their differences in a constructive manner.

Pending the peaceful settlement of territorial and jurisdictional disputes, the Parties concerned undertake to intensify efforts to seek ways, in the spirit of cooperation and understanding, to build trust and confidence between and among them, including

a. holding dialogues and exchange of views as appropriate between their defense and military officials;
b. ensuring just and humane treatment of all persons who are either in danger or distress;
c. notifying on a voluntary basis other Parties concerned of any impending joint/combined military exercise; and
d. exchanging on a voluntary basis relevant information.

6. Pending a comprehensive and durable settlement of the disputes, the Parties concerned may explore or undertake cooperative activities. These may include the following:

a. marine environmental protection;
b. marine scientific research;
c. safety of navigation and communication at sea;
d. search and rescue operations; and
e. combating transnational crime including but not limited to trafficking in illicit drugs, piracy and armed robbery at sea, and illegal traffic in arms.

The modalities, scope and locations, in respect to bilateral and multilateral cooperation should be agreed upon by the Parties concerned prior to their actual implementation.

7. The Parties concerned stand ready to continue their consultations and dialogues concerning relevant issues, through modalities being agreed upon by them, including regular consultations on the observance of this Declaration, for the purpose of promoting good neighborliness and transparency, establishing harmony, mutual understanding and cooperation, and facilitating peaceful resolution of disputes among them.

8. The Parties undertake to respect the provisions of this Declaration and to take actions consistent therewith.

9. The Parties encourage other countries to respect the principles contained in this Declaration.

10. The parties concerned reaffirm that the adoption of a code of conduct in the South China Sea would further promote peace and stability in the region and agree to work, on the basis of consensus, towards the eventual attainment of this objective.

Source: ASEAN, accessed at http://www.asean.org/external-relations/china/item/declaration-on-the-conduct-of-parties-in-the-south-china-sea.

Index

About the Author

Donald E. Weatherbee is the Donald S. Russell Distinguished Professor Emeritus at the University of South Carolina, where he specialized in the politics and international relations of Southeast Asia. A graduate of Bates College, he holds an MA and PhD from the Johns Hopkins School of Advanced International Studies. In addition to the University of South Carolina, Prof. Weatherbee has served on the faculty of the United States Army War College and has held teaching and research appointments at universities and institutes in Indonesia, Malaysia, Singapore, Thailand, Germany, the Netherlands, and England. He has an extensive list of publications on Southeast Asian international relations. His most recent book is *Indonesia in ASEAN: Vision and Reality* (2013). Other recent publications include *Historical Dictionary of United States–Southeast Asia Relations* (2008); "Strategic Dimensions of Economic Interdependence in Southeast Asia," in *Strategic Asia 2006–2007*; "Southeast Asia in 2006: Déjà vu All Over Again," in *Southeast Asian Affairs 2007*; "Political Change in Southeast Asia: Challenges for U.S. Strategy," in *Strategic Asia 2007–2008*; and "ASEAN's Identity Crisis," in *Legacy of Engagement in Southeast Asia* (2008). His professional recognition includes the US Army's Distinguished Civilian Service Medal for his contribution to strategic planning for post–Vietnam War Southeast Asian international relations.